The Construction of Mental
Representations During Reading

The Construction of Mental Representations During Reading

Edited by

Herre van Oostendorp
Utrecht University

Susan R. Goldman
Vanderbilt University

LAWRENCE ERLBAUM ASSOCIATES, PUBLISHERS
1999   Mahwah, New Jersey   London

Lawrence Erlbaum Associates, Inc., Publishers
10 Industrial Avenue
Mahwah, NJ 07430

Cover design by Kathryn Houghtaling Lacey

Library of Congress Cataloging-in-Publication Data
The construction of mental representations during reading / edited by Herre van Oostendorp and Susan R. Goldman.
p. cm.
Includes bibliographical references and indexes.
ISBN 0-8058-2428-6 (hardcover: alk. paper). — ISBN 0-8058-2429-4 (pbk. : alk. paper)
1. Reading, Psychology of. 2. Mental representation. I. Oostendorp, Herre van. II. Goldman, Susan R.
BF456.R2C64   1999   418'.4'019—dc21
98–13836   CIP

Books published by Lawrence Erlbaum Associates are printed on acid-free paper, and their bindings are chosen for strength and durability.

Printed in the United States of America
10 9 8 7 6 5 4 3 2 1

Contents

Introduction: Some Initial Considerations   vii

I: Models of Processing and Representation   1

1. Incrementality in Discourse Understanding   3
Simon Garrod and Anthony Sanford

2. Modeling Causal Integration and Availability of   29
Information During Comprehension of
Narrative Texts
Mark Langston and Tom Trabasso

3. The Landscape Model of Reading: Inferences and   71
the Online Construction of Memory Representation
Paul van den Broek, Michael Young, Yuhtsuen Tzeng, and
Tracy Linderholm

4. Toward a Theory of Documents Representation   99
Charles A. Perfetti, Jean-François Rouet, and M. Anne Britt

5. Context Models in Discourse Processing   123
Teun A. van Dijk

II: Processes and Strategies of Representation   149
Construction

6. The Intermediate Effect: Interaction Between Prior   151
Knowledge and Text Structure
Stéphanie Caillies, Guy Denhière, and Sandra Jhean-Larose

7. Building Representations of Informational Text: 169
   Evidence From Children's Think-Aloud Protocols
   Nathalie Coté and Susan R. Goldman

8. The Role of Illustrations in Text Comprehension: 195
   What, When, for Whom, and Why?
   Valérie Gyselinck and Hubert Tardieu

9. The Role of Situational Continuity in Narrative   219
   Understanding
   Joseph P. Magliano, Rolf A. Zwaan, Art Graesser

10. Learning From Text: Structural Knowledge   247
    Assessment in the Study of Discourse
    Comprehension
    Evelyn C. Ferstl and Walter Kintsch

III: Monitoring and Updating Representations   279

11. Metacognitive Monitoring of Text Cohesion in   281
    Children
    Marie-France Ehrlich

12. Modifying Mental Representations: Comprehending   303
    Corrections
    Hollyn M. Johnson and Colleen M. Seifert

13. Difficulties in Updating Mental Representations   319
    During Reading News Reports
    Herre van Oostendorp and Christiaan Bonebakker

14. Distinguishing Between Textbase and Situation   341
    Model in the Processing of Inconsistent
    Information: Elaboration Versus Tagging
    Isabelle Tapiero and Jose Otero

15. Conclusions, Conundrums, and Challenges for the Future   367
    Susan R. Goldman and Herre van Oostendorp

Author Index   377

Subject Index   385

Introduction:
Some Initial Considerations

Some of the earliest research on reading was concerned with how readers process a text and make meaning from the printed information. For example, Buswell (1920) was one of the first to investigate readers' eye movements during reading. His work was guided by the structural characteristics of the printed text, for example, where on the page readers fixated. His analytic descriptions were in terms of the parts of the line and page rather than on the informational or functional properties of the fixated text. Buswell's emphasis was consistent with the larger theoretical zeitgeist of that time, emphasizing structural approaches to language.

At a similar point in time, Bartlett, a social psychologist, was emphasizing a more reader-based aspect of the reading process. He was one of the first to point out the importance to the meaning-making process of the reader's knowledge and familiarity with the context and content of the material being read. With the publication of "Remembering" in 1932, Bartlett showed how readers' memories for what they had read changed over time to increasingly reflect their expectations about what the text should or could have said. These expectations were rooted in readers' prior knowledge of the experiences and situations described in the text. In essence, the inferences readers made were consistent with their prior knowledge. Successive "retellings" of the story they had read, "War of the Ghosts," increasingly resembled circumstances and events with which the readers were familiar rather than the culturally unfamiliar practices described in the story.

The early research directions reflected in Buswell's structural approach as compared to Bartlett's meaning-oriented approach continued to evolve and guide research in one form or another for the next 40 to 50 years. The effects of manipulations to the surface structure of the text were examined through various measures of memory for what had been read. As technologies for measuring reading time and eye movements became more sophisticated, studies of text processing, as well as memory for what was processed, began to emerge. Indeed, over the last 10 to 15 years, there has been an upsurge in efforts to understand the processing activities in which readers engage, with special emphasis on how they construct coherent representations of the textual input. Many of these studies support the conclusion that multiple levels of representation are involved in making meaning. For example, van Dijk and Kintsch (1983) distinguished among surface, textbase, and situation-model levels of representation. The surface code reflects features of the surface text (e.g., noun, determiner, verb, etc.). The textbase captures the meaning relations among elements within a sentence and across sentences in the text and reflects very minimal impact of prior knowledge. The situation model captures the referential meaning of the text, that is, the real or imaginary situation in the world that the text describes, and depends on the integration of information in the text with prior knowledge. Constructing coherent representations of text involves processing activities at these multiple levels.

The online processing activities involved in constructing representations from textual input are the theme of this volume. This book is divided into three substantive parts, as well as a concluding chapter. Part I deals with models of processing and representations. Parts II and III concentrate on specific empirical investigations of learners' attempts to construct coherent representations of narrative and instructional text material. In Part II, the chapters discuss processes of constructing situation model representations and the variables that affect this process. In Part III, the chapters have a specific focus on how we appropriately monitor and update representations. In the remainder of this chapter, we provide a brief overview of each of the sections.

PART I: MODELS OF PROCESSING AND REPRESENTATION

Part I consists of five chapters that describe different models of processing and representation. The models apply to different levels of representation, as well as to different text genres. However, all of the models are concerned with how coherence is achieved.

Coherence depends on being able to connect incoming information with the representation of the previous information from the text, with prior knowledge, or with both. The ability to connect elements in the text with one another is mediated by prior knowledge of content and of the role of various surface structure elements of the text. The following two-sentence sequence illustrates these processes.

> The Big Apple is a very popular place for tourists, especially in the summertime. New York City can often be humid but is generally cooler than many other parts of the country.

A reader who knows that "The Big Apple" and "New York City" refer to the same location will process these two sentences differently than a reader who does not know this. Specifically, readers who do not know that the two refer to the same place are likely to interpret the first clause of the second sentence as setting up a contrast between "The Big Apple" and another location called "New York City." After all, humidity is not something one typically associates with a pleasant place for touring. The remainder of the second sentence might produce a number of different effects. For example, these readers might restructure and reinterpret their representation. Alternatively, they might represent the information as referring to two separate and distinct locations. In contrast, readers who know that both sentences refer to the same location are likely to interpret the second sentence as providing an explanation of the claim made in the first sentence. They might be momentarily puzzled by the "negative" quality of life indicator (humidity) in the first clause but this puzzlement would be cleared up by the presence of the contrastive connector "but." This connector cues the fact that the second sentence is indeed providing a rationale for the claim in the first sentence.

The Big Apple example deals with establishing referential indices for the concepts present in the text. This is the issue of concern in chapter 1 by Garrod and Sanford. Pronominal reference is ubiquitous in text. When, and to what degree, readers place their bets on a particular representation is the subject of their chapter. They distinguish between the immediate recovery of candidate referents and the interpretive commitment to one of those. In discussing their scenario mapping and focus account, they argue that language processing is often incomplete and that partial interpretation is usually all that is necessary for satisfactory comprehension.

The next two chapters move the discussion to models of more extended discourses. The models developed by Langston and Trabasso (chap. 2) and by van den Broek, Young, Tzeng, and Linderholm (chap. 3) deal specifically with narratives and how readers construct the referential or situation model of the world described by the text. These models are impressive in that they attempt to account for indices of online processing as well as for the resulting representations as revealed through various types of memory tasks. In both models, concepts can be connected to one another if they are simultaneously active. The Langston and Trabasso model is a connectionist model that depends on discourse analysis of narrative and the centrality of causal connections. Langston and Trabasso validate the model with 12 data sets drawn from eight studies conducted by other researchers as well as by themselves. These data sets encompass five types of data on integrating antecedents during processing and their subsequent availability. Noteworthy in the chapter is a comparison with other activation-based models of comprehension, including the van den Broek et al. landscape model.

The van den Broek et al. landscape model is a processing model that emphasizes dynamic fluctuations in the activation of concepts and the concept networks of which they are a part. The memory representation is defined by the patterns of activation that occur during online processing. In this regard, it departs from other activation-based models (e.g., Goldman & Varma, 1995; Goldman, Varma, & Coté, 1996; Kintsch, 1988; Langston & Trabasso, chap. 2, this volume). Patterns of activation are determined by the text, readers' attentional capabilities, background knowledge (including causal relations among events), and criteria for comprehension. van den Broek et al. show that the landscape model predicts both the content and order of recall of narrative texts. They also provide an analysis of how the model accounts for a variety of other data in the literature on narrative processing.

Readers typically have a rich knowledge base to use in online processing of narratives, especially goal-directed stories such as the ones that have figured prominently in much of the work on comprehension (see, for discussion, Coté, Goldman, & Saul, 1998; Goldman, 1996). As the Langston and Trabasso and van den Broek et al. chapters reflect, much effort has gone into understanding the online construction of mental representations for narratives (cf. Graesser, Singer, & Trabasso, 1994; Zwaan & Radvansky, in press; Zwaan, Magliano, & Graesser, 1995). Less work has been directed toward models of the construction of coherent representations of text intended to provide readers with information, that is, text from which readers are supposed to learn new information (see Goldman et al., 1996, and McNamara & Kintsch, 1996). One property of learning from text that does not apply to story comprehension is that readers often consult multiple sources of information about the same topic or event. In constructing a coherent representation of the event, characteristics of the source itself often need to be taken into account. Indeed, in history, source information is critical to understanding the historical event. The need for a model of the documents, as well as a model of the historical situation, is the subject of chapter 4 by Perfetti, Rouet, and Britt.

Perfetti et al. define a documents model that represents how multiple sources are related to one another. They argue that doing history involves consulting multiple sources. Knowing the type of source is quite relevant to understanding and constructing the situation model. It is not uncommon for sources to disagree with one another. Perfetti et al. contend that what is needed for adequate representation construction is an intertext model that includes a node for each document and labeled links between documents and the situations they describe. This model has several interesting implications for detection of inconsistencies and updating, a subject that is discussed in chapter 15.

The first section of the book concludes with chapter 5 by van Dijk, in which he argues for the importance of an explicit model of context. Van Dijk distinguishes between experience models that are the experiential basis of personal knowledge as compared with models built in processing discourse, designated event models (but which other researchers refer to as *situation models*). Context models are the subset of experience models that deal with communicative aspects of the discourse. For the case of newspaper article processing, context includes credibility of journalists and newspapers, truthfulness of reports, and informativeness of the news. The documents model of Perfetti et al. seems to be a particular type of context model. Particularly important in van Dijk's proposal is the emphasis on a formal analysis of those aspects of prior knowledge that relate to the communicative context and explicit consideration of how they impact processing and the representation that readers construct.

PART II: PROCESSES AND STRATEGIES
OF REPRESENTATION CONSTRUCTION

The models and issues raised by the chapters in Part I of the book lay the groundwork for turning to Parts II and III, each of which concentrates on specific investigations of learners' attempts to construct coherent representations of narrative and instructional text material. In Part II, there are five chapters that deal with the process of constructing situation model representations and the variables that affect this process. Although all of the chapters have clear implications for reading to learn, only three of them specifically deal with instructional texts (Caillies, Denhière, & Jhean-Larose, chap. 6; Coté & Goldman, chap. 7; and Gyselinck & Tardieu, chap. 8, all this volume). Caillies, Denhiére, and Jhean-Larose report empirical results that indicate that the match between the structure of the text and the structure of the learners' knowledge in the domain determines what can be recalled. The implication for online processing is that it is easier to build a representation when the structure of the information is consistent with the structure of knowledge.

Coté and Goldman use think-aloud methodology to examine how children generate and update their evolving representations of texts typical of those found in school textbooks. Their data indicate that individuals used a range of processing strategies and did so in ways that were differentially successful for building coherent situation models that went beyond the specific text. They point out specific prior knowledge limits that place constraints on what *can* be understood, given the content and organization of a specific text. An important issue their work raises is how learners deal with constraints on learning that are imposed by the content and structure of the text in interaction with the content and structure of their text-relevant prior knowledge. Gyselinck and Tardieu suggest that, under certain conditions, illustrations may be useful in dealing with such constraints.

Gyselinck and Tardieu are particularly interested in when, for whom, and why illustrations and text interact so that the result is an elaborated representation of the text. Data from a recent study by Gyselinck (1995) are reported that demonstrate beneficial effects when pictures are presented concurrent with a text in the content area of physics and chemistry. They conclude with a discussion of the implications of these, and other findings, for understanding the processing mechanisms involved in picture enhancement effects. In particular, they propose that situation model construction is facilitated by the transparency of the structural relations reflected in the picture.

A different aspect of representation construction is the topic of the chapter by Magliano, Zwaan, and Graesser. Their work focuses on what kinds of situation models for narratives are constructed, and when. They propose and present data that validate four principles that govern processing and the construction of coherent situation models. Key to their argument is that the reader simultaneously attempts to monitor continuity across multiple dimensions of stories (e.g., characters, objects, time, space, causality, and goal intentionality). Shifts in any of these dimensions demand more effortful processing, with implications for measures of inference construction and reading time.

In the final chapter in Part II, Ferstl and Kintsch (chap. 10) propose a new method for assessing the representation constructed during reading. The method, Structural Knowledge Assessment, can be used appropriately either with narrative or instructional text materials. The gist of the method is that associative network structures are derived using data from a cued-association task. Network structures approximate text representations. Changes in the network structures after reading reflect what has been learned. Structural Knowledge Assessment makes significant advances over extant methods of examining network structures (e.g., multidimensional scaling). This is a promising technique, as Ferstl and Kintsch indicate, for examining the stability of observed changes and whether there are long-term effects on prior knowledge.

PART III: MONITORING AND UPDATING REPRESENTATIONS

Part III focuses specifically on the issue of how we appropriately update previously represented information either within a text currently being read or subsequently when we read text on the same topic. Although this issue is considered in several of the other chapters in the volume, none specifically treat it in detail empirically. The four chapters in this section of the book do so (Ehrlich, chap. 11; Johnson & Seifert, chap. 12; van Oostendorp & Bonebakker, chap. 13; and Tapiero & Otero, chap. 14, all this volume).

Several processes are involved in being able to update representations that are under construction or that have been constructed previously. Ehrlich's chapter reports data from children who were specifically asked to monitor the coherence of anaphoric reference during reading and to point out inconsistencies in the information in multiparagraph instructional passages. The results are discussed in terms of coherence standards, possible individual differences in these, and their impact on comprehension monitoring.

The remaining chapters in Part III deal with possible explanations for why adults have trouble updating information. Johnson and Seifert (chap. 12) propose a distinction between surface and global updating and suggest that readers may engage in surface updating, but not global updating. Global updating corresponds to updating at the situation model level. If a task does not require use of a situation model representation, it may appear that people have updated. Yet when the task taps the situation model, as in inference generation tasks, it will appear that no updating has occurred. Consistent with Johnson and Seifert's efforts to explain updating and inconsistency detection, van Oostendorp and Bonebakker (chap. 13) propose several factors and process models that might account for data showing that adults are not terribly good at updating representations even when corrections are repeated and alternate causal explanations are provided. Their favored explanation is an idea similar to Johnson and Seifert's (chap. 12) and consistent with Garrod and Sanford's (chap. 1) point about shallow processing: For most purposes, when adults read newspaper reports they do not apply stringent coherence criteria to the representations they construct.

Finally, Tapiero and Otero (chap. 14) capture the distinction between shallower and deeper processing, or surface and global updating, by distinguishing between whether the representation of the text or of the situation is affected. Information can be tagged as inconsistent in the text representation or it can be elaborated in the situational representation, depending on time constraints on performing the task. Furthermore, when testing for the occurrence of updating, tasks that tap only the text representation may show one thing, whereas those that tap the situational representation will show another. The empirical findings are very interesting, as are the modeling efforts they report.

Chapter 15, entitled "Conclusions, Conundrums, and Challenges for the Future," concludes the volume. As the name implies, in this chapter, we attempt to synthesize and describe commonalities and trends reflected in the various chapters. Although considerable progress has been made in understanding the processes of comprehension, there remain some conundrums and missing pieces in a complete and coherent theory of meaning construction. We treat several of these. Finally, we discuss a number of interesting challenges for future research.

REFERENCES

Bartlett, F. C. (1932). *Remembering: A study in experimental and social psychology.* Cambridge, England: Cambridge University Press.

Buswell, G. T. (1920). An experimental study of the eye-voice span in reading. *Supplementary educational monographs, 17.* Chicago: University of Chicago Press.

Coté, N., Goldman, S. R., & Saul, E. U. (1998). Students making sense of informational text: Relations between processing and learning. *Discourse Processes.*

Goldman, S. R. (1996). Writing as a tool for thinking and reasoning: A commentary on "Cognitive processes in children's writing: Developmental and individual differences" by Deborah McCutchen. *Issues in Education: Contributions From Educational Psychology.*

Goldman, S. R., & Varma, S. (1995). CAPping the construction-integration model of discourse comprehension. In C. Weaver, S. Mannes, & C. Fletcher (Eds.), *Discourse comprehension: Essays in honor of Walter Kintsch* (pp. 337–358). Hillsdale, NJ: Lawrence Erlbaum Associates.

Goldman, S. R., Varma, S., & Coté, N. (1996). Extending capacity-constrained construction integration: Toward "smarter" and flexible models of text comprehension. In B. K. Britton & A. C. Graesser (Eds.), *Models of text comprehension.* Hillsdale, NJ: Lawrence Erlbaum Associates.

Graesser, A. C., Singer, M., & Trabasso, T. (1994). Constructing inferences during narrative text comprehension. *Psychological Review, 101,* 371–395.

Gyselinck, V. (1995). *Les modèles mentaux dans la compréhension de textes: Le rôle des illustrations* [Mental models in text comprehension: The role of illustrations]. Unpublished doctoral thesis, University of Paris V.

Kintsch, W. (1988). The role of knowledge in discourse comprehension: A construction-integration model. *Psychological Review, 95,* 163–182.

McNamara, D. S., & Kintsch, W. (1996). Learning from texts: Effects of prior knowledge and text coherence. *Discourse Processes, 22,* 247–288.

van Dijk, T. A., & Kintsch, W. (1983). *Strategies of discourse comprehension.* New York: Academic Press.

Zwaan, R. A., & Radvansky, G. A. (in press). Situation models in language comprehension and memory. *Psychological Bulletin.*

Zwaan, R. A., Magliano, J. P., & Graesser, A. C. (1995). Dimensions of situation model construction in narrative comprehension. *Journal of Experimental Psychology: Learning, Memory, and Cognition, 21,* 386–397.

Part I

MODELS OF PROCESSING
AND REPRESENTATION

Chapter 1

Incrementality in Discourse Understanding

Simon Garrod
Anthony Sanford
University of Glasgow

Twenty years ago in the annual review of experimental psycholinguistics, Johnson-Laird (1974) defined the fundamental problem as that of establishing what happens when we understand sentences: what mental operations occur, when in relation to language perception, and in what order. So, psychologists have a long-standing interest in the time course of language processing, and it is against this background that we consider the issue of incrementality in discourse understanding.

The idea that human language comprehension is essentially incremental, continually adding to the interpretation as each word is encountered, is a very attractive one. In conversation, there is a strong impression that we know what our interlocutor is trying to say as it is being said; we may even be tempted, on occasion, to complete his or her sentence before he or she has finished speaking. Similarly, when reading, there is a strong impression that the interpretation is being built up continuously as each word is encountered. So, at the level of introspection, the idea of incremental language comprehension is compelling. There is also a sound psychological reason for the language-processing system to operate in this way, based on what is known about human memory and its poor capacity for dealing with uninterpreted information. Any well-adapted human language-processing system should favor incremental interpretation when possible.

However, although there is a large body of evidence to suggest that syntactic processing is essentially incremental (this is associated mainly with garden-path phenomena studied extensively since Bever, 1970), comparable evidence for incremental semantic analysis or incremental interpretation at the level of the discourse is much harder to find. The principal aim of this chapter, therefore, is to review the evidence on the precise time course of discourse comprehension and see what light can be thrown on the more general issue of incremental interpretation. In doing this, we come to the conclusion that it is important from a psychological point of view to distinguish two general modes of language processing: one concerned with building up an interpretation in an essentially incremental fashion and the other, lower-level process, concerned with matching patterns in the input against both local and global knowledge representations. We argue that the latter mode of processing, which is immediate but not incremental, can operate at any level from syntactic analysis right through to discourse comprehension.

The chapter is organized into three main sections. In the first, we draw a distinction between immediate *recovery* of information and immediate *integration,* and show how this can be applied at the level of sentence interpretation. The next section reviews the evidence on immediacy of discourse comprehension in the light of this distinction and uses it to sort out a number of apparent contradictions in the findings. An important issue that emerges is to what extent discourse processing may lead to only partial interpretations. This point is considered in the final section of the chapter.

IMMEDIACY, INCREMENTALITY, AND MODES OF PROCESSING

Immediacy of processing is well motivated from a psychological point of view because of the severe memory constraints that limit holding too much uninterpreted information. For this reason, Just and Carpenter (1980) argued for what they called the immediacy assumption in text comprehension. According to this assumption, readers interpret each content word of a text as it is encountered even at the expense of making guesses that sometimes turn out to be wrong. However, there are a number of ways in which immediate interpretation might operate, and it is important to specify these if we are to make sense of the experimental evidence on discourse understanding. The two main versions of immediacy that need to be considered are immediate recovery of information and immediate integration of information. To illustrate this distinction, consider the situation of syntactic parsing. As each word and phrase is encountered, it is generally assumed that the processor immediately recovers relevant syntactic information about the element in question, for example, its syntactic category, morphological structure, and so on. So, syntactic parsing is generally thought to be immediate at this low level of information recovery. However, most psychologists would want to argue that the immediacy of syntactic processing does not stop there; it also must involve some form of integration to specify the various syntactic relations between the words and phrases encountered. In other words, there must be both a process of immediate recovery and a process of immediate integration into the current phrase marker if the system is to be described as a truly incremental processor.

In general, research on the time course of parsing supports the view that syntactic processing is immediate and incremental in this stronger sense. For example, Frazier and Rayner (1982) demonstrated that readers confronted with certain kinds of structural syntactic ambiguity would commit themselves in the first instance to only one reading. Thus, when encountering the ambiguous sentence fragment in (1), readers typically treat the prepositional phrase *on the cart* as attached to the verb *loaded* rather than to the noun phrase *the boxes*.

(1) Sam loaded the boxes on the cart . . . . . .

They were able to demonstrate this by measuring the reader's eye movements with the two versions of a sentence containing this ambiguous fragment:

(2) Sam loaded the boxes on the cart before lunch.
(3) Sam loaded the boxes on the cart onto the van.

When presented with (3), readers encountered difficulty at the point where the prepositional phrase attachment was disambiguated. They spent substantially longer fixating this region of the sentence and were much more likely to refixate the ambiguous fragment shown in (1). Frazier and Rayner used this finding to argue that the syntactic parsing process was essentially incremental with the processor always attempting to increment a single syntactic analysis as each word is encountered. If in this process a potential syntactic ambiguity is encountered, the system will simply opt for the integration that yields the simplest structure, and in this case it is the structure involving minimal attachment.

From the present point of view, what is important about these findings is that they demonstrate a pressure toward immediate incremental analysis even at the risk of subsequent misunderstanding. At the same time, they illustrate the main pitfall of doing it this way, which arises from the problem of early commitment. The system will either be forced to track multiple alternative analyses or to make an early and risky commitment to following one line of interpretation over the other. In fact, Frazier and Rayner (1987) found other cases of local syntactic ambiguity associated with lexical categorization that do not trigger such immediate commitment.

For instance, when readers are given sentences such as (4) or (5) following, a different pattern of results emerges.

(4) I know that the desert trains young people to be especially tough.

(5) I know that the desert trains are especially tough on young people.

Here a potential syntactic ambiguity is present at the words *desert trains*, which could either be treated as noun plus verb (as in 4) or as adjective plus noun (as in 5). These sentences were compared with the unambiguous controls (4′ and 5′):

(4′) I know that this desert trains young people to be especially tough.

(5′) I know that these desert trains are especially tough on young people.

If the processor was always interpreting incrementally, even at the expense of making an early commitment, then readers should take just as long (if not longer) processing the ambiguous fragment *desert trains* in (4) and (5) as when processing the disambiguated fragment in (4′) and (5′). In fact quite the opposite pattern emerges. Readers spend more time fixating the words in the unambiguous case than in the ambiguous one, but then spend less time on the remainder of the sentence. This is consistent with a mechanism that holds off interpretation of the ambiguous information and attempts to look ahead for disambiguators before committing itself to an immediate incremental analysis. As Frazier and Rayner pointed out, the extent of such delaying may only be limited to one or two words, which will usually be quite sufficient to sort out this kind of syntactic category ambiguity. Nevertheless, the result does point to a certain amount of flexibility in relation to the immediate and incremental analysis of syntactic structure. Frazier and Rayner proposed that what might determine delayed processing is whether or not the analysis depends only on prestored information (e.g., syntactic categorization) or requires actual computation. The assumption is that computing alternative interpretations is more costly than recovering prestored alternatives. This same distinction between computing versus recovering prestored interpretations turns out to be important when considering incrementality at the level of discourse interpretation. However, first we need to look at evidence for incrementality in semantic processing.

With immediacy in relation to semantic processing, the picture turns out to be even more complicated. Readers can be garden pathed when they encounter radical lexical ambiguities, but not when they encounter ambiguities of sense. Frazier and Rayner (1990) set up a contrast between sentences like (6) and (7) containing the ambiguous word *pitcher* (vase vs.

baseball thrower), and sentence like (8) and (9) containing the word *record*, which is not lexically ambiguous, but does admit different senses (disc vs. account).

(6) Being so elegantly designed, the pitcher pleased Mary.

(7) Throwing so many curve balls, the pitcher pleased Mary.

(8) After they were scratched, the records were carefully guarded.

(9) After the political take-over, the records were carefully guarded.

In all cases the words were chosen so as to have one dominant and one subordinate meaning or sense. Hence, out of context, subjects tend to take *pitcher* to refer to a baseball thrower and *record* to refer to a disc. To establish whether the reader would immediately assign one interpretation over the other, they compared cases like (6) where the disambiguating phrase precedes the ambiguous word, with cases like (10) where it follows.

(10) Of course the pitcher pleased Mary, being so elegantly designed.

The results were quite striking. When the target word was lexically ambiguous (e.g., pitcher), there was generally a marked advantage in having the disambiguating phrase precede the target, and, if disambiguation was toward the nonpreferred meaning, readers spent a little extra time fixating the word, but soon recovered. However, if the disambiguating phrase followed the target, readers spent longer overall and experienced considerable extra difficulty in cases where the overall context favored the nonpreferred meaning of the word. So, for the lexically ambiguous cases, the pattern of results is consistent with the standard garden-path situation with syntactic ambiguity. When readers encounter a choice point in constructing an interpretation, they track one and only one meaning, and in the absence of prior disambiguating context, the meaning that they track corresponds to the dominant meaning of the word in question.

However, the results were different with materials containing the multiple-sense words like *record* or *newspaper*. In these cases, there was no detectable reading time difference overall between prior and postdisambiguation conditions. Having no context to select between different senses of the target word did not seem to lead to immediate adoption of one sense or the other. However, there was some evidence that when prior context was available readers would immediately adopt the appropriate reading. This came from a small but reliable effect of dominance immediately following the reading of the target word: in a context that selected the subordinate sense, readers would take slightly longer to integrate the information.

Frazier and Rayner explained this result in relation to what they called the immediate partial interpretation hypothesis. According to this hypothesis, the processor will generally operate in an immediate and incremental fashion but may delay its semantic commitments, if this does not result in either (a) a failure to assign any semantic value whatsoever to a word or major phrase, or (b) the need to maintain multiple incompatible values for a word, phrase, or relation. To account for the difference between lexical versus sense ambiguity, they assumed that meanings and senses relate to different kinds of underlying mental representations. Whereas there is no single representation for the two lexemes underlying an ambiguous word, different senses of the same word can be represented in a single more abstract form and so do not require maintenance of incompatible alternative semantic values at this level.

Whether Frazier and Rayner's account proves to be correct, the results of these studies illustrate some of the issues surrounding incremental processing. From a psychological point of view it would seem that there are two general constraints operating, both related to working memory limitations. The first is that of requiring some immediate interpretation for each element as it is encountered—to avoid holding uninterpreted material—and the second opposing constraint is that of only being able to track one particular sequential interpretation at a time—to avoid holding multiple incompatible interpretations of the same material. This latter constraint presumably reflects the system's inability to track alternative readings simultaneously and also guards against the risk of combinatorial explosion when trying to trace out all the possible alternative interpretations downstream of the initial ambiguity.

That these are genuine memory constraints is reinforced by Just and Carpenter (1992). They were able to demonstrate that subjects with high reading span, a measure of linguistic working memory capacity, were less susceptible to certain kinds of syntactic garden path. They argued that this was due to both being able to maintain multiple representations for longer (in a similar fashion to Frazier & Rayner's, 1987, subjects), and being able to take more account of other kinds of contextual constraint when assigning an appropriate syntactic interpretation. The significance of Just and Carpenter's findings is that incremental integration of linguistic information seems to be as much due to working memory constraints as to specific architectural features of the parsing system. If this is true, we would expect to find those same general constraints applying to language processing at a discourse level.

To see how such constraints might affect discourse processing, we need to consider what might correspond to information recovery and information integration at that level. By analogy with Frazier and Rayner's account, we then need to consider what constitutes a sufficient level of interpretation for the item to impose no special memory load.

IMMEDIACY IN RELATION TO DISCOURSE COMPREHENSION

Like syntactic parsing and semantic analysis, discourse processing can be viewed as requiring both recovery of information and integration of that information into an overall representation of the text. Garrod and Sanford (1994; see also Garrod, 1994) argued that it is essentially a process of anchoring interpretations of the sentence and its fragments (i.e., noun phrases, verb groups, etc.) into this representation. Within their framework, recovery of information corresponds to identifying the appropriate anchoring site in the representation, and integration corresponds to incorporating and linking (e.g., through various coherence relations) the current information in the sentence into that already represented at that site.

In certain respects this distinction is similar to Kintsch's (1988) construction versus integration contrast. In Kintsch's account, construction corresponds to recovering all the relevant information in memory associated with the expression under interpretation, whereas integration corresponds to selecting a single consistent interpretation for the clause. However, as we argue in the conclusion of this chapter, Kintsch (1988) did not explicitly address the question of incrementality and hence the extent to which parsing and discourse comprehension relate over time. The notion of discourse anchoring highlights this relationship.

The most straightforward examples of anchoring arise with anaphoric expressions such as pronouns or fuller definite noun phrases. Thus, in the following example, discourse level interpretation requires the reader to identify the co-indexed items in the two sentences:

(11) Bill wanted to lend $Susan_1$ some $money_2$.
(12) She_1 was hard up and really needed it_2.

In effect, the pronoun *she* identifies with the entity corresponding to *Susan* in the discourse representation and the pronoun *it* identifies with the entity corresponding to *some money*. But full discourse level interpretation of sentence (12) also requires integrating this information with the prior representation. For example, the reader needs to do this to be able to infer that the reason for Bill's wanting to lend the money to Susan was his recognition of her perilous financial state (see Garrod, 1994, for a fuller discussion).

In such a simple example it is easy to conceive the recovery process and the integration process as, in principle, independent of each other. The pronoun *she* will recover the antecedent *Susan* and *it* will recover the antecedent *money* solely on the basis of gender and number matching. But this is by no means always the case. For example, with the following variant of (11) and (12), the first pronoun is potentially ambiguous when considered in isolation.

(13) Bill$_1$ wanted to lend his friend$_2$ some money.

(14) He$_2$ was hard up and really needed it.

(15) However, he$_1$ was hard up and couldn't afford to.

With examples like (13, 14) and (13, 15), the processor is presented with the same problem encountered with lexical or sense ambiguities discussed previously: Integrating the appropriate interpretation depends on information only available downstream of the pronoun. This means that making a referential commitment to the interpretation of a pronoun or fuller NP is very much like making a semantic commitment to one particular sense of a word like *record*. To do this, the reader will have to integrate information recovered from the potential antecedents (i.e., Bill or his friend) into the sentence being interpreted, and test the coherence of the resulting interpretations. According to the immediate partial interpretation hypothesis we would expect the whole process to be similar to that of sense selection: In the presence of strong prior evidence, the processor should immediately make a referential commitment, whereas in its absence the processor should retain a more abstract representation reflecting only the semantic content of the anaphoric description. This contrasts with an immediate referential commitment hypothesis whereby the processor would always make an initial commitment to one referential interpretation but at the risk of subsequently being garden pathed. So, let us turn to the psychological evidence for immediacy in relation to anaphoric processing. First, we consider the evidence for immediate recovery in the sense just discussed, and then we examine the evidence for immediate integration.

Immediate Contextual Recovery for Pronouns and Fuller Noun Phrases

The main technique for drawing inferences about when contextual information is recovered during reading is antecedent probe recognition. The subject is presented with a text, usually one word at a time, and at a critical point a probe word is presented. He or she is then required to make a timed judgment of whether the probe matched a word in the prior text.

In one of the earliest studies of this kind, Dell, McKoon, and Ratcliff (1983) used texts like the following:

A burglar surveyed the garage set back from the street.
Several milk bottles were piled at the curb.
The banker and her husband were on vacation.
The criminal/A cat slipped away from the street lamp.

At the critical point following either the anaphor *the criminal* or the non-anaphor *a cat*, they presented the test word *burglar* for probe recognition. They found that recognition was primed immediately following *criminal* as compared to *cat*. They also obtained a similar enhancement for words drawn from the sentence in which the antecedent had occurred (e.g., *garage*). This finding, together with related findings from Gernsbacher (1989), suggests that the relevant antecedent information is recovered rapidly (at least within 150 ms) following exposure to an anaphor. Gernsbacher also demonstrated a similar pattern of results with proper-name anaphors. In this case, she was able to show a reliable differential between positive priming for the antecedent and inhibition for a nonantecedent relative to a point just before the anaphor.

Hence, there is evidence for immediate recovery of contextual information, at least for explicit anaphors such as repeated names and definite descriptions. In the case of pronouns, the situation is somewhat more complicated. In a spoken cross-modal version of the priming task, Shillcock (1982) demonstrated some early effects following presentation of an unambiguous pronoun, but only in terms of suppression of the nonantecedent control word. Gernsbacher (1989), on the other hand, did not find evidence of either enhancement or suppression immediately after an unambiguous pronoun (see also Greene, McKoon, & Ratcliff, 1992). The only clear effects in her study emerged at the end of the sentence.

However, this apparent contradiction in the findings for the fuller anaphors versus pronouns may have something to do with the nature of the probes that were used. Cloitre and Bever (1988) reported a number of experiments that suggest that noun anaphors only immediately activate surface information about their antecedents, whereas pronouns activate deeper conceptual information. The experiments compared priming effects using a number of different tasks. In general, they found that tasks that tapped recovery of conceptual information about the antecedent, such as category decision, produced earlier effects following the pronoun than the noun anaphors, whereas the opposite was true for a lexical decision task that taps surface information. Furthermore, secondary effects associated with conceptual properties of the antecedent, such as its concreteness, emerged in the immediate responses following the pronoun but not the noun anaphors. So the different referential devices are recovering different types of information from the prior discourse, with pronouns having a privileged status in terms of access to conceptual information.

A recent set of experiments by Vonk, Hustinx, and Simon (1992) also suggested that topicalization may play an important role in pronoun antecedent recovery. They used materials in which the antecedent was clearly established as the thematic subject or topic of the preceding text. The target sentence then contained either a pronoun or definite description identifying this character. Under these circumstances, they found evidence for earlier recovery of information following the pronoun as compared to the fuller description. This result fits well with previous findings that topicalization and antecedent focusing are especially important for pronoun resolution (Gordon, Grosz, & Gilliom, 1993; Sanford, Moar, & Garrod, 1988).

In relation to the first criterion of immediacy—that of immediate information recovery—anaphoric processing seems to behave in a similar fashion to other sentence internal semantic processes such as sense selection. However, antecedent probe recognition studies are not without their problems. In particular, presenting texts in a piecemeal word-by-word fashion is a poor simulation of the normal reading process and may well interfere with the time course of the sentence resolution. A second issue that turns out to be particularly important for interpretation of pronouns is the degree to which they identify a focused antecedent in the discourse representation, hence the conflict between the Vonk et al. (1992) results and those from Gernsbacher (1989).

A less invasive procedure for establishing what is happening during reading is to track eye movements, and there have been a few studies that have used this technique to look at recovery of contextual information. The first study we consider looked at the interpretation of unambiguous pronouns with antecedents either close in the text or far removed. By measuring the amount of time the reader spent fixating the pronoun and subsequent regions of the sentence, Ehrlich and Rayner (1983) were able to demonstrate an antecedent distance effect. When the antecedent was distant, readers spent a reliably longer time fixating the region immediately after the pronoun and for a few words beyond it as compared to the other condition. This result is consistent with the idea that a pronoun immediately triggers access to its antecedent, but recovery takes longer when the antecedent is distant, and so presumably out of focus.

The second eye-tracking study that has some bearing on the time course of antecedent recovery looked at the interpretation of definite description anaphors. This study, reported by Garrod, O'Brien, Morris, and Rayner (1990) and based on an earlier study by O'Brien, Shank, Myers, and Rayner (1988), explored the effects of role restriction constraints on the time taken to interpret the anaphors. Various contexts were constructed that could impose a potential restriction on the nature of an antecedent referent. An example set is shown here:

(23) He assaulted her with his weapon
(24) He stabbed her with his weapon
(25) He assaulted her with his knife
(26) He stabbed her with his knife

After a further intervening sentence, subjects were presented with one of the following target sentences, and their eye movements were recorded:

(27) He threw the knife into the bushes, took her money and ran away.
(28) He threw a knife into the bushes, took her money and ran away.

The basic question of interest was how the different types of contextual restriction on the antecedent weapon affect the subsequent fixation time for the anaphoric reference to *the knife* in sentence (27) as compared to the non-anaphoric reference to *a knife* in (28). In sentences (25) and (26) the antecedent is explicitly introduced as *a knife*, whereas in sentence (24) as opposed to (23), the verb implicitly restricts the weapon to be knife-like. One question that the study addressed was how these two forms of restriction affect the amount of time the reader actually fixates the subsequent anaphor *the knife*.

With the anaphoric target (27), gaze duration on *knife* was equally reduced by either implicit restriction of the antecedent weapon by the verb, as in sentence (24), or lexical specification of the weapon as a knife, as in (25) and (26). So, the only case where there was a reliably longer gaze duration was when neither restriction applied, as in (23). However, with non-anaphoric controls, there was only a gaze duration advantage when the antecedent exactly matched the lexical specification of the target noun. Contexts (25) or (26) led to shorter reader times than did contexts (23) or (24), but the implicit restriction from the verb had no effect whatsoever.

This experiment clearly demonstrates that an anaphor immediately recovers the contextual information in the antecedent. Although there was a lexical priming effect observed for the non-anaphoric control, there was no effect associated with the role restriction imposed by the verb or other part of the sentence. The role restriction effect observed in the anaphoric materials must therefore come from attempting to interpret a definite description that signals some coherent link between antecedent and anaphor.

In conclusion, both the priming studies and the few eye-tracking experiments reported to date indicate that the recovery of contextually relevant information occurs at the time of encountering a fuller anaphor. In the case of pronouns, the evidence is not quite so clear cut. The priming studies indicate that the form of the antecedent may not be so rapidly accessed with pronouns as with the fuller anaphors, but at the same time they suggest that deeper conceptual information can be recovered more rapidly.

In relation to our opening discussion, it would therefore seem that discourse interpretation proceeds immediately with respect to recovery of relevant antecedent information or identifying the site in the discourse representation where subsequent information is to be anchored. However, this still leaves open the issue of incrementality in the stronger sense of immediate integration. We turn to this in the next section.

Immediacy in Relation to Information Integration

Establishing that contextually relevant information has been recovered immediately following an anaphor does not license the stronger assumption that this information is immediately integrated into the interpretation of sentence and discourse. In order to establish immediate integration we need to be able to show that the interpretation of the sentence or sentence fragment has been directly affected by the prior discourse context at that point.

An example of such an online study was reported by Tyler and Marslen-Wilson (1982). In their experiment, subjects were required to name a visually presented probe (either the pronoun *him* or *her*) following one of the auditorily presented text fragments (a, b, or c) illustrated in the following:

As Philip was walking back from the shop, he saw an old woman trip and fall flat on her face. She seemed to be unable to get up again.

(a) Philip ran toward . . . him/her

(b) He ran toward . . . him/her

(c) Running toward . . . him/her

The probes were chosen in such a way that one (e.g., *her*) was always pragmatically consistent with the contextual interpretation of the fragment at that point, whereas the other (e.g., *him*) was not. They reasoned that any advantage in terms of naming latency for the appropriate probe could only arise if the listener had already established the contextual significance of the subject of the clause at that point and integrated this with the interpretation of the verb. The experiment showed that in all conditions, such an advantage occurred. The most interesting result is that associated with condition (c), because it suggests that the listener assigns the agent of the verb purely on the basis of pragmatic inferences about the most likely discourse antecedent in that context. So, antecedent recovery and integration can occur even when there is no explicit anaphor in the sentence. In a more recent study, Marslen-Wilson, Tyler, and Koster (1993) were able to replicate this finding and demonstrate that discourse focus, lexical information in the pronoun, and pragmatic inference associated with the verb all interact to support this early resolution.

Although their result is certainly consistent with the early involvement of inference that is so important for immediate integration, the technique does suffer from the disadvantage that it only enables a test somewhat downstream of the anaphor. In other words, it does not give incontrovertible evidence for immediate integration in the way that the other experiments demonstrate immediate recovery. Also, it may be possible that the naming task itself somehow forces integration at that point.

Garrod, Freudenthal, and Boyle (1994) reported an eye-tracking study that overcomes these methodological limitations. It was based on materials like those shown here:

CONTEXT: A dangerous incident in the pool

Elizabeth1/Alexander2 was an inexperienced swimmer and wouldn't have gone in if the male lifeguard3 hadn't been standing by the pool. But as soon as she1/he2 got out of her1/his2 depth she1/he2 started to panic and wave her1/his2 hands about in a frenzy.

TARGET SENTENCES

(a) Within seconds she1 sank   into the pool +F+G+C
(b) Within seconds she1 jumped into the pool +F+G–C
(c) Within seconds he3 jumped into the pool –F+G+C
(d) Within seconds he3 sank   into the pool –F+G–C
(e) Within seconds he2 sank   into the pool +F–G+C
(f) Within seconds he2 jumped into the pool +F–G–C

(+F = Matches focused antecedent, +G = Gender differentiated, & +C = consistent verb. The '–' conditions represent the converse situation)

Like the Marslen-Wilson et al. passages, each introduced two characters who could either be gender differentiated or not (i.e., Elizabeth + male lifeguard or Alexander + male lifeguard) and where one character was always the thematic focus of the text (i.e., the named characters Elizabeth or Alexander). The crucial manipulation was then on the verb in the target sentence: Each verb was always only contextually consistent with one of the characters. For example, whereas Elizabeth can sink at that point in the story, she cannot jump; whereas the lifeguard can jump, he cannot sink. The crucial question then is how early this inconsistency can be detected. With the eye-tracking procedure it is possible to measure the point in the sentence when the reader first detects such an anomaly by comparing the first-pass gaze durations and immediate regressive eye movements on matched contrasting materials (e.g., (a) and (b), or (c) and (d)). If you can discover a differential effect at the verb, then it means that the subjects must have integrated the information from the context into the interpretation at that point. So the technique gets at the same point as the Marslen-Wilson et al. naming procedure, but gives a more immediate test in a normal reading task.

It turned out that there was strong evidence for very early detection of inconsistency, but only in the case where the pronoun was both gender disambiguating and maintained reference to the focused antecedent (conditions +F+G+/−C as in sentences (a) and (b)). The magnitudes of the consistency effects are shown in Fig. 1.1a, represented as differences in fixation time between consistent and inconsistent verb conditions. This result is in marked contrast to the situation when the pronouns were replaced with explicit repeated name or definite description anaphors (e.g., having Elizabeth in (a) and (b) and the lifeguard in (c) and (d)). As is shown in Fig. 1.1b, here the inconsistency was only detected downstream of the verb.

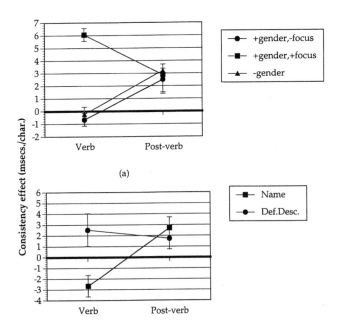

FIG. 1.1.   Consistency effects for pronouns (a) and full anaphors (b) under various conditions (from Garrod, Freudenthal, & Boyle, 1994).

Nevertheless, in all anaphor conditions, there were marked effects of consistency appearing in the second-pass fixations for the verb and subsequent regions. Although it is clear that the readers all ultimately detect the anomaly, it seems that it is only in the case where the pronoun identifies the focused thematic subject of the passage that there is an immediate attempt to integrate the contextual information.

Taken together, these results indicate that the immediate resolution of pronouns comes about through an interaction between the syntactic (gender) information in the pronoun and the focus state of the prior discourse representation. If an antecedent is focused and the pronoun uniquely identifies it through gender matching, then the system makes an early commitment to the full interpretation. When either of these conditions does not hold, commitment is delayed until after the verb has been encountered. Presumably this arrangement makes best use of coherence-checking mechanisms to fix the final interpretation of the pronoun.

The outcome for the fuller noun phrases is much more surprising. On the one hand, there is clear evidence from the antecedent-priming literature discussed previously that the fuller anaphors immediately recover some information about their antecedents, but on the other hand this does not seem to lead to immediate commitment on the part of the processing system to this particular referential interpretation. One possible explanation for the apparent discrepancy comes from considering the degree to which the fuller forms presuppose that particular interpretation.

Full definite descriptions, unlike pronouns, only occasionally take their meanings from explicitly introduced antecedents. Fraurud (1990) found that more than 60% of definites in a large corpus of written text were first mentions without discourse antecedents. This arises because in many cases the definite identifies an implicitly defined role in the discourse situation (see Garrod & Sanford, 1982, 1990, 1994). The difference in presupposition between the pronoun as opposed to the fuller definite can be illustrated with the aforementioned materials where the target sentences containing the fuller descriptions would be perfectly acceptable without explicit discourse antecedents. Thus, the following amended version of the example material is a well-formed text with the definite description but not with the associated pronoun:

> Elizabeth wouldn't have gone in if her sister had not been standing by the pool. But as soon as she got out of her depth she started to panic and wave her hands about in a frenzy. Within seconds, the lifeguard/he* jumped into the pool.

The passage can be understood and is perfectly coherent even when the fuller description does not have an explicit antecedent in the prior text. This is clearly not the case with the pronoun version. One possible consequence of the differences in contextual presupposition might be in terms of the requirements for immediate commitment to one particular referential interpretation. A second related issue concerns the degree to which it is possible to formulate a partial interpretation for the pronoun as opposed to the fuller definite that would satisfy the immediate interpretation constraint discussed in the previous section. If there is no effective partial interpretation for the pronoun, then holding it in memory while attempting to process the rest of the sentence may impose a heavy memory load on the system.

The fact that it is possible to differentiate experimentally between immediate recovery and immediate integration of antecedent discourse information motivates drawing a distinction between anaphor bonding and anaphor resolution. As Sanford (1985a; also Sanford & Garrod, 1989) suggested, anaphors may immediately set up bonds with potential antecedents without necessarily forcing a commitment to referential resolution at that stage. Consider the following sentence pair:

(16) Sailing to Ireland was eventful for Harry. It sank without a trace.

The second sentence sounds odd with the pronoun even though a potential referent *boat* is easily inferred from the context. It gives a compelling impression that it was Ireland that sank without a trace, even though this is ruled out in the ultimate interpretation (the "sounds-like" effect). Sanford, Garrod, Lucas, and Henderson (1983) showed that reading times were longer for such sentences than for their counterparts in which bonding is ruled out by gender and number cues, and where no sounds-like effect is reported:

(17) Being arrested was embarrassing for Andy. They (the police?) took him to the station in a van.

A sentence may be said to be "bond enabling" if there is a suitably foregrounded element that can serve as a false antecedent for a pronoun, by virtue of a match in number and gender. Now it might be supposed that (16) creates a problem as compared to (17) because there is an incorrect but immediate resolution of the pronoun *it*, constituting a semantic garden path. However, as Sanford (1985b) showed, a similar problem does not arise with sentence pairs like (18) and (19):

(18) Sailing to Ireland was eventful for Jim. It was a really windy day.
(19) John had a fearful headache. It was Dr. Brown who had prescribed the wrong pills.

In order to accommodate the difference between the effects of (16) and (18), the distinction between bonding and resolution was proposed. To explain the sounds-like effect in (16), we have to assume that the possibility of coreference was entertained at some point. But because there is no such effect with sentences like (18), immediate false reference resolution seems to be ruled out. On encountering the pronoun, and even later in most of the materials, the processor would have no way of knowing that (16) and (18) were different syntactic and semantic forms. Our argument was that early bonding takes place when a pronoun is encountered that has a suitable (but possibly false) antecedent. The bond simply associates the pronoun with the possible antecedent word, without assigning any specific semantic relation to the association, hence the term *bond*. If the predicate then indicates that the pronoun is being used coreferentially, as in (16), the association is tested as a probable site for instantiation as an anaphor. If it does not, as in (18), then further processing of the bond does not occur. So, it is only in the former case that the sounds-like effect occurs. Of course, under normal circumstances where an anaphoric relation is intended, bonding will facilitate resolution by providing early identification of the locus for the relation.

So, in processing terms, bonding amounts to locating where in the representation relevant information may be found, whereas resolution involves commitment to one particular interpretation at that point in the process. Such a commitment would in effect pipe the relevant contextual information through to the processing system and so enable it to integrate subsequent information in the sentence directly into the discourse representation. In the same way that the syntactic processor may be loath to always make early commitments, as in the Frazier and Rayner (1987, 1990) experiments, it seems that the sentence resolver may also be loath to make such immediate referential commitments except under rather special conditions.

With respect to the whole question of incrementality of discourse processing, this would indicate that truly incremental processing is possible but may be subject to strategic manipulation. The results also raise more broad-ranging questions about the extent to which evidence for immediacy should always be taken as indicative of incrementality in processing. We end by considering this more general question in the light of the evidence from syntactic parsing, semantic processing, and processing at the level of the discourse as a whole.

IMMEDIACY, INCREMENTALITY, AND PARTIAL PROCESSING

We are now in a better position to say something about the general question of how immediacy in processing relates to incrementality. We can start with the two general psychological processing constraints identified at the beginning of this chapter: the constraint that the system should avoid trying to maintain uninterpreted information, and the competing constraint that it should avoid having to track multiple incompatible interpretations of the sentence as a whole. Whereas evidence for tracking only one interpretation at a time is well documented in a range of garden-path phenomena, less is known about the operation of the first constraint on the depth of the immediate analysis.

The main issue raised by this constraint concerns the criterion for interpretation: Just how complete does the interpretation of any unit of input have to be to satisfy it? At the syntactic level this would seem to be moderately straightforward, but even here there may be problems. For example, Perfetti (1990) argued that the parser may on occasion only immediately compute partial interpretations that leave certain aspects of the syntactic representation vague. Thus, he argued that local constituents such as prepositional phrases may be constructed incrementally without necessarily committing the system to remote attachments for the phrases at that time. This would enable the processor to avoid having to opt for one particular high-level syntactic analysis in the absence of clear syntactic triggers, while complying with the second processing constraint against tracking multiple incompatible interpretations. Questions about partial or incomplete interpretation are particularly relevant to processing at the semantic and discourse levels, because it is often not clear what constitutes a complete interpretation at these levels.

There are quite a few studies that give evidence for incomplete or shallow semantic processing. For example, consider the extent to which the full meaning of a word may be ignored when constructing sentence meaning. One well-known example of such partial processing is the "Moses Illusion" (Ericson & Mattson, 1981), in which readers routinely fail to notice the anomaly in the question, How many animals of each sort did Moses put on the ark? (It wasn't Moses, it was Noah.) Barton and Sanford (1993) investigated several constraints controlling detection of a related type of anomaly:

(20) Suppose that there is an airplane crash with many survivors who were European. Where should they be buried?

More than half of the subjects failed to notice this anomaly. In contrast, many more noticed it in the following version:

(21) Suppose that there was an airplane crash with many survivors. Where should they be buried?

Not only does this result show that processing of the expression "survivors" is shallow (i.e., it is partial or incomplete), it also shows that when the context sentence contains information that is relevant to answering the question, deeper analysis does not take place. In the present case, that information is present in (20) where we are told that the survivors are European, but not in (21) (see Barton & Sanford, 1993, for other conditions supporting this analysis). So, depth of processing depends in part on the overall goals of the comprehension process. In this case, the aim is to determine where the people should be buried. Consequently, when the relevant information is available, it is processed. However, when it is not available, the earlier information must be re-analyzed at a deeper level to find an answer.

Barton and Sanford (1993) also tested predictions based on the idea that the contribution a word makes to a discourse representation is very much a function of context. In a context where the term *survivors* is highly salient, it is to be expected that the impact of the word itself (or the amount of processing of its semantic representation) will be low. In one experiment, they compared a scenario in which death and survival are only weakly implied, as in a bicycle race crash, with the standard aircrash scenario, and readers were considerably more successful at detecting the anomaly. So, it is clear that the scenario has a strong influence on the degree of interpretation. However, the results of a further experiment suggest that the influence of context is not strictly incremental. Barton and Sanford varied the order of presentation of the background information relative to the anomalous target item. If the scenario's effect is incremental, then one would expect order of presentation to be important, because it would only be once the scenario had been established that the full interpretation of the anomalous item should be blocked. The following comparisons were made, and the detection rates are given for each of them:

Early scenario, passive VP 26%
(When an aircraft crashes, where should the survivors be buried?)
Early scenario, active VP 44%
(When an aircraft crashes, where should you bury the survivors?)
Late scenario, passive VP 31%
(Where should the survivors be buried after an aircrash?)
Late scenario, active VP 37%
(Where should you bury the survivors of an aircrash?)

The results showed no overall tendency for reduced detection of the anomaly when the scenario came late. So they concluded that a strictly incremental buildup of constraints was not taking place.

Of course, it might be assumed that these examples are unusual and do not reveal much about normal processing. However, it would be difficult to show that the present results are the outcome of unusual processing.

Furthermore, shallow processing of the Moses Illusion type is well established (e.g., Reder & Kusbit, 1990), and there are several other examples of incomplete processing that have been reviewed elsewhere (e.g., Sanford & Garrod, 1994), including further cases where pragmatics appears to override local semantics, as in the so-called "depth-charge sentences" of Wason and Reich (1979):

(24) No head injury is too trivial to be ignored.

(25) No missile is too small to be banned.

In (24) the usual reading is "however trivial a head injury, it should not be ignored." In (25) the reading is "however small a missile, it should be banned." A little reflection shows that these two readings are incompatible with one another, and that the first case is an instance where local semantics has been overridden by situational expectancies. The difficulty some people have with spotting the problem in the question, Can a man marry his sister's widow? points to a similar situational override.

What all of this suggests is that semantic processing can be shallow, but never so shallow that the word in question does not matter. We suggest that the effects parallel the bonding/semantic integration distinction discussed with respect to reference. If the superficial semantics of a word fit top-down constraints, then it is not processed in great detail. Such superficial semantics might be based on whether the word is relevant to the contextual domain (paralleling a "bond"). If the focal structure of the sentence, or other requirements of coherence, force it, then the bond is used as a site of elaboration. The account implies that much processing is in fact shallow, yet comprehension clearly takes place. This is no dilemma if it is assumed that the normal structure of messages is tuned to shallow comprehension mechanisms.

In summary, the evidence is for immediate or early shallow analysis, with very selective and often delayed elaborated interpretation. Rather than meanings being combined incrementally, the evidence is for early immediate processing, such processing being incomplete. Elsewhere, we have argued that the language-comprehension process is designed to anchor utterances to knowledge of specific situations (Garrod & Sanford, 1982, 1990; Sanford & Garrod, 1981, 1994). For instance, stereotypic knowledge about the treatment of head injuries or the banning of missiles should be accessed by the kinds of statements studied by Wason and Reich. Our working hypothesis is that it is this sort of mapping that enables messages to be understood, and that such mappings are primary in the sense that all else depends on them (see Sanford, 1987, for a broader discussion). It therefore makes sense for the processor to identify such background-knowledge anchors as early as possible. But because there appears to be no obvious rule about what it takes in an input to identify an appropriate piece of situation-specific knowledge, there is at present no way of clearly specifying how immediacy should apply with this process, let alone what incrementality might amount to.

We should point out that shallow processing is an important general phenomenon, and we have used it to argue for a process in which the applicability of a word to a situation is first tested; if the fit is good, then further processing may be shallow unless the word is in a focused part of the sentence. Van Oostendorp (1994) put forward a different proposal in which the semantic relatedness of the elements of a sentence determine whether deep or shallow processing takes place. In a sentence like "The cat caught a mouse in the kitchen," the interword semantic relatedness was deemed high, whereas with "The cat seized a mole in the field," the relatedness was deemed lower. In the high-related cases, the time to verify attributes like *cat has claws* was longer than for the low-related cases (once the complication of imageability had been partialled out). Van Oostendorp proposed that when semantic relatedness is high, semantic processing and the building of situation models is reduced, which is quite different from what we are proposing. We propose that if the mapping of a sentence to background knowledge is high, then further processing will tend to be low. The answer depends on whether Van Oostendorp's examples of high semantic relatedness correspond to more stereotyped situations.

CONCLUSIONS

The analysis of immediacy and incrementality given in this chapter is intended to be as free from constraints imposed by existing theories as possible. But of course, a detailed specification of immediate and incremental processing would go a long way toward specifying a process model of text comprehension. Despite the pervasiveness of incrementality and immediacy as a theoretical issue, they are only indirectly addressed in the majority of current theories, such as the minimalist account (McKoon & Ratcliff, 1992) and the construction-integration (CI) account (Kintsch, 1988).

In contrast, the Sanford and Garrod (1981; Garrod & Sanford, 1994; Sanford & Moxey, 1995) scenario-mapping and focus (SMF) account is based on the strong assumption that language input is related to world knowledge at the earliest opportunity, with the subsidiary assumption that much world knowledge is organized as packages useful for real-world situations, and that once such a package (scenario) becomes active, it serves an interpretative function. Thus, although specifying the conditions for immediacy of access to background knowledge may be a problem, once it has been accessed, interpretations with respect to it should be immediate, subject to the limitations of the previous section. According to this account, the global problem of immediacy is one of getting the interpreter to work as soon as possible, which means identifying a scenario as soon as possible. Within such a framework, there is no initial determination of a text base, except as a sketchy and possibly underdetermined syntactic structure for the sentence under interpretation. Such an account predicts that situation-specific (scenario) knowledge can override local semantic and syntactic interpretations of sentences.

This sounds superficially different from minimalism, where perhaps the main assumption about immediacy is that elaborative inferences are seldom made, and even bridging inferences may not be made. But the contrast is not that clear. Recruiting situation-specific knowledge within SMF means identifying sites of reference in LTM (recovery) where interpretation (integration) may take place. This is not the same as creating an inference that has a propositional status and incorporating it into a text base. In fact, to the extent that an inference is to be equated with a text proposition that just happened to come from general knowledge, we would agree with McKoon and Ratcliff's general position that such inferences are seldom made (cf. Garrod, 1985). But we do recognize the need to operationalize the distinction between scenario mapping and inference making more clearly than is the case at present.

The idea of developing full-blown elaborated mental models on the basis of discourse is different again. It is clearly possible to construct such models on the basis of text, but it is debatable whether they result immediately from reading any text. In SMF theory, the discourse-based model is the mapping between discourse fragments and the appropriate background scenario; a more complex "mental model" may follow (cf. Sanford & Moxey, 1995, for details).

Finally, Kintsch's CI model is cast in terms of successive cycles and so should carry a number of implications about immediacy and incrementality. Superficially, construction and integration sound like the recovery and integration described here. However, they are not. Recovery is the process of identifying sites in a representation where further processing may occur should it be required, whereas integration refers to this further processing. On the other hand, Kintsch uses the term *construction* to refer to a bottom-up component of network construction, in which word meanings are activated, propositions are formed, and inferences and elaborations are produced without regard to discourse context. Once this has happened, the net is treated to a connectionist-style relaxation to form an interpretation. Although this sounds like a two-stage process, and therefore capable of analysis within an immediacy framework, we do not believe it is, because Kintsch (1988) also claims that "It would be quite possible to apply the relaxation procedure . . . repeatedly in each cycle, as propositions are being constructed" (p. 168). It is thus difficult to extrapolate from Kintsch's position to the analysis in the present chapter.

Stepping back somewhat from these high-level descriptions, and focusing more closely on the detail of immediacy and incrementality, we can summarize our observations. This chapter started out promising general conclusions about incrementality in language processing based on evidence from the study of discourse comprehension. Two general points emerge— one methodological and the other more theoretical. The methodological point is that evidence for immediacy does not always license the stronger conclusion about incrementality in processing. As we have seen, comprehension can occur through immediate recovery of prestored information without necessarily requiring the information to be combined at that point with what has come before. So, evidence of immediacy does not necessarily constitute evidence for incrementality. The second, theoretical, point comes from the observation that human language processing may often be incomplete and that partial interpretation can occur at almost any level of analysis. This has consequences for how one might want to evaluate an essentially incremental processing system. Most theories start out with the assumption that to understand something is to give it a full interpretation and the question of incrementality simply concerns the order in which this full interpretation is built up relative to the order of the expressions in an utterance. Hence, evidence that a listener makes partial commitments is taken as evidence against a strictly incremental processing system. But, of course, this assumes that those partial commitments will at some time be converted into full commitments and as we have seen, this may not always be the case.

REFERENCES

Barton, S. B., & Sanford, A. J. (1993). A case study of anomaly detection: Shallow semantic processing and cohesion establishment. *Memory and Cognition, 21*(4), 477–487.

Bever, T. (1970). The cognitive basis for linguistic structures. In J. R. Hayes (Ed.), *Cognition and the development of language* (pp. 279–360). New York: Wiley.

Cloitre, M., & Bever, T. G. (1988). Linguistic anaphors, levels of representation and discourse. *Language and Cognitive Processes, 3*, 293–322.

Dell, G. S., McKoon, G., & Ratcliff, R. (1983). The activation of antecedent information during the processing of anaphoric reference in reading. *Journal of Verbal Learning and Verbal Behaviour, 22*, 121–132.

Ehrlich, K., & Rayner, K. (1983). Pronoun assignment and semantic integration during reading: Eye-movements and immediacy of processing. *Journal of Verbal Learning and Verbal Behaviour, 22*, 75–87.

Ericson, T. A., & Mattson, M. E. (1981). From words to meaning: A semantic illusion. *Journal of Verbal Learning and Verbal Behaviour, 20*, 540–552.

Fraurud, K. (1990). Definiteness and the processing of NPs in natural discourse. *Journal of Semantics, 7*, 395–434.

Frazier, L., & Rayner, K. (1982). Making and correcting errors during sentence comprehension: Eye movements in the analysis of structurally ambiguous sentences. *Cognitive Psychology, 14*, 178–210.

Frazier, L., & Rayner, K. (1987). Resolution of syntactic category ambiguities: Eye movements in parsing lexically ambiguous sentences. *Journal of Memory and Language, 26*, 505–526.

Frazier, L., & Rayner, K. (1990). Taking on semantic commitments: Processing multiple meanings vs. multiple senses. *Journal of Memory and Language, 29*, 181–201.

Garrod, S. (1985). Incremental pragmatic interpretation versus occasional inference during reading. In O. Rickheit & H. Stroner (Eds.), *Inferences in text comprehension* (pp. 161–183). Amsterdam: North Holland.

Garrod, S. (1994). Resolving pronouns and other anaphoric devices: The case for diversity in discourse processing. In C. Clifton, Jr., L. Frazier, & K. Rayner (Eds.), *Perspectives on sentence processing*. Hillsdale, NJ: Lawrence Erlbaum Associates.

Garrod, S., Freudenthal, D., & Boyle, E. (1994). The role of different types of anaphor in the on-line resolution of sentences in a discourse. *Journal of Memory and Language, 33*, 39–68.

Garrod, S., O'Brien, E. J., Morris, R. K., & Rayner, K. (1990). Elaborative inferencing as an active or passive process. *Journal of Experimental Psychology: Learning, Memory and Cognition, 16*, 250–257.

Garrod, S., & Sanford, A. J. (1982). Bridging inferences in the extended domain of reference. In A. Baddeley & J. Long (Eds.), *Attention and performance IX* (pp. 331–346). Hillsdale, NJ: Lawrence Erlbaum Associates.

Garrod, S., & Sanford, A. J. (1990). Referential processing in reading: Focusing on roles and individuals. In D. A. Balota, G. B. Flores d'Arcais, & K. Rayner (Eds.), *Comprehension processes in reading* (pp. 465–486). Hillsdale, NJ: Lawrence Erlbaum Associates.

Garrod, S., & Sanford, A. J. (1994). Resolving sentences in a discourse context: How discourse representation affects language understanding. In M. Gernsbacher (Ed.), *Handbook of psycholinguistics* (pp. 675–698). New York: Academic Press.

Gernsbacher, M. A. (1989). Mechanisms that improve referential access. *Cognition, 32*, 99–156.

Gordon, P. C., Grosz, B. J., & Gilliom, L. A. (1993). Pronouns, names, and the centering of attention in discourse. *Cognitive Science, 17*, 311–347.

Greene, S. B., McKoon, G., & Ratcliff, R. (1992). Pronoun resolution and discourse models. *Journal of Experimental Psychology: Learning, Memory and Cognition, 18*, 266–283.

Johnson-Laird, P. N. (1974). Experimental psycholinguistics. *Annual Review of Psychology, 25.*

Just, M., & Carpenter, P. (1980). A theory of reading: From eye fixations to comprehension. *Psychological Review, 87*, 329–353.

Just, M., & Carpenter, P. (1992). A capacity theory of comprehension: Individual differences in working memory. *Psychological Review, 99*, 122–149.

Kintsch, W. (1988). The role of knowledge in discourse comprehension: A construction-integration model. *Psychological Review, 95*, 163–182.

Marslen-Wilson, W. D., Tyler, L. K., & Koster, C. (1993). Integrative processes in utterance resolution. *Journal of Memory and Language, 32*(5), 647–666.

McKoon, G., & Ratcliff, R. (1992). Inference during reading. *Psychological Review, 99*, 440–446.

O'Brien, E. J., Shank, D. M., Myers, J. L., & Rayner, K. (1988). Elaborative inferences during reading: Do they occur on-line? *Journal of Experimental Psychology: Learning, Memory and Cognition, 14*, 410–420.

Perfetti, C. A. (1990). The co-operative language processors: Semantic influences in an autonomous syntax. In D. A. Balota, G. B. Flores d'Arcais, & K. Rayner (Eds.), *Comprehension processes in reading* (pp. 205–228). Hillsdale, NJ: Lawrence Erlbaum Associates.

Reder, L. M., & Kusbit, G. W. (1990). Locus of the Moses illusion: Imperfect encoding, retrieval, or match? *Journal of Memory and Language, 30*, 385–406.

Sanford, A. J. (1985a). Aspects of pronoun interpretation. In G. Rickheit & H. Strohner (Eds.), *Inferences in text processing* (pp. 183–205). North Holland: Elsevier Science Publishers.

Sanford, A. J. (1985b). Pronoun reference resolution and the bonding effect. In G. Hoppenbrouwers, P. Seuren, & A. Weijters (Eds.), *Meaning and lexicon*. Dordrecht, Netherlands: Foris.

Sanford, A. J. (1987). *The mind of man*. Brighton, England: Harvester Press.

Sanford, A. J., & Garrod, S. (1981). *Understanding written language: Explorations in comprehension beyond the sentence*. Chichester: Wiley.

Sanford, A. J., & Garrod, S. (1989). What, when and how?: Questions of immediacy in anaphoric reference resolution. *Language and Cognitive Processes, 4*, 263–287.

Sanford, A. J., & Garrod, S. C. (1994). Selective processing in text understanding. In M. Gernsbacher (Ed.), *Handbook of psycholinguistics* (pp. 699–719). New York: Academic Press.

Sanford, A. J., Garrod, S., Lucas, A., & Henderson, R. (1983). Pronouns without explicit antecedents. *Journal of Semantics, 2*, 303–318.

Sanford, A. J., Moar, K., & Garrod, S. (1988). Proper names as controllers of discourse focus. *Language and Speech, 31*, 43–56.

Sanford, A. J., & Moxey, L. M. (1995). Aspects of coherence in written language: A psychological perspective. In T. Givon & M. Gernsbacher (Eds.), *Coherence in spontaneous text*. Philadelphia: John Benjamins.

Shillcock, R. (1982). The on-line resolution of pronominal anaphora. *Language and Speech, 24*, 4.

Tyler, L. K., & Marslen-Wilson, W. D. (1982). Processing utterances in discourse contexts: On-line resolution of anaphors. *Journal of Semantics, 1*, 297–315.

Vonk, W., Hustinx, L., & Simons, W. (1992). The use of referential expressions in structuring discourse. *Language and Cognitive Processes, 7*, 301–335.

Van Oostendorp, H. (1994). Text processing in terms of semantic cohesion monitoring. In H. van Oostendorp & R. A. Zwaan (Eds.), *Naturalistic text comprehension* (pp. 35–55). Norwood, NJ: Ablex.

Wason, P., & Reich, R. S. (1979). A verbal illusion. *Quarterly Journal of Experimental Psychology, 31*, 591–597.

Chapter 2

Modeling Causal Integration and Availability of Information During Comprehension of Narrative Texts

Mark Langston
Tom Trabasso
The University of Chicago

In this chapter, we report on an approach to the study of comprehension that employs a combination of discourse analysis and connectionist modeling. In so doing, we provide a theoretical account for how readers make causal inferences and construct dynamic representations of the text over the course of processing sentences. We focus on how clause information is accessed and integrated during reading. The basis for availability and integration of clauses is the use of knowledge about events, agents, emotions, intentions, goals, plans, actions, and outcomes to understand what happens in narratives. The discourse analysis, based on logical criteria, is used to identify the causal relations that might be inferred by readers between the clauses of the narrative text. The connectionist model integrates each new clause into a narrative context of prior clauses via causal connections between clauses.

The model's integration over successive clauses builds a dynamic representation of the narrative context during processing. As each clause is integrated, the model updates the connection strengths of the clauses with one another. This dynamic process continues until all the narrative clauses are integrated. A clause's connection strength at any moment thus reflects its history of processing and indexes its availability. The psychological validity of the model is assessed by how well it can mimic a variety of empirical findings on reading comprehension and memory.

Our approach provides a basis for understanding and quantifying *accessibility* through causal reasoning and *availability* of information stored in a memory representation during comprehension. Comprehension, in our approach, depends on relating ideas and connecting information from text clauses in a meaningful way, storing, and using the results of integration in further processing of the text. For us, the main way of relating narrative clauses meaningfully and achieving coherence in understanding is through the use of causal reasoning (Mackie, 1980). Causal reasoning about events requires the making of inferences that relate the events portrayed in the narrative. Hence, our assumption that readers use knowledge of human intention and causation to relate clauses that refer to states, actions, and events in narratives. This knowledge (or its lack thereof) constrains the kinds of inferences that readers make over the course of reading and understanding a narrative text. However, the knowledge that readers access during comprehension is, in turn, constrained by information in the text and by the inferences that are or have been made to earlier clauses. Thus, knowledge, text, and inferences are all important to construction and use of changing memory representations of what is being read. They are particularly important to the *integration* of new clauses into the existing narrative context. The construction of the representations, however, depends on whether such knowledge and information are accessible and available to readers.

We propose a discourse analysis and connectionist model that, together, provides a quantitative account for accessing and making available information from clauses over the course of understanding a text. The availability of prior information changes each time a new clause is integrated. The present model indexes this differential availability over the course of processing through its computations of connection strengths of nodes that represent information from the clauses. One index of availability is the strength of connections between a pair of clauses. Another is the average connection strength that one clause has to all the clauses that have been processed up to that point. Accessing and retrieving information from a prior clause, then, depends primarily on its connection strength to information from other clauses. A large number of empirical studies have been reported during the past decade on how accessible or available is information to readers during and after reading (Graesser, Millis, & Zwaan, 1997). The validity of connection strength as an index of the availability of information is assessed in how well it mimics several of these findings on reading comprehension.

INTRODUCTION

General Assumptions

When readers experience a series of events through reading of the text, they do not experience these events as a series of random happenings, but as a coherent sequence. How do the readers achieve this feeling of coherence? Coherent understanding of a discourse requires considerable knowledge and numerous inferences (Graesser, Singer, & Trabasso, 1994). The discourse provides data that activates the necessary relevant knowledge. It also enables the generation of inferences that relate the ideas expressed in clauses or sentences. The reader uses the activated knowledge and inferences to construct a coherent memory representation of the discourse. This memory representation is important to later use of what was acquired from the discourse.

Comprehenders experience events over time. Integration of these events by the reader into the memory representation provides the basis for coherence and subsequent use of information. The first event provides a *context* in which one can understand a subsequent event. The understanding of the second event affects the understanding of the first event. Comprehension, then, may be viewed as dynamic and interactive over time. In general terms, the understanding of each new event occurs in the context of all of its preceding events, and at the same time, the new event can affect how the prior events are understood. Events in a sequence, then, are mutually constraining and one has to "update" one's understanding as each new event is processed. One goal of the present research is to take into account quantitatively this kind of dynamic understanding.

In *narrative discourse*, in particular, inferences entail the use of knowledge of psychological and physical causality. The use of knowledge about human goals, plans, and actions is central to making relevant inferences. We assume that people have considerable expertise to make sense of what they read or hear about human behavior. Causal explanations or predictions are the kind of inferences that connect the events in the narrative. Because very young children exhibit the use of knowledge of goals and plans in interpreting events that they witness as they encode pictorial events (Trabasso & Nickels, 1992; Trabasso, Stein, Rodkin, Munger, & Baughn, 1992), we may be safe in assuming that adults are equally or more expert in being able to understand the motives and actions of others.

Situation Models and Causal Connections

Researchers differ as to which aspects they have chosen to include in their analyses of situation models of narrative understanding. The focus may be on objects located in space over time (Glenberg, Myer, & Linden, 1987; Morrow, Greenspan, & Bower, 1987), the temporal sequencing of actions in a script (Schank & Abelson, 1977), the motivations and causes of the actions (Schank, 1975; Trabasso, van den Broek, & Suh, 1989), the spatial perspective and location of the experiencer in the story world (Segal, 1995), interacting agents (Graesser et al., 1997) or the emotions experienced by the characters and the experiencer (Stein & Levine, 1989, 1990; Tan, 1996).

Perhaps the most comprehensive and systematic study of what affects the ease of constructing a situation model is that put forth by Zwaan and his colleagues (Zwaan, Langston, & Graesser, 1995; Zwaan, Magliano, & Graesser, 1995). In construction of a situation model, the reader "indexes" and monitors concurrently several natural, literary text properties that contribute to situation continuity: temporal, spatial, characters, intentions, and causes. Changes in these properties, from sentence to sentence, were identified by Zwaan and his colleagues and entered into multiple regression analyses of the time it took to read each sentence. Temporal and causal breaks had significant, unique effects on variation in reading time: the larger the change in temporal or causal continuity, the longer it took readers to read the sentence. These findings were replicated in the first and second reading of literary passages scored for temporal, spatial, and causal continuity by the same procedures.

In a related study, Magliano, Trabasso, and Langston (1995) had participants rate each sentence as to how well the sentence fit into the preceding context. Fit ratings were obtained on a first and again on a second reading of narratives, 13 to 18 sentences in length. Reading times were obtained from an independent group of participants who read the same narratives. Magliano et al. found that causal continuity correlated with the fit ratings and reading times of the sentences, whereas temporal and spatial factors were not consistently significant. They also found that both distal and proximal causal relations accounted for substantial unique variance in fit judgments and reading times.

Thus, in contexts of reading narrative texts that vary in properties important to the construction of a situation model, readers monitor and are affected by the presence or absence of potential causal connections between sentences, both locally and at a distance.

Empirical Evidence on Causal Connections
in Discourse Comprehension

The fact that causal connections affect comprehension of text is widely established. Here, we cite a selected set of studies that have focused on causality and provide evidence for this fact. Furthermore, the studies cited provide the set of empirical findings for which we wish to provide a theoretical account. The findings are that (a) causal connections affect judgments of causal relatedness between sentences, speed of understanding a consequent sentence after reading its cause, and the likelihood of recalling a causal consequent, given its cause as a cue (Myers, Shinjo, & Duffy, 1987); (b) causal connections affect judgments of importance of sentences (Trabasso & Sperry, 1985); (c) causal connections affect priming of a causal antecedent by the reading of its causal consequent (Lutz & Radvansky, in press; Rizzella & O'Brien, in press; Suh & Trabasso, 1993); (d) causal connections affect judgments of ease of understanding or "fit" of a current sentence into a story context (Magliano et al., 1995); (e) causal connections affect recall of individual sentences and whole stories (Trabasso, Suh, & Payton, 1994; Trabasso, Suh, Payton, & Jain, 1994); (f) causal connections affect judgments of story coherence (Trabasso, Suh, & Payton, 1994).

MODELING INTEGRATION DURING COMPREHENSION

Goals of Our Approach

Our main goal is to provide a theoretical account for empirical findings on causal connectivity and discourse comprehension. To do this, we advocate and use a discourse analysis of the text materials in an experiment to identify a priori causal connections that *could be made by the readers* during the processing of a discourse. We use a connectionist model to simulate how people might use their "expert" knowledge of psychological and physical causation to make these causal connections during understanding and to represent their interpretations of events and event relations in memory. The model is used to simulate the integration of causal connections during understanding as well as after all of the events have been understood. The model's measures of clause connection strength are assumed to assess the availability of information from a clause during or after processing. The validity of the discourse analysis and the model is tested by quantitative comparisons between the model's measures of clause connection strength with empirical findings.

Outline of the Approach

Figure 2.1 begins with a *text* that a reader experiences as connected discourse. The discourse of interest here is that of a narrative text. We semantically analyze the text a priori to determine possible causal relationships that could be inferred between clauses. A discourse analysis is used to identify these potential, necessary, causal connections between the conceptualizations that underlie the sentences. For us, meaning is defined in terms of the conceptualizations (interpretations) of sentences that are related by comprehenders via connecting, causal inferences. For example, "anger" as a state may be understood in terms of its precipitating event and what the person wanted as well as its associated affect and the goals and plans that stem from it (Stein & Levine, 1990; Stein, Trabasso, & Liwag, 1994).

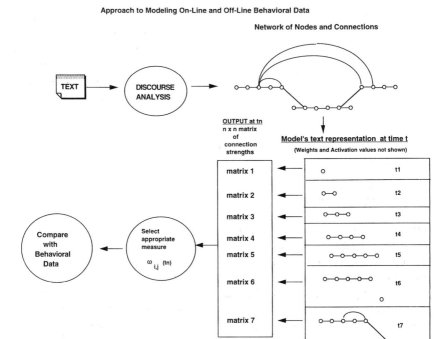

FIG. 2.1. Schematic outline of approach to the study of discourse comprehension.

From the discourse analysis, we *construct* a "semantic representation" of
the text. This representation is realized as a network of nodes that represent
clause or sentence content and the connections between the nodes that
represent causal inferences. The inferences themselves may represent
clause chains that readers make to bridge clauses (cf. Trabasso & Magliano,
1996, for think-aloud methods for revealing causal inference reasoning
chains that integrate text). We then implement the connectionist model
by providing the model, as input, a matrix of nodes and connections from
which the model constructs text representations. We simulate processing
of sentences as their integration into text representations constructed by
the model as it processes each clause or sentence. The model receives one
new sentence or clause and its connections to prior sentences or clauses
at a time. Each new sentence or clause is represented in the matrix as a
node and its connections to the previously represented nodes. The model
integrates the input information into a quantitative representation of the
text. The integration is quantified in output matrices that reflect changes
in the text representation with each sentence or clause input. From the
model's outputs, different quantitative measures are derived for validation

against data on human comprehension. Which measures are used requires a psychological analysis of the tasks and processes that lead to the empirical data.

To the extent that measures output by the model "mimic" or correspond to empirical findings, the theoretical account has "predictive validity." The validation is a test of the assumed constructive and integrative processes (i.e., the discourse analysis's identification of a network of causal connections), the model used to integrate them, and the particular measures of integration that are derived from the model. It is important to recognize that the model's measures depend on the discourse model for input but quantification of the discourse analysis's output is necessary for comparisons against empirical data on availability during or after processing.

Discourse Analysis. To understand the logical basis of the discourse analysis, assume that when the comprehender makes causal inferences between the contents of clause A and clause B, the comprehender constructs a conceptual dependency between clause A and clause B. This dependency may be tested by counterfactual reasoning. Clauses A and B refer to events A and B in a set of circumstances. The set of circumstances are important because "causes" are selected conditions from sets of individually necessary but jointly sufficient conditions. Narrators select causal content from these sets of conditions and present it in a narration. If so, then the occurrence of A is said to be necessary, in the circumstances, for the occurrence of B. This provides for a logical, counterfactual test of the form: if not-A, then not-B (Mackie, 1980). That is, if event A is removed from the circumstances of the narrative and things are allowed to go on from there, event B will not occur. It is also possible that causal connections meet criteria of "weak" sufficiency (Mackie, 1980). That is, if event A is put into the circumstances of the narrative and things are allowed to go on from there, then event B will occur. In either case, event A is one part of a set of individually necessary but jointly sufficient conditions for the occurrence of event B. Note that we do not assume that readers engage in this kind of logical reasoning. The criteria of necessity and sufficiency are used in discourse analysis to test intuitively for conceptual dependencies between events A and B (see van den Broek, 1990, for a detailed discussion of necessity and sufficiency criteria in identifying causal relations).

To identify potential causal relations among a set of events in a narrative, candidate causes may be found by posing why or how questions on each event in the sequence (Graesser, 1981; Graesser & Clark, 1985). The candidates will be causally prior clauses. Each candidate is tested counterfactually. If the counterfactual test is passed, we infer that a conceptual dependency exists between the candidate antecedent clause and the consequent clause. The counterfactual analysis is used to identify direct causal connections. That is, no other cause should intervene between the candidate antecedent clause and its consequent. However, indirect causal relationships can be inferred from direct connections by transitivity. Furthermore, the connectionist model computes connection strengths between all clauses.

Episodic categorization of clauses also can aid in identifying causal relations of different kinds. In the following example, an Initiating Event psychologically causes a Goal (see Trabasso et al., 1989, for a more complete description of identifying causal relations and episodic structures of narratives):

Text sentence B: "Ivan was determined to kill the giant"

Candidate A: "Ivan heard that a giant was terrifying people in his village"

Test: If Ivan had not heard that a giant was terrifying people in his village, he would not, in the circumstances of the story, be determined to kill the giant.

Causal Network Representations. When the discourse analysis is completed, an $n \times n$ matrix of directly connected clauses results. Given this matrix, the model, described here, computes strengths for the direct connections. The direct connections are used to discover indirect connections between clauses. The connections in the matrix are bidirectional.

Each node in the matrix has an initial self-connection strength of 7. All direct connections have initial strengths of 6. Indirect connections decline from 5 to 0, depending on the number of intervening clauses. These initial values are arbitrary. They serve to weight differentially causal relationships by distance in the surface text between clauses (see Kintsch, Welsch, Schmalhofer, & Zimny, 1990).

The matrix can be represented graphically as a causal network of nodes and connections. Figure 2.2 shows the causal networks that were used by Suh (1988) to construct two kinds of stories with substantially the same content. The episodic structures in Fig. 2.2 follow the notation of Trabasso et al. (1989).

In the "Goal Fail–Success" story, for example, a warrior, Ivan is introduced in a setting (S1) and he learns that a giant has been terrorizing and killing villagers (E1). As a result, he is motivated (G1) to kill the giant and he shoots an arrow (A1) but the giant is only wounded and not killed (O1). A famous swordsman comes to Ivan's village (E2) and Ivan decides to learn how to use a sword (G2), practices and trains with the swordsman (A2a and A2b), becomes a skilled swordsman (O2), and his teacher then rewards him with a new sword (R2). The outcome of his training enables Ivan to find the giant and attack him with his sword (A3a and A3b), resulting in the giant's death (O3). The villagers are overjoyed and welcome him back to the village (R3).

GOAL FAIL-SUCCESS STORY NETWORK

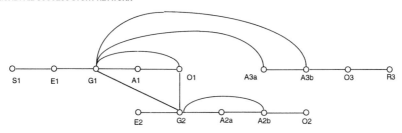

GOAL SUCCESS STORY NETWORK

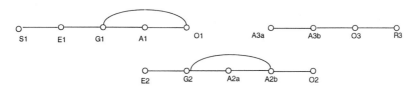

FIG. 2.2.   Network representation of two versions of a story.

In the "Goal Success" story, for example, Ivan kills the giant with an arrow (O1). He then learns to become a swordsman and so on and ends up being welcomed back to the village.

In Fig. 2.2, the goals (G1 and G2) have more connections in the Goal Fail–Success version than in the Goal Success version (5 vs. 2 for Goal 1 and 5 vs. 3 for Goal 2). Although Suh (1988) and Trabasso and Suh (1993) termed these stories "Hierarchical" and "Sequential" because of the overall structures of the stories, it should be apparent that their main differences in structure are reflected in their goal and overall connectivity (see also Goldman & Varnhagen, 1985; van den Broek, 1988, for analyses and studies on stories that have hierarchical or linear structures).

The next step in our approach is to present the network representation to the model for processing each node and connection. We now introduce the model and its assumptions.

Components of the Model.   The model contains one main storage area called the *text representation.* The text representation of the model contains nodes, connections between nodes, and quantitative values that change over time as each new node is processed. The nodes in the text representation correspond to clauses or sentences from the discourse being modeled. Each node in the text representation has associated with it some *activation value* that changes over time as the text representation is constructed. Each connection represents the relationship between a pair of sentences in the text, as identified by the discourse analysis described earlier. Each connection has associated with it a *connection strength* that also changes over time as new nodes and their connections are integrated into the existing text representation. The activation values and connection strengths reflect, through processing, both the current memory representation of the reader and the history of her comprehension.

The model performs two main computations: It *spreads activation* among nodes in the text representation and it *adjusts connection strengths* based on the results of the activation spread. Collins and Quillian (1969; see also Anderson, 1983; Fletcher, 1981; McKoon & Ratcliff, 1980, 1984; Meyer & Schvaneveldt, 1976) proposed the spread of activation among concepts in memory as a fundamental psychological process involved in memory retrieval and concept association. This process has been instantiated in many successful models of psychological processes (Goldman & Varma, 1995; Goldman, Varma, & Coté, 1996; Just & Carpenter, 1992; van den Broek, 1990; van Dijk & Kintsch, 1983). Spreading activation results in quantities that reflect the overall structure of a network representation, accounting for both direct and indirect connections between nodes. This property allows the use of activation values to modify connection strengths between nodes so they more accurately reflect the current state of the representation. To achieve this, a form of correlation learning rule is used. This type of rule was originally specified by James (1890) as a mechanism for learning concepts, and by Hebb (1949) as a neurological learning mechanism. The correlation rule specifies that connection strengths should be modified by the activation of the nodes at either end of the connection. This implies that if two nodes become highly active at the same time, the connection between them will be strengthened to reflect this context-sensitive dependence. In relation to our model, when two sentences become highly active due to some change in the text representation (e.g., the introduction of a consequence that was necessitated by an antecedent sentence), the connection between those two sentences would be strengthened to reflect their relationship to each other as well as their relationship to the rest of the text representation.

Together, the spreading activation mechanism and the correlation strength update rule operate over causal network representations to provide a model capable of accounting for a range of online and offline comprehension measures. The main psychological implication of our model is that the integration of a new sentence and its relations into an existing memory representation changes the entire memory representation. Examining these representational changes, as described by connection strengths over time, provides us with a parsimonious account of the construction of context and the mechanisms implicated in discourse comprehension.

How the Model Integrates a Text.   To understand how the model processes a text and computes the connection strengths and activation values, consider the text representation depicted in Fig. 2.3a. Assume that at time *t*,

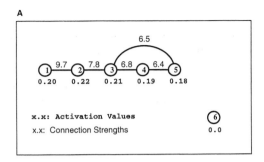

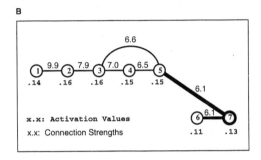

FIG. 2.3. A: The text representation at time t, consisting of six nodes and their connections. B: The text representation at time $t + 1$, consisting of the original six nodes and their connections from time t, plus a new node and its connections.

the text representation consists of six previously processed nodes, their connections, and the numerical values representing their state at time t. Each node in the representation represents one clause or sentence from the text being processed.

At time $t + 1$, the next sentence in the text is processed, causing a new node and its connections to be entered into the existing text representation. This is illustrated in Fig. 2.3b. The new node has an initial activation value of 1.0. Its connections also have initial connection strengths of 7.0. The values associated with the nodes and connections must be updated, because the addition of the new node changes the structure of the existing text representation. This update occurs via a spread of activation among the nodes in the current representation. The new activation value for each node is computed according to the strength of its connections and the activation values of the nodes to which it is connected. Formally, this may be stated as:

$$a_{i(t+1)} = \Sigma a_{j(t)} w_{ij(t)} \tag{1}$$

where $a_{i(t+1)}$ is the activation of node i at time $t + 1$, $a_{j(t)}$ is the activation of node j at time t, and $w_{ij(t)}$ is the strength of the connection between node i and node j at time t. Activation values therefore depend on connection strengths between nodes.

After Formula 1 has been applied, the resulting activation values are converted to percentages of total activation. This normalization is needed to keep the activation values from increasing exponentially.

This procedure is repeated until the total change between the normalized activation values just computed and the normalized activation values previously computed falls below some arbitrarily small value n. This may be stated as:

$$\Sigma a_{i(x)} - \Sigma a_{i(x-1)} < n \tag{2}$$

where $\Sigma a_{i(x)}$ is the sum of the activation values from the current spread of activation, $\Sigma a_{i(x-1)}$ is the sum of activation values from the previous spread of activation, and n is an arbitrarily small value. Therefore, Formula 2 requires that Formula 1 is computed at least twice. Once the inequality in Formula 2 has been satisfied, the activation values for the text representation are considered to have *settled*.

After the activation values have settled, it is necessary to adjust the text connection strengths to reflect the change in the text representation brought about by the addition of the new node and its connections at time $t + 1$. Just as activation values depend on connection strengths, connection strengths depend on activation values. After the activation values have settled, the connection strengths are updated by adding the product of the activation of two nodes and the strength of the connection between them to the current connection strength. Formally this is written as:

$$w_{ij(t+1)} = w_{ij(t)} + (w_{ij(t)} * a_i * a_j) \tag{3}$$

where $w_{ij(t+1)}$ is the new strength of the connection between node i and node j, $w_{ij(t)}$ is the old strength of the connection between node i and node j, a_i is the activation of node i, and a_j is the activation of node j. Once Formula 3 has been applied for all nodes in the text representation, processing is finished for time $t + 1$. If the node just processed was that for the last sentence in the text, processing stops. If not, a new node is entered into the representation and the process repeats.

Assumptions of the Model. There are several computational assumptions that affect how the model processes information. Each assumption is either psychologically or computationally motivated, and together they provide the constraints within which the model operates. First, when a new node is introduced to the model, each new direction connection is given an initial strength of 6.0 before any processing occurs. The processing the model performs over the text representation is responsible for adjusting this value to reflect more correctly the strength of association at a given time between any two sentences.

Second, when a new node is introduced to the model, it is assigned an initial activation value of 1.0. This implies that each new sentence comes into memory with some activation with which it may influence other areas of the text representation via the spread of activation among nodes.

Third, we assume that all nodes are allowed to participate in every processing cycle. The number of nodes and connections over which computations are performed is not limited, as is the case in other computational models of text comprehension (Goldman & Varma, 1995; Goldman et al., 1996; Kintsch, 1988). This assumption was motivated by recent work by Ericsson and Kintsch (1995), who proposed that expertise in a particular task or domain requires a highly efficient organization of long-term memory. This organization allows retrieval and processing of items from memory that does not reflect the constraints of short-term memory. In our model, we assume the representation being used is that of an expert in narrative comprehension, possessing expert-level knowledge of agent-oriented causation. Furthermore, we assume that the data we predict was produced by subject who are also expert comprehenders. This assumption will be supported and discussed later in the chapter, when and after we examine data from various experiments.

Fourth, activation values are converted to percentages after each iteration of Formula 1. This is necessary to constrain activation values to a reasonable range. Without such normalization, activation values would increase exponentially and quickly become unmanageable.

Fifth, we assume that if activation values have not settled after 100 iterations of Formula 1, the settling process is halted and the current values are used in Formula 3. This assumption was necessitated by the types of networks we modeled. Occasionally, the model will receive as input a node that has no connections to the rest of the text representation (e.g., Fig. 2.3a, node #6). When this situation arises, settling cannot be guaranteed. Typically, if the activation values have not settled after 100 iterations, one node is oscillating between two activation values and the settling criterion will never be satisfied. However, the activation values have reached some minimum, and this minimum provides sufficient values for the modification of connection strengths.

Sixth, all settled activation values found at time $t - 1$ are carried over to the next processing cycle. When a new node is introduced to the model, it receives an initial activation value of 1.0. All previously existing nodes begin the new processing cycle with the activation values they had at the end of processing at time $t - 1$. Therefore, a new node begins with 50% of the total activation of the current network, because all activation values were normalized to percentages at the end of time $t - 1$. This may seem excessive, but it has been demonstrated mathematically (Golden, January 23, 1996, personal communication) that the final activation values do not depend on the initial activation values.

In summary, the model receives a network derived from a causal discourse analysis of a text. The causal network is processed one node at a time, to simulate reading. The model incorporates each new node and its connections into an existing text representation, and spreads activation among the nodes. Once activation has settled, the activation values are used to adjust the strengths of the connections between the nodes. At any time during or after this processing, we may extract values from the matrix of connection strengths. These strengths are then used to predict behavioral data.

Model Measures and Behavioral Measures. To determine which values are extracted from the matrix, we must understand the psychological assumptions underlying both the model and the behavioral measures we wish to predict. The psychological assumption underlying connection strengths is that they reflect the change in availability of a node over time. Activation values are computed based on the structure of the text representation at a given point in time, and thus reflect the relative importance of a node with respect to the rest of the representation. This relative importance is used to adjust connection strengths, which come to reflect the overall *availability* of a node given its history of participation in processing. Furthermore, the connection strength between a prior node and a current node is an index of availability of the prior node after processing the current node. Thus, we have a psychological foundation for the selection of one or more kinds of connection strengths for comparison to behavioral data.

It is also necessary to understand the psychology underlying the behavioral measures themselves. For example, in a word-naming task, the subject is probed at a certain point during comprehension with some word or phrase related to the prior text, and asked to respond in some way (e.g., judge whether the probe is a word or non-word). The time necessary to respond to the probe is then recorded. It is assumed that the probe will be responded to quickly if the target is readily available in memory, and slowly if the target is less available. To simulate this, we may extract the strength of the connection between the location of the probe and the location of the target and compare it to the subject's response time. To illustrate this procedure further, consider the probability of recalling individual sentences from a text. The recall probability reflects the overall availability in memory for each sentence of a text after comprehension. In this case, we would compute the mean connection strength for each node in the text representation and compare these means to the recall probabilities for each sentence. By analyzing the psychological assumptions of both the model and the behavioral measures, we are able to obtain model data that accurately reflect the behavioral data. We now turn to that task and present a series of studies that investigated a wide variety of comprehension measures. After each study, we demonstrate the model's ability to account for the data.

VALIDATION OF THE MODEL

We use 12 sets of data from 8 studies to test the psychological validity of our approach. These data test how valid three components of our approach are for accounting for experimental findings on comprehension. The three components are (a) the semantic construction of causal networks via the discourse analysis of texts, (b) the integration of the network representations of sentences and relations into a text representation by the model, and (c) the particular measures derived from the model's text representation to predict the data. The success of the model's measures to mimic behavioral data could be attributable to all three components, but a failure may result from any one component. The three components are thus jointly necessary and sufficient for success but individually necessary for failure.

Five types of data are used to test the validity of our approach: (a) time taken to integrate sentences into a text representation, (b) availability of antecedents during integration, (c) availability of antecedents retrieved during integration, (d) judgments based on integration, and (e) memory for what was integrated into the text representation.

Integration time data come from studies on sentence reading time (Myers et al., 1987). Data on availability of antecedents during integration come from think-aloud protocols that reveal inferences during reading (Suh & Trabasso, 1993; Lutz & Radvansky, in press). Data on availability of antecedents retrieved during integration time come from studies on the time taken to verify prior text sentences (Suh & Trabasso, 1993; Lutz & Radvansky, in press), and the time taken to name a prior text word (Rizzella & O'Brien, in press). Data on judgments based on integration come from studies where readers rate the causal relatedness of sentence pairs (Myers et al., 1987), the importance of individual sentences (Trabasso & Sperry, 1985), or the fitness of sentences into a story context (Magliano et al., 1995). Memory for what was integrated is reflected in data from studies where the readers have read and integrated sentences into the text representation, such as in re-reading and rating sentence fits (Magliano et al., 1995), in recalling sentences that are cued by other sentences (Myers et al., 1987), in free recall of sentences or entire stories (Trabasso, Suh, Jain, & Payton, 1994), or in rating the coherence of an entire story (Trabasso, Suh, & Payton, 1994).

The validation of the model is thus organized according to the integration of the discourse that is assumed to occur in each experimental task. In each application of our approach, we first analyze the text materials used in the experiments according to the discourse model of Trabasso et al. (1989). From the discourse analysis, we construct a causal network representation of each text. We then integrate the causal network by presenting each successive sentence and its connections with previous sentences to the model. The model produces a text representation of nodes, connections, and connection strengths after integrating each sentence input. The text representations change with each sentence, t, and thus represent updating of connection strengths until all sentences have been integrated. To examine correspondences between the model's output and behavioral data, we obtain from the model's text representation connection strengths between two nodes, or the mean connection strength of a node after processing sentence t or after processing all the text sentences.

Time Taken to Integrate Sentences
Into a Text Representation

Reading Time. The first measure of processing during comprehension is that of the time taken to read a sentence in the context of another sentence. A reader should integrate a sentence more quickly if the sentence is directly related to its antecedent. In the model, if a network is linear in structure, outputs for direct connections are stronger than indirect connections and the connection strength between nodes decreases as a function of the number of intervening nodes. Therefore, the shorter the (causal) distance between two sentences in the text, the stronger the connection strength between the pair of sentences, and the shorter should be the time taken to integrate the second sentence with the first.

Myers et al. (1987) reported a study on causal relatedness and cued recall in which they controlled for sentence length. Myers et al. generated 32 stories with five sentences that were causally related in a temporal sequence. An example story is:

(1) Cathy had begun working on a new project.
(2) Cathy worked overtime to finish her project.
(3) Cathy worked very hard and became exhausted.
(4) Cathy felt very dizzy and fainted at her work.
(5) She was carried unconscious to a hospital.

In Experiment 1, participants read pairs of sentences, one sentence at a time. In the pairs, the second sentence was always the last sentence of the story and the first sentence was one of the four preceding sentences. Thus, one pair might be:

Sentence 1: Cathy felt very dizzy and fainted at her work.
Sentence 2: She was carried unconscious to a hospital.

Participants read the sentences knowing that they would be cued for recall of the second sentence by the first (see the following). The time taken to read each sentence was recorded.

We found causal networks for each story of Myers et al. (1987). For example, the discourse analysis of the five sentences of the Cathy story yielded a linear, temporal-causal network: (1) → (2) → (3) → (4) → (5). Causal networks were found for all 32 stories. Of these, 17 were linear and 15 were nonlinear. Each story's network was represented as a 5 × 5 sentence matrix of causal connections. The matrices were processed by the model one sentence (and its connections to antecedents) at a time. The connection strengths between pairs of sentences, (1)–(5), (2)–(5), (3)–(5), and (4)–(5) were found. The correlation between sentence pair connection strength and time to read the second sentence of the pair was negative and significant, $r = -.32$; $F(1, 126) = 14.41$, $p < .01$.

Because the five sentences form a linear, causal chain, the "causal distance" of Myers et al. (1987) was defined in terms of the number of sentences intervening between a pair of sentences. The causal distances thus were: 3, 2, 1, and 0 for pairs (1)–(5), (2)–(5), (3)–(5), and (4)–(5), respectively. Figure 2.4 displays the relationships among mean causal connection strength, causal distance, and reading time for the second sentence of a pair of the Myers et al. study.

Mean connection strength of a pair is linearly and inversely related to causal distance in the network and to the amount of time it took to read the second sentence of the pair. In this case, the model measure of connection strength reflects how many intervening causes readers needed to infer in order to bridge the first and second sentences and successfully integrate them. We present further evidence on connection strength, causal distance, causal relatedness, and recall from the Myers et al. (1987) study next.

Availability of Antecedents During Integration

Think-Aloud Protocols. Suh and Trabasso (1993) varied the number and distance of connections of the first goal in two kinds of stories. Figure 2.2 illustrates the networks used by Suh (1988) to generate these stories. In the Goal Success story, the first goal meets with success after one or two attempts by the protagonist, and had no further connections. In Goal Fail–Success

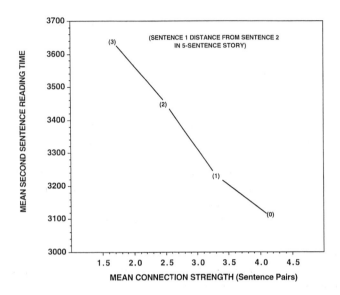

FIG. 2.4.   Time (in msec.) to read the second sentence of a pair after reading the first sentence as a function of the connection strength between the pair of sentences. The distance (number of intervening sentences in a five-sentence story) between the first and second sentence is shown in parentheses. The data are from Myers, Shinjo, and Duffy (1987).

stories, the protagonist initially fails to attain his goal, and generates a subordinate goal that motivates attempts that succeed and then enable him to attain his first goal. Consequently, the first goal has many more connections in the Goal Fail–Success story than in the Goal Success story. The first goal should be more available in the Goal Fail–Success stories than in the Goal Success stories, especially after sentences that are causally connected to it (e.g., attempts motivated by the goal).

Suh and Trabasso (1993) had college students read Goal Fail–Success and Goal Success stories, one sentence at a time, with the instruction to try to understand each sentence in the story and to report to the experimenter their understanding. The "think-aloud" protocols were scored for references made by readers to Goal 1 statements at each sentence in the story. Figure 2.5 shows the proportion of subjects who referred to Goal 1 during thinking aloud about sentences that occurred between Goal 1 and the final outcome of the story for the Goal Success and Goal Fail–Success versions. The percentage values are given on the right ordinate of each graph.

In Goal Success versions, Goal 1 is causally connected to sentences only in the first episode. In the Goal Fail–Success stories, the connections are to initial attempt(s) (A1) of the first episode, the goal of the second episode

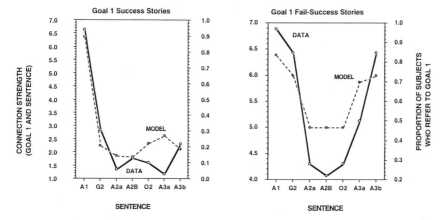

FIG. 2.5. Proportion of subjects who make references to the first goal in think-aloud protocols during understanding of a sentence as a function of connection strength between the first goal and the same sentence after it was integrated. Data are from Suh and Trabasso (1993).

(G2), and to the last two attempts (A3a and A3b). The model was applied to the networks of the eight different Goal Success and eight matching Goal Fail–Success stories used as materials in the Suh and Trabasso (1993) study.

To estimate the availability of Goal 1 after the integration of a sentence, Goal 1's connection strength to each sentence was found after that sentence's entry in each story. The connection strength between Goal 1 and each sentence was then averaged across the same sentences for the respective eight Goal Success and eight Goal Fail–Success stories. The values of these connection strengths are given on the left ordinate of the graphs in Fig. 2.5.

The functions for each measure are similar to the empirical data in each graph of Fig. 2.5. For Goal Success, the proportion of readers who refer to Goal 1 and the connection strength each decline rapidly and reach asymptote at sentence A2a. Furthermore, the two functions coincide, for the most part, over the sentences. For the Goal Fail–Success, each function is U-shaped. However, the connection strengths are higher at sentences A2a, A2b, O2, and A3a, suggesting that the model overpredicts these data. Overprediction (as well as underprediction) of data by the model in this and all the cases is discussed later after presentation of all comparisons of the model with data.

Using the proportion of readers who made reference to goals in the Goal Fail–Success stories, Suh and Trabasso (1993) also traced the fate of the superordinate Goal 1 and its subordinate Goal 2 over the four attempt (A) statements of the second and third episodes. In the second episode,

Goal 2 is directly connected to attempts A2a and A2b, whereas Goal 1 is indirectly connected to these attempts through Goal 2. In the third episode, Goal 1 is directly connected to attempts A3a and A3b, whereas Goal 2 is not. Figure 2.6 displays two graphs, one for the model and one for the Suh and Trabasso (1993) data. The proportion of readers who refer to each goal in their think-aloud protocols are shown in the left graph of Fig. 2.6. The model's connection strength of Goal 1 or Goal 2 with each attempt are shown in the right graph of Fig. 2.6.

The functions in the two graphs are similar in that both show a crossover interaction between availability of goals over the four attempts. Each goal is more available at the attempts to which it is directly connected.

Lutz and Radvansky (in press) replicated and extended the Suh and Trabasso (1993) think-aloud study. Lutz and Radvansky retained and modified the eight stories used by Suh and Trabasso and added new stories. In the initial, "pilot" study, the Goal Success story was renamed "Short," and the Goal Fail–Success story, "Long." Lutz and Radvansky added another structural variation, called "Neutral," where Goal 1 was immediately satisfied by an outcome in the first episode. This change was made to examine the availability of Goal 1 information under two conditions of successful and one of initial failure in completion. Readers read each of 12 stories and typed their "thoughts" into a computer.

Lutz and Radvansky (in press) scored whether a reference to Goal 1 was made at each sentence, from the first goal to the last outcome. We carried out our discourse analysis on each of the 12 Lutz and Radvansky

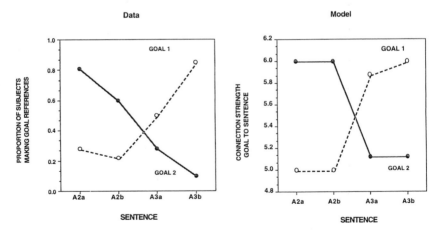

FIG. 2.6. The left graph shows the proportion of readers who referenced the first or second goal (G1 or G2) after reading each of four attempt (A) sentences in the second and third episodes of Goal Fail–Success stories. The right graph shows the connection strength of each goal to each attempt after integration of the attempt. Data are from Suh and Trabasso (1993).

stories for each condition. The obtained causal networks indicated that the three conditions varied in causal connectivity of the stories. For example, the average number of Goal 1 connections was 1.44, 4.44, and 6.56 for the Neutral, Short, and Long versions, respectively. The networks were submitted to the model and the connection strength between Goal 1 and each sentence after its entry was found. Given the differences in connectivity of Goal 1 between the conditions, we expected that Goal 1's availability, as measured by its connection strength to individual sentences, would decline the fastest in the Neutral condition, followed by the Short condition. In the Long condition, it should remain or become more available because, unlike the other two conditions, it is connected to sentences in the second and third episodes.

In order to compare the model's performance with that of readers, we constructed double-Y plots of the two measures with the sentences as the abscissa. Figure 2.7 thus displays, for each condition, the observed proportion of readers who refer to Goal 1 during understanding each sentence with the model's measure of Goal 1's connection strength to the same sentences. The values for the proportion of references is on the right ordinate and the connection strengths are shown on the left ordinate.

The functions of the model and the data are similar within each of the three conditions. For the Neutral condition, the rate of reference and connection strength decline rapidly, reflecting the low connectivity of Goal 1. For the Short condition, the two measures also decline, but more slowly than that observed in the Neutral condition, reflecting the increase in connectivity of Goal 1 to the initial attempts and outcomes. In the Long condition, the model and data decline and show increases later at Goal

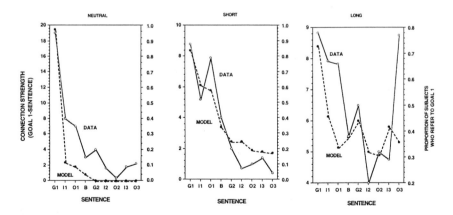

FIG. 2.7. Proportion of readers who referenced the first goal while thinking aloud during reading compared with connection strength of the first goal with each sentence after its integration. Data are from Lutz and Radvansky (in press).

2, once again reflecting Goal 1 connectivity. Thus, as far as functions and different rates of decline over time, the model qualitatively mimics the data. We were unable to evaluate the model quantitatively against the data via correlation analysis because we had access only to mean sentence data from the published report of Lutz and Radvansky (in press). The model's measures, however, underestimate the data of the Neutral and Long conditions. Readers made more references to Goal 1 than the model's measures indicate. These underestimation findings are discussed next.

Availability of Antecedents Retrieved During Integration

Sentence Verification Time. "Priming" of target words or sentences is a method used to infer whether certain information was made available as the result of reading a piece of text. If a sentence is connected to a prior sentence, then information from the prior sentence should be more available after its integration than when the current sentence is not connected to the prior one. In line with this expectation, Suh and Trabasso (1993) found that verification of Goal 1 sentences were faster in Goal Fail–Success than in Goal Success stories. For example, Ivan's goal of killing the giant was verified faster after reading that Ivan learned how to use a sword where Ivan still had the goal of wanting to kill the giant than when he had previously killed the giant.

Suh and Trabasso (1993) presented each story to readers one sentence at a time. After the reader read sentences at certain locations such as A1, G2, A2a, A2b, O2, A3a, or A3b of Fig. 2.2, they were asked to recognize whether or not a target sentence had occurred in the previously read text. The key target sentence was Goal 1 and was located at different places in the stories across three independent experiments with different readers. Because the target sentence was the same in Goal Fail–Success and Goal Success stories, the difference in recognition times for Goal 1 provides the priming data of interest.

The connection strength of Goal 1 to each sentence prior to the Goal 1 recognition test was found. The difference in connection strengths for the matching Goal-sentence pair of the two story structures was then found. This difference in connection strength should reflect the difference in availability of Goal 1 information after the processing of the sentence that preceded the recognition test sentence. Connection strength between Goal 1 and the "priming" sentence, then, should mimic the priming data of Suh and Trabasso (1993; see Fig. 2.8).

The model's measures correspond well, in general, to the amount of priming at different sentences across three experiments. In Experiment 1, the model mimics the shape of the priming function, although the model's values are higher for the right three targets. In Experiment 2, the model and data slopes are in the same direction. In Experiment 3, the model predicts

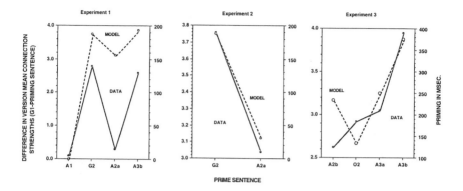

FIG. 2.8. Recognition time differences between targets (Priming) and differences in connection strength between Goal 1 and Priming Sentences for Goal Fail–Success and Goal Success stories. The priming data are from Suh and Trabasso (1993).

the observed increase from the outcome (O2) to the two successive attempts (A3a and A3b) but it overpredicts at A2b (as it did for the think-aloud data of Experiment 1). These overpredictions are discussed next.

In their Experiment 2, Lutz and Radvansky (in press) also tested for facilitation in recognition of Goal 1 statements. In order to test for the availability of Goal 1 information after reading a priming sentence, they probed for recognition of Goal 1 statements (e.g., "Did Ivan want to kill the giant?") at the attempt just before the final outcome in the third episode. Lutz and Radvansky used 18 stories, including those of their pilot study. Three story structure variations were compared. The "Neutral" condition had early goal success and thus fewer connections. Their "Completed Goal" condition corresponds to Suh and Trabasso's (1993) Goal Success version. Finally, their "Failed Goal" condition corresponds to Suh and Trabasso's (1993) Goal Fail–Success version. Their findings are shown in Fig. 2.9. The data show that the reading time was shortest for the Failed Goal condition and longest for the Neutral condition.

Nodes with high connection strengths are more available than those with low connection strengths. Reading time, in turn, should reflect this differential availability of nodes. In the Lutz and Radvansky (in press) study, Goal 1 availability is greater in the Failed Goal than in the Neutral condition. The model reflects this in the connection strengths between Goal 1 and the test sentence across conditions. Therefore, the inverse relationship in Fig. 2.9 shows that the model corresponds to the data very well.

Word Naming Time. Another measure of availability of antecedent information after integration of the current sentence with those in prior text is the amount of time it takes to name a target word (see Keenan,

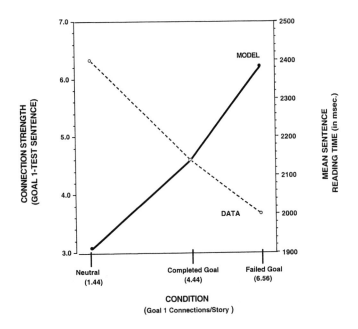

FIG. 2.9. Reading time for first goal sentence verification after reading an attempt related to the first goal for three story Conditions that vary in length and connectivity. The data are from Lutz and Radvansky (in press).

Potts, Golding, & Jennings, 1990; McKoon & Ratcliff, 1990, for reviews of word priming methods). The more available the information related to the target word, the faster the naming of the target word.

Rizzella and O'Brien (in press) studied availability of distant causal antecedents for consequent events. Two early antecedent causes were elaborated by adding new but related sentences to the story text. Participants named a target word presented at the end of the story. The target word came from either the early or late antecedent in a set of two sentences. The elaboration of the early causal antecedents led to faster naming time of the target word than when it was not elaborated. The naming time data are shown for Experiment 1 of their study in the right-hand graph of Fig. 2.10.

We performed a discourse analysis on the published story example of Rizzella and O'Brien for each of the four conditions of Experiment 1 and submitted the resulting causal networks to the model for computation. The discourse analysis showed that the causal antecedents defined by Rizzella and O'Brien were highly connected with the sentences that elaborated it. From the model's output, consistent with the Rizzella and O'Brien

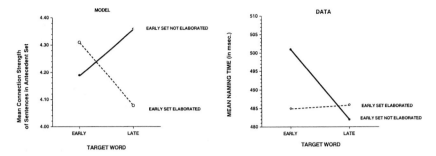

FIG. 2.10. The effect of elaborating a set of early antecedent sentences on the naming times of a target word at the end of the story. The target word was from the early or late set of antecedent sentences. Data are from Rizzella and O'Brien (in press).

identification of antecedents, we found the mean connection strength of the early and of the late antecedent sentences. The data are shown in the left-hand graph in Fig. 2.10.

The model predicts an interaction between elaboration or no elaboration and early or late antecedent words. Connection strengths of early antecedent sentences and, hence, their word availability, are stronger when the early antecedent sentences were elaborated. Strength (availability) should be inversely related to speed of naming. In line with this expectation, in Fig. 2.10, the model's measures were inversely related to the naming time data. However, the model, based on only one story discourse analysis, underpredicts the facilitation of the late word naming in the early elaboration condition. It is possible that these data reflect a floor effect and that readers were naming the target words too fast for differences to emerge between conditions. In order to evaluate this, we would have to perform a discourse analysis on all of the Rizzella and O'Brien stories.

Judgments Based on Integration

Importance Rankings of Sentences. Trabasso and Sperry (1985) analyzed the causal connections of six Chinese folk tales used by Brown and Smiley (1977) to study judgments of importance of sentences. Brown and Smiley had readers sort sentences into quartiles of importance. They then found the average rank of importance for each sentence based on its quartile (1 through 4). Trabasso and Sperry's (1985) criteria for a causal connection was that of necessity in the circumstances, following Trabasso, Secco, and van den Broek (1984). Their original causal network for each Chinese folk tale was processed, one node at a time, by the model and the mean connection strength of each sentence was found. Connection strength of a sentence just after it was processed was found as an online measure, and connection strength of each sentence was found after all sentences of the story were processed.

In the Brown and Smiley (1977) study, the readers processed the entire text and then re-read the sentences several times in order to assign ranks of importance. As a result, they should be sensitive to both antecedent and consequent connections of each sentence. Thus, we would expect that a sentence's mean connection strength after all of the sentences have been processed would be a better predictor of the ratings than its connection strength just after its first, online integration.

Both measures were positively correlated with the rankings of importance of the 348 sentences of the six folk tales (the first sentence of each story was excluded). Thus, as the importance of a sentence increased, so did its connection strength. The correlations between connection strength for a sentence after it was processed with its mean importance ranking was $r = .19$ ($p < .01$). Connection strength at the end of the story rose, $r = .31$ ($p < .01$) and was significantly higher than that for the strength after the sentence was initially integrated (correlated $t = 2.08$, $df = 347$, $p < .05$). This measure of connection strength correlated positively with that after the sentence, $r = .42$, $F(1, 348) = 72.78$, $p < .01$. However, the measure of connection strength at the end of the story accounted for a significant percentage of unique variance in the residuals after the connection strength at sentence integration was partialled out. The latter did not account for any unique variance. The respective correlations with residuals after entering the other connection strength measure were $r = .23$ versus $r = .07$.

Connection strength of sentences after complete story integration, which reflects all the sentence's connections, was therefore a best predictor of the data. The mean connection strength obtained after processing each sentence the first time through the story reflects only antecedent connections, whereas connection strength at the end of the story reflects all connections. This result is in line with the assumption that the readers have read the complete story and took into account the antecedent and consequent connections of a sentence in their rankings of importance.

Figure 2.11 shows the relationship between the number of connections per sentence with their associated mean importance rankings and mean connection strength after complete processing of the story. The sentence mean importance rank and mean number of connections are both related linearly to mean connection strength.

Rating of Causal Relatedness. Myers et al. (1987) had participants read and rate pairs of sentences on a seven-point scale of "causal relatedness." The pairs came from the five-sentence stories just described. The last

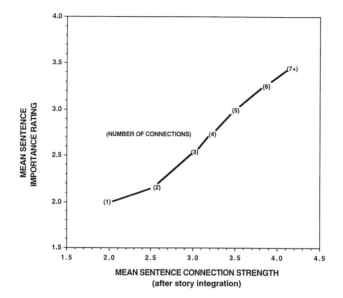

FIG. 2.11. Mean sentence importance ratings compared with number of causal connections (in parentheses) and mean connection strengths after story integration. Importance rating data are from Brown and Smiley (1977). The causal connections are from Trabasso and Sperry (1985).

sentence of each story was paired with each of its four antecedents. There were 32 stories with ratings on each of four pairs from each story.

We found that the model's measure of connection strength between pairs of sentences correlated highly and positively with ratings of causal relatedness, $r = .76$, $F(1, 126) = 166.86$, $p < .01$. Sentence pair connection strength thus accounted for 58% of the variance in participants' ratings of causal relatedness. The right graph of Fig. 2.12 shows the relationship among mean connection strength, causal distance, and causal relatedness of the sentence pairs. All of the relationships are linear.

Readers appear to use both temporal and causal information in judging causal relatedness. Because they are judging the causal relatedness of a pair of sentences that differ in their causal distance, their ratings take into account the number of intervening causes necessary to bridge an antecedent sentence with its consequent sentence.

Myers et al. (1987) defined causal distance in terms of the surface distance or number of other sentences (0 to 3) between a pair of sentences. We found that pairs of the same distance varied in their causal connectivity and, hence, their connection strength. The right-hand graph of Fig. 2.12 compared with that on the left shows that the causal relatedness was more

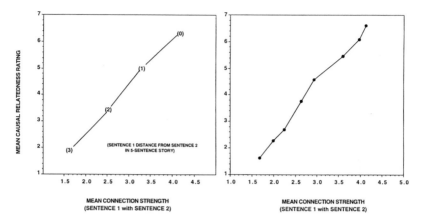

FIG. 2.12. Causal relatedness and connection strength of sentence pairs after integration of the last sentence. The left graph shows causal relatedness and distance in the five-sentence story. The right graph shows the relationship without distance. The data are from Myers, Sinjo, and Duffy (1987).

finely differentiated by variation in connection strength than by the number of intervening sentences in the surface text.

Judgments of Sentence "Fit" Into Story Contexts During First and Second Readings

Magliano et al. (1995) had readers read each story of Suh and Trabasso (1993) and rate "how well each sentence fit into the context of the story" on a 5-point scale where a 5 was defined as *fit very well.* Readers read the story, sentence by sentence, and rated each sentence's fit during their first reading and again during a second reading. The mean fit judgment over readers for each of the 220 sentences (excluding the first sentence in each story) during first and second readings were respectively correlated with mean sentence connection strength, obtained either after integration of each sentence or at the end of the story.

For the fit judgments during the first reading, the correlations were high, positive, and significant [after sentence $r = .40$, $F(1, 218) = 41.37$, $p < .01$; end of story $r = .41$, $F(1, 218) = 42.80$, $p < .01$]. Each measure thus accounted for approximately 16% of the variance in the sentence ratings. For the second reading fit judgments, the correlations with both measures were also significantly positive, though somewhat lower [after sentence $r = .28$, $F(1, 218) = 17.91$, $p < .01$; after story $r = .34$, $F(1, 218) = 38.39$, $p < .01$]. The model's measures did not differ from one another for either reading ($ts = 0.54$ and 1.56, $df = 217$, $p > .05$).

Figure 2.13 shows the plots of the mean connection strength after each sentence was integrated with the mean for the first reading fit judgments (on the left) and mean connection strength after story integration with second reading fit judgments (on the right). Connection strength has a curvilinear relationship with the first reading and a linear relationship with second reading fit judgments. The first reading judgments appear to asymptote at midrange of connection strengths, whereas the second reading fit judgments continue to rise through the whole range of strengths. Readers were more sensitive to average differences in connection strength after having read the whole story.

Modeling Episodic Structure Over the Course of the Story. Figure 2.2 shows that the stories studied by Magliano et al. (1995) had three episodes. Episode 1 includes sentences S1 through O1; Episode 2, sentences E2 through R2; Episode 3, sentences A3a through R3. In Fig. 2.2, there are causal coherence breaks between the Outcome (O1) in Episode 1 and the Initiating Event (E2) in Episode 2. For the Goal Success stories, there is a coherence break between the Outcome (O2) in Episode 2 and the first Attempt (A3a) of Episode 3.

We examined qualitatively whether readers, in the two sets of fit judgments obtained by Magliano et al. (1995), were sensitive to episodic structure and to the breaks in causal coherence. The left graph in Fig. 2.14 displays the mean fit judgments made by readers during their first readings of the stories. These data reveal that readers were indeed sensitive to episodic structure and coherence breaks in evaluating the ease of a sentence's fit into

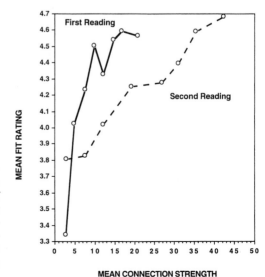

FIG. 2.13. Mean sentence fit rating during first and second readings of a story as a function of sentence connection strength after sentence integration (first reading) or after story integration (second reading). Fit data are from Magliano, Trabasso, and Langston (1995).

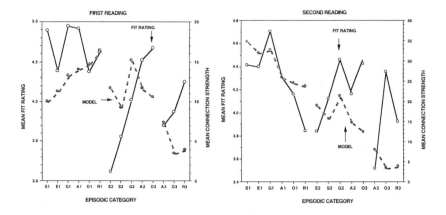

FIG. 2.14. Mean fit rating for sentences in their episodic location and category over the story. First reading fit rating is compared with sentence connection strength after its integration in the left graph. Second reading fit is compared with sentence connection strength after story integration in the right graph.

the prior story context. There are clear drops in the ratings between Episodes 1 and 2 (i.e., between R1 and E2) and between Episodes 2 and 3 (i.e., between R2 and A3). Furthermore, the first reading fit judgments increase within Episodes 2 and 3 but are at ceiling in Episode 1.

How well do the connection strengths of a sentence obtained after its initial integration correspond to these empirical results? The model's measures mimic the changes in the first-reading empirical data across episodic boundaries. However, the model's measures do not capture the within-episode changes.

In Fig. 2.14, the right graph displays the findings for the second reading. Here, readers are more sensitive, but in a different way, in their fit judgments to the episodic structure and appear to be using knowledge acquired about the story structure during the first reading. However, they do not reflect the coherence break at the beginning of the second episode. The model thus mimics some changes in fit judgments over the first two episodes. It underestimates the data in the third episode in both graphs.

Figure 2.14 also reveals a general property of a class of connectionist models (e.g., Goldman & Varma, 1995; Goldman et al., 1996; van den Broek, Risden, Fletcher, & Thurlow, 1996), namely, that during the course of processing, the mean connection strengths tend to decline. This "primacy" effect accounts for the correlations with the fit measures but also for the model's failure to account for increases in ratings near the end of the story. We discuss the "primary effect" and the Goldman and Varma (1995) and van den Broek et al. (1996) studies next.

Memory for What Was Integrated Into the Text Representation

After reading a text, readers may be asked to answer questions, make judgments, summarize, and/or remember parts or all of what they have read (Omanson, 1982; Trabasso & van den Broek, 1985). Although these tasks require retrieval processes, the availability of the text information is affected by what occurred during reading and comprehension. In particular, sentences that were highly integrated into the text representation should be more available. In our model, connection strength reflects the degree of integration of a sentence into the story context. Connection strength should correspond to comprehension or recall measures that index availability of text information. In this section, we examine how integration during reading affects processing of texts after reading is completed.

Cued Recall. Myers et al. (1987) had readers recall the second sentence of a pair cued by presentation of the first sentence. Myers et al. plotted the cued recall as a function of the pair's causal relatedness. In so doing, they grouped the data into eight sets. The mean connection strengths between groups of pairs correlated highly and positively with mean cued recall ($r = .68$, $df = 7$, $p < .05$). Thus, the probability of retrieving the second sentence given the first sentence as a cue corresponded to the mean connection strength of the pair.

Immediate and Delayed Recall of Sentences. Trabasso, Suh, Jain, and Payton (1994) and Trabasso, Suh, and Payton (1994) had readers read sets of eight stories originally studied by Suh and Trabasso (1993). The readers read each story at their own pace and rated the story's coherence. Four of the stories were recalled immediately after the rating was completed. The readers came back 2 days after the first session and were asked to recall the remaining four stories. For the 220 sentences of the 16 total stories ($M = 14.57$ sentences per story), we correlated the proportion of subjects who recalled each sentence, either immediately or after a delay of 2 days, with the sentence's connection strength.

Immediate recall was statistically independent of connection strength after sentence integration [$r = -.03$, $F(1, 218) < 1$]. On the other hand, connection strength after story integration was positively related to the amount of recall when the recall *was delayed for two days* [$r = .21$, $F(1, 218) = 9.79$, $p < .01$]. These data indicate that long-term but not short-term retention is a result of integration of sentences during reading into a relatively permanent text representation.

In order to examine the rate of retention, we subtracted the delayed from the immediate recall proportions. The resulting differences were

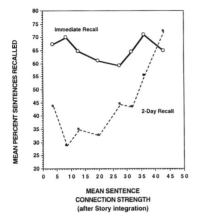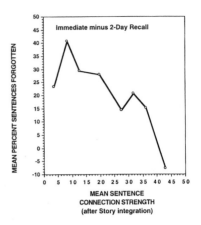

FIG. 2.15. The left graph shows immediate and 2-day recall of sentences as a function of sentence connection strength after story integration. The right graph displays forgetting as the difference between immediate and 2-day recall as a function of sentence connection strength after story integration.

inversely correlated with sentence connection strength $[r = -.22, F(1, 218) = 11.30, p < .01]$. Those sentences with higher connection strengths were retained best, whereas those with low connection strengths were forgotten.

Figure 2.15 shows plots of recall and forgetting as a function of sentence connection strength after story integration. The left graph in Fig. 2.15 shows that immediate recall was high (averaging 67%) and independent of sentence connection strength. Recall 2 days later, however, increased with connection strength. The graph on the right side of Fig. 2.15 shows that the rate of forgetting (difference between immediate and 2-day recall) declined with connection strength. Our analyses thus show that the retrieval of sentences is dependent on integration during reading.

Recall and Coherence of the Whole Story. The preceding analysis was at the level of the *sentence.* In this section, *the story as a whole* is the level of analysis. We examine correspondences between the model and two holistic behavioral measures, namely, coherence ratings and recall of whole stories.

Trabasso, Suh, Jain, and Payton (1994) and Trabasso, Suh, and Payton (1994) obtained coherence ratings of the 16 stories of Suh and Trabasso (1993) prior to recall. In order to predict the coherence and the recall of stories as a whole, we obtained the mean sentence connection strength per story and correlated these measures with the average coherence rating per story and average proportion of sentences recalled per story, both for immediate and 2-day recall. As before with sentences, the model failed to account for immediate recall of the stories. The correlation between the mean connection strength of all the sentences of the story with mean proportion of sentences recalled per story was not significant [$r = -.09$, $F(1, 14) < 1$]. On the other hand, story mean connection strength accounted for substantial variance in both 2-day (long-term) recall and overall coherence ratings. The respective correlations were $r = .51$ for delayed recall [$F(1, 14) = 5.02$, $p < .05$] and $r = .71$ for mean coherence rating per story [$F(1, 14) < 14.5$, $p < .01$]. The correlation plots for the recall and coherence data are shown in Fig. 2.16 along with identification of the story as a Goal Fail–Success (F) or Success (S).

In Fig. 2.16, note that the Goal Fail–Success (F) stories are separable from the Goal Success (S) stories, both in recall and in coherence ratings. For the coherence ratings, there is no overlap between F and S stories. The reason that the model discriminates between the hierarchical and sequential structural differences of the F and S stories is that these structures differ in their causal connectivity and, hence, in their mean connection strength. The categorization of these stories merely describes their structure, but the connection strength quantifies the degree of their integration and predicts their recall and judged coherence.

DISCUSSION

Model Evaluation

In this section, we evaluate the performance of the connectionist model in mimicking empirical findings (see also Goldman et al., 1996). In reporting the correspondences between the model and data, we evaluated the model statistically through regression analyses. In addition, we compared the model against the data graphically in terms of the correspondence

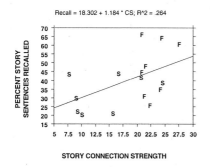
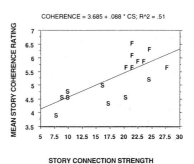

FIG. 2.16. The left scatterplot is of delayed recall and story connection strength. The right scatterplot is of coherence ratings and connection strengths of whole stories. Data are from Trabasso, Suh, Jain, and Payton (1994) and Trabasso, Suh, and Payton (1994).

between empirical functions. We found that the model predicted the data quite well, in general, but also overpredicted or underpredicted some of the data.

Overprediction. One reason for overprediction is that the discourse analysis identifies all possible direct causal relationships between clauses or sentences. If readers make fewer causal inferences than those identified by the discourse analysis, the data will be overpredicted (see, e.g., Fletcher & Bloom, 1988, for indirect evidence that readers make some but not all goal-based inferences). This is what may have occurred in the data of Suh and Trabasso (1993) for Goal Fail–Success stories (see Figs. 2.5, 2.6, & 2.8).

One solution to this problem would be to allow inferences to be made on a probabilistic basis. Thus, differences in knowledge, development, or strategies could be quantified. That is, the likelihood of a connection being made by the model would be less than unity. Although this quantitative adjustment would yield better fits of the data, it is unsatisfactory in that it merely reflects reader differences rather than explains them. Another solution would be to obtain empirical estimates of the likelihood of making inferences and use them in prediction. These estimates might be obtained by question asking (Graesser, 1981) or by think-aloud protocols (Trabasso & Magliano, 1996). Empirical estimates of reader differences in making inferences could be used to improve the accuracy of the fit of the model for particular texts. The empirical estimates would also provide a basis for assessing individual reader differences in age or other indices of knowledge or ability.

The model also overpredicted how well a sentence fit into a story for some causal coherence breaks between episodes (see Fig. 2.14). The model takes into account all connections through its integration rule. As a result, sentences that have no antecedent or no consequent (i.e., lie on a "dead-end"; see Trabasso et al., 1984; Trabasso & Sperry, 1985; Trabasso & van den Broek, 1985) receive more activation and strength than they should. Again, one could adjust the model to give less weight to nodes that have only one connection. However, this post hoc adjustment is unsatisfactory, would constitute "data fitting," and would have no theoretical motivation.

Underprediction. The model, in Fig. 2.7, underpredicted the think-aloud data of Lutz and Radvansky (in press). Readers made *more* goal-based inferences than were expected by the discourse analysis. These results are in contrast with the overprediction of think-aloud data obtained by Suh and Trabasso (1993). These behavioral differences could lie in the fact that Lutz and Radvansky used different methods of data collection and scoring than Suh and Trabasso. Lutz and Radvansky's readers typed their inferences into the computer whereas Suh and Trabasso's subjects reported verbally their inferences to an experimenter. Readers may have been more conservative in reporting inferences in conversation because of pragmatic constraints or limitations of working memory. In scoring goal inferences, Lutz and Radvansky included the superordinate goal and the last outcome sentences in their analysis whereas Suh and Trabasso did not include these sentences. Goals always contain, and outcomes frequently contain, explicit goal information. Inclusion of goal information in the text could inflate what is scored as goal references by readers. Trabasso and Magliano (1996) found that readers frequently paraphrase the current sentence content. If readers paraphrase goal statements and outcome statement content that include goal objects (e.g., "thanking Ivan for killing the giant"), then actual inferences about goals would be highly overestimated in the protocols. Unfortunately, Lutz and Radvansky's protocols were not available to us for analysis so that this issue is undecided. Analyses of them and the sentence content by the criteria used by Suh and Trabasso could help to decide this issue.

Underestimation also occurred in Fig. 2.14 where the model was compared with the fit data of Magliano et al. (1995). Readers gave very high, near-ceiling ratings to early sentences during their first reading. As readers gained more information from the text, they were more discriminating and were not at ceiling in their ratings.

Another reason for underestimation stems from a property of the mathematical model. Other things being equal, the longer a sentence stays in the network, the more strength it accumulates. Sentences integrated later will, in general, be lower in strength than those integrated earlier. The exceptions to this declining trend are those sentences that have more connections (e.g., subordinate goals). The general tendency for later sentences to be lower in connection strength leads to underestimation of empirical data. There is a class of models, based on spreading activation, that gives more weight to sentences that stay in the model longer. This "primacy" bias is found in two models that mathematically resemble our model (Goldman & Varma, 1995; van den Broek et al., 1996). Goldman and Varma discussed at length this aspect of their model. We now discuss each of these models with respect to this issue in comparison to our model.

Comparison With Other Models. Goldman and Varma (1995) developed a computational model that combined the Construction-Integration model of Kintsch (1988, 1992) and the CAPS model of Just and Carpenter (1992). The model is called the Capacity Constrained Construction-Integration (3CI) model. The connection strengths obtained from the 3CI model correlated with some data on adult and child recall and summarization. The texts modeled by Goldman and Varma were parsed into propositions. This parsing yielded one or more nodes for each sentence of the text. An argument overlap and a proposition embedding measure were each computed between pairs of propositions. These measures provided the basis for connecting the propositions. The text representation was fed to the 3CI model, one sentence at a time, and activation was spread among the propositions. After the activation values settled, the connection strengths between each pair of nodes that participated in processing were updated, and the nodes for a new sentence were entered. This procedure was repeated until the entire text was processed.

There are representational and mathematical differences between our model and the 3CI model of Goldman and Varma (1995). We represented information from the text in terms of clauses, whereas Goldman and Varma used propositions. Our connections are causal and are between clauses whereas theirs are based on argument overlap and proposition embedding, both within and between clauses. The difference in focus on clauses versus propositions necessitates different processing assumptions. Whereas a clause or sentence in our approach is represented by a single node, its propositions may require several nodes and thus require assumptions regarding a "working memory" limitation on how many propositions are processed in a cycle. The single-clause assumption avoids the need for a working-memory level limitation (Ericsson & Kintsch, 1995).

The working-memory limitation affects the way in which 3CI computes the spread of activation. Whereas our model allowed activation to spread among all nodes currently in the text representation, the 3CI model used production rules which themselves accrued activation. These production rules limited the spread of activation among only those nodes whose activation surpassed some threshold. This caused the model to eliminate connections that existed between weakly activated nodes, thus simulating a variable-capacity "working memory" within which processing occurred. Although there is no explicit, working-memory limitation in our model, differential availability of nodes for processing occurs. Differential availability is regulated by the connectivity and prior history of a node rather than by an arbitrary restriction on the number of nodes allowed to participate in processing. The effect of a node on processing of current sentences is proportional to its connection strength. This differential availability mimics a working-memory limitation in a graded manner and as an all-or-none threshold.

We noted that the 3CI model exhibited a "primacy effect" as did our model. This fact was observed and commented on by Goldman and Varma (1995) and Goldman, Varma, and Coté (1996). The primacy effect is that connection strengths between nodes are biased toward nodes entered early in processing. Although there is currently no complete explanation for this effect, it appears to be attributable to three factors: the high relative connectivity of early nodes, the normalization of values in each processing cycle, and the increased complexity of the representation over time. Langston, Trabasso, and Magliano (in press) explored processing of hierarchical and linear networks and found that this primacy effect occurred regardless of structure. When the representation is small and relatively non-complex, small differences in connectivity can greatly affect the activation values and subsequent connection strength changes for a node. As the representation grows and becomes more complex, small changes in the number and strength of connections for a node have a smaller impact, and a greater change in connectivity is required to produce activation and strength changes similar to those earlier in processing.

Van den Broek, Risden, Fletcher, and Thurlow (1996) also had success with a model in the same class as ours, using connection strengths to predict probability of word recall. This model, however, computed activation based on both anaphoric and causal relationships, and allowed activation to decay over time. Once again, the model was successful in predicting probability of word recall based on word connection strength, and also demonstrated the "primacy effect" for connection strength, in that those nodes early in the text had a higher mean connection strength than those later in the text.

These studies together provide support for activation-mediated connection strengths as predictive of various behavioral measures of comprehension. They also demonstrate that the "primacy effect" in connection strengths is not limited to our particular model, but is an inherent behavior of the class of models that employs spreading activation as a mechanism for updating connection strengths. Despite this primacy bias, it is evident that this class of models is capable of producing a set of measures, namely, connection strengths, that mimic a range of comprehension measures.

How Necessary Is the Computation Model?   The success of the model in predicting data did not depend on the mathematical rules of the model alone. The semantic component of the discourse analysis was necessary to the computation of connection strength. Given the success of a network of causal connections in predicting the data, the question arises as to how necessary was the model to the approach? An $n \times n$ matrix of connections was input to the model and converted into connection strengths that had psychological interpretations in various contexts. The model is one of many possible transformations of the (1, 0) entries in the $n \times n$ matrix. Any computation on the connectivity matrix could be used but each one would constitute a theory of processing (e.g., distance between nodes in terms of a graph, number of direct connections, or number of indirect connections). In line with this, Trabasso and Sperry (1985) simply counted the total number of connections of a clause and correlated its sum with the importance ranking. Their correlations are comparable to those of the model.

In future work, we plan to compare how well this and other simple metrics do in comparisons with the model on those situations where the whole story has been integrated (e.g., judgments and recall). On the other hand, the model's assessment of updating of strength is not easily available to simple counting metrics or to identification of a causal connection where integration is occurring. For example, the increases in connection strength and in priming over the last three points of Suh and Trabasso's (1993) verification priming data (Fig. 2.8) are not easily captured by presence or absence or sums of connections. In any event, working with activation-mediated models requires some kind of mathematical model for operating on networks.

CONCLUDING COMMENTS

Our identification of causal relations between clauses and their integration by the model together were highly successful in simulating findings on reading comprehension across eight different studies and a variety of tasks. Integration based on causal relationships between clauses provides a robust account of data on comprehension of narrative texts. Connection strength accounted for the time to integrate sentences, the availability of antecedent information during the integration of a current sentence, judgments of importance, causal relatedness, fitness of sentences, coherence of stories as a whole, cued recall and long-term retention and forgetting of sentences, and recall and coherence judgments of stories as a whole. These results were found across studies using reading time, priming, naming time, think-aloud verbal protocols, rating scales, and cued or free recall.

The robustness of the predictions support the idea that readers construct meaning by accessing and relating ideas causally during comprehension. Causal inferences facilitate integration of sentence information into memory representations that are lasting and useful. We are encouraged by the fact that one property, namely causal connectivity, proved so robust in uniting a wide variety of findings.

Our combined use of a discourse analysis to identify, a priori, causal connections, and a connectionist model to integrate clauses via causal connections into a dynamic representation allowed us to trace the availability and retrievability of clause information during and after processing the text. The model enabled us to quantify the strength of relationships between clauses that varied in distance over the text. Further, the model also enabled us to quantify retention. Finally, the model enabled us to measure effects of reading and re-reading on integration of causal antecedents and consequents separately.

ACKNOWLEDGMENT

The research reported here was supported by a grant from the Spencer Foundation to T. Trabasso.

REFERENCES

Anderson, J. R. (1983). *The architecture of cognition.* Cambridge, MA: Harvard University Press.

Brown, A. L., & Smiley, S. S. (1977). Rating the importance of structural units of prose passages: A problem of metacognitive development. *Child Development, 48,* 1–8.

Collins, A. M., & Quillian, M. R. (1969). Retrieval time from semantic memory. *Journal of Verbal Learning and Verbal Behavior, 8,* 240–247.

Ericsson, K. A., & Kintsch, W. (1995). Long-term working memory. *Psychological Review, 102,* 211–245.

Fletcher, C. R. (1981). Short-term memory processes in text comprehension. *Journal of Verbal Learning and Verbal Behavior, 20,* 564–574.

Fletcher, C. R., & Bloom, C. P. (1988). Causal reasoning in the comprehension of simple narrative texts. *Journal of Memory and Language, 27,* 235–244.

Glenberg, A. M., Meyer, M., & Linden, K. (1987). Mental models contribute to foregrounding during text comprehension. *Journal of Memory and Language, 26,* 69–83.

Goldman, S. R., & Varma, S. (1995). CAPping the construction-integration model of discourse comprehension. In C. A. Weaver, III, S. Mannes, & C. R. Fletcher (Eds.), *Discourse comprehension: Essays in honor of Walter Kintsch* (pp. 337–358). Hillsdale, NJ: Lawrence Erlbaum Associates.

Goldman, S. R., Varma, S., & Coté, N. (1996). Extending capacity-constrained construction integration: Toward "smarter" and flexible models of text comprehension. In B. K. Britton & A. C. Graesser (Eds.), *Models of understanding text* (pp. 73–113). Mahwah, NJ: Lawrence Erlbaum Associates.

Goldman, S. R., & Varnhagen, C. K. (1985). Memory for embedded sequential story structure. *Journal of Memory and Language, 25,* 401–418.

Graesser, A. C. (1981). *Prose comprehension beyond the word.* New York: Springer-Verlag.

Graesser, A. C., & Clark, L. F. (1985). *Structures and procedures of implicit knowledge.* Norwood, NJ: Ablex.

Graesser, A. C., Singer, M., & Trabasso, T. (1994). A constructionist theory of inference generation during narrative text comprehension. *Psychological Review, 101,* 371–395.

Graesser, A. C., Millis, K., & Zwaan, R. A. (1997). Discourse comprehension. *Annual Review of Psychology, 48,* 163–189.

Hebb, D. O. (1949). *The organization of behavior.* New York: Wiley.

James, W. (1890). *Principles of psychology* (Vol. 1). New York: Holt.

Just, M. A., & Carpenter, P. A. (1992). A capacity theory of comprehension: Individual differences in working memory. *Psychological Review, 99,* 122–149.

Keenan, J. M., Potts, G. R., Golding, J. M., & Jennings, T. M. (1990). Which elaborative inferences are drawn during reading? A question of methodologies. In D. Balota, G. Flores d'Arcais, & K. Rayner (Eds.), *Comprehension processes during reading* (pp. 377–402). Hillsdale, NJ: Lawrence Erlbaum Associates.

Kintsch, W. (1988). The role of knowledge in discourse comprehension: A construction-integration model. *Psychological Review, 95,* 163–182.

Kintsch, W. (1992). How readers construct situation models for stories. The role of syntactic cues and causal inferences. In A. F. Healy, S. M. Kosslyn, & R. M. Shiffrin (Eds.), *Essays in honor of William K. Estes* (pp. 135–155). Hillsdale, NJ: Lawrence Erlbaum Associates.

Kintsch, W., Welsch, D., Schmalhofer, F., & Zimny, S. (1990). Sentence memory: A theoretical analysis. *Journal of Memory and Language, 29,* 133–159.

Langston, M. C., Trabasso, T., & Magliano, J. P. (in press). Modeling on-line comprehension. In A. Ram and K. Moorman (Eds.), *Computational models of reading and understanding.* Cambridge, MA: MIT Press.

Lutz, M. F., & Radvansky, G. A. (in press). The fate of completed goal information in narrative comprehension. *Journal of Memory and Language.*

Magliano, J., Trabasso, T., & Langston, M. (1995, November). *Cohesion and coherence in sentence and story understanding.* Paper presented at the meetings of the Psychonomic Society, Los Angeles, CA.

Mackie, J. L. (1980). *The cement of the universe.* Oxford, England: Clarendon.

McKoon, G., & Ratcliff, R. (1980). Priming in item recognition: The organization of propositions in memory for text. *Journal of Verbal Learning and Verbal Behavior, 19,* 369–386.

McKoon, G., & Ratcliff, R. (1984). Priming and on-line text comprehension. In D. Kieras & M. Just (Eds.), *New methods in reading comprehension research* (pp. 119–128). Hillsdale, NJ: Lawrence Erlbaum Associates.

McKoon, G., & Ratcliff, R. (1990). Textual inferences: Models and measures. In D. Balota, G. Flores d'Arcais, & K. Rayner (Eds.), *Comprehension processes during reading* (pp. 403–422). Hillsdale, NJ: Lawrence Erlbaum Associates.

Meyer, D. E., & Schvaneveldt, R. W. (1976). Meaning, memory structure, and mental processes. *Science, 192,* 27–33.

Morrow, D. G., Greenspan, S. L., & Bower, G. H. (1987). Accessibility and situation models in narrative comprehension. *Journal of Memory and Language, 26,* 165–187.

Myers, J. L., Shinjo, M., & Duffy, S. A. (1987). Degree of causal relatedness and memory. *Journal of Memory and Language, 26,* 453–465.

Omanson, R. C. (1982). The relation between centrality and story category variation. *Journal of Verbal Learning and Verbal Behavior, 21,* 326–337.

Rizzella, M. L., & O'Brien, E. J. (in press). Accessing global causes during reading. *Journal of Experimental Psychology: Learning, Memory, & Cognition.*

Schank, R. C. (1975). The structure of episodes in memory. In D. G. Bobrow & A. M. Collins (Eds.), *Representation and understanding: Studies in cognitive science* (pp. 237–272). New York: Academic Press.

Schank, R. C., & Abelson, R. P. (1977). *Scripts, plans, goals and understanding.* Hillsdale, NJ: Lawrence Erlbaum Associates.

Segal, E. W. (1995). Narrative comprehension and the role of deictic shift theory. In J. F. Duchan, G. A. Bruder, & L. E. Hewitt (Eds.), *Deixis in narrative: A cognitive science perspective* (pp. 3–19). Hillsdale, NJ: Lawrence Erlbaum Associates.

Stein, N. L., & Levine, L. (1989). The causal organization of emotional knowledge: A developmental study. *Cognition and Emotion, 3,* 343–378.

Stein, N. L., & Levine, L. (1990). Making sense out of emotional experience: The representation and use of goal-directed knowledge. In N. L. Stein, B. Leventhal, & T. Trabasso (Eds.), *Psychological and biological approaches to emotion* (pp. 45–73). Hillsdale, NJ: Lawrence Erlbaum Associates.

Stein, N. L., Trabasso, T., & Liwag, M. D. (1994). The Rashomon phenomenon: Personal frames and future-oriented appraisals in memory for emotional events. In M. M. Haith, J. B. Benson, R. J. Roberts, Jr., & B. F. Pennington (Eds.), *The development of future oriented processes* (pp. 409–435). Chicago: University of Chicago Press.

Suh, S. (1988). *Converging evidence for causal inferences during comprehension.* Unpublished doctoral dissertation, The University of Chicago, Chicago, IL.

Suh, S., & Trabasso, T. (1993). Inferences during on-line processing: Converging evidence from discourse analysis, talk-aloud protocols, and recognition priming. *Journal of Memory and Language, 32,* 279–301.

Tan, E. S. (1996). *Emotion and the structure of narrative film: Film as an emotion machine.* Mahwah, NJ: Lawrence Erlbaum Associates.

Trabasso, T., & Magliano, J. P. (1996). Conscious understanding during comprehension. *Discourse Processes, 21,* 255–287.

Trabasso, T., & Nickels, M. (1992). The development of goal plans of action in the narration of picture stories. *Discourse Processes, 15,* 249–275.

Trabasso, T., Secco, T., & van den Broek, P. (1984). Causal cohesion and story coherence. In H. Mandl, N. L. Stein, & T. Trabasso (Eds.), *Learning and comprehension of text* (pp. 83–111). Hillsdale, NJ: Lawrence Erlbaum Associates.

Trabasso, T., & Sperry, L. L. (1985). Causal relatedness and importance of story events. *Journal of Memory and Language, 24,* 595–611.

Trabasso, T., Stein, N. L., Rodkin, P. C., Munger, G. P., & Baughn, C. (1992). Knowledge of goals and plans in the on-line narration of events. *Cognitive Development, 7,* 133–170.

Trabasso, T., & Suh, S. (1993). Understanding text: Achieving explanatory coherence through on-line inferences and mental operations in working memory. *Discourse Processes, 16,* 3–34.

Trabasso, T., Suh, S., & Payton, P. (1994). Explanatory coherence in communication about narrative understanding of events. In M. A. Gernsbacher & T. Givon (Eds.), *Text coherence as a mental entity* (pp. 189–214). Amsterdam: John Benjamins.

Trabasso, T., Suh, S., Payton, P., & Jain, R. (1994). Explanatory inferences and other strategies during comprehension and their effect on recall. In R. Lorch & E. O'Brien (Eds.), *Sources of coherence in text comprehension* (pp. 219–239). Hillsdale, NJ: Lawrence Erlbaum Associates.

Trabasso, T., & van den Broek, P. (1985). Causal thinking and the representation of narrative events. *Journal of Memory and Language, 24,* 612–630.

Trabasso, T., van den Broek, P., & Suh, S. (1989). Logical necessity and transitivity of causal relations in stories. *Discourse Processes, 12,* 1–25.

van den Broek, P. (1988). The effect of causal relations and goal failure position on the importance of story statements. *Journal of Memory and Language, 27,* 1–22.

van den Broek, P. (1990). The causal inference marker: Toward a process model of inference generation in text comprehension. In D. Balota, G. Flores d'Arcais, & K. Rayner (Eds.), *Comprehension processes in reading* (pp. 423–445). Hillsdale, NJ: Lawrence Erlbaum Associates.

van den Broek, P., Risden, K., Fletcher, C. R., & Thurlow, R. (1996). A "landscape" view of reading: Fluctuating patterns of activation and the construction of a stable memory representation. In B. K. Britton & A. C. Graesser (Eds.), *Models of understanding text* (pp. 165–187). Mahwah, NJ: Lawrence Erlbaum Associates.

van Dijk, T. A., & Kintsch, W. (1983). *Strategies of discourse comprehension.* New York: Academic Press.

Zwaan, R. A., Langston, M. C., & Graesser, A. C. (1995). The construction of situation models in narrative comprehension: An event-indexing model. *Psychological Science, 6,* 292–297.

Zwaan, R. A., Magliano, J. P., & Graesser, A. C. (1995). Dimensions of situation model construction in narrative comprehension. *Journal of Experimental Psychology: Learning, Memory, & Cognition, 21,* 386–397.

Chapter 3

The Landscape Model
of Reading: Inferences
and the Online Construction
of a Memory Representation

Paul van den Broek
University of Minnesota

Michael Young
University of Iowa

Yuhtsuen Tzeng
Tracy Linderholm
University of Minnesota

How do readers construct a memory representation from the texts they read? How does the actual process of going through a text and comprehending individual sentences translate into a mental representation of the text that lingers far after the reader has put down the book? In this chapter we present a detailed description of the way in which cognitive processes during reading allow the gradual emergence of a memory representation. Central to this description is the notion that concepts and propositions fluctuate in their activation as the reader progresses through the text. Using core notions from research on human memory and memory access, we show how this landscape of activations results in a memory representation.

In the first section of this chapter, we describe the central conceptual properties of the landscape view of reading. In the second section, we illustrate the general model by implementing it in a specific theory of reading comprehension (based on the assumption that readers attempt to maintain coherence) and by empirically testing the implementation's validity. In the third section, we pursue implications of this model by describing how it captures specific phenomena and current issues in the area of discourse processing.

THE LANDSCAPE MODEL OF COMPREHENSION
AND MEMORY FOR TEXTS

Three Generations of Cognitive Research in Reading

In the early days of cognitive research on reading, the focus was on what readers remember from the texts that they read. This focus reflected a realization, fueled by anthropological work on the structure of narratives (e.g., Colby, 1973; Propp, 1928), that memory for texts is systematic rather than random. The purpose of this first generation of cognitive research in text comprehension was to determine the defining features of what readers recall and to draw conclusions about the nature of the memory representation that results from reading. One set of models developed in this generation of research emphasized top-down influences on memory, focusing on the role of text elements in the overall structure of the text. Examples include story grammars (e.g., Mandler & Johnson, 1977; Stein & Glenn, 1979) and script theory (Schank & Abelson, 1977) for narrative texts, and hierarchical theories (e.g., Meyer, 1975) for expository texts. A second set of models focused on bottom-up effects, that is, the role that each text element plays in maintaining coherence with other individual elements. These models emphasize that readers attempt to construct mental representations that are coherent in terms of their referential (e.g., Kintsch, 1988; Kintsch & van Dijk, 1978) and causal structure (e.g., Trabasso, Secco, & van den Broek, 1984; see also Goldman & Varnhagen, 1986; Graesser & Clark, 1985).

With the development of methodologies for measuring online activities and activations (eye-tracking techniques, probing techniques, etc.) in the mid-1980s, attention shifted from the product of reading, the memory representation, to the actual process of reading itself. The purpose of this second generation of research was to describe and understand what readers do as they proceed through a text. Here, the focus was on the balancing act that the reader must perform: On the one hand the reader needs to make inferences in order to comprehend the text, on the other hand he or she has limited attentional or working memory resources available to do so. Models in this generation describe the cognitive processes that take place online: What are the inferences that readers routinely make (and what are those they do *not* make), how do the conflicting constraints of limited attentional resources and the need for comprehension interact during reading, and so on. Examples of such models are the Current State Strategy (Fletcher & Bloom, 1988), the Causal Inference Maker (van den Broek, 1990a), the Construction-Integration model (Kintsch, 1988), minimalist theories (e.g., McKoon & Ratcliff, 1992), constuctionist theories (e.g., Graesser, Singer, & Trabasso, 1994; Singer, Graesser, & Trabasso, 1994), and the Structure Building Framework (Gernsbacher, 1990).

Both generations of research continue to exist, yielding important new insights into reading comprehension and memory. However, in the mid-1990s a third generation of research developed. The purpose of research in this generation is to integrate the online and offline aspects of reading (e.g., Goldman & Varma, 1995; Goldman, Varma, & Coté, 1996; Langston & Trabasso, this volume; van den Broek, Risden, Fletcher, & Thurlow, 1996). Thus, the focus is on comprehension processes *and* memory representation and, most importantly, on the relation between the two. This relation is complex and bidirectional because not only is the representation constantly modified as the reader encounters and comprehends new text, but the developing representation itself provides an important resource for the reader in understanding subsequent text. Thus, comprehension of new information updates the memory representation, which, in turn, influences subsequent comprehension. The landscape model presented in this chapter attempts to capture the online processes and the offline representation as well as their dynamic interaction.

The Reading Process: A Landscape of Fluctuating Activations

As a reader proceeds through a text, he or she activates concepts represented by the text and relations among these concepts. Because attentional resources are very limited, however, a reader can only attend to a subset of all the words, concepts, or relations in the text at any one time (Just & Carpenter, 1992; Kintsch & van Dijk, 1978). What determines which concepts are activated? At each reading cycle (i.e., with each new sentence, proposition, or whatever one takes as the unit of text analysis) there are four potential sources of activation. One source is the text that is currently being processed. A second consists of the immediately preceding reading cycle: As the reader commences a new cycle, information that was activated in the preceding cycle is likely to be, at least in part, carried over and available for processing. Third, readers may reactivate concepts that were processed in even earlier reading cycles (of course, these concepts themselves originally would have been derived from any of the four sources). Fourth, they may access and activate background knowledge.

The role of the current text is obvious, but there is also ample evidence that the other three sources indeed influence activation of concepts during reading. Evidence of carryover from previous cycles is found throughout the memory literature (see Klatzky, 1980, for a review) and has been featured strongly in the study of reading, both in theories (e.g., Fletcher & Bloom, 1988; Kintsch & van Dijk, 1978; van den Broek, 1990a) and in empirical findings (e.g., Fletcher, Hummel, & Marsolek, 1990). Likewise, readers frequently reactivate information that was activated in prior reading cycles either because it is required for comprehension (e.g., Goldman & Saul, 1990; O'Brien, Albrecht, Hakala, & Rizella, 1995; O'Brien, Duffy, & Myers, 1986; Suh & Trabasso, 1993; van den Broek, Rohleder, & Narvaez, 1996; van den Broek & Thurlow, 1990) or because it is strongly associated with information in the current cycle (Albrecht & O'Brien, 1993; McKoon & Ratcliff, 1980; O'Brien & Albrecht, 1992). Such reactivation may involve reinstatement of information that was explicitly mentioned in the prior text or that was originally retrieved from background knowledge (Trabasso & Suh, 1993; van den Broek, 1990a). Finally, there is ample evidence that readers routinely—and often automatically—activate background knowledge that is associated with what they read (e.g., Kintsch, 1988; McKoon & Ratcliff, 1992; Sharkey & Sharkey, 1992) or that is required for comprehension (Lucas, Tanenhaus, & Carlson, 1990; O'Brien, Shank, Myers, & Rayner, 1988; van den Broek, Rohleder, & Narvaez, 1996).

Thus, it is clear that readers have each of these four sources available to activate concepts as they read. That is not to say that investigators agree on which sources actually are used in a particular instance. Much current research is stimulated by different views on the circumstances in which each source is accessed (e.g., the debate between "minimalists" and "constructionists"; Graesser et al., 1994; McKoon & Ratcliff, 1992; Singer et al., 1994). Here the important point is that most, if not all, researchers agree that readers at various times activate concepts from each of these four sources.

Together, limited attentional capacity and access to these sources of activation cause text elements constantly to fluctuate in activation as the reader proceeds through a text. With each reading cycle, new concepts are activated, some old ones are retained, and others are removed from the focus of attention or working memory (cf. Kintsch & van Dijk, 1978). These fluctuations are central to the proposed model of reading. By simultaneously considering the activation "peaks" and "valleys" for each concept across reading cycles, one obtains a "landscape" of activations (van den Broek, Risden, et al., 1996).[1] Figure 3.1 provides an example of such a landscape. This particular landscape is derived for the short narrative in Table 3.1 using certain assumptions about the factors that determine the activations of concepts. We return to these assumptions later in this section, but for the moment we simply illustrate a landscape and its general properties. On the vertical axis is the level of activation (here arbitrarily depicted on a 0–5 scale);

---

[1]We are not the first to use a landscape metaphor. In 1890, William James described concept activation during sentence reading in a similar fashion (*Principles of Psychology*, pp. 279–283).

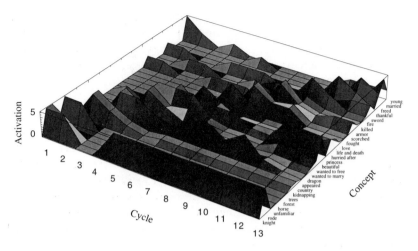

FIG. 3.1. Landscape of activations for the knight story.

TABLE 3.1
The Knight Story

1. A young knight rode through the forest.
2. The knight was unfamiliar with the country.
3. Suddenly, a dragon appeared.
4. The dragon was kidnapping a beautiful princess.
5. The knight wanted to free her.
6. The knight wanted to marry her.
7. The knight hurried after the dragon.
8. They fought for life and death.
9. Soon, the knight's armor was completely scorched.
10. At last, the knight killed the dragon.
11. He freed the princess.
12. The princess was very thankful to the knight.
13. She married the knight.

On one horizontal axis are the concepts relevant to the text,[2] and on the other horizontal axis are the reading cycles. A cross-section at a reading cycle shows which concepts are activated during that cycle, whereas a cross-section at a concept captures the concept's activation history over the course of reading. A cross-section at a vertical plane shows which concepts exceed a particular activation threshold, and when they do so.[3]

---

[2]Only concepts directly relevant to the text are included. A complete depiction would include *all* concepts that a person possesses. Most of the additional concepts would, of course, receive zero activation. Those with non-zero activation result in context-dependent learning.

[3]One might speculate, for example, that consciousness consists of those concepts that exceed a certain threshold of activation (Baars, 1988).

In the current model, the dynamic properties of the shifting landscape are captured in a computational, connectionist model. The technical details of this model have been presented elsewhere (van den Broek, Risden, et al., 1996; van den Broek, Young, & Risden, 1996). Here we focus on the major conceptual aspects of the model.

Levels of Activation and Processing Resources. Central to the Landscape—indeed to any—model of reading is the nature of activation. In the Landscape model, activation is conceptualized in accordance with recent models of working memory (e.g., Just & Carpenter, 1992). First, the Landscape model assumes that concepts can be activated to different degrees. This dimensional view differs from all-or-none views according to which a concept is either activated or not activated. Thus, some concepts can be squarely in the center of attention while others are hovering in the background, still activated but less so.

Second, readers are assumed to have available a limited pool of activation that can be distributed over concepts. Thus, if a reader activates a few concepts very strongly, the pool that is available for other concepts declines and either only a few additional concepts can be activated or their activations will be small. This view of attentional resources contrasts with views in which attention or working memory consists of a determinate number of slots. An interesting consequence of the pool-of-activation feature is that as readers proceed through a text and accumulate more information, they either have to spread the available resources more thinly or more selectively, or they have to recruit more resources (e.g., by increasing concentration).[4]

Retrieval From Background Knowledge or From Prior Cycles: Cohort Activation. At times, readers may import concepts that are not mentioned in the current sentence. This occurs when concepts are retrieved from background knowledge or from the reader's emerging representation of the text itself. Such retrieval is likely to happen in two circumstances: When the to-be-imported concepts are strongly associated with concepts in the current processing cycle, and when the concepts are retrieved for a specific purpose, for example to allow comprehension of the current sentence. We discuss such specific purposes later. For now, our concern is with the mechanics of retrieval regardless of its origin.

---

[4]In the implementations of the model discussed later, no explicit limits are imposed on the available pool of activation. There are two reasons for this. First, the texts used to illustrate and test the models are simple and unlikely to challenge any limited resources. Second, it allows us to show how the competition learning curve (described in the next section) already considerably constrains the flow of activation.

A central feature of the Landscape model is that the processing of a concept is accompanied by *cohort activation*: When a concept is activated, other concepts that are connected to it (i.e., its cohorts) will be somewhat activated as well. This view is closely related to the explicit/implicit focus theory of memory retrieval developed by Garrod and Sanford (1990; see also Ericsson & Kintsch, 1995; Kintsch, 1988; Ratcliff & McKoon, 1988). In the Landscape model, the amount of activation for a secondarily retrieved concept is a function of the strength of its relation to the primarily retrieved concept and of the amount of activation that the primary concept received. Furthermore, it is a function of a cohort-activation parameter that captures the extent to which activation of a primary concept is transferred to members of its cohort. This parameter can range from 0 (no cohort activation) to 1 (activation of cohort concepts is maximal).

As the reader's mental representation for a text emerges during reading, new concepts are added and new associations are formed. Thus, a concept's cohort at one point in the text differs from its cohort at another point and, hence, so will the activations it triggers. In this way, the emerging representation exerts a powerful influence over the online process, which, in turn, influences further changes in the representation.

Carryover From Preceding Cycles and Decay. Part of a concept's cohort is the concept itself. Thus, a concept can maintain its own activation through cohort activation. When the cohort-activation parameter is less than 1.0, concepts exhibit a gradual decrease in activation over subsequent cycles, thus mimicking decay. Like any other member of its cohort, the concept's activation in subsequent cycles is a function of the concept's activation in the preceding cycle and the strength of its self-connection, which we designate its *node strength*. A concept with high node strength is more likely to remain in memory for a while, whereas one with low node strength is more likely to fade quickly after its initial activation.

This description of the activation dynamics for a concept over reading cycles applies to the situation in which the original concept is not reactivated in the subsequent cycles. If the concept is rementioned or for some reason is retrieved from background knowledge or reinstated from preceding cycles, then such reactivation would override the carryover function.

The Sources of Activation and the Landscape Model. The Landscape model in its general form is impartial to the sources of activation. Therefore, it can accommodate any combination of the four sources of activation discussed earlier and, indeed, of any other source of activation one might hypothesize. In this chapter, we present an implementation of the model that includes all four sources. Central to such implementations is the notion that the pattern of activations and deactivations is not just a reflection of the text itself. Instead, it is the result of an interaction among the text, the reader's attentional capacities, his or her background knowledge, and the reader's criteria for comprehension and hence for retrieval.[5]

The Reading Product: The Landscape Builds a Mental Structure

The outcome of a successful reading process is a coherent mental representation of the text. Prior research on memory for texts indicates that such representations resemble networks of interrelated concepts (propositions, sentences, etc.). Memory for a particular concept is a function of its individual properties as well as of its relations to other concepts. Among the individual properties, the number of times a concept is mentioned and its salience are important (Kintsch & van Dijk, 1978; Mandler & Johnson, 1977; Miller & Kintsch, 1980; Perfetti & Goldman, 1974; Stein & Glenn, 1979; Trabasso & van den Broek, 1985). With respect to relations, a concept's number of connections to other concepts has been found to be a particularly powerful predictor of memory strength (Fletcher & Bloom, 1988; Graesser & Clark, 1985; O'Brien & Myers, 1987; Trabasso & Suh, 1993; Trabasso & van den Broek, 1985; van den Broek, 1988; van den Broek & Lorch, 1993; van den Broek & Trabasso, 1986).

The Learning Process: Building Nodes and Connections. How do the online activations result in such a memory representation? In the Landscape model, the online activation vectors dynamically and gradually construct the representation. The changes in activation vectors are captured in the mental representation in such a way as to permit storage of a memory for these changes that is as efficient as possible. The emerging representation tries to encode the ordered associations among the story's concepts and their appropriate levels of activation. This encoding is captured by a network of directional connections among the concepts, including the aforementioned self-connections (i.e., node strengths). The construction of connections between concepts allows the model to anticipate and encode the activation of one concept on the basis of the activation of other concepts. These connections, in turn, enable the model to reconstruct the original input during recall. Both encoding and retrieval are probabilistic, so this reconstruction is likely to be approximate only.

In earlier versions of the Landscape model, the accumulation of node and connection strengths at a reading cycle depended only on the activation of the concepts involved. A concept's node strength increased pro-

---

[5]The comprehension processes themselves can be automatic or strategic.

portional to the amount of its activation. If a concept was highly activated, its salience in the memory representation increased more than when it was weakly activated. Likewise, the increase in connection strength between two coactivated concepts was a multiplicative function of the activation of each. Thus, if both were strongly activated in a cycle, then the increase in their connection strength would be large, whereas if both were weakly activated, the increase in connection strength would be small.

In this (Hebbian) view, each time a reader encounters a concept or pair of concepts of a given activation, the amount of change in node or connection strength is the same. However, this is an unlikely scenario. First, such linear accumulation has no limit: Concepts and concept relations would become stronger ad infinitum, thereby quickly overwhelming the processing system. Second, there is ample evidence of expectancy or surprisingness effects: The first occurrence of an event is likely to bring about a larger change in representation than a subsequent occurrence, other things being equal. For example, imagine that a reader encounters a connection between two concepts, say between a porcelain vase falling and it breaking, in one of two contexts. In the first context, the reader already has experienced this connection many times. In the second context, the reader has rarely or never experienced this connection. The change in the representation is much larger in the second context than in the first: If one has never seen a porcelain vase fall and break, the change in knowledge status is much larger than if one has already seen that sequence of events take place many times.

The graded effect of multiple experiences is captured in the current version of the model by an *asymptotic (modified Delta) learning rule*. According to this rule, the change in a connection's strength is proportional to the surprisingness of a concept's activation level. If a concept's activation level was perfectly predicted by the existing representation of an ongoing story, there is no reason to change the representation. In contrast, if a concept's activation level was not well anticipated, the network's connectivity needs to change to better capture the dynamics of the story's activation vectors.

A final major effect on the change in connection between two concepts is exerted by the connections of each to other concepts. This is because the concepts "compete" for the privilege of predicting another concept. This *cohort competition* has profound effects on the representation that is constructed with each consecutive reading cycle; it serves to efficiently represent the story dynamics, avoiding redundancies when possible. Cohort competition perhaps is best illustrated by some examples. If a concept has become strongly associated to another concept (i.e., its activation and connections accurately predict activation of the other concept), then there is little room for a third concept to build a connection as well. Consider the story in Table 3.1. If *knight* always predicted *dragon* early in the story, its connection to *dragon* would approach asymptote. If later in the story *knight* was always paired with *princess* and together they predicted *dragon*, there would be little if any learning of a direct princess → dragon association because it would be redundant. A different form of competition occurs when a group of concepts tends to predict the activation of another concept. In this case, the concepts must share the total associative strength available. In other words, they jointly predict the other concept, but in the absence of other members of the group the prediction would not be as strong.

As a result of the asymptotic learning rule, the connections between two concepts tend to be asymmetrical, with the predictive relation between the two concepts being stronger in one direction than in the other. The resulting asymmetric connectivity matrix contrasts with the symmetric matrices that emerge from the use of Hebbian learning in the earlier version of our model and in other existing models (e.g., Goldman & Varma, 1995; Kintsch, 1988; Landauer & Dumais, 1997; Langston & Trabasso, this volume). The connection asymmetry encodes the ordered relations among the concepts, enabling the model to recall concepts in the order in which they were originally read (cf. Golden, 1994).

Updating the Memory Representation. Together, these three factors—the activation of individual concepts, the asymptotic learning rule, and cohort competition—determine the updating of the strengths of individual concepts and connections at each cycle. Over the entire reading process, the reader gradually learns the various concepts and their interconnections and builds an episodic memory representation of the text.[6] As a result, the representation changes during reading. To illustrate, Fig. 3.2 shows two snapshots of part of the developing network for the Knight story in Table 3.1 and Fig. 3.1, one after three reading cycles (top panel) and the other after the final cycle (bottom panel). Varying node strengths are represented as circles of different sizes, and connections as links of different thickness. A comparison between the two panels shows that both node strengths and the relative strengths of connections change dynamically as the reader moves through the text.

Several aspects of the updating process are worth highlighting because they may not be immediately obvious from consideration of nodes and connections in isolation. First, the updating process extends beyond the

---

[6] The focus here is on the construction of an episodic representation of the text. Note, however, that the contents of the reader's semantic memory (i.e., background knowledge) are updated in a similar fashion, for example by comprehension of a text. In light of the asymptotic learning curve, discussed later, the modifications in semantic memory caused by a single text are likely to be small, though, unless a concept or set of concepts receives massive and/or repeated attention.

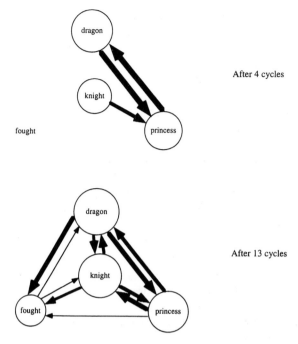

After 4 cycles

After 13 cycles

FIG. 3.2. Partial memory representation of the knight story, after three reading cycles (top panel) and after the final cycle (bottom panel).

modification of individual nodes and connections. As a result of cohort activation and competition, a change in node strength or connection density of one concept will reverberate throughout the representation and affect the properties of other concepts. Thus, with each reading cycle, the online activation of concepts results in a restructuring or reconfiguring of the entire representation. One might find that concepts and connections that were prominent at one point had retreated to the middle of the pack in the next cycle, and vice versa. This is illustrated in Fig. 3.2 as well. For example, the predictive connection between *princess* and *dragon* initially was strong, but declined as the connection between *knight* and *dragon* increased. The fact that restructuring extends beyond individual nodes and connections becomes even clearer when we consider situations in which the updating is more complicated than sheer accumulation of strengths of nodes and connections, for instance when the reader is confronted with information that is inconsistent with information earlier in the text or when the text corrects an earlier statement. In such situations, restructuring is even more extensive. We discuss the model's handling of these situations in a later section.

A second central aspect of the updating process is that the developing representation affects subsequent activation vectors and, hence, the impact that new input has on updating the representation. Again, the three factors of cohort activation, cohort competition, and asymptotic learning are responsible for this. Cohort activation dictates, in part, what activation vector will result from the new input, whereas cohort competition and asymptotic learning dictate the amount of change that the activation vector achieves. This state of affairs has an important implication, namely that the effect of reading a new sentence (proposition, etc.) depends on the history of all involved concepts and connections over the course of reading the preceding text.

In summary, textual input and developing memory representation interact in updating the node and connection strengths of concepts. The connectivity matrix, in turn, captures the temporal dynamics of the changing landscape. The recursive nature of this process ensures that the updating involves the representation as a whole rather than just individual nodes and connections. The resulting representation of the text can be used as a source for retrieval mechanisms suited for various tasks, such as the recapitulation of the original activation dynamics during recall or as a speeded response in a probe-reaction time experiment.

Retrieving Concepts From the Mental Representation. The network representation can be accessed both during and after reading. In the current version of the Landscape model, the retrieval cue is an activation vector (Fletcher, van den Broek, & Arthur, 1996; van den Broek, Young, et al., 1996; cf. Raaijmakers & Shiffrin, 1981). Through cohort activation, the initial pattern of activation generated by the cue will trigger patterns of activation in the network that can be used as the retrieval cues for subsequent patterns. The details of this process can be captured in different mechanisms, but the important point is that the pattern of retrieval depends on (a) the structure (i.e., nodes, node strengths, and connections) of the representation that is completed at the time that the retrieval takes place and (b) the activation vector that is used as the starting point or trigger for retrieval. Exactly what is retrieved and the order in which this happens depends on these two aspects and on their interaction.

IMPLEMENTING AND TESTING THE LANDSCAPE MODEL

In this section, we implement the Landscape model and test its psychological validity. To do so we must make a final decision, namely what factors determine the actual contents of the activation vectors. As mentioned earlier, this is an important source of differences among theorists' views of the reading process. Most researchers agree that readers access all four sources of activation (i.e., text, carry-over, reinstatement from prior cycles, background knowledge) in *some* circumstances, but they differ about what those circumstances are and whether they occur during normal reading. These disagreements are particularly strong with respect to access of background knowledge and reinstatements (e.g., Graesser et al., 1994; McKoon & Ratcliff, 1992; Singer & Ritchot, 1996; cf. van den Broek, Fletcher, & Risden, 1993). In principle, any of these theoretical positions can be implemented in the Landscape model. Indeed, as we discuss later, different implementations can be used to compare the predictive power of each position.

For our implementation, we take a *functional*, coherence-driven, view of the reading process (van den Broek, 1990a; van den Broek, Risden, & Husebye-Hartman, 1995). According to this view, readers attempt to maintain a certain level of understanding as they proceed through a text.[7] Whether they retrieve information (from memory for prior cycles or from background knowledge) depends on whether that information is functional in maintaining/attaining comprehension. Readers are relatively unlikely to exert effort to access background information or memory for prior cycles unless that effort is likely to bring them closer to the desired level of coherence. Standards of coherence may vary across individuals as well as within an individual (e.g., as a function of differences in motivation, reading goals, instructions, fatigue) but there is considerable agreement that two standards of coherence are employed by most readers in normal reading situations—*referential* and *causal* (see Singer, 1994; van den Broek, 1994). Referential coherence has been obtained when the reader has clearly identified the reference for the objects, persons, and so forth, in the sentence that is currently being read (e.g., Gernsbacher, 1990; Kintsch & van Dijk, 1978; O'Brien, 1987). Thus, the sentence pair, "The lady gave the waiter 10 dollars. He returned to give her the change," is referentially coherent if the reader recognizes that "he" refers to the waiter and "her" to the lady. Causal coherence is established when, in the eyes of the reader, the event described in the current sentence has a causally sufficient explanation (Trabasso & van den Broek, 1985; van den Broek, 1990a). In the previous example, the lady's giving the waiter 10 dollars is not causally sufficient for the waiter's returning with change unless one also infers (from background knowledge or prior cycles) that the lady gave too much money to the waiter.

The standards of referential and causal coherence can be incorporated in the implementation of the Landscape model. In essence, this implementation models a reader who steadily moves along, making inferences

---

[7]A reader need not be aware that he or she is engaging in this attempt or that he or she is employing any particular criteria/standards for coherence.

when they are required for comprehension but not when they are just there to be made. As a result, the vector of activation at each reading cycle is determined by the current text and carryover from the preceding cycle, as well as by retrieval from prior cycles or background knowledge *when such retrieval is required for referential and/or causal coherence* (for methods to determine referential coherence, see Turner & Greene, 1978; for determining causal coherence, see Trabasso, van den Broek, & Suh, 1989; van den Broek, 1990b). The memory representation that results captures the causal and referential contingencies between the concepts in the text. The activation landscape depicted in Fig. 3.1 and the (partial) emerging memory representation in Fig. 3.2 are based on this causal-referential implementation.

As mentioned, the notion that referential and causal coherence determine online activations has considerable support in the research literature. For example, during reading, concepts that are necessary for referential or causal coherence indeed are reactivated from background knowledge or memory for prior cycles (e.g., Casteel, 1993; Gernsbacher, 1990; Myers, 1990; O'Brien, 1987; Trabasso & Suh, 1993; van den Broek, Rohleder, et al., 1996). Likewise, there is ample evidence that causal and referential relations play an important role in readers' memory representations of a text. For example, these relations are strong predictors of frequency of recall, perceived importance, speed of retrieval, and answers to questions (e.g., Goldman, 1985; Goldman & Varnhagen, 1986; Miller & Kintsch, 1980; O'Brien & Myers, 1987; Trabasso & van den Broek, 1985; van den Broek, 1988; van den Broek & Lorch, 1993).

These studies have limited utility as tests of the Landscape model, however. In the online studies, for example, probing occurs at only one or two locations in the text, and only one concept is probed at each location. The Landscape model makes predictions concerning the activation of multiple concepts at all locations in the text. Thus, the real test for a model of the reading process requires assessing activations throughout the text and of all potentially relevant concepts. The offline studies, too, have limitations: The theoretical memory representations that are used to predict task performance are based on a static analysis of the text without consideration of the online process that supposedly yielded the representations. In summary, although bits and pieces of the causal-referential landscape model had been supported in the existing body of literature, the model as a whole remained to be tested.

Two experiments in which the online and offline components of the Landscape model were tested directly are reported in van den Broek, Risden, et al. (1996). The purpose of the first experiment was to investigate online fluctuations in activation. Participants read texts such as in Table 3.1 line by line, at their own pace. After each sentence, they were presented with a list consisting of all concepts related to the text and an equal number of unrelated distractors. For each concept, participants indicated on a five-point scale how strongly they thought it was activated. Averaging participants' ratings yielded an empirical landscape of activations for all concepts over the course of the text. This landscape was compared to theoretical landscapes based on a simplified version[8] of the causal-referential implementation. The empirical and theoretical landscapes were strongly correlated, $r = .73$ ($p < .01$). To put this correlation in perspective, note that the average correlation between participants' landscapes was .79. Thus, the theoretical model predicted participants' behavior about as well as it possibly could have.

The model's predictions about the mental representation that results from the fluctuating activations during reading were tested in a second experiment. Participants read and recalled the same texts as were used in the first experiment. Recall protocols were compared to the final mental representations produced by the simplified Landscape model. The network properties of concepts were used in hierarchical regression analyses to predict frequency of recall. The empirical and theoretical memory representations were closely related. A concept's node strength strongly predicted frequency of recall, $R^2 = .49$ ($p < .01$). Predictive power was even greater when the strength of the relations that a concept had to other concepts—its connection density—was entered as an additional factor, bringing the total R^2 to .64 (the increase, .15, is significant at $p < .01$).

The theoretical networks not only predicted frequency but also order of free recall. The first text element to be recalled almost inevitably (94%) was the one that had received the largest total of activation across cycles. The conditional probability of subsequent mention was predicted by the strength of relations between concepts, $R^2 = .34$ ($p < .01$): The second element to be recalled usually was the one that had the strongest connection to the first recalled element, the third element was strongly related to the second one, and so on. Node strength had an additional effect, increasing R^2 to .44 (the increase, .10, is significant at $p < .01$): If two or more concepts were equally related to the last-recalled concept then the strongest of the candidate concepts tended to be recalled next. Thus, it appears that readers first retrieve the concept that is most prominent in strength and relations in the mental representation and then trace their representation along the strongest relational paths to subsequent concepts, using concept strengths as tie-breakers.

These results indicate that the Landscape model captures important aspects of the cognitive processes that take place during reading, and of the mental representation that emerges. These tests are based on a causal-

---

[8] The simplified version did not include cohort activation and used a Hebbian learning rule rather than an asymptotic learning curve.

referential implementation and, thus, also provide evidence that much inference making during reading occurs when such inferences are necessary to establish referential and causal coherence. Other implementations could have been chosen. Indeed, the Landscape model can be used to contrast alternative theoretical accounts of the reading process. Risden (1996), for example, implemented four theories of inference making in the current Landscape model: constructionist (in which readers are assumed to generate virtually all possible inferences), minimalist (in which readers are assumed to generate inferences only rarely), causal-referential, and order-only (in which no inferences are generated). Of the four implementations, the causal-referential one best predicted online and offline behavior. These results support the causal-referential model and, more importantly for the present purpose, they show how the Landscape model can be used to compare and test different reading theories.

IMPLICATIONS OF THE LANDSCAPE MODEL

In the previous section, we illustrated that the model captures general reading phenomena such as concept activation levels and frequency and order of recall. Here we explore specific features of the Landscape model in the context of phenomena that currently are receiving attention in the literature on cognitive processes in reading.

Constructing the Memory Representation

Effects of Input Order. In the Landscape model, the relation between fluctuating activations and episodic representation of the text is reciprocal. At each point during reading, the existing representation is updated on the basis of the current activation vector, but this vector itself is partly influenced by the representation as it has emerged so far. An important implication of this reciprocal relation is the existence of *order effects*. The history of a concept during the reading process affects its properties in the mental representation: Present the same information in different orders and different representations will result. Examples can be found in children's *Choose-your-own-adventure* books or in Julio Cortazar's (1966) *Hopscotch.* In both cases, the events in the texts can be read in one or more orders, each resulting in a different interpretation of the events, personality traits, how events are connected, and so on.

Resolving Contradictions and Corrections. Texts frequently contain inconsistencies or explicit corrections of earlier information. The Landscape model provides a detailed description of what happens in these situations.

According to the model, incompatibilities are noticed by the reader if the two pieces of incompatible information are activated simultaneously. For this to occur, the information in the prior cycle needs to be reactivated. As described earlier, the likelihood of reactivation is a joint function of the memory representation as it has developed so far and the current activation vector. Both influence the likelihood that a contradiction is detected. On the one hand, the more strongly the earlier information is represented in memory (i.e., the greater its node and connection strengths), the more likely it is to be retrieved at a later cycle. Thus, if a concept is repeated or connected to many other concepts through elaboration, its chances of being retrieved later are great.

On the other hand, the more effective the current activation vector is in reactivating the conflicting information, the more likely the two conflicting pieces of information are to be co-activated. In the case of explicit correction, the incompatible information from the earlier cycle is directly restated and hence reactivation is almost guaranteed. In the case of an implicit inconsistency, reactivation of the incompatible information occurs in two circumstances. First, reactivation may occur as part of an effort to establish coherence for the information in the current cycle. In this case, the model stumbles on the inconsistent information as it executes another process. Second, reactivation may result from a passive flow of activation from the current cycle to the preceding concept through cohort activation. Here, the greater and more direct the association between the two pieces of contradictory information is, the more likely they will be activated simultaneously.[9]

Once an inconsistency is detected, the reader needs to restructure the mental representation to re-establish coherence. This process, similar to that observed during wrap-up at the end of a text or sentence, takes time and hence reading slows down. In the case of a correction, the reader knows in what way the representation needs to be revised, whereas in the case of a contradiction the reader needs to resolve the conflict him- or herself. In either case the new connection enters into the updating process. The old, erroneous, connections can be dealt with in one of two ways. They can be deleted through some form of inhibition or suppression or they can remain in the representation. The Landscape model favors the second possibility: Connections—once established—continue to exist in the representation although over the course of reading they are likely to lose relative prominence as the correct connections gain in strength. The two possibilities lead to different predictions: In the first scenario the

---

[9]In this respect, the Landscape model shares many features with the Resonance model (O'Brien & Albrecht, 1992). Unlike the Resonance model, however, the Landscape model explicitly allows for the possibility that reactivation and hence inconsistency detection may take place as a side effect of other processes, such as an effort to comprehend the current sentence.

incorrect (and now deleted) connections should not have an influence on later activations, whereas in the second scenario the incorrect connections may still surface in later comprehension. The preponderance of evidence supports the second scenario (e.g., Johnson & Seifert, 1994; van Oostendorp & Bonebakker, this volume; Wilkes & Leatherbarrow, 1988). This explains the informal observation that connections, once laid, often are hard to undo. Examples abound in politics and advertising.

Forward Inferences. Forward inferences generally are considered to be less frequent than backward, coherence-building inferences (e.g., McKoon & Ratcliff, 1989; Singer & Ferreira, 1983; van den Broek, 1990a). Although the results of initial studies led researchers to conclude that in the absence of specific reading goals they are not produced at all, it has become clear since that forward inferences *are* drawn but only when the preceding text provides compelling semantic constraints (Klin & Myers, 1993; van den Broek, 1990a; van den Broek & Huang, 1995; Vonk & Noordman, 1990).

The Landscape model captures the role of constraints in the generation of forward inferences through cohort activation. At a particular reading cycle, the activated concepts spread activation to other concepts to which they are associated (in episodic memory for the text or in background knowledge). If the spreading activation converges on a particular concept, then this event will be activated even if it has not occurred yet (cf. Kintsch, 1988). Examples can be found readily. For example, after reading the first few sentences of the story in Table 3.1, participants frequently activated concepts such as *fighting, killing,* and *marrying the princess* even though none of these concepts had been mentioned yet.

The generation of a forward inference depends not only on the presence but also the timing of adequate constraints. On the one hand, constraints take time to accumulate: Retrieval from episodic memory as well as activation of background knowledge is a slow process (e.g., Balota & Lorch, 1986; Bloom, Fletcher, van den Broek, Reitz, & Shapiro, 1990; Kintsch, 1988; Till, Mross, & Kintsch, 1988). On the other hand, constraints decline when the supporting activation vector dissipates, for example as the time since the last reading cycle increases. Thus, there may be a small window of opportunity during which all the required constraints are present to allow the forward inference. The results of recent research suggest that this is indeed the case (Keefe & McDaniel, 1993; van den Broek & Huang, 1995). The transient nature of forward inferences has implications not only for theories but also for investigative procedure: Tests of whether a particular inference is made or not are valid only if the inference is probed inside the window of opportunity.

In the Landscape model, a forward inference may influence the generation of backward inferences later in the text. Once generated, the inference becomes part of the new activation vector. As a result, it influences the updating of the developing mental representation and the processing of subsequent text. Imagine a sentence describing someone accidentally dropping a porcelain vase. A reader may well activate background knowledge such as the fragility of porcelain and the forward inference that the vase will break. These inferences will become part of the memory representation. If the text in a later cycle describes an event that begs explanation, for example that the protagonist pays damages to the homeowner, the explanation that the vase broke is readily retrieved. The opposite occurs if the forward inference conflicts with information in a later cycle, for example if the text cycle later mentions that the homeowner sold the vase for a large amount of money. Thus, forward inferences can interact with later backward inferences. The possibility of this interaction has been noted (van den Broek, 1990a; Whitney & Budd, 1996) but has not yet been investigated empirically. Again, this has practical implications as well. Investigations of backward inference generation need to eliminate the possibility that results are confounded by forward inferences.

Top-Down Processing: Activations of Schemas. In the description of cohort activation, we have focused on individual concepts. At times, however, multiple concepts may seem to be activated instantaneously as a unit. This occurs when concepts are interconnected so tightly that activation of one member evokes activation of the others. Such a conglomerate of concepts often consists of knowledge that has been accumulated and generalized over individual experiences, constituting a *schema* (also called script, generalized knowledge structure, etc.; see Graesser & Clark, 1985; Mandler, 1984; Schank & Abelson, 1977; Stein & Glenn, 1979). Activation of a schema results in top-down processes, that is, the generation of extensive expectations and inferences. For example, when a reader is told that he or she will read a fairy tale, general knowledge about the content and structure of fairy tales may be activated and influence the interpretation of the text that follows (e.g., McDaniel & Einstein, 1989; Zwaan & Brown, 1996).

In the Landscape model, such knowledge structures are activated in the same way as other groups of concepts are, namely through cohort activation. The activation vector that serves as the starting point or cue for the cohort activation of an abstract knowledge structure may originate before the reading process starts (e.g., from instructions) or once the reading process is on its way (e.g., when the first sentence is "Once upon a time, in a faraway land . . ."). In either case, the schema will be activated, become part of the new activation vector, and henceforth exert a strong influence on the processing of subsequent text. Thus, the Landscape model parsimoniously captures both top-down and bottom-up processes through the same mechanisms.

Individual Differences in Reading Comprehension

Individuals differ in their attentional capacities, knowledge, and comprehension processes. As a consequence, the same text may be processed, interpreted, and remembered very differently by different individuals. Indeed, even within the same individual, comprehension processes may differ from one reading situation to the next—for example, as a result of different reading goals, motivation, and fatigue (see van den Broek et al., 1993). Here, we illustrate some of the sources for inter- and intra-individual variation. By implementing these variations in the Landscape model, one gains important insights into the reading process in general as well as into the origins of individual differences.

Background Knowledge. One source of individual differences is background knowledge. In the Landscape model, background knowledge is one of the major factors in determining the activation vectors that occur during reading. The more knowledge a reader has, and the more densely interconnected this knowledge is, the more easily and extensively it is accessed through processes such as cohort activation (e.g., Ericsson & Kintsch, 1995). Thus, background knowledge affects the activation vectors that, in turn, affect the eventual memory representation (e.g., Chi, Feltovich, & Glaser, 1981; Chiesi, Spilich, & Voss, 1979; Ericsson & Kintsch, 1995).

Aside from differences in the amount of background knowledge, individuals may differ in the extent to which they tend to access background knowledge. At one extreme would be a reader who attempts to stay as close to the text as possible and to avoid augmenting the memory representation by activating background knowledge, whereas at the other extreme would be a reader who attempts to connect every aspect of the text to his or her background knowledge. The resulting memory representations would be quite different. For the first reader it would consist mainly of the textual units and their direct interconnections, whereas for the second it would contain extensive world knowledge. These representations constitute what are often called the *textbase* and *situation model*, respectively (e.g., van Dijk & Kintsch, 1983). Most readers will likely fall between the two extremes of the continuum, mixing text information with background knowledge (see McNamara & Kintsch, 1996).

Variation in background knowledge use may occur within an individual as well. For example, just like two readers with differences in expertise in an area construct different activation vectors and memory representations, so does a reader at two different stages in the development of his or her knowledge. With respect to textbase and situation model, a reader may sometimes aim to stay close to the text and at other times engage in extensive activation of background knowledge.

Standards for Coherence and Reading Strategies. As described earlier in this chapter, the contents of the activation vectors during reading depend, in part, on the reader's standards for coherence. These standards determine when adequate coherence is attained and when additional retrieval from prior reading cycles or from background knowledge is necessary (Lorch, Lorch, & Klusewitz, 1993; van den Broek et al., 1995; see also Goldman & Saul, 1990). If a reader is interested in minimal comprehension (see McKoon & Ratcliff, 1992), the standards for coherence are met relatively easily and little reactivation or background-knowledge retrieval takes place. In contrast, if a reader is interested in attaining a thorough understanding of the text, then the standards for coherence are very demanding: Reading will be relatively slow and involve extensive recruiting of background knowledge or of information from the mental representation that has been constructed so far (e.g., van Oostendorp, 1991). The resulting differences in activation vectors are reflected, in turn, in the updated memory representation and hence in performance in subsequent comprehension and memory tasks. In the implementations of the Landscape model described in this chapter, the standards are assumed to be causal and referential coherence. These standards were chosen because they have been found to be shared by individuals and across reading situations. However, there can be little doubt that readers frequently adopt additional standards, particularly in light of a particular task (e.g., exam preparation, literary analysis, trying to identify who's done it in detective stories). These additional standards and the relations among standards have not yet been investigated, but could easily be implemented in the Landscape model.

A reader's standards for coherence are closely related to his or her reading strategies. On the one hand, a reader's standards determine when the reader feels that comprehension is achieved (which may, of course, differ from what a teacher considers adequate comprehension). On the other hand, a reader's reading strategies and metacognitive skills determine whether he or she can attain the standards for coherence. A reader may realize that a standard of comprehension is not attained but lack the strategies to remedy the problem.

Processing. Readers may differ in various aspects of the processing described by the Landscape model. For example, readers may differ in the amount of attentional resources they have available (e.g., Just & Carpenter, 1992; Singer, Andrusiak, Reisdorf, & Black, 1992; Whitney, Ritchie, & Clark, 1991). As a second example, readers may differ in the extent to which the cohorts of concepts in the current vector are activated. If cohort activation is strong, the textual information will be strongly integrated with all prior information as well as with background knowledge and hence the predictive association between any two concepts will be weak. Conversely, if cohort activation is weak, few connections are built, but those that are will have strong predictive power. As a last example, readers may differ in the slope of their learning curves, attaining the maximum more quickly or more slowly. Activation vectors (and the resulting representation) will be affected by differences in these processing properties.

Retrieval

Retrieval of information from the mental representation can take various forms. It may occur during reading or after reading; it may occur as a general attempt to retrieve the entire text or in an effort to locate specific information. In the Landscape model the process of retrieval is identical, regardless of timing and purpose, but the outcome is not. The reason is that at any one time retrieval is determined by two factors: the current activation vector and the memory representation. The ease and speed with which one can respond to a task (e.g., a speeded laboratory task, wanting to relate a story to a friend, recalling instructions read in a manual) is influenced by the combination of the two sources. As the memory representation changes (e.g., at different points in the reading process) so does information retrieval. Thus, using *knight* as a prompt, *dragon* is activated more easily after the third cycle in the story than at the end of the story (see connection strengths in Fig. 3.1). Likewise, the activation vector that is the starting point for retrieval influences the ease with which a particular piece of information is retrieved. Thus, the manner in which an activation vector prompts retrieval depends on its content. For example, if the retrieval cue is "tell me all you can remember about the story about the knight," the network will be accessed in a slightly different way than if the retrieval cue were "tell me all you can remember about the story about the princess." Even more different outcomes will be observed with retrieval cues that contain two concepts or that elicit entirely different activities (e.g., following directions versus recall of an instruction manual). Evidence that different tasks elicit different retrieval patterns comes from text research (e.g., Trabasso & van den Broek, 1985; van den Broek, 1988) and from general memory research (see Klatzky, 1980).

Retrieval after reading also varies as a function of whether it is immediate or delayed. If retrieval is initiated immediately after reading has been completed, the activation vector for the last cycle is still active and will enter into the equation of the retrieval process, but if recall is delayed it will play no role. These predictions are consistent with findings that, with delay, the influence of overall text structure increases with delay whereas that of surface properties decreases (e.g., Trabasso et al., 1984; see also Sachs, 1967). Likewise, O'Brien and Myers (1987) observed that retrieval differs as a function of whether the process is started immediately on completion of reading or after a delay.

In summary, retrieval of textual information is a function of the structure of the memory representation that is being accessed as well as of the current activation vector. These two factors, and their interaction, determine both the content and the order of what is retrieved.

CONCLUSION

In this chapter, we have proposed a model of reading comprehension that captures the cognitive processes that take place during reading as well as the memory representation that results. This model exemplifies the third generation of research in reading, in which the insights gained from the first two generations—with a focus on memory representation and online activations, respectively—are combined to yield an integrated theoretical description of process and product in reading comprehension. We have shown that the Landscape model has considerable psychological validity, predicting online activations and both frequency and order of recall. Furthermore, we have illustrated how the model captures specific features of memory and comprehension of text, such as the resolution of contradictions, and generates testable hypotheses on topics ranging from the interaction between forward and backward inferences to the effects of individual differences.

We have illustrated and tested the model by assuming that readers attempt to attain causal and referential coherence as they proceed through a text. This assumption seems a reasonable one, given that it has ample support in the research literature and is embraced by many investigators. It should be pointed out, though, that the Landscape model can be used to implement other assumptions as well. For example, one could model a comprehender who does not care (or have the skills) to attain causal coherence. Or, one could add emotional valence of events as a factor in determining online activations. These are just a few examples, but they illustrate how the Landscape model constitutes a general platform for testing and comparing theoretical notions about the sources for activation.

The model is general in another sense as well. In this chapter, we have focused on comprehension of narrative texts, but the model has generality that extends beyond narratives. For other types of texts, the factors that determine the content of the vectors and hence the connections that result may differ but the processes of translating the vectors into a memory representation will be the same (cf. Goldman & Varma, 1995; Goldman et al., 1996). Indeed, the Landscape model can be applied to the processing of any type of temporarily distributed information, not just reading. Striking similarities have been observed between processing of narrative texts and that of information presented in television programs (van den Broek,

Lorch, & Thurlow, 1996) or movies (Magliano, Dijkstra, & Zwaan, 1996; Sharp, Bransford, Goldman, Risko, Kinzer, & Vye, 1995). Application of the model to these diverse settings will allow us to determine the commonalities and differences in the comprehension skills that people bring to bear in different aspects of their lives (see Gernsbacher, 1990; van den Broek, Lorch, et al., 1996).

ACKNOWLEDGMENTS

We thank Susan Goldman, Valerie Gyselink, Herre van Oostendorp, and Sashank Varma for their comments on an earlier version of this chapter. The research described in this chapter was supported by the Center for Cognitive Sciences at the University of Minnesota through a grant from the National Institute of Child Health and Human Development (HD-07151).

REFERENCES

Albrecht, J. E., & O'Brien, E. J. (1993). Updating a mental model: Maintaining both local and global coherence. *Journal of Experimental Psychology: Learning, Memory, and Cognition, 19*, 1061–1070.

Baars, B. J. (1988). *A cognitive theory of consciousness.* New York: Cambridge University Press.

Balota, D. A., & Lorch, R. F. (1986). Depth of automatic spread activation: Mediated priming effects in pronunciation but not in lexical decision. *Journal of Experimental Psychology: Learning, Memory, and Cognition, 12*, 336–345.

Bloom, C. P., Fletcher, C. R., van den Broek, P. W., Reitz, L., & Shapiro, B. P. (1990). An on-line assessment of causal reasoning during text comprehension. *Memory & Cognition, 18*, 65–71.

Casteel, M. A. (1993). Effects of inference necessity and reading goal on children's inferential generation. *Developmental Psychology, 29*, 346–357.

Chi, M. T. H., Feltovich, P. J., & Glaser, R. (1981). Categorization and representation of physics problems by experts and novices. *Cognitive Sciences, 5*, 121–152.

Chiesi, H. L., Spilich, G. J., & Voss, J. F. (1979). Acquisition of domain related information in relation to high and low domain knowledge. *Journal of Verbal Learning and Verbal Behavior, 18*, 257–274.

Colby, B. N. (1973). A partial grammar of Eskimo folktales. *American Anthropologist, 75*, 645–662.

Cortazar, J. (1966). *Hopscotch.* Random House.

Ericsson, K. A., & Kintsch, W. (1995). Long-term working memory. *Psychological Review, 102*, 211–245.

Fletcher, C. R., & Bloom, C. P. (1988). Causal reasoning in the comprehension of simple narrative texts. *Journal of Memory and Language, 27*, 235–244.

Fletcher, C. R., Hummel, J. E., & Marsolek, C. J. (1990). Causality and the allocation of attention during comprehension. *Journal of Experimental Psychology: Learning, Memory, and Cognition, 16*, 233–240.

Fletcher, C. R., van den Broek, P. W., & Arthur, E. (1996). A model of narrative comprehension and recall. In B. K. Britton & A. C. Graesser (Eds.), *Models of understanding text* (pp. 141–163). Mahwah, NJ: Lawrence Erlbaum Associates.

Garrod, A., & Sanford, S. (1990). Referential processing in reading: Focusing on roles and individuals. In D. A. Balota, G. B. Flores d'Arcais, & K. Rayner (Eds.), *Comprehension processes in reading* (pp. 465–484). Hillsdale, NJ: Lawrence Erlbaum Associates.

Gernsbacher, M. A. (1990). *Language comprehension as structure building.* Hillsdale, NJ: Lawrence Erlbaum Associates.

Golden, R. M. (1994). Analysis of categorical time-series text recall data using a connectionist model. *Journal of Biological Systems, 2*, 283–305.

Goldman, S. R. (1985). Inferential reasoning in and about narrative texts. In A. C. Graesser & J. B. Black (Eds.), *The psychology of questions* (pp. 247–276). Hillsdale, NJ: Lawrence Erlbaum Associates.

Goldman, S. R., & Saul, E. U. (1990). Flexibility in text processing: A strategy competition model. *Learning and Individual Differences, 2*, 181–219.

Goldman, S. R., & Varma, S. (1995). CAPping the construction-integration model of discourse comprehension. In C. A. Weaver, S. Mannes, & C. R. Fletcher (Eds.), *Discourse comprehension: Essays in honor of Walter Kintsch* (pp. 337–358). Mahwah, NJ: Lawrence Erlbaum Associates.

Goldman, S. R., Varma, S., & Coté, N. (1996). Extending capacity-constrained construction-integration: Toward "smarter" and flexible models of text comprehension. In B. K. Britton & A. C. Graesser (Eds.), *Models of understanding text* (pp. 73–114). Mahwah, NJ: Lawrence Erlbaum Associates.

Goldman, S. R., & Varnhagen, C. K. (1986). Memory for embedded and sequential story structures. *Journal of Memory and Language, 25*, 401–418.

Graesser, A. C., & Clark, L. F. (1985). *The structures and procedures of implicit knowledge.* Norwood, NJ: Ablex.

Graesser, A. C., Singer, M., & Trabasso, T. (1994). Constructing inferences during narrative text comprehension. *Psychological Review, 101*, 371–395.

James, W. A. (1890). *Principles of psychology.* New York: Holt.

Johnson, H. M., & Seifert, C. M. (1994). Sources of the continued influence effect: When discredited information in memory affects later inferences. *Journal of Experimental Psychology: Learning, Memory, and Cognition, 20*, 1420–1436.

Just, A. M., & Carpenter, P. A. (1992). A capacity theory of comprehension: Individual differences in working memory. *Psychological Review, 99*, 122–149.

Keefe, D. E., & McDaniel, M. A. (1993). The time course and duration of prediction inferences. *Journal of Memory and Language, 32*, 446–463.

Kintsch, W. (1988). The role of knowledge in discourse comprehension: A construction-integration model. *Psychological Review, 95*, 163–182.

Kintsch, W., & van Dijk, T. A. (1978). Towards a model of text comprehension and production. *Psychological Review, 85*, 363–394.

Klatzky, R. L. (1980). *Human memory structures and processes.* San Francisco, CA: Freeman & Company.

Klin, C. M., & Myers, J. L. (1993). Reinstatement of causal information during reading. *Journal of Experimental Psychology: Learning, Memory, and Cognition, 19*, 554–560.

Landauer, T. K., & Dumais, S. T. (1997). A solution to Plato's problem: The latent semantic analysis theory of acquisition, induction, and representation of knowledge. *Psychological Review, 104*, 211–240.

Lorch, R. F., Jr., Lorch, E. P., & Klusewitz, M. A. (1993). College students' conditional knowledge about reading. *Journal of Educational Psychology, 85*, 239–252.

Lucas, M. M., Tanenhaus, M. K., & Carlson, G. N. (1990). Levels of representation in the interpretation of anaphoric reference and instrument inference. *Memory & Cognition, 18*, 611–631.

Magliano, J. P., Dijkstra, K., & Zwaan, R. A. (1996). Predictive inferences in movies. *Discourse Processes, 22*, 199–224.

Mandler, J. M. (1984). *Stories, scripts, and scenes: Aspects of schema theory.* Hillsdale, NJ: Lawrence Erlbaum Associates.

Mandler, J. M., & Johnson, N. S. (1977). Remembrance of things parsed: Story structure and recall. *Cognitive Psychology, 9,* 111–151.

McDaniel, M. A., & Einstein, G. O. (1989). Material appropriate processing: A contextualistic approach to reading and studying strategies. *Educational Psychology Review, 1,* 113–145.

McKoon, G., & Ratcliff, R. (1980). Priming in item recognition: The organization of propositions in memory for text. *Journal of Verbal Learning and Verbal Behavior, 19,* 326–338.

McKoon, G., & Ratcliff, R. (1989). Semantic associations and elaborative inferences. *Journal of Experimental Psychology: Learning, Memory, and Cognition, 15,* 326–338.

McKoon, G., & Ratcliff, R. (1992). Inferences during reading. *Psychological Review, 99,* 440–466.

McNamara, D. S., & Kintsch, W. (1996). Learning from text: Effects of prior knowledge and text coherence. *Discourse Processes, 22,* 247–287.

Meyer, B. J. F. (1975). *The organization of prose and its effects on memory.* Amsterdam: North-Holland.

Miller, J. R., & Kintsch, W. (1980). Readability and recall of short prose passages: A theoretical analysis. *Journal of Experimental Psychology: Human Learning and Memory, 6,* 335–354.

Myers, J. L. (1990). Causal relatedness and text comprehension. In D. A. Balota, G. B. Flores d'Arcais, & K. Rayner (Eds.), *Comprehension processes in reading* (pp. 361–375). Hillsdale, NJ: Lawrence Erlbaum Associates.

O'Brien, E. J. (1987). Antecedent search processes and the structure of text. *Journal of Experimental Psychology: Learning, Memory, and Cognition, 13,* 278–290.

O'Brien, E. J., & Albrecht, J. E. (1992). Comprehension strategies in the development of a mental model. *Journal of Experimental Psychology: Learning, Memory, and Cognition, 18,* 777–784.

O'Brien, E. J., Albrecht, J., Hakala, C., & Rizzella, M. (1995). Activation and suppression of antecedents during reinstatement. *Journal of Experimental Psychology: Learning, Memory, and Cognition, 21,* 626–634.

O'Brien, E. J., Duffy, S. A., & Myers, J. L. (1986). Anaphoric inference during reading. *Journal of Experimental Psychology: Learning, Memory, and Cognition, 12,* 346–352.

O'Brien, E. J., & Myers, J. L. (1987). The role of causal connections in the retrieval of text. *Memory & Cognition, 15,* 419–427.

O'Brien, E. J., Shank, D., Myers, J. L., & Rayner, K. (1988). Elaborative inferences during reading: Do they occur on-line? *Journal of Experimental Psychology: Learning, Memory, and Cognition, 14,* 410–420.

Perfetti, C. A., & Goldman, S. R. (1974). Thematization and sentence retrieval. *Journal of Verbal Learning and Verbal Behavior, 13,* 70–79.

Propp, V. (1928). *Morphology of the folktale.* Austin: University of Texas Press.

Raaijmakers, J. G. W., & Shiffrin, R. M. (1981). Search of associative memory. *Psychological Review, 88,* 93–134.

Ratcliff, R., & McKoon, G. (1988). A retrieval theory of priming. *Psychological Review, 21,* 139–155.

Risden, K. (1996). *Causal inference in narrative text comprehension.* Unpublished doctoral dissertation, University of Minnesota, Minneapolis.

Sachs, J. (1967). Recognition memory for syntactic and semantic aspects of connected discourse. *Perception & Psychophysics, 2,* 437–442.

Schank, R. G., & Abelson, R. P. (1977). *Scripts, plans, goals, and understanding.* Hillsdale, NJ: Lawrence Erlbaum Associates.

Sharkey, A. J. C., & Sharkey, N. E. (1992). Weak contextual constraints in text and word priming. *Journal of Memory and Language, 31,* 543–572.

Sharp, D. L. M., Bransford, J. D., Goldman, S. R., Risko, V. J., Kinzer, C. K., & Vye, N. J. (1995). Dynamic visual support for story comprehension and mental model building by young, at risk children. *Educational Technology Research and Development, 43,* 25–42.

Singer, M. (1994). Discourse inference processes. In M. A. Gernsbacher (Ed.), *Handbook of psycholinguistics* (pp. 479–515). New York: Academic Press.

Singer, M., Andrusiak, P., Reisdorf, P., & Black, N. L. (1992). Individual differences in bridging inference processes. *Memory & Cognition, 20,* 539–548.

Singer, M., & Ferreira, F. (1983). Inferring consequences in story comprehension. *Journal of Verbal Learning and Verbal Behavior, 22,* 437–448.

Singer, M., Graesser, A. C., & Trabasso, T. (1994). Minimal or global inference during reading. *Journal of Memory and Language, 33,* 421–441.

Singer, M., & Ritchot, K. F. M. (1996). The role of working memory capacity and knowledge access in text inference processing. *Memory & Cognition, 24,* 733–743.

Stein, N. L., & Glenn, C. G. (1979). An analysis of story comprehension in elementary school children. In R. O. Freedle (Ed.), *New directions in discourse processing* (pp. 53–120). Hillsdale, NJ: Lawrence Erlbaum Associates.

Suh, S., & Trabasso, T. (1993). Inference during on-line processing: Converging evidence from discourse analysis, talk-aloud protocols, and recognition priming. *Journal of Memory and Language, 32,* 279–301.

Till, R. E., Mross, E. F., & Kintsch, W. (1988). Time course of priming for associate and inference words in a discourse context. *Memory & Cognition, 16,* 283–298.

Trabasso, T., Secco, T., & van den Broek, P. W. (1984). Causal cohesion and story coherence. In H. Mandl, N. L. Stein, & T. Trabasso (Eds.), *Learning and comprehension of text* (pp. 83–111). Hillsdale, NJ: Lawrence Erlbaum Associates.

Trabasso, T., & Suh, S. Y. (1993). Using talk-aloud protocols to reveal inferences during comprehension of text. *Discourse Processes, 16,* 3–34.

Trabasso, T., & van den Broek, P. W. (1985). Causal thinking and the representation of narrative events. *Journal of Memory and Language, 24,* 612–630.

Trabasso, T., van den Broek, & Suh, S. Y. (1989). Logical necessity and transitivity of causal relations in stories. *Discourse Processes, 12,* 1–25.

Turner, A., & Greene, E. (1978). *Construction and use of a propositional text base.* Journal Supplement Abstract Service Catalogue of selected documents in psychology. (Ms. No. 1713)

van den Broek, P. W. (1988). The effects of causal relations and hierarchical position on the importance of story statements. *Journal of Memory and Language, 27,* 1–22.

van den Broek, P. W. (1990a). The causal inference marker: Towards a process model of inference generation in text comprehension. In D. A. Balota, G. B. Flores d'Arcais, & K. Rayner (Eds.), *Comprehension processes in reading* (pp. 423–446). Hillsdale, NJ: Lawrence Erlbaum Associates.

van den Broek, P. W. (1990b). Causal inference and the comprehension of narrative text. In A. C. Graesser & G. H. Bower (Eds.), *Inferences and text comprehension* (pp. 175–194). San Diego, CA: Academic Press.

van den Broek, P. W. (1994). Comprehension and memory of narrative texts: Inferences and coherence. In M. A. Gernsbacher (Ed.), *Handbook of psycholinguistics* (pp. 539–588). San Diego, CA: Academic Press.

van den Broek, P. W., Fletcher, C. R., & Risden, K. (1993). Investigation of inferential processes in reading: A theoretical and methodological integration. *Discourse Processes, 12,* 169–180.

van den Broek, P. W., & Huang, Y. (1995). *Forward inferences during text comprehension: The role of causal constraint.* Paper presented at the 36th annual meeting of the Psychonomic Society, Los Angeles, CA.

van den Broek, P. W., & Lorch, R. F., Jr. (1993). Causal relations in memory for narrative text: Evidence from a priming task for network representations. *Discourse Processes, 16,* 75–98.

van den Broek, P. W., Lorch, E. P., & Thurlow, R. (1996). Children's and adults' memory for television stories: The role of causal factors, story-grammar categories, and hierarchical level. *Child Development, 67,* 3010–3028.

van den Broek, P. W., Risden, K., & Husebye-Hartman, E. (1995). The role of readers' standards for coherence in the generation of inferences during reading. In R. F. Lorch Jr. & E. J. O'Brien (Eds.), *Sources of coherence in reading* (pp. 353–373). Mahwah, NJ: Lawrence Erlbaum Associates.

van den Broek, P. W., Risden, K., Fletcher, C. R., & Thurlow, R. (1996). A "landscape" view of reading: Fluctuating patterns of activation and the construction of a stable memory representation. In B. K. Britton & A. C. Graesser (Eds.), *Models of understanding text* (pp. 165–187). Mahwah, NJ: Lawrence Erlbaum Associates.

van den Broek, P. W., Rohleder, L., & Narvaez, D. (1996). Causal inferences in the comprehension of literary texts. In R. J. Kreuz & M. S. McNealy (Eds.), *The empirical study of literature* (pp. 179–200). Mahwah, NJ: Lawrence Erlbaum Associates.

van den Broek, P. W., & Thurlow, R. (1990). *Reinstatements and elaborative inferences during the reading of narratives.* Paper presented at the 31st annual meeting of the Psychonomic Society, New Orleans, LA.

van den Broek, P. W., & Trabasso, T. (1986). Causal networks versus goal hierarchies in summarizing text. *Discourse Processes, 9,* 1–15.

van den Broek, P. W., Young, M., & Risden, K. (1996). *The competitive cohort model.* Unpublished manuscript.

van Dijk, T. A., & Kintsch, W. (1983). *Strategies for discourse comprehension.* New York: Academic Press.

van Oostendorp, H. (1991). Inferences and integrations made by readers of script-based texts. *Journal of Research in Reading, 14,* 3–20.

Vonk, W., & Noordman, L. G. (1990). On the control of inferences in text understanding. In D. A. Balota, G. B. Flores d'Arcais, & K. Rayner (Eds.), *Comprehension processes in reading* (pp. 447–463). Hillsdale, NJ: Lawrence Erlbaum Associates.

Whitney, P., & Budd, D. (1996). Think-aloud protocols and the study of comprehension. *Discourse Processes, 21,* 341–351.

Whitney, P., Ritchie, B. G., & Clark, M. B. (1991). Working memory capacity and the use of elaborative inferences in text comprehension. *Discourse Processes, 14,* 133–145.

Wilkes, A. L., & Leatherbarrow, M. (1988). Editing episodic memory following the identification of error. *Quarterly Journal of Experimental Psychology, 40,* 361–387.

Zwaan, R. A., & Brown, C. M. (1996). The influence of language proficiency and comprehension skill on situation-model construction. *Discourse Processes, 21,* 289–327.

Chapter 4

Toward a Theory
of Documents Representation

Charles A. Perfetti
University of Pittsburgh

Jean-François Rouet
University of Poitiers

M. Anne Britt
University of Pittsburgh

In this chapter, we add some considerations to existing theories of text, moving beyond the notions of text base and situation model to outline a theory of documents. The essential idea of this theory—actually a framework for a theory—is that the intelligent use of texts entails mental representations of specific texts, situations described in texts, and relations among texts. Our aim is to explain some of the ways this claim is correct and to show some of the features required of a richer model of text representation. As part of this effort, we first critically examine the important distinction between situations and texts.

TEXT AND SITUATION MODELS

A distinction between the semantic content of texts and the situations they describe is at once obvious and difficult. van Dijk and Kintsch (1983) observed the need for theories of text understanding to honor this distinction, and, at least in principle, they do. The distinction is not without difficulty, however. The problem with the text-situation distinction is not that it is not a valid distinction, but that it is difficult to test. The reason has to do with propositional representations. van Dijk and Kintsch, following Anderson (1983), supposed that situations can be represented as propositions, just as text meanings are. Situations can also be represented as linear or spatial arrays, depending on the text and the reader's task, allowing some possibility of separation. However, for many texts and for many mundane tasks, such separation is very difficult. For example, when the reader's task is only vaguely specified as a request to read for "comprehension," it is not clear what kinds of representation will result. In such cases, both texts and situations may be represented as propositions and to that extent are indistinguishable. Attempts to demonstrate clear separation come from tasks that encourage subjects to construct nonpropositional representations. For example, Perrig and Kintsch (1985) presented subjects with texts written to provide spatial relation in either route or survey form. They were able to show a divergence between a text-based process of recall and a situation-based process of inference-based understanding. A related approach has been to demonstrate spatial analog processes in texts, assuming that such processes have operated on nonpropositional spatial representations (Glenberg, Meyer, & Lindem, 1987; Haenggi, Kintsch, & Gernsbacher, 1995; Morrow, Greenspan, & Bower, 1987). In short, the main approach has been to show that readers can construct spatial and nonpropositional representations that are not based on the explicit content of the text. Such demonstrations, however, do not address directly the existence of multiple representations of situations versus texts *qua* texts. They merely show that the information readers represent includes information of various kinds, and that some of this information is derivative of the text rather than explicitly in it.

   Some of this problem of text versus situation disappears if one abandons the text base, assuming no level of shallow semantic representation (Johnson-Laird, 1983). This possibility, which represents text at a syntactic level and restricts semantic representations to situations, has some advantage: It allows a single level of shallow representation, a syntactic-semantic surface form to be used to construct a richer, inference-rich model of relationships. The advantage of the two-level proposal is that the distinction between surface forms and meaning is more readily established than that between two types of meaning, which is what the more standard approach to text requires. Thus, if the main goal were to be able to discriminate semantic-syntactic representations from situation representations, a model that includes just these two levels would help. Comprehension could be described as the transformation of syntactic strings (sentences) having only limited semantic interpretations (e.g., thematic role interpretations) into meaning-rich situation models.

   However, text research has been reluctant to move to this two-level representation system: For one thing, the level of propositional representation has proved very successful in its empirical consequences. Measures of reading time, text recall and summarization, and text comprehensibility are all predicted by quantitative assessment of text propositions (Kintsch, 1974; Kintsch & van Dijk, 1978). The relative success of such predictions compared with alternatives that include a syntactic and non-propositional semantic level has not been a target of research. Thus, the propositional text base has proved its practical theoretical value more clearly than its representational assumptions. The propositional text base also allows a natural way to describe a relatively superficial level of comprehension, one that may have more lexical-conceptual meaning than is commonly represented in syntax.

We have discussed this issue here because it is important for theories of text representation, and ours is a representational model. We have, on balance, concluded that a propositional level is a practical starting point for the kind of model we propose. The problem we address requires generally richer text representations rather than more impoverished ones. The assumption that one of these representations includes a level of "barebones" text meaning without form is consistent with this assumption, and it seems prudent to include it. Our goal requires that we be able to attribute text meaning to multiple texts, and a propositional level serves that purpose. More generally, we assume there must be multiple levels of intermediate analysis of texts during comprehension. These include a level of form representation that provides syntactically parsed inputs for whatever atomic meaning processes assemble the basic meaning representations of a text. This syntactic level is essential, although it is typically ignored in accounts of text processing, except as a means to signal meaning importance (Kintsch, 1992; see Perfetti & Britt, 1995). We ignore it, too, but only because we focus on a level of representation that is well beyond both the syntactic and the propositional. The motivated learner who reads texts, as opposed to one text, acquires rich representations of texts and situations from the atomic and intermediate representations, whatever their form.

If we are correct about the value of rich multitext models, some of the difficulty in seeing situation models through texts disappears. It is difficult to separate the semantic representation of a single text from that of the situation it describes. The distinction between the two, however, becomes more visible with multiple texts. This is especially the case when two or more texts deal with what is ostensibly the same "situation." We return to this point later.

Text and Texts

The world of multiple texts differs from the world of the single text in an even more obvious way. Reading multiple texts produces representations that include connections between the texts. These connections can be of many different kinds. In many cases, the connections are only implicit and may be unrecognized by the reader. In a fairly common case, one text has information that builds on information learned through previous texts, essentially "updating" a situation model (Larsen, 1983; van Dijk, 1988; van Oostendorp, 1996a, 1996b). A good deal of successful learning from text has exactly this property.

A different case arises from texts that explicitly contradict each other, forcing the reader to recognize the connections between the texts. For example, Perfetti, Marron, and Foltz (1996) presented an example of an oppositional connection based on an actual syndicated newspaper column about Holocaust deniers and a published reply. In effect, the column and the reply constitute a set of opposing arguments. In such a case, the connection between the texts is explicit and unidirectional. The second text replies to the first text by referring to it directly, and then setting down an immediate opposition to it. But the connections between two oppositional texts are also implicit and bidirectional, because they also have links to a situation model. Thus, the first text can be said to oppose the second text despite being written prior to it. It directs the reader to build a situation model that contradicts the situation model made by the second text. In short, explicit connections between texts arise through citation; implicit connections can arise through the situation(s) connected to each text.

We have also explored this issue through research on document sets about historical controversies (Britt, Rouet, Georgi, & Perfetti, 1994; Rouet, Britt, Mason, & Perfetti, 1996). This research demonstrated that an adequate representation of multiple, contradictory conclusions based on documents must incorporate information about the document itself, for example, the document type (primary source vs. second-hand account), author's identity and/or role in the events, date of publication, and so forth. In an essay-writing task, this information is used to connect a piece of information to its source (e.g., "according to author X . . .") and to state the rhetorical relationships among texts (e.g., "based on Y, author X claims that . . .", "Document X contradicts document Y . . ."). These observations led us to hypothesize the existence of a potentially rich documents representation, which integrates partial, conflicting situation models built from multiple texts. Although the texts describe overlapping events, a single updated situation model would not be sufficient because the texts are describing contradictory models of the situation.

THE DOCUMENTS MODEL

The general Documents Model has two components or submodels: The Intertext Model represents the relationships among documents and among a document and elements of the situation; the Situations Model represents situations very broadly construed—both real situations and hypothetical ones; and, importantly, multiple interrelated situations. When the Situations Model and the Intertext Model are interconnected, then we have a full Documents Model.

Illustration of the Intertext Model

We illustrate a small piece of the intertext portion of a Documents Model by reference to a piece of cognitive psychology literature. The document space, shown as Fig. 4.1, arises from an interview by one of us (CP) with a document author (who is also one of the authors of this chapter). The author was asked to recall her dissertation, published in 1994, and to answer a few questions about it: "What was the main claim of the published paper? Name the most important papers on this problem at the time. What were their claims?" Other questions might be asked, with the general purpose of getting information that locates named documents in a document space, from which we derive a specific Documents Model. Of course, this is a retrospective procedure and is offered here only to illustrate a general approach to Intertext Models.

To paraphrase what the model represents, the 1994 paper by Britt (Britt, 1994) reported research on a topic treated in other documents (the influence of discourse context on syntactic attachment decisions), thus organizing a document space. There are many more texts in the discourse space than the five represented in Fig. 4.1, but this subset represents a set of connections that are psychologically salient to experts in this field. These documents are connected through a set of document predicates that specify

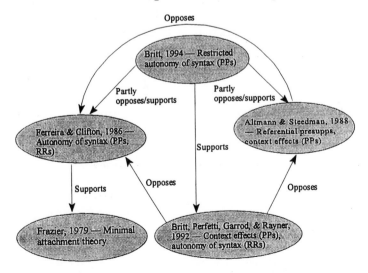

FIG. 4.1. An Intertext Model of five parsing texts.

the functional relations (as opposed to merely temporal or formal relations) among the documents. Thus, a relationship of opposition exists between two of the documents. Altmann and Steedman (1988) argued that because syntactic structures pick out discourse referents, the use of certain structures presupposed referential situations. Discourse contexts, thus, could be arranged to bias parsing decisions. This argument opposes the claim that parsing attachments are initially controlled only by syntactic principles, as represented by minimal attachment theory (Frazier, 1979) and supported by experiments by Ferreira and Clifton (1986), which were criticized by Altmann and Steedman through a widening circle of evidence and argument.

In illustrating the Intertext Model with this particular document set, we do not suggest that it is only in scholarship that Intertext Models are built. They merely provide especially clear examples of such models. Such models will be part of any content domain and may include all kinds of documents.

The Intertext Model

Document Nodes. The Intertext Model includes a node for each document and labeled links between documents and the situations they describe. Figure 4.2a illustrates a template for a Document Node in the Intertext Model. Every node has available variables or slots for Source, Rhetorical Goals, and Content, each of which can be further subdivided. The value for a given slot may or may not be indicated. Whether a slot is filled in will be partially determined by several factors including: the task, discriminability among sources, immediate cognitive demands and time constraints, knowledge of the particular situation, and knowledge of sourcing in general. For example, a novice history student lacking knowledge of the particular

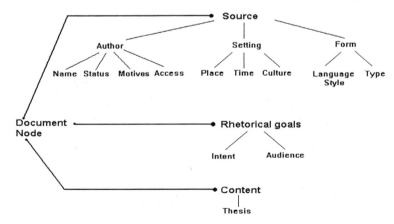

FIG. 4.2a. Template of a Document Node for an Intertext Model.

historical controversy and being only vaguely aware of how to source and why, may only represent the most salient information (i.e., the author's name). However, as shown in Fig. 4.2a, the source variables include a wider range of source information that indicates author identification, setting identification, and document form. Author identification variables identify the author, his or her characteristics, and motives. This includes a slot for the author's name, status or credentials (e.g., President, scholar), motivations in conveying the content (e.g., fame, fortune, posterity), and access to information recorded (e.g., witness, participant, student of). Source information can often be identified through the setting or context, especially information concerning historical setting (i.e., place in which document is created, date and historic period, and cultural context). Finally, document form variables can indicate information pertaining to source identification including the language style (e.g., legal, diplomatic, conversational) and the document type (e.g., treaty, letter, textbook). Of course, there could be additional features that provide important elaboration—distinguishing characteristics of a source that would aid in answering questions about the veracity and significance of a document—but the selected characteristics provide a framework for the type of source information that could be identified and later used in evaluation of the content of the document. Each Document Node may also include information about the document's rhetorical goals. Often the rhetorical goals are not explicitly stated and must be inferred by the reader based on prior knowledge. Rhetorical goals important for evaluating the source of information include the intents of the author (e.g., to inform, persuade, record, illustrate) and the intended or inferred audience for the document (i.e., friend, government agency, newspaper readers). Wineburg (1994) referred to these goals as a document's subtext.

Finally, each Document Node will include a content variable slot, which is a text abstraction of the main point or thesis of the document. For an argumentative text, this could be a summary of the author's main claim or position advocated. For a treaty, the content slot may include the general purpose of the contract agreed on. Because the content of the node is a matter of the reader's knowledge of the document, the content information will be highly variable and will probably not be filled in until after the entire document has been read.

Notice that one might do away with at least the content node as part of the Intertext Model, and assign all such information to the situation model. In such a case, the content of the document would be the situation it describes. Indeed, in a full Documents Model, one with situations as well as documents, this content information must be represented as part of a situation. However, we have decided in favor of some redundancy. A document summary is a characteristic of the document, even as it is also a claim about a situation. Thus, we have essentially duplicated the duality assumption that gives both text-based and situation-based representations: In effect, some part of the text-base macrostructure is represented as a document node. The situation it asserts is separately represented. This duality is subtly different from the usual distinction between text and situation and may be free of the problems we noted in our introduction: Our claim is not that there is a privileged level of representation that is exclusively propositional. Rather, the Documents Model assumes that a summary (or some fragment, topic, etc.) is available as part of what a reader can come to know about a text. This knowledge may actually have come through the building of a situation model based on the text.

To further illustrate a Document Node for an Intertext Model, consider Fig. 4.2b. This is a fully elaborated Document Node for a hypothetical source used in our prior research, which we refer to again later in this chapter. This source is Professor Norman's historical essay published in 1988. His main intent is to inform readers and to persuade them with arguments that the United States supported a revolt in Panama. It would be very rare that a student would be able to or willing to fill in each slot of the Document Node.

Intertext Predicates. Intertext predicates represent relations between documents and relations between a document and a situation model event or causal relation. They include a range of relationships that can hold between document pairs. As we have noted, these intertext predicates often pivot on a solidarity dimension. Thus, the illustration in Fig. 4.1 includes both links of agreement and opposition between pairs of articles on the role of context in parsing. At this level, however, such links are quite superficial:

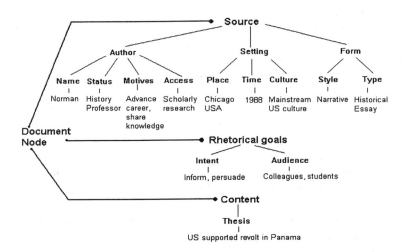

FIG. 4.2b. A Document Node representing Norman's document.

They do not reflect the detailed knowledge an informed reader, especially an expert, can have about the relations between the documents. Thus, an informed reader may represent whether an opposition arises from methodological or interpretational considerations and whether the opposition is more apparent than real, owing to a deeper understanding of the entire document space. However, there is something intuitively right (to us) about this superficial level of representation for many purposes. It appears to capture the level that even an expert might have for many purposes (e.g., summarizing the intertext space) and it may correspond to what survives in memory for the Intertext Model as memory for details fades.

The relations between texts constitute part of a reader's Documents Model, which links texts and situations. The links that label the connections between documents in a particular model can vary widely over many intertext predicates. In many text problems, the predicates are dominated by a solidarity dimension (e.g., *support* vs. *oppose, agrees with* vs. *disagrees with, gives evidence for* vs. *gives evidence against,* etc.). Such cases are prominent when the documents deal with a controversial issue, such as historical controversy (Rouet et al., 1996), but also in normal scientific discourse. (The practice of scholarly journals to publish comments on articles exemplifies direct and explicit connections of this type.) Other intertext predicates include those that capture incremental relations between texts (*based on*), familial-temporal relations (*predecessor–successor*), intellectual or aesthetic relations (*in the spirit of*), mere referring relations (*cites*), and imprecise relationships (*relevant to*).

These intertext predicates are usually marked explicitly in a text. To the extent they are marked, the reader's Intertext Model mirrors an Intertext Model expressed by a text author. To the extent they are not marked, the reader must infer an Intertext Model based on additional knowledge of the texts. Thus, good scholarly texts are of the first type— authors acknowledge explicitly the connections in the document space. By contrast, for example, an expert reading a student paper expects to find fewer explicit connections, and must build the document space entirely from his or her base of expertise. The nonexpert, of course, may fail to build a good Documents Model because of insufficient knowledge of the document space.

The Situations Model

An Intertext Model, although it can be accessed as a separate component, will ordinarily be connected to situations. The connections then provide a fuller Documents Model, one with texts and situations. In a simple and idealized case, one can think of the reader as learner, using a text to build a mental model of some real or hypothetical world asserted by the text.

With multiple documents, an idealized goal may be to arrive at the most complete and accurate representation of a situation. An alternative practical goal might be to learn which documents support a learner's own beliefs about a situation.

In the case of history texts, a given author may convey a single coherent situation model of a series of events and their causes. However, multiple texts provide multiple situations. A second author may try to convince the reader that certain events had a greater causal impact than those argued by the first author, or that some other perspective on "the situation" should be privileged. In this two-text case, both authors are likely to refer to a core of events and some of their assumptions about causal connections overlap. However, some events and connections may be made by only one of the authors. In order for a reader to be able to represent adequately all the significant events and possible causes that were part of the text content, the reader must be able to access earlier event representations and build on them when reading further elaborations of the events.

Given the potential range of relationships among documents and variability in expertise and motivation of a reader, there is corresponding variability in what the reader comes to understand from a set of texts. To stay with the case of history, a serious learner may not be content to use the documents to build a single unique model of the events. Rather, the learner can come to represent the events and proposed causes in complexes of ambiguous (multiple) situations, along with document support for interpretations of these situations. Alternatively, a reader may strive to integrate information fully from the multiple stories into a single coherent situation model of a single set of events. Still another reader may simply take a given text as the privileged source for a situation model, effectively avoiding the complexity of multiple documents. For the expert, however, the goal is more typically to develop a coherent interpreted situation model based on multiple documents, with a representation of the document sources that support that model.

To represent the complexity that accompanies the use of these richer document sets while allowing for at least the potential of a unitary situational representation, additional information must be added to a causal-temporal representation of events. This could be in the form of propositions attached to (or marking) relevant nodes or links in the causal-temporal structure. We illustrate the building of a simple Documents Model with two fictitious passages derived from the materials used in the Rouet et al. (1996) study.

Table 4.1a provides a brief account of the 1903 revolt in Panama from a single author. From this passage, a reader may build a representation of the situation analogous to the causal-temporal network shown in Fig. 4.3. Causal-temporal networks of this kind have been shown to represent ac-

TABLE 4.1a
Norman's Text Describing U.S. Acquisition of a Canal in Panama

The U.S. wanted to build a canal to make travel between the east and west coasts safer and faster. A congressional committee recommended the territory of Panama as a site. To obtain permission, they began negotiations with Colombia, the owner of the province of Panama. The negotiations led to a treaty that was ratified by the U.S. Congress but was rejected by the Colombian Congress. A Panamanian revolutionary who had come to Washington to ask for assistance met with the U.S. President and Secretary of State. The U.S. President did not officially offer support but during the Panamanian revolt, a U.S. military ship was parked in the Panamanian harbor and failed to help the Colombians maintain power. The U.S. presence aided in the success of the revolution. Within three days the U.S. recognized Panama's independence and within 2 months they signed a treaty with the new nation of Panama enabling the U.S. to build and control a canal through Panama.

TABLE 4.1b
James' Text Describing U.S. Acquisition of a Canal in Panama

The U.S. wanted a canal in the Central American region. They created a committee to look for possible locations, and this committee eventually recommended Colombia's province of Panama as the prime location. The negotiations with Colombia led to a treaty that was ratified by the U.S. Senate but was rejected by the Colombian Congress. **The rejection of the treaty increased the Panamanian citizens' desire for independence. They worried about losing the financial benefits of the canal. The angry Panamanians planned and carried out a revolution against Colombia. The U.S. happened to have a ship in the area, but the Panamanians took the U.S. presence as a sign of support, and carried out their revolt.** It was successful. Several days later, the U.S. and Panama negotiated and signed a treaty permitting the U.S. to build a canal in their territory.

curately what people remember from simple narratives (Trabasso & van den Broek, 1985). Britt et al. (1994) and Perfetti, Britt, and Georgi (1995) discussed the relevance of causal-temporal networks for historical accounts. The causal-temporal network connects the events described in the passage and may be used to answer questions such as "Why was there a revolution in Panama?" or "Did the United States participate in the planning of the revolution?"

The Document Node for this document is represented by the circle labeled "Norman" and could contain information similar to that found in Fig. 4.2b. The document-to-situation links (i.e., a link from the event to the Document Node for that document) of the Intertext Model are represented by the dark dotted lines. Note that not every event is marked or linked to the source. Preliminarily, we suggest that the first event and several controversial events critical to the author's interpretation are marked. This would vary depending on the reader's prior knowledge and the task demands. These Intertext Model links can then be used to answer questions such as "Who argued that the United States intervened based on the 1846 treaty?" or "What

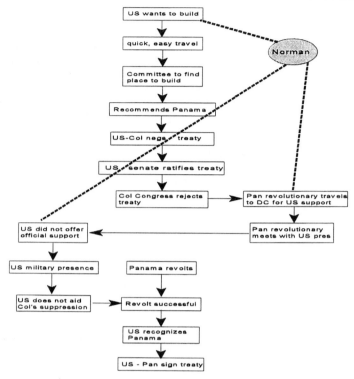

FIG. 4.3.   Representation of situation (boxes and solid arrows) and intertext links (dotted lines) to a Document Node (shaded oval) representing Norman's account. See Fig. 4.2b for a fully elaborated form of Norman's Document Node (shaded oval).

evidence did Norman cite to demonstrate U.S. involvement in the revolution?" Whether readers represent an intertext node and links after reading Norman's passage depends on many factors, including context and reader expertise in the discipline of history. We return to these factors later.

The need for a Documents Model appears more clearly if one now considers the passage presented in Table 4.1b, which presents a similar account of the Panama events, except for the sentences in boldface suggesting that the Panamanians, not the United States, were responsible for the revolution. If James' text were presented in isolation, the passage could result in a simple causal-temporal network similar to the one shown in Fig. 4.4. However, when asked to read both Norman's and James' accounts, the reader must resolve the contradiction about the role of the United States in the revolt. The simplest way would be to build a separate causal-temporal network for James' passage, as one would do on the assumption of one-to-one mapping of texts and situations. This would result in two separate causal-temporal networks (see Figs. 4.3 & 4.4).

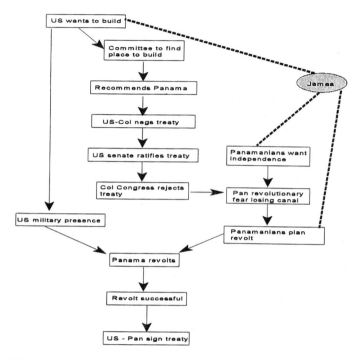

FIG. 4.4. Representation of situation (boxes and solid arrows) and intertext links (dotted lines) to a Document Node (shaded oval) representing James' account.

Integrated Documents Model

Under certain circumstances, the reader may try to integrate the information in the two texts, including the discrepant information. In this case, the first sentence of the passage may lead to a search through memory for possible relevant knowledge, activating a representation of the Norman document (see Fig. 4.3; Mannes, 1994; Mannes & Hoyes, 1996). This representation can then be used as a model of the situation on which to scaffold new information, guided by evaluation heuristics to resolve contradictions. This may be done by connecting critical events and causes to the appropriate Intertext Document Node (e.g., Norman or James). Figure 4.5 illustrates a possible Documents Model for the integrated situation model described by the two texts. There are several important things to note in this figure. First, the situational model events (i.e., boxes) and the links (i.e., arrows) vary in their strength. Those mentioned by both authors are strengthened and therefore represented by darker elements. Second, the two authors are indicated by the shaded circles. Each of these Docu-

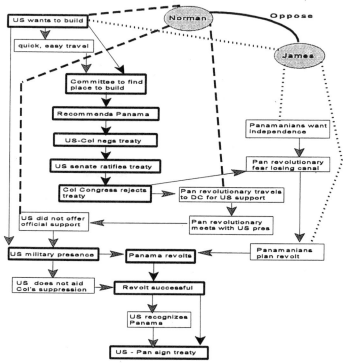

FIG. 4.5. Representation of a model of the combined situation (boxes and solid arrows) and intertext links (dotted lines) to Norman's and James' Document Node (shaded ovals). Strength of the nodes and links are represented by the darkness of the boxes and arrows.

ment Nodes would have some of their respective Source, Rhetorical goals, or Content slots filled in. Third, the darker dotted lines signify Norman's document-to-situation links and the lighter dotted lines signify James' document-to-situation links. Finally, there is a single link between the two documents shown by the dark solid line and labeled "Oppose" because the two authors argue opposing theses.

Given this type of Documents Model representation, the reader may use these Intertext links to signal the origin of information to the reader. For instance, if the reader is asked to account for the Panama revolt, he or she may use phrases such as "according to Norman," or "based on James' essay" to mark the connection between some events and a particular source. The reader may use similar connectors to state the connection between the claim made in a particular document and supporting evidence for this claim (e.g., "Based on the 1846 treaty, James argues that the United States had a right to block the railroad"). Finally, the reader can use other rhetorical predicates to mark the intertext connections (e.g., "Norman disagrees with James as regards the role of the United States"). The information present in the intertext document node (see Figs. 4.2a and 4.2b) is critical to make this kind of connection.

Assuming the reader builds a Documents Model along the lines just sketched, an interesting question is what he or she comes to believe about the situation. In our example, we account only for the Documents Model, including the links between documents (depicted by a solid line in Fig. 4.5) and between situations and documents (depicted by dotted lines in Fig. 4.5). This is ample for a learner to answer a range of questions about the events in the text and positions of authors regarding these events and their interpretation. It is also useful to capture what the learner will be able to access to write countless variations of essays of the form, "What was the cause of the Panamanian revolution?" It does not represent a "true" situation, nor a "believed" situation, which, of course, for the believer are the same thing. An expert who has studied a complete set of documents may come to have (an always tentative) best-guess true-situation model. And nonexperts, of course, can readily come to have (believed) "true" models without substantial document support, although this is less likely with the Panama story than with other stories more emotionally important to the individual. In short, we emphasize that a Documents Model is a model of the document and situation space. It can be accommodated to build individual belief models, but that is not part of what we want to demonstrate at this point.

EMPIRICAL CONDITIONS ON BUILDING DOCUMENTS MODELS

So far, we have focused on an abstract theoretical framework. We turn now to the question of what influences the construction of integrated document models. In general terms, what are the contextual and learner factors that make a difference?

An important general question concerns the extent to which a reader's situation model, as constructed on an initial reading, is affected by subsequent readings. There has been evidence pointing to the possibility that once formed, a reader's understanding of a situation is resistant to being overturned by contradictory information, at least under some circumstances. Readers continue to make inferences based on information read earlier, even when later information has discredited this information (Johnson & Seifert, 1994; however, van Oostendorp, 1996b, reached a different conclusion about this "continued influence effect"). More generally, the question is the conditions under which readers "update" a situation model based on subsequent information. van Oostendorp (1996a) reported that subjects who read newspaper articles on the U.N. action in

Somalia had difficulty updating information; when given a second article that included new information, they were not very accurate in judging the accuracy of information based on the new information, especially when the information was highly relevant. It is not clear how to interpret this result, partly because the level of performance that would have occurred in the absence of a first text is unknown. However, it is interesting that subjects who had developed accurate situation models based on the first article were more likely to update this model accurately with information from the second article. This suggests that whatever difficulty there might be in integrating information over multiple texts, the formation and up-dating of a single coherent situation model can occur with skill, or other variables affecting text comprehension. We also suspect that learners are more likely to build relationships among situations when the texts them-selves are separately represented, such that an actual Documents Model is formed.

The Role of Learners' Tasks and Goals

The learner's goals, and the task context in which they are realized, are important in influencing the construction and use of a Documents Model. The goal or purpose of reading multiple documents normally includes more than just learning the propositional content of the documents. In-deed, as we emphasized, the goal of a learner goes beyond both text models and situation models. Readers generally want to use document information in order to perform a specific task (e.g., solve a problem or answer a question). In some situations, including school learning, these tasks are defined through explicit assignments, study directions, or queries. We expect these tasks to matter for multiple-document learning, just as they do for single-text learning, where several kinds of research supports the assumption that the task has a strong influence on how readers read, evaluate, memorize, and use information from multiple sources.

The first type of evidence comes from research on the comprehension of single texts. Based on the van Dijk and Kintsch (1983) model of text comprehension, several studies have shown that the nature of the reading task (e.g., learning vs. memorizing information) can promote the building of either a literal or elaborative memory trace (Mannes, 1988; Schmalhofer & Glavanov, 1986). In addition, a number of studies showed that specific study directions can influence the selection and hierarchization of text information in memory (Baillet & Keenan, 1986; Pichert & Anderson, 1977). Thus, the relation between the text content and the reader's cog-nitive representation may change as a function of task requirements.

For multiple documents, however, the problem is more complex for two reasons. First, the multiple-documents case brings an increase in text diversity and task complexity. Second, the issue of information selection and ordering must be considered both at the within-document and between-document levels. Several studies have found an influence of the task faced by readers on their understanding of document information. For example, Wiley and Voss (in press) asked college students to study a text presented in one condition as a single text and in another condition as multiple texts. After studying, readers were asked to write either a narrative or an argumentative account of the situation described in the text(s). Wiley and Voss reported that the combination of multiple sources and the argumentative writing task resulted in more causal, connective, and transformed information in the written account. They concluded that constructive understanding of a historical situation can be promoted through argument-centered writing tasks. In terms of a Documents Model, this effect can be said to reflect the learner's distribution of attention between the two major components of the document space, the Intertext Model and the situations model. The multiple document space allows an Intertext Model to be constructed; and the argumentative task encourages the development of an integrated Documents Model—one in which the intertext components and the situations are interconnected, at least during the writing task. By contrast, narrative writing appears to encourage the construction of a single situation model.

A second kind of task effect comes from a study by Rouet and Britt (1996), who found evidence that study directions can affect the accuracy of readers' memory for information sources. Their study investigated the effects of situation versus argument-centered instructions on 17-year old French students' memory for information sources. The participants read four documents about revolts in post-World War I Europe. Students who were instructed to compare Soviet and Western interpretations (i.e., argument centered) tended to remember primary sources better, whereas students instructed to learn what happened (i.e., situation centered) remembered secondary sources better. This distinction between primary and secondary sources is interesting from the perspective of the Documents Model. Secondary sources are narrative accounts that draw on primary sources, which themselves are of various types. (Some can be narrative, but many are not.) Thus, when the task is to learn what happened, the student may attend more to texts that provide an account of the situation (i.e., a narrative). When the task is to compare interpretations, the student may attend more to texts that provide the source of interpretative differences. This suggests the construction of the intertext portion of the Documents Model.

Task effects may also be involved in producing superficial discrepancies in the research on multiple document understanding. Wineburg (1991) compared history graduates' and high-school students' understanding of a set of documents about the Battle of Lexington, one of the first military events of the American war for independence. The results showed that, contrary to the novices, history experts use elaborate reasoning heuristics while reading, and hierarchize information as a function of source parameters. However, Rouet et al. (1996) found that college students with little experience in history were able to understand and use primary documents when reasoning about an unfamiliar controversy. One difference between these two studies was in the study directions given to participants. Wineburg (1991) instructed the students to read in order to find out what happened in Lexington on that day, with no explicit mention that information may be inconsistent or conflicting across sources. Rouet et al., in contrast, instructed their subjects to read in order to form an informed opinion about a controversial topic. More explicit directions may have directed students' attention toward information sources (as opposed to content) and toward the interpretations presented in the documents (as opposed to factual information).

In general, task effects reflect the interaction between a learner's goals and the document space in the construction of a Documents Model. Tasks that encourage attention to documents, as opposed to situations, should lead to the construction of an Intertext Model, and thus a functioning Documents Model. Such tasks might include instructions to compare documents, to cite arguments of a specific text author, to describe the types of documents read, and so on. By contrast, tasks that direct attention to producing simple causal event sequences may encourage the development of a situation model, but not necessarily an Intertext Model. Such tasks may include summarization, recall, and certain kinds of question answering. These may indirectly lead to a relatively impoverished Documents Model, one that contains mainly or only situations. The distinction between the two classes of tasks is roughly between questions about "what was said by whom?" versus "what happened?"

As a practical matter, it is possible that the situation models come rather easily, even when there is some emphasis on documents. Because situation models have the advantage of resting on familiar, highly used cognitive structures that center on narrative and causal-temporal event chains, they may need less specific instructions. Intertext representations may be less likely to be formed without specific guidance, but, in the course of constructing document representations, situation models may come as natural bonuses. If so, tasks that focus on situations lead to poor document representation, whereas tasks that focus on documents will not have a corresponding negative effect on students' understanding of situations.

Other contextual variables, such as the amount of time devoted to studying, the document presentation format (e.g., printed text vs. computer-based hypertext), availability of expanded source information, and other between-document organizers may also play a critical role on the organization of multiple documents in memory. However, there is so far too little empirical evidence to support a discussion of these aspects of context on the construction of integrated Documents Models.

The Role of Reader Expertise

Studies of single-text processing have either assumed or demonstrated that domain knowledge allows domain experts to build up richer text representations (e.g., Dee Lucas & Larkin, 1988; Spilich, Vesonder, Chiesi, & Voss, 1979). However, when looking at multiple texts it is obvious that domain knowledge is only one among several sources of knowledge involved in the comprehension process. Other sources include knowledge about texts as sources of information, and knowledge about how to use texts for a specific purpose or problem (see, e.g., Dillon, 1991). Rather than examine all possibilities for different kinds of knowledge, we exemplify this class of knowledge influences by referring to the reader's initial discipline knowledge. By discipline knowledge, we refer to an undifferentiated knowledge that includes specific domain knowledge and trained experiences with the texts in that domain.

We suggest that readers' ability to build comprehensive Documents Models varies as a function of the reader's initial discipline knowledge. Given a set of documents and a problem, some readers will tend to build a simple narrative model, with few connections to information sources, whereas others will construct a model in which the story(ies) will be embedded in the Intertext Model.

We consider the two short essays presented in the Appendix to illustrate this suggestion. These essays were collected as part of previous studies (Rouet et al., 1996; Rouet, Favart, Britt, & Perfetti, in press). The two essays were written by students with different backgrounds but under similar study conditions. The students were asked to read a set of documents about the 1903 United States military intervention in Panama, with the purpose of answering a controversial question (i.e., to what extent was the United States intervention justified?). Then the students were asked to write their opinion about the controversy.

Essay 1 was written by a first-year college student from an American university. It contains a selection of facts ordered so as to make a coherent story. The gist of the story contained in the student essay is as follows: A revolution was about to break out in Panama, American lives were threatened, which resulted in a limited intervention on the part of the U.S. military. The intervention was successful even though the Marines were outnumbered, probably because some Colombian leaders were corrupt. There is no explicit reference to documents, nor any mention of the controversy. In terms of the Documents Model framework, there is no explicit connection between the situation model and the Intertext Model. In fact, there is no evidence that the student has acquired an Intertext Model. Rather, it seems that a subset of consistent information was selected from a subset of sources, and a story reconstructed from this selection of information. Such an essay may indicate the student's efforts to reduce a complex, inconsistent situations model into a single, simplified situation model.

Essay 2 was written by a graduate history student from a French university. The essay introduces the structure of the Documents Model immediately (i.e., two opposed interpretations triggered by the same set of events and supported by various kinds of evidence). No attempt is made to provide a single, coherent story. Instead, there are many references to the documents and a clear effort to present the contribution of each document. In terms of the Documents Model, the student is describing both the Intertext Model and the critical connections between the Intertext Model and the Situations Model.

It is important to note that the problem statement, the document set, and the study conditions were similar for the two students. Of course, many individual factors can explain the differences in the essays—cultural or ideological background, amount of academic training, expertise in the discipline of history. Our purpose here is not to discuss the relative importance of these factors. We suggest only that studying multiple documents can lead a reader to various types of representations, which vary in the extent to which connections between content and sources of information are established. Experts are more likely to develop a detailed situation model from a text in their area of expertise (Kintsch, Welsch, Schmalhofer, & Zimny, 1990). Additionally, Rouet et al. (in press) suggest that experts are more likely to develop a connection between situations and text sources, at least during comprehension. Discipline expertise does not lead to the construction of simple narrative situational models, but to a more interconnected Documents Model.

We emphasize, however, the likelihood that differences between experts and nonexperts can be affected by the task. The task used by Rouet et al. (1996) encouraged attention to documents. As we suggested in the previous section, such a task should promote the construction of an Intertext Model, compared with tasks that require the student to "tell what happened." With such instructions, differences between experts and nonexperts might be even larger. Experts may typically choose to build an Intertext Model in their area of expertise, even when not encouraged to do so. Indeed, they may prefer to do so even in areas outside their immediate expertise as was suggested by Rouet et al. (in press; see also Perfetti et al., 1995).

SUMMARY AND CONCLUSIONS

Most text-comprehension theories assume the existence of two basic levels of representation: a textbase and a situation model. It has been previously argued that the building of a situation model is critical for tasks that involve text learning or text-based problem solving (e.g., Kintsch, 1986; Schmalhofer & Glavanov, 1986). In this chapter, we described a theoretical framework that accounts for tasks that involve reading multiple texts. We argued that in such cases, an additional level of representation may be needed. This additional level, the Documents Model, includes a mental representation of each text, each situation described in a text, relations among texts, and also relations between texts and situations.

The Documents Model includes two major components, the Intertext Model and the Situations Model. The Intertext Model represents all relevant information attached to a text (i.e., information about source, content, and rhetorical goals) and the relationships among texts (i.e., references embedded in text and solidarity relationships—confirms, opposes). The Situations Model represents the situations, facts, and events described in the texts. Some parts of a Situations Model can be connected to the Intertext Model, for instance, when several texts provide conflicting accounts or interpretations of the same events. When this is done, there is a rich Documents Model, one that represents not only a single situation, but a range of possible situations tied to the documents. Whether such a model is actually constructed by a learner is influenced by a number of factors, including the learner's goals and the demands of the task, as well as expertise, discipline training, dispositions toward learning, and other factors that can influence the extent to which an individual will be motivated to make connections between texts and situations.

APPENDIX

Two opinion essays based on a unique document set.

CONTROVERSY: To what extent was the November 1903 U.S. military intervention in Panama justified?

Essay 1 (U.S. First-Year Student)

United States military intervention was minimal. Only 42 marines were on the USS Nashville. They only came onto Panama when American lives were threatened. The revolution was bound to happen. Colonel Shaler was the one that [sic] shut down the railroad to the Colombian troops. I think he would have done this even if Colonel Hubbard didn't request/demand the action. The Panamanians wanted to revolt. The United States had forty-two marines in the harbor, while the Colombians had four hundred troops at their disposal. I think the Colombians [sic] leaders were corrupt and there was some type of payoff/scandal involved that we will never know about. So, I believe the limited intervention was justified.

Essay 2 (French History Graduate Student)[1]

The U.S. intervention in Panama gave birth to two radically opposed theses: One defending the intervention, the other one not supporting it. The opposition between the two viewpoints is evidenced from the time of the U.S. landing (Carmack/Roosevelt) but it continues till the present times since two historians deliver different interpretations of the events.

However the arguments proposed in each thesis do not "weight" the same. The U.S. President as well as historian Wilson seem to consider [past events] as a unique criterion. It is the past (the numerous interventions in Panama, the relations with Colombia) that justifies the [1903] intervention. This argument, which poorly explains the sudden necessity of [another] intervention, is buried into a discourse that uses tricks to convince the reader or hearer that their point of view is correct. Whereas the thesis that does not defend the U.S. intervention is supported by arguments selected in the very text that rules the relations between Colombia and the U.S.: the 1846 Treaty. It is on the basis of a text of international law that they argue; and they consider that there was a violation of the Treaty.

ACKNOWLEDGMENTS

Preparation of this chapter was supported by a grant from the James S. McDonnell Foundation's program in Cognition and Education for Document-Supported History Instruction. Some of the research on which the chapter is based was supported by the Learning Research and Development Center's Center for Student Learning, which was partially supported by OERI.

REFERENCES

Altmann, G., & Steedman, M. (1988). Ambiguity, parsing strategies, and computational models. *Langauge and Cognitive Processes, 3*, 73–97.
Anderson, J. R. (1983). *The architecture of cognition.* Cambridge, MA: Harvard University Press.

---

[1]This is translated from the French.

Baillet, S. D., & Keenan, J. M. (1986). The role of encoding and retrieval processes in the recall of text. *Discourse Processes, 9,* 247–268.

Britt, M. A. (1994). The interaction of referential uniqueness and argument structure in parsing prepositional phrases. *Journal of Memory and Language, 33,* 251–283.

Britt, M. A., Rouet, J.-F., Georgi, M. C., & Perfetti, C. A. (1994). Learning from history texts: From causal analysis to argument models. In G. Leinhardt, I. L. Beck, & C. Stainton (Eds.), *Teaching and learning in history* (pp. 47–84). Hillsdale, NJ: Lawrence Erlbaum Associates.

Campanario, J. M., & van Oostendorp, H. (1996, September). *Updating mental representations when reading scientific text.* Paper presented at the International Seminar on Using Complex Information Systems, Poitiers, France.

Dee Lucas, D., & Larkin, J. H. (1988). Novice rules for assessing importance in scientific texts. *Journal of Memory and Language, 27,* 288–308.

Dillon, A. (1991). Readers' models of text structures: The case of academic articles. *International Journal of Man–Machine Studies, 35,* 913–925.

Ferreira, F., & Clifton, C., Jr. (1986). The independence of syntactic processing. *Journal of Memory and Language, 25,* 348–368.

Frazier, L. (1979). *On comprehending sentences: Syntactic parsing strategies.* Bloomington: Indiana University Linguistics Club.

Glenberg, A. M., Meyer, M., & Lindem, K. (1987). Mental models contribute to foregrounding during text comprehension. *Journal of Memory and Language, 26,* 69–83.

Haenggi, D., Kintsch, W., & Gernsbacher, M. A. (1995). Spatial situation models and text comprehension. *Discourse Processes, 19,* 173–199.

Johnson, H. M., & Seifert, C. M. (1994). Sources of the continued influence effect: When misinformation in memory affects later inferences. *Journal of Experimental Psychology: Learning, Memory, and Cognition, 20*(6), 1420–1436.

Johnson-Laird, P. N. (1983). *Mental models.* Cambridge, MA: Harvard University Press.

Kintsch, W. (1974). *The representation of meaning in memory.* Hillsdale, NJ: Lawrence Erlbaum Associates.

Kintsch, W. (1986). Learning from text. *Cognition and Instruction, 3,* 87–108.

Kintsch, W. (1992). How readers construct situation models for stories: The role of syntactic cues and causal inferences. In A. F. Healy, S. M. Kosslyn, & R. M. Shiffrin (Eds.), *From learning processes to cognitive processes: Essays in honor of William K. Estes* (Vol. 2, pp. 261–278). Hillsdale, NJ: Lawrence Erlbaum Associates.

Kintsch, W., Welsch, D., Schmalhofer, F., & Zimny, S. (1990). Sentence memory: A theoretical analysis. *Journal of Memory and Language, 29,* 133–159.

Kintsch, W., & van Dijk, T. A. (1978). Toward a model of text comprehension and production. *Psychological Review, 85,* 363–394.

Larsen, S. F. (1983). Text processing and knowledge updating in memory for radio news. *Discourse Processes, 6,* 21–38.

Mannes, S. (1988). A theoretical interpretation of learning vs memorizing texts. *European Journal of Psychology of Education, 3,* 157–162.

Mannes, S. (1994). Strategic processing of text. *Journal of Educational Psychology, 86,* 377–388.

Mannes, S., & Hoyes, S. M. (1996). Reinstating knowledge during reading: A strategic process. *Discourse Processes, 21,* 105–130.

Morrow, D. G., Greenspan, S. L., & Bower, G. H. (1987). Accessibility and situation models in narrative comprehension. *Journal of Memory and Language, 16,* 165–187.

Perfetti, C. A., & Britt, M. A. (1995). Where do propositions come from? In C. A. Weaver III, S. Mannes, & C. R. Fletcher (Eds.), *Discourse comprehension: Essays in honor of Walter Kintsch* (pp. 11–34). Mahwah, NJ: Lawrence Erlbaum Associates.

Perfetti, C. A., Britt, M. A., & Georgi, M. C. (1995). *Text-based learning and reasoning: Studies in history.* Mahwah, NJ: Lawrence Erlbaum Associates.

Perfetti, C. A., Marron, M. A., & Foltz, P. W. (1996). Sources of comprehension failure: Theoretical perspectives and case studies. In C. Cornoldi & J. Oakhill (Eds.), *Reading comprehension difficulties: Processes and intervention* (pp. 137–165). Mahwah, NJ: Lawrence Erlbaum Associates.

Perrig, W., & Kintsch, W. (1985). Propositional and situational representations of text. *Journal of Memory and Language, 24,* 503–518.

Pichert, D. E., & Anderson, R. C. (1977). Taking different perspectives on a story. *Journal of Educational Psychology, 69,* 309–315.

Rouet, J.-F., & Britt, M. A. (1996, July). *Remembering information from multiple documents: Effects of task demands and source information.* Paper presented at the meeting of the Society for Text and Discourse, San Diego, CA.

Rouet, J.-F., Britt, M. A., Mason, R. A., & Perfetti, C. A. (1996). Using multiple sources of evidence to reason about history. *Journal of Educational Psychology, 88,* 478–493.

Rouet, J.-F., Favart, M., Britt, M. A., & Perfetti, C. A. (in press). Studying and using multiple documents in history: Effects of discipline expertise. *Cognition and Instruction.*

Schmalhofer, F., & Glavanov, D. (1986). Three components of understanding a programmer's manual: Verbatim, propositional and situational representations. *Journal of Memory and Language, 25,* 279–294.

Spilich, G. H., Vesonder, G. T., Chiesi, H. L., & Voss, J. F. (1979). Text processing of domain-related information for individuals with high and low domain knowledge. *Journal of Verbal Learning and Verbal Behavior, 18,* 275–290.

Trabasso, T., & van den Broek, P. (1985). Causal thinking and the representation of narrative events. *Journal of Memory and Language, 24,* 612–630.

van Dijk, T. A. (1988). *News as discourse.* Hillsdale, NJ: Lawrence Erlbaum Associates.

van Dijk, T. A., & Kintsch, W. (1983). *Strategies of discourse comprehension.* New York: Academic Press.

van Oostendorp, H. (1996). Updating situation models derived from newspaper articles. *Medienpsychologie, 8,* 21–33.

Wiley, J., & Voss, J. F. (in press). The effects of "playing historian" in history. *Applied Cognitive Psychology.*

Wineburg, S. S. (1991). Historical problem solving: A study of the cognitive processes used in the evaluation of documentary and pictorial evidence. *Journal of Educational Psychology, 83,* 73–87.

Wineburg, S. S. (1994). The cognitive representation of historical texts. In G. Leinhardt, I. L. Beck, & C. Stainton (Eds.), *Teaching and learning in history* (pp. 85–135). Hillsdale, NJ: Lawrence Erlbaum Associates.

Chapter 5

Context Models in Discourse Processing

Teun A. van Dijk
University of Amsterdam

THE NEGLECT OF CONTEXT IN PSYCHOLOGY

Linguists, discourse analysts, and psychologists generally agree that context crucially influences the structures and processing of text and talk. However, whereas they have developed sophisticated theories of discourse structure and comprehension, the detailed structures of context and how these constrain language use have received much less explicit attention.

If context is taken into account in the psychology of text processing at all, it is usually reduced to one or more independent variables that are assumed to affect text understanding, such as goals, task demands, previous knowledge, gender, age, or different types of readers. Although interest in contextual constraints is increasing in psychology, contextual analysis itself remains marginal when compared to the attention to the role of variable text structures and genres, inferences, knowledge, and their mental processing (Graesser & Bower, 1990; van Oostendorp & Zwaan, 1994; Weaver, Mannes, & Fletcher, 1995). Thus, the notion of context may be wholly absent in the subject index of representative recent books on text understanding (Britton & Graesser, 1996).

Linguists and discourse analysts have paid a great deal of attention to the role of context, but have failed to develop explicit theories of text–context relationships. As is the case in psychology, most sociolinguistic accounts tend to examine such relationships in terms of simple covariation, instead of analyzing the precise nature and strategies of contextual influence. Following the early work of Dell Hymes and his SPEAKING model of context (Hymes, 1962), ethnographic approaches have so far been most interesting (Auer & Di Luzio, 1992; Duranti & Goodwin, 1992; Gumperz, 1982). In another development influenced by anthropological linguistics, functional-systemic linguistics and social semiotics show how the structures of discourse are to be defined in terms of the main dimensions of the context of situation or register, such as ongoing action, participant roles, channel, and symbolic purpose (Halliday, 1978; Martin, 1992).

The most extensive work on context has been carried out in the social psychology of language (Brown & Fraser, 1979; Giles & Coupland, 1991), following various approaches to the social psychology of situations (Argyle, Furnham, & Graham, 1981; Furnham & Argyle, 1981; Forgas, 1979, 1985). Thus, Brown and Fraser (1979) presented a situation schema consisting of components such as Scene—consisting of Setting (Bystanders, Locale, Time) and Purpose (goals, tasks, topic)—and Participants and their various properties and relationships. Wish and Kaplan (1977), using multidimensional scaling, identified five basic dimensions people use in the interpretation of social situations: (a) co-operative—competitive, (b) intense—superficial, formal—informal, (d) dominant—equal, and (e) task-oriented—nontask-oriented (see also Forgas, 1985; Giles & Coupland, 1991).

Against this background of theory formation in psychology, linguistics, and discourse analysis, the present chapter first argues that, strictly speaking, *contexts do not directly influence discourse or language use at all.* Rather, it is the *subjective interpretation* of the context by discourse participants that constrains discourse production, structuration, and understanding (see also Giles & Coupland, 1991). That is, given a communicative event in some social situation, its participants actively and ongoingly construct a mental representation of only those properties of this situation that are currently *relevant* to them. Herbert Clark (1996) recently developed a theory of some elements of such represented situations in terms of the common ground participants share and extend during joint discursive and other action (see also Barwise, 1989; Cohen & Siegel, 1991).

Second, extending earlier work on mental models, it is argued that such subjective interpretations of contexts are to be represented in specific models stored in episodic memory (viz., context models). Such context models are assumed to exercise the crucial overall and local control over all processes of discourse production and comprehension. A detailed analysis of these control strategies does not merely show *that* context (indirectly) shapes text and talk, but also *how* this happens exactly. In other words, context models are the necessary cognitive interface between text and context.

Thirdly, I show that context models are a special case of a more general kind of model (viz., experience models). Such experience models represent the ongoing, subjective interpretation of everyday episodes in the lives of social actors. They are discussed against the background of earlier work on event interpretation and on episodic and autobiographical memory. It is stressed that both context models and experience models should not be confused with, or reduced to, the familiar situation models of current theories of text processing. Whereas the latter provide the cognitive base for the semantics of the text, the former control its pragmatic, stylistic, and other properties that vary as a function of the communicative situation.

In order to focus our theoretical discussion, we use (the processing of) *news discourse* in the press as the specific genre for which more specific observations may be made. We use news discourse as an example because, besides everyday conversation and professional discourse, it is the kind of discourse most of us are confronted with most frequently. Also it is undoubtedly the kind of discourse from which we learn most about the world. Moreover, it is the discourse genre I have worked on most extensively, both theoretically and empirically, so that I have some insights into its contextual constraints (van Dijk, 1988a, 1988b, 1991).

It should be stressed that it cannot be the aim of this chapter to examine in detail all the context categories or properties that have been discussed (or ignored) in the literature, nor to propose an exhaustive list or a foundational theory of the discursive relevance of these categories. Rather, our much more modest objective is to stress that contexts are discursively relevant for language users only through their mental modeling, and to examine how such context models influence discourse processing. Also, our contribution is theoretical. Furthermore, empirical (experimental and other) research needs to be carried out to test and elaborate the various assumptions of the theoretical framework.

EVENT MODELS

Earlier work on mental models in episodic memory was limited to mental representations of what events, episodes, or situations discourses are *about* (Garnham, 1987; Johnson-Laird, 1982; Oakhill & Garnham, 1996; van Dijk & Kintsch, 1983). Such situation models (which I now prefer to call *event models* to avoid confusion with the communicative situation represented by context models) account for reference, co-reference, coherence, inferences, and other semantic aspects of discourse processing. Event models represent the subjective interpretation of discourse, the mental starting point of production, and what people later (correctly or falsely) remember of a discourse. Through generalization and abstraction, the information represented in event models provides the basis of socially shared knowledge. And conversely, during understanding, these models are constructed from information derived from discourse and from such instantiated sociocultural knowledge. Much experimental work has confirmed and extended the basic tenets of this mental model theory (Morrow, 1990, 1994; Morrow, Bower, & Greenspan, 1989; see also Britton & Graesser, 1996; Lorch & O'Brien, 1995; van Oostendorp & Zwaan, 1994).

Instead of further detailing this theory of situation or event models, it may be pointed out that most current approaches disregard such models' embodiment of evaluative beliefs about events, that is, opinions (but see, e.g., Graesser, Singer, & Trabasso, 1994). The subjectivity of mental models is most typically represented not only by how people selectively interpret and represent events about which they communicate, but also by what opinions they have about the events.

The same is true for emotion. Thus, while reading a news report about genocide in Bosnia, we combine (a) new factual beliefs about historical events with (b) applied general information about genocide, (c) opinions about (failing) international intervention, as well as (d) emotions of sympathy with the victims. Each of these types of information may later act as a search and retrieval cue in recall of such complex event models.

For obvious contextual reasons that we spell out later, event models are typically richer in information than the discourses that express them: Most known information about an event may be uninteresting, irrelevant, inappropriate, or already known to the recipients and should therefore remain implicit. This means that we need categories in a context model that can handle such criteria of interestingness, relevance, and mutual knowledge and that can act as the communicative interface between event models and discourse structures. That is, pragmatic context models not only monitor how discourses are structured to make them appropriate to the context, but also regulate the relations between semantic event models and discourse (Robinson & Swanson, 1990).

EXPERIENCE MODELS

Context models are a special case of a more general type of model, which I call experience models. Experience models ongoingly represent, and make sense of the many episodes of our everyday life. Communicative events are not only functionally embedded in such episodes, they are themselves such daily episodes. The context models language users build to understand and manage communicative situations may therefore be expected to have the overall structure of such general experience models.

Before we list some properties of experience models (EMs), it should be emphasized that they should not be confused with event models construed for discourse processing, which may be about any event (e.g., the news events we read about in the press). EMs and event models only are the same for autobiographical discourse, such as personal stories about past experiences. However, because of the primacy of personal experiences and daily routines of building EMs, the structure of event models may well be built in analogy with EMs. Also, it is plausible that event models that are similar to EMs are more accessible (Larsen & Plunkett, 1987). Where no comparable EMs are available to help understand discourse, instantiations of more generally socially shared knowledge, such as scripts (e.g., about wars, catastrophes, etc.) will be used to construct event models.

Let us now summarize some of the properties of experience models:

1. Experience models are subjective, unique interpretations of the specific episodes in which particular people participate daily.

2. EMs are stored in episodic memory (Tulving, 1983; but see McKoon, Ratcliff, & Dell, 1986). Together they define people's personal, autobiographical memory (Robinson & Swanson, 1990; Rubin, 1986; Thompson, Skowronski, Larsem, & Betz, 1996; Trafimow & Wyer, 1993).

3. EMs are the experiential basis of, but are distinct from, more general, context-free personal knowledge stored in episodic memory (Nelson, 1993). Such personal knowledge may be relevant for the construction of many different EMs at various moments of one's life, and may, for example, include personal scripts. Thus, "My shopping of this morning" represents an EM, whereas "My shopping" (or "My neighbor") would represent personal knowledge. Thus, personal scripts are typically derived from personal routines, that is, repeated mundane EMs.

4. As long as people are awake and conscious, they continuously are engaged in the construction of EMs. However, EMs themselves are *discrete*, and segment the activities of everyday life in a sequence of separate, meaningful episodes of different levels and sizes (Newtson, 1973). This process may be compared to the meaningful segmentation and interpretation of ongoing discourse as different units at various levels.

5. EMs consist of various kinds of propositional and analogical information organized by a limited number of categories defining an efficient model schema (Barclay & Subramaniam, 1987). Typical categories are Setting (Time, Location, Circumstances), Participants in various roles, Goals, and various types of Activities, as well as their properties.

6. Although EMs are different from scripts (which represent general, socially shared knowledge and not unique personal experiences) their schematic structure may be similar to the structure of scripts for routine activities (Graesser & Nakamura, 1982; Schank & Abelson, 1977). As episodic structures, therefore, EMs are closer to so-called MOPS (Schank, 1982; see also the earlier work of Schank on the representation of episodes, e.g., Schank, 1975).

7. Social scripts may be acquired through processes of generalization, abstraction, decontextualization, and social normalization of EMs. Conversely, once acquired, scripts will typically be applied and instantiated in order to construct routine EMs. It is still a matter of debate when, how, and how much social knowledge (and inferences derived from it) are integrated into EMs and other episodic models (Graesser & Bower, 1990; Trafimow & Wyer, 1993). Instead of integrating applied social knowledge in the models themselves, one might assume that the models merely feature pointers to such general knowledge. I assume, however, that EMs feature specific, situation-bound, that is, adapted instantiations of social knowledge—those and only those that are relevant for the current interpretation of ongoing episodes.

8. EMs are ongoingly construed in an effective *strategic* way, for example, online, tentatively, and hence possibly erroneously, using different information of various levels at the same time (van Dijk & Kintsch, 1983).

9. EM construction strategically uses and combines the following kinds of information: (a) interpreted sense data, (b) personal knowledge and scripts, including Self, (c) old EMs (personal memories of previous episodes), and (d) instantiated and adapted social knowledge and attitudes.

10. *Segmentation* of EM sequences is based on changes in the information stored under one of the category nodes (e.g., a change of place, time period, participants, or (overall) activity type).

11. EMs are typically segmented, understood, and recalled at (or above) some *prototypical middle-range* level, such as "my taking a shower" or "my having breakfast" rather than "my opening the door" or "my starting the car." Lower-level and basic actions are only attended to, separately stored, remembered, and talked about later in situations of trouble or when they otherwise become interesting or salient.

12. Model schema categories, together with higher-level *macrorepresentations* of activities, may also be used in the overall *organization* of EMs in episodic memory (e.g., "My time as a student," "My vacation in Spain," or "My life with Claudia," etc.; Anderson & Conway, 1993; Seifert, Abelson, McKoon, & Ratcliff, 1986). That is, EMs may be further organized at various levels into compound, complex, and higher-level EMs (Hanson & Hirst, 1989; Neisser, 1986).

13. Self is a central category in EMs. However, the unique *hic et nunc* nature of EMs requires that the actually constructed Self in an EM is also a unique construct. That is, it is a specific instantiation of a more general, abstract, and more permanent Self represented in episodic memory (Barclay & Subramaniam, 1987; Kihlström, 1993; Markus, 1977; Srull & Wyer, 1993). Again, this distinction shows the difference between EMs and more permanent episodic knowledge. The Self category organizes many of the

other categories of the EM schema, such as relations between participants, perspective, and so on.

14. As is the case for all models, EMs feature *opinions* and *emotions*, especially because of the personal relevance or involvement of the Self in these experiences (Neisser & Fivush, 1994). In the same way that scripts may be derived from abstracted, generalized, and socially normalized EMs, socially shared *attitudes* may be derived from EMs that feature personal opinions. And vice versa, attitudes may be instantiated in the construction of opinions in EMs (e.g., "My opinion now about this abortion" from "My group's opinion about abortion"). Obviously, as is the case for all personal instantiations of socially shared cognitions, EMs will always be unique and adapted to the current circumstances. Hence the individual variation of EMs.

15. EMs not only define the details of our personal past and present, they also represent overall designs of future actions, such as *plans, tasks,* and *goals,* which may also be used to retrieve EMs (Anderson & Conway, 1993; Wyer & Bodenhausen, 1985).

16. As forms of concurrent thought, EMs may represent unfinished business that gives rise to our everyday, involuntary *ruminations* (worries, regrets, anxiety, anticipation, etc.), especially when their goals have not yet been realized (Martin & Tesser, 1996; Singer, 1993; Wyer, 1996).

17. When being recalled, EMs may become the typical stuff of everyday *storytelling,* especially if they are relatively exceptional or otherwise interesting for recipients. However, stories are not only shaped by EMs but also by relevant *context models* that define the specific communicative goals and circumstances of storytelling. That is, for contextual reasons, storytellers may transform their EMs in many ways (Brewer, 1982; Bruner, 1987, 1994; Edwards & Middleton, 1986; Kerby, 1991; Labov & Waletzky, 1967; Lieblich & Josselson, 1994; Loftus, 1979; Means & Loftus, 1991; Nelson, 1989; Polanyi, 1985).

18. Changes of episodes in EMs may be represented in discourse by a change of underlying semantic episodes, each governed by a topic or macroproposition. Such a change, for example, of participants, setting, overall action, or perspective, is typically expressed by beginning a new paragraph in written texts (van Dijk, 1982).

These summarizing features of experience models each need to be developed in detailed theories. However, the idea of experience models is persuasive and nicely occupies a theoretical niche left open between such earlier notions as *situation model, script, autobiographical memory, personal knowledge, Self,* and the like. Indeed, experience models explain some of the relationships between these notions, while providing the basis for a more explicit theory of episodic and personal memory.

CONTEXT MODELS

As suggested, context models are special kinds of experience models. They represent communicative episodes in which we participate, often as part of other everyday episodes (conversation at breakfast, meeting at work, etc.). Because, among other elements of the situation, context models represent ongoing action, they are of course dynamic: They will be continuously *updated* during the processing of text or talk.

Different participants in a communicative event each have their own, personal context model, defining their personal interpretation of the current situation. However, discursive interaction and communication is possible only when such models are at least partly *shared*, synchronized, or negotiated. Indeed, participants may jointly produce and ongoingly update each other's models. Speakers may have partial models of the context models of recipients and vice versa, especially about the knowledge they share. Such mutual beliefs about each other's models are theoretically infinite, but in practice are constrained by contextual relevance (for details about mutual knowledge in language users, see Clark, 1996).

Context models have the same overall *schematic structure* as other experience models, but with specific categories tuned to communicative events. So far, these categories have only partly been made explicit in discourse analysis (e.g., age, gender, ethnicity, class, roles, power, goals, or beliefs of participants, as well as setting characteristics, such as time, location, and circumstances).

To distinguish explicitly between contexts and the full complexity of social situations (Argyle et al., 1981; Furnham & Argyle, 1981), we define contexts as the structure of all properties of the social situation that are *systematically relevant* for the production, comprehension, or functions of discourse and its structures.

Relevance may be both personal and social in this case, and is defined by the current context model (Sperber & Wilson, 1986). That is, it is not objective age, ethnicity, sex, or similar social features that constitute the context, but their socially based and mentally represented constructions as they are made or taken to be relevant by social members in interaction. This does not mean that anything goes. Despite personal and contextual variation, the relevance criterion is socially based while grounded in social rules and strategies. Precisely in order to distinguish between the theoretically infinite complexity of the social situation and the context constructed out of this situation, language users have learned to focus on those properties of the social situation that are *systematically* relevant for discourse in a given culture. For instance, they know that speakers may vary formal discourse properties (such as pronouns) as a function of their (represented) age or gender rather than as a function of hair color or height. Moreover, efficiency and strategic processing demands also require that the number of systematically relevant situation properties be relatively small.

The Structure of Context Models

Against the background of earlier work on context in discourse studies and psychology (see references given previously), I provisionally assume that context models are organized at least by the following schematic categories (definition and illustration of these categories are given later for news processing):

   I. DOMAIN
  II. SITUATION
      A. Setting
         A.1. Time
         A.2. Location
             A.2.1. Props
         A.3. Circumstances
      B. Events
         B.1. Participants
             B.1.1. Roles
                 B.1.1.1. Social roles
                 B.1.1.2. Interactional roles
                 B.1.1.3. Communicative roles
         B.2. Action/Discourse
             B.2.1. Action types, Genres
         B.3. Cognition
             B.3.1. Aims, goals, or purposes
             B.3.2. Knowledge
             B.3.3. Opinions
             B.3.4. Emotions

The point of this model schema is to organize and reduce the complexity of the social situation in such a way that language users have an efficient device to contextualize discourse production and comprehension. As suggested before, the criterion of inclusion of each category is defined in terms of systematic relevance for a given language or culture: Properties of discourse have to be able to vary according to the information stored under each category of the schema.

The schema should be read as follows: A social situation is part of a social domain (such as politics, education, or law) and consists of a number of events in a spatiotemporal setting. These events themselves consist of participants with different roles and with different mental properties (e.g., goals and knowledge) engaging in various kinds of actions, of which the verbal action is the crucial one for the definition of a social situation as a context (for details, see following sections).

The seeming simplicity of this schema might hide the fact that each category may itself cover fairly complex representations. Because context models are a special type of experience models, they might for instance feature possibly complex person models of participants. Such participant models might be constructed from the extensive general (lay) knowledge people have about themselves and other persons (Markus, 1977). However, it is here assumed that for the construction of efficient context models for language use, it is sufficient that the participants know the relevant (a) identities (roles), (b) ongoing actions, (c) current beliefs of themselves and other participants in the situation, and (d) various properties of the setting.

Note that given the richness of the social situation in which people discursively interact, many other categories may be proposed for inclusion in the schema. For instance, participants may be aware of, and orient to, one or more objects in the situation, and such (possibly joint) awareness may be signaled by deictic expressions (Clark, 1996). However, for several theoretical reasons, we prefer to represent the world or situation talked *about* separately, as in the event model discussed previously. One of these reasons is that we do not want to make a fundamental theoretical distinction between the representation of the referents (objects, people, etc.) that are part of the communicative situation itself and those that are not. However, this example does suggest that event models and context models may overlap. This is obviously necessary in order to account for all other expressions that refer to elements of the context.

Context Models in Text Processing

One of the first interesting implications of the context model schema just presented is that the mental representation of the ongoing discourse itself should be part of the context model. This is true because context models were assumed to represent ongoing action, and discourse is merely one specific type of such action and an inherent part of the whole communicative event and situation. The traditional distinction between text and context is therefore only an analytical one, based on a notion of a (completed) discourse being abstracted from its context. Thus, especially in spoken discourse, the (representation of the) previous part of a dialogue becomes automatically part of the context model that influences what is currently being said and done. In other words, we here encounter a first link between the notion of Text Representation in earlier theories of text processing, and the notion of context model proposed here: Both are continuously and jointly constructed and strategically updated as representations in episodic memory.

The fact that text representations are part of context models does not mean, however, that event models and context models collapse: People distinguish between the information they get from a discourse, on the one hand, and the contextualized occurrence of the discourse itself, on the other hand. That is, we should also theoretically distinguish between personal *knowledge* as represented in event models, and autobiographical *memories* of past communicative events as represented in context models. After all, knowledge may also be acquired through means other than discourse. Moreover, source forgetting and other forms of decontextualization are common phenomena: Of most things we know, we later do not remember when and how we heard or read about them (Thompson et al., 1996).

Contextual Constraints on Semantic Representations

To understand how context models monitor discourse production and comprehension, we first need to know how they regulate the relations between event models and semantic representations. Under what contextual constraints should particular information in event models be included in the meaning of the text, or be presupposed, left implicit, or simply kept from expression? What explicit information should be marked as more or less important or relevant? And conversely, in comprehension processes, what does the semantic representation of a text tell us about the event and context models of the writer/speaker, and how does it influence the construction of a context model of the reader/hearer? For instance, presuppositions tell us something about the knowledge of the speaker, and implicit meanings tell us something about what a speaker may not want to say explicitly for some contextual reason (e.g., appropriateness, politeness, impression management, or face keeping).

With the various parameters of the context and experience models discussed here, we now examine some of the contextual constraints on the relations between event models and meanings of discourse. By way of example, we pay special attention to the production and comprehension of news discourse in the press (for details on news discourse, see Fairclough, 1995; Fowler, 1991; van Dijk, 1988a, 1988b, 1991).

Unfortunately, there are as yet very little experimental or other empirical data on the role of specific context models in news processing. The vast bulk of the literature on news production deals with the social and practical aspects of newsmaking (Gans, 1979; Tuchman, 1978). Of course, such evidence may be used as a basis for the theory of journalistic context models of newsmaking and how they influence news discourse. Psychological work on news largely focuses on comprehension and reproduction.

Although some of this work refers to mental models, it hardly shows how these are controlled by context models, apart from the influence of the usual independent variables (gender, age, etc.) on memory for news (Findahl & Höijer, 1985; Graber, 1984a; Gunter, 1987; Harris, 1989; Larsen, 1988). There is, however, recent work on story understanding that deals more explicitly with some of the conditions (e.g., those of genre knowledge) of event model construction (Zwaan, 1994).

Note that when we refer to the ways context models regulate or monitor the transformation of event model information into discourse meanings, this should be understood as a process that affects both production and comprehension. In production, it tells the journalist what information of an event model to select for inclusion in the news report. In comprehension, the context model of the reader specifies the relevant information to derive from the text and hence what to include in the event model. The context model also explains what information or opinion is made explicit and which information is presupposed, and what inferences can thus be made about the knowledge and opinions or other social characteristics of the journalist.

Let us now examine each of the categories of the context model schema and briefly indicate how they constrain the semantic representations of news discourse in news production, or the construction of event models given the meaning of a text in processes of comprehension.

The first overall category controlling all other category information involved in news production and comprehension (viz., Social Domain) features information such as *Media* or *Mass communication*. It regulates knowledge about typical settings (e.g., newspaper reading, watching TV), typical participants (journalists, readers), typical genres (news reports, talk shows, etc.), and so on. Both in production and comprehension, it tells the participants that the event model expressed in a news report is intended to be shared as public knowledge. This implies, among other things, that most socioculturally known information may be left implicit. Also, in production by reporters, such domain knowledge (e.g., about the social functions of news) regulates which information about an event is newsworthy, publicly relevant or interesting, and what information is not (Bridges, 1991).

More specifically, contextual knowledge about the *type of communicative* event or genre, such as news report, talk show, sitcom, or editorial, tells the participants what specific communicative functions these genres have and what event model information is or should be most relevant to accomplish that function. For instance, for expression in editorials, it is the editor's opinions about an event that should be selected, and not the details of the event itself. More generally, genre information regulates the choice of specific topics and their hierarchical importance (Tenney, 1989;

see also Zwaan, 1994). For news understanding, the *medium* is relevant. Depending on their social roles and knowledge, recipients may find newspaper news to be more credible or reliable than TV news (or vice versa). The contextual Time category is of course crucial for the processing of news. It defines recency as an essential feature of news, regulates the expression and comprehension of datelines, and forms the basis of the semantic content of news structure categories such as Recent Events, Previous Events, and Historical Background (van Dijk, 1988a). Similarly, time of reading may affect recall (Furnham & Gunter, 1987). Finally, the Time category regulates specific media and presentation forms of news, such as the Morning Paper or the Late Night Show.

Similar observations hold for the contextual category of Location (of journalists or readers). This category defines the content of broad news categories, such as local, national, and international news. Geographical closeness of events has always been an important news value: We may expect more news and especially more details (i.e., more of the event model expressed in the news report) about events that are close to and hence more relevant to the reader (Galtung & Ruge, 1965).

The Location category also defines spatial perspective of descriptions (for the representation of spatial information in mental models, see, e.g., Morrow, 1986, 1990, 1994). Thus, there are many ways reporters may semantically represent events known to them, also depending on the news genre. They may describe them explicitly from their own (spatial) viewpoint, or that of witnesses or other news participants. They may thus also display bias when they spatially side with (take the point of view of) one group of news actors (e.g., the police) rather than another (e.g., demonstrators; Glasgow University Media Group, 1976, 1980; van Dijk, 1988b).

The Circumstances category requires that news meanings and their event models be relevant to ongoing social and political events (or for the readers, the social circumstances of their lives). Trivially, during a general strike for instance, both journalists and readers will want respectively to write or read details about that strike. This means that the Circumstances category regulates the urgency and priority of the inclusion of specific event model information in actual news discourse meanings, the macrostructural hierarchy (topicality) of semantic representations, as well as the prominence with which such meanings are expressed in the paper, in the program, on the page or screen.

When writing about what they know about an event, people are more or less aware of their various roles—the communicative role of writer or anchor person, their professional role as journalist, or their social roles as men or women. In many cases such social identities are taken for granted, that is, contextually not very relevant. Depending on such roles and the associated structures of interest, experience, or ideologies, some information of the model may be focused on and selected for expression in news reports, what is newsworthy and what is found interesting for the readers. Thus, White journalists may self-servingly focus only on specific events of a racial conflict, or present the conflict from a White perspective (Balon et al., 1978; Dines & Humez, 1995; Mazingo, 1988; van Dijk, 1991; van Zoonen, 1994; Wilson, 1991; Wodak, 1987b).

Conversely, in their context models about journalists, readers may infer from news meanings possible judgments about credibility or political orientation, and hence about whether the event model journalists express is biased or not (Austin & Dong, 1994). Thus, it has been found that Black readers tend to focus more on civil rights issues than do Whites, and their contextual self-representation influences the ways news meanings are interpreted as relevant models (Burgoon, Burgoon, & Shatzer, 1987; Iyengar & Kinder, 1987; see also Johnson, 1987). Finally, it is well known that differences of class, education, and knowledge also play a role in news selection and understanding (Graber, 1984a; Wodak, 1987a).

Recall that it is not social group membership itself, but social construction and personal modeling that is relevant for the process of understanding news. Thus, in many contexts, men and women, Whites and Blacks, or young and old, will show more personal variation than group variation in the processing of news (Graber, 1984a). More generally, current research on media reception emphasizes the rather autonomous interpretive role of audiences and their construction of personal, social, and cultural interests, relevancies and goals (Liebes & Katz, 1990; Neumann, Just, & Crigler, 1992). This again shows the vital role of context models (and in particular of readers' self-models) in the interpretation of news. In other words, we cannot substitute personal context models simply by more general and abstract mental representations shared by a group.

Social relations are obviously relevant in news production and mass media communication. Journalistic or editorial power based on position and on resources such as expertise and information influences what event knowledge will or will not be included in the news, what opinions or critique (e.g., of politicians) will be expressed or not, and what news meanings will be found credible in the construction of event models by the readers. Context models show how journalists actually interpret such power relations, and how they manage (defy or comply with) them in the actual production of news discourse meanings. Besides their beliefs about reader knowledge and interests, and about newsworthiness of events, these represented forms of journalistic or political power and dominance may be the most influential contextual criterion that regulates what and how information of journalistic event models is actually included in the semantic representation of the news discourse they write (Altschull, 1984; Lee & Solomon, 1990).

The contextual representation of newsmaking as *interaction* (e.g., in interviews, press conferences, or editorial meetings) in many ways shapes the meaning of the news (Clayman, 1990; Tuchman, 1978; van Dijk, 1988a). Thus, information from earlier interaction may be included as relevant quotes in the text, other information may be presented as "off the record," and specific topics may be expressed or suppressed as a function of such interaction characteristics (editorial preferences, legal and political constraints, politeness, etc.). This will also affect the *aims* and *goals* of newsmaking, which may ideologically vary between informing the public and criticizing the powerful and thus serving as a "watchdog of society." The very function of revelations implements this relation between what is known (models) and what is actually meant and said in the news.

Perhaps most crucial for the transformation of event models into discourse meaning is the role of *knowledge* of journalists and readers. As suggested before, sociocultural knowledge and opinions that journalists presuppose to be shared by the readers will not generally be fully expressed, but merely signaled. New knowledge and opinions, as is typical for news reports and editorials, however, need to be made explicit or argued for. Relevant for the construction of models of the production context are also the beliefs of journalists about their readers, beliefs that have generally been found to be rather erroneous (Gans, 1979; Gunter, 1987; Neuman et al., 1992). That is, more generally, the specific situational knowledge represented in the context models of participants is part of the more general common ground that is necessary for discursive interaction (Clark, 1996).

Conversely, readers need to call on vast amounts of social and political knowledge in order to derive their event models from the meanings of news discourse (Graber, 1984a; Perry, 1990). Relevant expertise in this case may simply be identified with sociopolitical knowledge (Hsu & Price, 1993; Lau & Sears, 1986). Experts may thus interpret and learn differently, depending on whether they already know the information and can use their own knowledge to better organize new information. Similarly, we should examine what exactly happens when previous knowledge of readers is inconsistent with that expressed in the text (Hacker, Coste, Kamm, & Bybee, 1991; Zanna, Klosson, & Darley, 1976). Indeed, in our terms, what kind of event model will be formed when readers construct the source as wrong or biased? To solve such problems, given the variety and complexity of knowledge, one should analytically distinguish between personal memories of participating in communicative events (experience models), personal knowledge, knowledge about events (event models), socially shared historical knowledge, and general, abstract knowledge, which may have very different influences on understanding news (Kintsch & Franzke, 1994).

Readers' *opinions*, *emotions*, *attitudes*, and *ideologies* will be brought to bear in specific judgments both about the events and about the newspaper and the journalists, and hence about the credibility or reliability of event models being conveyed (Perry & McNelly, 1988; Schoenbach & Baran, 1990). One major factor frequently found to facilitate news comprehension and retention is that of personal *interest*, an attribute that we define as motivation to acquire knowledge about a specific topic. We may locate this attribute in the self-schema of readers (Graber, 1988). Together with self-modeling of social group membership, thus, the personal and social cognitions of readers (and even a collection of features defining lifestyle) that define their context models are a major factor in news comprehension, that is—in our terms—how mental event models are derived from news meanings (Graber, 1988). Opinions and emotions are especially relevant in the appreciation of *literature*, and thus may contribute to specific forms of comprehension and context model construction (see, e.g., Kreuz & MacNealy, 1996; van Oostendorp & Zwaan, 1994).

Conversely, it needs little further argument that the instantiation of group attitudes and ideologies in context models of journalists fundamentally regulates what and how information of event models will be included in news meanings. The general strategy here is that positive information about the ingroup and negative information about the outgroup will be included or highlighted, whereas negative information about the ingroup and positive information about the outgroup will tend to be suppressed or downgraded (e.g., from topical macroposition to lower-level detail of the semantic microstructure; van Dijk, 1995).

After this brief analysis of the context models involved in news processing, we now have some elementary insight into the transformation of event models into text meaning, and vice versa. The overall strategy is that no model information should be expressed that is *inappropriate* in the present context. The conditions that define such appropriateness may be varied and are formulated in terms of the information stored in the respective categories of the context model. Thus, information may be excluded, presupposed, or downgraded because it is already known, because it may be inferred from what is known, because it is irrelevant, uninteresting, unprofessional, disrespectful, illegal, too specific or too general, and so on, given the overall goals and functions of news reporting in the domain of the mass media.

Contextual Control of Surface Structures

If event models provide the information that will be partly or implicitly included in semantic representations, and context models monitor how this happens, we may expect such context models to be especially relevant in the control of discursive surface structures. Indeed, given the semantic representation of a discourse as described previously, we now need to know exactly how this is being *formulated* (for the other processes involved in formulation, see Levelt, 1989). We need to have a controlling mechanism for selection of speech acts and genre, for schematic discourse organization (such as news schemata), as well as for lexicalization, word order, sentence structure, and the properties of sounds or graphics. We might summarize these variations under the general label of style—the contextually variable expression of more or less the same meaning of a text.

Some of these contextual constraints are autonomous, that is, when they control discourse structure immediately. For instance, the news report genre requires conventional categories of a news report schema (e.g., a headline) independently of content or meaning. In other cases, the input to surface structure variation is *dependent* on both meaning and context features, as is the case for lexicalization. Let us briefly summarize a few typical cases of contextual constraints on the forms or style of news reports. In other words, when are the formulations of news (found to be) more or less appropriate in the specific communicative events of the mass media, as distinct from expression of the same meaning in, for instance, everyday conversation or a scholarly article.

Instead of taking context model categories as our starting point, as we have done until now, we now reason backward. That is, like a reader in news comprehension, we interpret surface structures in terms of possible contextual constraints (for general discussion of these news structures and their contextual explanations, see, e.g., Fairclough, 1995; Fowler, 1991; Fowler, Hodge, Kress, & Trew, 1979; van Dijk, 1988a, 1988b, 1991; Glasgow University Media Group, 1976, 1980, 1982).

Given the selection and conceptualization of event model information in semantic representations, *lexicalization* is intuitively the most obvious way such meaning is expressed in the surface structure of discourses in a specific language. In news production (and interpretation), choice of words is a function of contextual features such as domain (media jargon), genre categories (e.g., the use of a short word like "bid" instead of "attempt" in headlines), expert knowledge, and especially journalistic opinions, attitudes, and ideologies (e.g., "freedom fighter" vs. "terrorist"; Davis & Walton, 1983; Herman, 1992). Similarly, *nominalizations* instead of full clauses may be used to obscure responsible agency, for example, as a function of the opinion of the journalist (e.g., "pollution" and "discrimination" instead of information about who does the polluting or the discriminating; Fowler, 1991; van Dijk, 1991). Verb tenses are obviously a function of the contextual Time category, and verb aspect also of the opinions of journalists. More generally, the formality of lexicalization in news is a function of both genre and domain, participant roles and knowledge.

Deictic expressions ("today," "now," "here," "abroad," etc.) signal several context parameters such as time of news production and location of reporters. At the same time, they may express social roles, social relations, group membership, and attitudes, as in the well-known "Us" versus "Them" pair denoting ingroups and outgroups.

Semantic representations may be expressed by different *word order* or *clause structure*, depending on journalistic beliefs about agency, involvement, or responsibility of agents or other participants in the news. Thus, passive clauses may downplay responsible agency of ingroup members (we, middle class, White, western, male, etc.), and conversely, negative outgroup agency (e.g., of minorities) may be emphasized by active clauses and syntactic fronting of words designating such groups. Similarly, special headline syntax (omission of articles and auxiliaries) may be typical of contextual genre constraints (Fowler et al., 1979; Jucker, 1992).

Rhetorical devices such as hyperboles, similes, metaphors, or euphemisms, among many others, especially have a persuasive function in the expression of meaning, and thus especially signal journalistic opinions (Roeh, 1982). Outgroups may thus be conceptualized by negative metaphors and by hyperboles of negative properties, whereas the opposite will be true for ingroup members (van Dijk, 1991). As elsewhere in the expression of opinion in news reports, such opinions will in turn be a function of social group membership, that is, with what social groups journalists identify.

News reports are globally organized by a characteristic genre *schema* or superstructure, featuring such categories as Summary (Headline + Lead), Recent Events, Previous Events, Context, Historical Background, Verbal Reactions, and Commentary (Duszak, 1995; van Dijk, 1988a). Obviously, the schema itself is a function of genre, whereas some of its categories specifically relate to other contextual features (Recent Events presupposes Time; Commentary the Opinion of the journalist, etc.). Changes of the schema may indicate special importance or relevance accorded to specific information, viz., as a function of the opinions or perspective of the journalist or the reader (Fredin & Tabaczynski, 1993). Specific categories, such as Headlines that express a summary and that define the situation, or quotes (as Verbal Reactions), may also differentially affect perception of social and political issues (Gibson & Zillmann, 1993; Perfetti et al., 1987).

Finally, graphical structures, such as size and type of headlines, the use of pictures and photos, position in the newspaper or on the page or page layout, signal genre and especially the opinions of journalists about the importance, relevance, or interest of events. As is the case for the other surface structures mentioned, the use of such features may also influence (and bias) the formation of event and context models of the readers.

The Context Models of News Processing

Surface structures of discourse are primarily a function of semantic representations, which in turn realize parts of event models. However, we have seen that many properties of discourse are also a *direct* function of the various categories of context models we have discussed, such as setting, knowledge, opinion, and emotions of speakers, group membership, social position and status, as well as current aims, such as those of persuasion. Generalizing over much variation, we may conclude that all information that is contextually relevant, important, or in our best interests will be included in the text and/or structurally highlighted, and vice versa.

That is, during news comprehension, readers do much more than construct models about political and social events. They also construct a model of the communicative event, with themselves as readers, and journalists as writers and in other roles. For the readers, this context model defines their regional location and hence the interestingness of close or distant events; time and recency; their knowledge and the informativeness of the news; opinions and the relevance and persuasiveness of the news; the credibility of journalists and newspapers; the truthfulness of reports; the groups or peoples in the news with whom they identify, and so on.

Indeed, context models define the very social situations of newsmaking and newsreading. They explain why people read the paper in the first place. They regulate what information will be focused on, be believed and accepted, or what reports will be selected for reading.

In news production, context models and their relevant categories organize the vastly complex communicative process of newsmaking, the organization of beats, interaction with colleagues, editorial conferences, interviews, press conferences, reading of other media, and a host of other daily routines geared toward the production of news reports (Tuchman, 1978).

Our brief description of context models in news processing has only begun to scratch the surface of how journalists manage the complex daily episodes that define newsmaking, and how these context models and their structures control the structures of news reports themselves as well as their comprehension and uses by the readers.

Theory and Practice of Context Modeling

The relations described between context models and the ways they monitor the specific structures of discourse (or how discourse structures may be used to help construct context models in comprehension) have been formulated in general, and relatively abstract terms. Actual production and comprehension is of course more complicated and messy, and more strategic and goal directed. People make errors, have incomplete information to construct or derive context models, or given their context models they make errors in discourse production and comprehension. In news processing, journalists may have insufficient knowledge about the events they cover, little or misguided information about the knowledge, opinions, or interests of the readers, or they may confuse the constraints of several professional or social roles.

Similarly, readers may have insufficient knowledge to understand the news. They almost always will do so from their own perspective and in their own interests, thus producing relevant, but possibly incomplete or biased event models. Mostly they also lack detailed knowledge about the production context of news (e.g., who control and have access to news-making) so that they may be easily manipulated into accepting suggested event models or the positive self-presentation strategies and credibility tactics of both journalists and their sources.

CONCLUSIONS

Despite its success in the psychology of text processing, the theory of mental models is still in its infancy. We know very little about the internal organization of such models, and how exactly they are formed, updated, and used in comprehension and knowledge acquisition. We need to know how they are related to other personal episodic information, such as personal experiences, opinions, emotions, knowledge about the Self, and socially shared knowledge and opinions.

This chapter has argued that within the general framework of a theory of episodic models, situation or event models need to be coupled with context models in order to explain how discourse is understood and produced. Such context models are the mental representations of the subjective interpretations language users construct of the relevant features of the communicative situation. Among many other things, they explain what information of situation or event models are to be included in the meaning of a discourse, and how, conversely, event models are derived from discourse. Moreover, they specify the many pragmatic, stylistic, and other context-sensitive properties of text and talk that are still too often ignored in much psychology of discourse processing.

Because communicative situations are part of our everyday experiences, context models were theoretically formulated as a special case of the models people build for the interpretation of their daily activities—so-called experience models. These models of everyday experience at the same time function as the episodic basis of personal storytelling, that is, as personal event models.

These various types of episodic models suggest that we need an integrated theory of the episodic representation of personal events, activities, experiences, and their relations to socially shared beliefs. A full-fledged theory of discourse processing presupposes such a more sophisticated theoretical framework.

Relevant to this suggestion is the final observation that various directions of research in cognitive and social psychology as well as in discourse studies might fruitfully cooperate. Unfortunately, current practice shows a deplorable division of labor (and even worse: mutual ignorance) between researchers in the various fields of research referred to here (text processing, autobiographical memory, event understanding, self-schemata, specific genre theories, and so on). Despite differences of object and method, a general theory of understanding, representation, and memory for events, actions, and discourse should then be a more feasible task.

REFERENCES

Altschull, J. H. (1984). *Agents of power: The role of the news media in human affairs.* New York: Longman.

Anderson, S. J., & Conway, M. A. (1993). Investigating the structure of autobiographical memories. *Journal of Experimental Psychology: Learning, Memory, and Cognition, 19,* 1178–1196.

Argyle, M., Furnham, A., & Graham, J. A. (1981). *Social situations.* Cambridge, England: Cambridge University Press.

Auer, P., & Di Luzio, A. (Eds.). (1992). *The contextualization of language.* Amsterdam: Benjamins.

Austin, E. W., & Dong, Q. W. (1994). Source v. content effects on judgments of news believability. *Journalism Quarterly, 71,* 973–983.

Balon, R. E., et al. (1978). How sex and race affect perceptions of newscasters. *Journalism Quarterly, 55,* 160–163.

Barclay, C. R., & Subramaniam, G. (1987). Autobiographical memories and self-schemata. *Applied Cognitive Psychology, 1,* 169–182.

Barwise, J. (1989). *The situation in logic.* Stanford, CA: Center for the Study of Language and Information.

Brewer, W. F. (1982). Stories are to entertain. A structural-affect theory of stories. *Journal of Pragmatics, 6,* 473–486.

Bridges, J. A. (1991). Daily newspaper managing editors perceptions of news media functions. *Journalism Quarterly, 68*(4), 719–728.

Britton, B. K., & Graesser, A. C. (Eds.). (1996). *Models of understanding text.* Mahwah, NJ: Lawrence Erlbaum Associates.

Brown, P., & Fraser, C. (1979). Speech as a marker of situation. In K. R. Scherer & H. Giles (Eds.), *Social markers in speech* (pp. 33–62). Cambridge, England: Cambridge University Press.

Bruner, J. (1987). Life as narrative. *Social Research, 54*(1), 11–32.

Bruner, J. (1994). The "remembered" self. In U. Neisser & R. Fivush (Eds.), *The remembering self: Construction and accuracy in the self-narrative. Emory symposia in cognition, 6* (pp. 41–54). New York: Cambridge University Press.

Burgoon, M., Burgoon, J. K., & Shatzer, M. J. (1987). Ethnic differences in the evaluation of newspaper image. *International Journal of Intercultural Relations, 11*(1), 49–64.

Clark, H. H. (1996). *Using language.* Cambridge, England: Cambridge University Press.

Clayman, S. E. (1990). From talk to text: Newspaper accounts of reporter–source interactions. *Media, Culture and Society, 12,* 79–103.

Cohen, R., & Siegel, A. W. (Eds.). (1991). *Context and development.* Hillsdale, NJ: Lawrence Erlbaum Associates.

Davis, H., & Walton, P. (Eds.). (1983). *Language, image, media.* Oxford: Blackwell.

Dines, G., & Humez, J. M. M. (Eds.). (1995). *Gender, race, and class in media: A text-reader.* CA: Sage.

Duranti, A., & Goodwin, C. (Eds.). (1992). *Rethinking context: Language as an interactive phenomenon.* Cambridge, England: Cambridge University Press.

Duszak, A. (1995). On variation in news-text prototypes: Some evidence from English, Polish, and German. *Discourse Processes, 19,* 465–483.

Edwards, D., & Middleton, D. (1986). Joint remembering: Constructing an account of shared experience through conversational discourse. *Discourse Processes, 9,* 423–459.

Fairclough, N. L. (1995). *Media discourse.* London: Edward Arnold.

Findahl, O., & Höijer, B. (1985). Some characteristics of news memory and comprehension. *Journal of Broadcasting and Electronic Media, 29*(4), 379–396.

Forgas, J. P. (1979). *Social episodes.* London: Academic Press.

Forgas, J. P. (1985). Language and social situations: An introductory review. In J. P. Forgas (Ed.), *Language and social situations* (pp. 1–28). New York: Springer-Verlag.

Fowler, R. (1991). *Language in the news. Discourse and ideology in the press.* London: Routledge.

Fowler, R., Hodge, B., Kress, G., & Trew, T. (1979). *Language and control.* London: Routledge & Kegan Paul.

Fredin, E. S., & Tabaczynski, T. (1993). Media schemata, information-processing strategies, and audience assessment of the informational value of quotes and background in local news. *Journalism Quarterly, 70*(4), 801–814.

Furnham, A., & Argyle, M. (Eds.). (1981). *The psychology of social situations.* Oxford: Pergamon Press.

Furnham, A., & Gunter, B. (1987). Effects of time of day and medium of presentation on immediate recall of violent and non-violent news. *Applied Cognitive Psychology, 1*(4), 255–262.

Galtung, J., & Ruge, M. H. (1965). The structure of foreign news. *Journal of Peace Research, 2,* 64–91.

Gans, H. (1979). *Deciding what's news.* New York: Pantheon Books.

Garnham, A. (1987). *Mental models as representations of discourse and text.* Chichester, England: Ellis Horwood.

Gibson, R., & Zillmann, D. (1993). The impact of quotation in news reports on issue perception. *Journalism Quarterly, 70*(4), 793–800.

Giles, H., & Coupland, N. (1991). *Language: Contexts and consequences.* Milton Keynes, England: Open University Press.

Glasgow University Media Group. (1976). *Bad news.* London: Routledge & Kegan Paul.

Glasgow University Media Group. (1980). *More bad news.* London: Routledge & Kegan Paul.

Glasgow University Media Group. (1982). *Really bad news.* London: Writers and Readers.

Graber, D. A. (1984a). *Processing the news.* New York: Longman.

Graber, D. A. (Ed.). (1984b). *Media power in politics.* Washington, DC: CQ Press.

Graesser, A. C., & Bower, G. H. (Eds.). (1990). *Inferences and text comprehension: The psychology of learning and motivation, Vol. 25.* New York: Academic Press.

Graesser, A. C., & Nakamura, G. V. (1982). The impact of a schema on comprehension and memory. In G. H. Bower (Ed.), *The psychology of learning and motivation: Advances in research and theory* (Vol. 16, pp. 60–109). New York: Academic Press.

Graesser, A. C., Singer, M., & Trabasso, T. (1994). Constructing inferences during narrative text comprehension. *Psychological Review, 101,* 371–395.

Gumperz, J. J. (Ed.). (1982). *Language and social identity.* Cambridge, England: Cambridge University Press.

Gunter, B. (1987). *Poor reception: Misunderstanding and forgetting broadcast news.* Hillsdale, NJ: Lawrence Erlbaum Associates.

Hacker, K. L., Coste, T. G., Kamm, D. F., & Bybee, C. R. (1991). Oppositional readings of network television news: Viewer deconstruction. *Discourse & Society, 2,* 183–202.

Halliday, M. A. K. (1978). *Language as social semiotic—The interpretation of language and meaning.* London: Edward Arnold.

Hanson, C., & Hirst, W. (1989). On the representation of events: A study of orientation, recall, and recognition. *Journal of Experimental Psychology-General, 118,* 136–147.

Harris, R. J. (1989). *A cognitive psychology of mass communication.* Hillsdale, NJ: Lawrence Erlbaum Associates.

Herman, E. S. (1992). *Beyond hypocrisy. Decoding the news in an age of propaganda: Including a doublespeak dictionary for the 1990s.* Boston: South End Press.

Hsu, M. L., & Price, V. (1993). Political expertise and affect: Effects on news processing. *Communication Research, 20*(5), 671–695.

Hymes, D. (1962). The ethnography of speaking. In T. Gladwin & W. C. Sturtevant (Eds.), *Anthropology and human behavior* (pp. 13–53). Washington, DC: Anthropological Society of Washington.

Iyengar, S., & Kinder, D. R. (1987). *News that matters: Television and American opinion.* Chicago: University of Chicago Press.

Johnson, E. (1987). Believability of newscasters to Black television viewers. *Western Journal of Black Studies, 11*(2), 64–68.

Johnson-Laird, P. N. (1983). *Mental models.* Cambridge, England: Cambridge University Press.

Jucker, A. H. (1992). *Social stylistics: Syntactic variation in British newspapers.* Berlin: Mouton de Gruyter.

Kerby, A. P. (1991). *Narrative and the self.* Bloomington: Indiana University Press.

Kihlström, J. F. (1993). What does the self look like? In Thomas K. Srull, & Robert S. Wyer (Eds.), *The mental representation of trait and autobiographical knowledge about the self: Advances in social cognition* (Vol. 5, pp. 79–90). Hillsdale, NJ: Lawrence Erlbaum Associates.

Kintsch, W., & Franzke, M. (1994). The role of background knowledge in the recall of a news story. In R. Lorch & E. O'Brien (Eds.), *Sources of coherence in text comprehension* (pp. 321–333). Hillsdale, NJ: Lawrence Erlbaum Associates.

Kreuz, R. J., & MacNealy, M. S. (Eds.). (1996). *Empirical approaches to the study of literature and aesthetics.* Norwood, NJ: Ablex.

Labov, W., & Waletzky, J. (1967). Narrative analysis. Oral versions of personal experience. In J. Helm (Ed.), *Essays on the verbal and visual arts* (pp. 12–44). Seattle: University of Washington Press.

Larsen, S. E. (1988). Remembering without experiencing: Memory for reported events. In U. Neisser & E. Winograd (Eds.), *Remembering reconsidered: Ecological and traditional approaches to the study of memory* (pp. 326–355). Cambridge, England: Cambridge University Press.

Larsen, S. F., & Plunkett, K. (1987). Remembering experienced and reported events. *Applied Cognitive Psychology, 1,* 15–26.

Lau, R. R., & Sears, D. O. (Eds.). (1986). *Political cognition.* Hillsdale, NJ: Lawrence Erlbaum Associates.

Lee, M. A., & Solomon, N. (1990). *Unreliable sources: A guide to detecting bias in news media.* Carol Pub. Group.

Levelt, W. J. M. (1989). *Speaking: From intention to articulation.* Cambridge, MA: MIT Press.

Liebes, T., & Katz, E. (1990). *The export of meaning: Cross-cultural readings of "Dallas."* New York: Oxford University Press.

Lieblich, A., & Josselson, R. (Eds.). (1994). *Exploring identity and gender: The narrative study of lives.* Thousand Oaks, CA: Sage.

Loftus, E. F. (1979). *Eyewitness testimony.* Cambridge, MA: Harvard University Press.

Lorch, R. F. J. E., & O'Brien, E. J. E. (Eds.). (1995). *Sources of coherence in reading.* Hillsdale, NJ: Lawrence Erlbaum Associates.

Markus, H. (1977). Self-schemata and processing information about the self. *Journal of Personality and Social Psychology, 35,* 63–78.

Martin, J. R. (1992). *English text: System and structure.* Amsterdam: Benjamins.

Martin, L. L., & Tesser, A. (1996). Some ruminative thoughts. In R. S. Wyer (Ed.), *Ruminative thoughts* (pp. 1–47). Mahwah, NJ: Lawrence Erlbaum Associates.

Mazingo, S. (1988). Minorities and social control in the newsroom: Thirty years after Breed. In G. Smitherman-Donaldson & T. A. van Dijk (Eds.), *Discourse and discrimination* (pp. 93–130). Detroit, MI: Wayne State University Press.

McKoon, G., Ratcliff, R., & Dell, G. S. (1986). A critical evaluation of the semantic-episode distinction. *Journal of Experimental Psychology: Learning, Memory, and Cognition, 12,* 295–306.

Means, B., & Loftus, E. F. (1991). When personal history repeats itself: Decomposing memories for recurring events. *Applied Cognitive Psychology, 5,* 297–318.

Morrow, D. G. (1986). Places as referents in discourse. *Journal of Memory and Language, 25,* 676–690.

Morrow, D. G. (1990). Spatial models, prepositions, and verb-aspect markers. *Discourse Processes, 13,* 441–469.

Morrow, D. G. (1994). Spatial models created from text. In H. van Oostendorp & R. A. Zwaan (Eds.), *Naturalistic text comprehension* (pp. 57–78). Norwood, NJ: Ablex.

Morrow, D. G., Bower, G. H., & Greenspan, S. L. (1989). Updating situation models during narrative comprehension. *Journal of Memory and Language, 28,* 292–312.

Neisser, U. (1986). Nested structure in autobiographical memory. In D. C. Rubin (Ed.), *Autobiographical memory* (pp. 71–81). Cambridge, England: Cambridge University Press.

Neisser, U., & Fivush, R. (Eds.). (1994). *The remembering self: Construction and accuracy in the self-narrative.* Cambridge, England: Cambridge University Press.

Nelson, K. (Ed.). (1989). *Narratives from the crib.* Cambridge, MA: Harvard University Press.

Nelson, K. (1993). Events, narratives, memory: What develops. *Minnesota Symposia on Child Psychology, 26,* 1–24.

Neuman, W. R., Just, M. R., & Crigler, A. N. (1992). *Common knowledge: News and the construction of political meaning.* Chicago: University of Chicago Press.

Newtson, D. (1973). Attribution and the unit of perception of ongoing behavior. *Journal of Personality and Social Psychology, 28,* 28–38.

Oakhill, J., & Garnham, A. (Eds.). (1996). *Mental models in cognitive science: Essays in honour of Phil Johnson-Laird.* Hove, England: Psychology Press.

Perfetti, C. A., Beverly, S., Bell, L., & Rodgers, K., et al. (1987). Comprehending newspaper headlines. *Journal of Memory and Language, 26,* 692–713.

Perry, D. K. (1990). News reading, knowledge about, and attitudes toward foreign countries. *Journalism Quarterly, 67*(2), 353–358.

Perry, D. K., & McNelly, J. T. (1988). News orientations and variability of attitudes toward developing countries. *Journal of Broadcasting & Electronic Media, 32*(3), 323–334.

Polanyi, L. (1985). *Telling the American story: A cultural and structural analysis.* Norwood, NJ: Ablex.

Robinson, J. A., & Swanson, K. L. (1990). Autobiographical memory: The next phase. *Applied Cognitive Psychology, 4,* 321–335.

Roeh, I. (1982). *The rhetoric of news.* Bochum, Germany: Studienverlag.

Rubin, A. M. (1986). Television, aging and information seeking. *Language & Communication, 6,* 125–137.

Rubin, D. C. (Ed.). (1986). *Autobiographical memory.* Cambridge, England: Cambridge University Press.

Schank, R. C. (1975). The structure of episodes in memory. In D. G. Bobrow & A. Collins (Eds.), *Representation and understanding: Studies in cognitive science* (pp. 237–272). New York: Academic Press.

Schank, R. C. (1982). *Dynamic memory: A theory of reminding in computers and people.* Cambridge, England: Cambridge University Press.

Schank, R. C., & Abelson, R. P. (1977). *Scripts, plans, goals, and understanding: An inquiry into human knowledge structures.* Hillsdale, NJ: Lawrence Erlbaum Associates.

Schoenbach, K., & Baran, S. J. (1990). Mass media effects on political cognition: How readers' images of journalists shape newspaper impact. In S. Kraus (Ed.), *Mass communication and political information processing: Communication* (pp. 85–97). Hillsdale, NJ: Lawrence Erlbaum Associates.

Seifert, C. M., Abelson, R. P., McKoon, G., & Ratcliff, R. (1986). Memory connections between thematically similar episodes. *Journal of Experimental Psychology: Learning, Memory, and Cognition, 12,* 220–231.

Singer, J. L. (1993). Experimental studies of ongoing conscious experience. In Ciba Foundation (Eds.), Experimental and theoretical studies of consciousness. *Ciba Foundation Symposium, 174* (pp. 100–122). Chichester, England: John Wiley & Sons.

Sperber, D., & Wilson, D. (1986). *Relevance: Communication and cognition.* Cambridge, MA: Harvard University Press.

Srull, T. K., & Wyer, R. S. (Eds.). (1993). The mental representation of trait and autobiographical knowledge about the self. *Advances in social cognition, Vol. 5.* Hillsdale, NJ: Lawrence Erlbaum Associates.

Tenney, Y. J. (1989). Predicting conversational reports of a personal event. *Cognitive Science, 13,* 213–233.

Thompson, C. P., Skowronski, J. J., Larsem, S. F., & Beta, A. L. (1996). *Autobiographical memory: Remembering what and remembering when.* Mahwah, NJ: Lawrence Erlbaum Associates.

Trafimow, D., & Wyer, R. S. (1993). Cognitive representation of mundane social events. *Journal of Personality and Social Psychology, 64*(3), 365–376.

Tuchman, G. (1978). *Making news: A study in the construction of reality.* New York: Free Press.

Tulving, E. (1983). *Elements of episodic memory.* Oxford: Oxford University Press.

van Dijk, T. A. (1980). *Macrostructures: An interdisciplinary study of global structures in discourse, interaction, and cognition.* Hillsdale, NJ: Lawrence Erlbaum Associates.

van Dijk, T. A. (1982). Episodes as units of discourse analysis. In D. Tannen (Ed.), *Analyzing discourse: Text and talk* (pp. 177–195). Washington, DC: Georgetown University Press.

van Dijk, T. A. (1988a). *News as discourse.* Hillsdale, NJ: Lawrence Erlbaum Associates.

van Dijk, T. A. (1988b). *News analysis: Case studies of international and national news in the press.* Hillsdale, NJ: Lawrence Erlbaum Associates.

van Dijk, T. A. (1991). *Racism and the press.* London: Routledge.

van Dijk, T. A. (1995). Discourse semantics and ideology. *Discourse and Society, 6*(2), 243–289.

van Dijk, T. A., & Kintsch, W. (1983). *Strategies of discourse comprehension.* New York: Academic Press.

van Oostendorp, H., & Zwaan, R. A. (Eds.). (1994). *Naturalistic text comprehension.* Norwood, NJ: Ablex.

van Zoonen, L. (1994). *Feminist media studies.* London: Sage.

Weaver, C. A., Mannes, S., & Fletcher, C. R. (Eds.). (1995). *Discourse comprehension: Essays in honor of Walter Kintsch.* Hillsdale, NJ: Lawrence Erlbaum Associates.

Wilson, C. C. (1991). *Black journalists in paradox: Historical perspective and current dilemmas.* New York: Greenwood Press.

Wish, M., & Kaplan, S. (1977). Toward an implicit theory of interpersonal communication. *Sociometry, 40,* 234–246.

Wodak, R. (1987a). "And where is the Lebanon?" A socio-psycholinguistic investigation of comprehension and intelligibility of news. *Text, 7*(4), 377–410.

Wodak, R. (1987b). Wie über Juden geredet wird: Textlinguistische Analyse öffentlichen Sprachgebrauchs in den Medien im Österreich des Jahres 1986 [How Jews are being talked about: Textlinguistic analysis of public language use in the Austrian media of the year 1986]. *Journal füer Sozialforschung, 2,* 105–125.

Wyer, R. S. (Ed.). (1996). *Ruminative thoughts.* Mahwah, NJ: Lawrence Erlbaum Associates.

Wyer, R. S., & Bodenhausen, G. V. (1985). Event memory: The effects of processing objectives and time delay on memory for action sequences. *Journal of Personal Social Psychology*, *49*, 304–316.

Zanna, M. P., Klosson, E. C., & Darley, J. M. (1976). How television news viewers deal with facts that contradict their beliefs: A consistency and attribution analysis. *Journal of Applied Social Psychology*, *6*, 159–176.

Zwaan, R. A. (1994). Effect of genre expectations on text comprehension. *Journal of Experimental Psychology: Learning, Memory, and Cognition*, *20*, 920–933.

Part II

PROCESSES AND STRATEGIES OF REPRESENTATION CONSTRUCTION

Chapter 6

The Intermediate Effect: Interaction Between Prior Knowledge and Text Structure

Stéphanie Caillies
Guy Denhière
Centre de Recherche en Psychologie Cognitive

Sandra Jhean-Larose
Université de Champagne–Ardennes

Many studies have shown that remembering and learning from text depend on both textual characteristics and the cognitive properties of readers (Denhière & Rossi, 1991). Kintsch (1994) demonstrated that with explanatory texts, remembering, and even learning, was better or occurred more quickly when the exposed concepts were just beyond the current state of the reader's knowledge. McNamara, Kintsch, Songer, and Kintsch (1996) showed that when the coherence of text was weakened, that is, when nouns were replaced by pronouns, and descriptive elaborations and connectives were removed, the readers with prior knowledge used compensatory comprehension processes to infer the relations not stated in the text. However, according to these authors, readers without relevant prior knowledge need to read a fully coherent, very explicit text in order to construct an efficient representation of the text base, which may in turn be necessary for the subsequent construction of a situation model (van Dijk & Kintsch, 1983). Kintsch and Franzke (1995) studied the construction of a situation model about the civil war in Sri Lanka by subjects with various degrees of special knowledge (i.e., the political goal of the war) and with the same level of general knowledge (i.e., the war's schema). They found that only subjects who were given information about the political goal of the war were able to reproduce a fair amount of information about the political situation and to form an adequate situation model. They concluded that "the reader's war schema was sufficient to understand one part of the text, at least superficially, whereas the politics schema was useless by itself and needed to be combined with specific prior information in order to support comprehension" (p. 331).

Although the effect of prior knowledge on text comprehension is well documented (Chiesi, Spilich, & Voss, 1979; Denhière & Mandl, 1988; Means & Voss, 1985; Voss, Vesonder, & Spilich, 1980), a puzzling, counterintuitive result called the *intermediate effect* was repeatedly obtained by Patel and Groen (1991a, 1991b) and Schmidt and Boshuizen (1993). These authors studied the effect of prior knowledge on the recall of clinical cases in three types of subjects: novices, intermediates, and experts in medicine. Although Patel and Groen (1991b) assumed that expertise is a continuum with intermediate levels, they showed that the intermediate subjects recalled more information about a clinical case than did the experts. It is therefore difficult indeed to interpret this result within the framework of expertise as a continuum. Patel and Groen (1991a, 1991b) suggested that the experts must have selected and recalled the relevant information using the macrostructure, whereas Schmidt and Boshuizen (1993) explained this result as the expert encapsulation of knowledge, with the detailed propositions initiated during comprehension being encapsulated into concepts of greater generality.

The main goal of this chapter is to demonstrate that this intermediate effect results from the interaction between semantic text coherence and prior knowledge structure: We assume that advanced, intermediate, and beginner subjects differ not only in the quantity of prior knowledge they possess, but also in the organization of that knowledge. According to previous results we obtained, the knowledge of advanced subjects is organized in a hierarchical goal–subgoal structure, whereas that of intermediates and beginners is organized in a temporocausal chain. We therefore compare the effect of two types of textual semantic coherence—teleological and causal—on the organization of the mental representation constructed after reading by three groups of learners with different levels of prior knowledge. Two domains are investigated: car mechanics and use of a word processing text editor.

Baudet and Denhière (1991) studied the structure of the representation in long-term memory of a complex functional system—an automobile starter system with an electromagnetic switch. They first described the units composing the system and the relations between these units in terms of a causal path and then prepared a teleological description of the system organized as a tree of goals–subgoals (Denhière, Legros, & Tapiero, 1993). The first description of the functional system considered the relations among actions, events, and states according to the causal attribute (Trabasso & Sperry, 1985). The sequences of actions, events, and states expressed the chronological order of the system's functioning. The second description considered these sequences of actions, events, and states as a hierarchical structure of goals–subgoals. The nodes subordinate to the original node represented the subgoals of the system; attainment of these subgoals was a condition for the realization of the main goal of the system. Baudet and Denhière (1991) studied the structure of the mental representation of this complex system in three groups of students with different levels of knowledge in car mechanics. To do so, they constructed four types of task that differed in the kind of activities required to retrieve information stored in memory: free interview, causal questioning, supplying the second event in a three-events sequence, and a recognition task. The results were consistent with the hypothesis of a mental representation organized in a functional system and showed that the acquisition of knowledge may be characterized by (a) more information units stored in memory and (b) greater structuring of the information in the system. The construction of a hierarchical, teleological organization presupposes the construction of an organization based on the temporal and causal ordering of actions. Although the beginner group could not differentiate between the system and the causal subsystems during these tasks, the group with high knowledge constructed a representation that was organized into only one functional system structured into subsystems.

Based on this result, we assume that advanced learners have a mental representation of the domain organized in a teleological structure, whereas beginner and intermediate learners have a mental representation organized in a causal path. If this is the case, we can infer that the teleological organization of textual information to be learned will facilitate the comprehension of the advanced learners because it is close to their representation in long-term memory, whereas the temporocausal organization will facilitate, all other factors being equal, the comprehension of beginners and intermediates trying to induce causal relations between the elements of the text. To test this hypothesis, two versions of an explanatory text, causal and teleological, were constructed. These texts contained the same information (i.e., the same list of actions, events, and states) but differed in their semantic coherence (Legros, Baudet, & Denhière, 1993). The texts were presented to three groups of learners. We predicted that (a) the recall performance of the advanced learners would be higher after reading the teleological version compared to the causal version of the text; (b) the recall of the intermediate and beginner learners would be higher after reading the causal version; and (c) advanced performance would be similar to that of intermediates after reading the causal text. We thus hypothesized that the intermediate effect depends on the interaction between the type of semantic textual coherence and the organization of prior knowledge of the learners. From this point of view, the intermediates in the experiments of Patel and Groen (1991a, 1991b) and Schmidt and Boshuizen (1993) may have performed at a higher level than the experts because the experimental text structure was closer to their representations in long-term memory than to that of the experts.

This hypothesis of the similarity in structure of prior knowledge and semantic textual coherence was tested in two experiments. The first experiment compared the free recall performance of beginner, intermediate, and advanced learners in car mechanics, and the second experiment was designed to replicate the results in another study domain—use of a word processing text editor—with a less difficult retrieval task than free recall, namely, cued recall. Free and cued recall allow us to define the representations constructed after reading, from which we can infer the organization of the mental representation in long-term memory based on the learner's level of expertise. Given that text recall includes both automatic and deliberate components of the search for information in memory, and that the deliberate component involves the use of a macrostructure (Guindon & Kintsch, 1984; Walker & Kintsch, 1985), we assumed that to achieve efficient information retrieval, the macrostructure reflected in recall should match the organization of knowledge in memory. Thus, for advanced learners the teleological text structure should serve as the most efficient macrostructure, whereas the causal text structure should be most efficient for beginner and intermediate learners.

EXPERIMENT 1

Results of previous research obtained in the domain of car mechanics (Baudet & Denhière, 1991; Jhean-Larose, 1991) indicated that advanced learners have a mental representation of the domain organized in a functional system in a goal–subgoals hierarchical structure, whereas beginner and intermediate learners have a mental representation organized in a causal path. If this is the case, the results should indicate a significant interaction between the semantic coherence of texts and prior knowledge: for the advanced learners, recall of the teleological text will be better, whereas for the beginner and intermediate learners, recall of the causal text will be better. Moreover, we predict that the intermediate recall of the causal text will be equal to or better than that of advanced learners and that advanced learners will recall more information than intermediates after reading the teleological text.

Method

Material. Two types of text were constructed: a causal text in which information was causally organized and a teleological text in which information was hierarchically organized. Their common goal was to introduce 14

TABLE 6.1
Presentation Order of the 14 Events in Causal and Teleological Texts

Event	1	2	3	4	5	6	7	8	9	10	11	12	13	14
Causal Text	1	2	3	4	5	6	7	8	9	10	11	12	13	14
Teleological Text	8	7	6	5	4	3	2	1	14	13	12	11	10	9

TABLE 6.2
Example of a Causal Text and of a Teleological Text

Excerpt of the Causal Text

The user inserts the ignition key into anti-theft switch.
It follows that
The user turns the ignition key to the start position
Consequently
The electric current comes into the cable which goes from the anti-theft switch to the
electromagnetic contactor's coil.
Thus,
The electric current will circulate in the electromagnetic contactor's coil.

Excerpt of the Teleological Text

To start the flywheel, it's necessary for:
The pinion's starter to gear into the starting crown.
For this
The gearing system of starter's pinion moves on helicoïdal way.
To do that
The positive control lever tilts.
To this end
The plunger core moves on in a rectilinear way.
To do this
The solenoid electromagnetizes itself.

events and 2 actions chosen about the starter system with an electromagnetic switch, using the same verbal expressions and composed of the same number of electrical and mechanical items. They differed in terms of semantic coherence and the presentation order of the expressions (see Table 6.1).

Two excerpts of the causal and teleological text are presented in Table 6.2. The causal text starts presenting the events: 1, 2, 3, 4, and the teleological text starts by the 8, 7, 6, 5 events.

Subjects. One hundred and twenty students participated in this experiment: 40 beginners, eighth graders in car mechanics having had 1 year of mechanics but never having studied the starter with an electromagnetic switch; 40 intermediates, first- and second-year students in C.A.P. (vocational training certificate) or B.E.P. (technical school certificate) programs in car mechanics;[1] and 40 advanced learners, second-year students in a B.T.S. (vocational training certificate after the age of 18) program in car mechanics. The subjects in each of the three groups were randomized into two subgroups assigned to read either the causal or the teleological text.

Procedure. The experiment was administered to small groups of 5 to 10 students. The texts were presented in booklet form. The subjects read the text twice at their own pace and then immediately following the second reading, they performed a free recall task limited to 15 minutes.

Analysis of Recall Protocols. The analysis of recall protocols concerned the 83 propositions common to both texts. The propositions recalled were either identical to the text proposition or paraphrases. The criteria chosen for accepting a proposition as paraphrase were the hyponomy and cohyponomy of the predicate and argument.

Results

The percentage of propositions recalled by each subject, identical or similar, constitutes the dependent variable. The results analyzed by means of an analysis of variance (ANOVA) showed that the percentage of recalled propositions varied significantly with the level of expertise: $F(2, 114) = 107.00$, $p < .01$. The planned comparisons showed that the performance of the advanced and intermediate groups was similar: 51.66% versus 53.61%, and was significantly higher than that of the beginners (18.48%): $F(1, 114) = 170.02$, $p < .01$. The interaction between Text and Expertise factors was significant: $F(2, 114) = 10.88$, $p < .01$. For the advanced learners, the recall of the teleological text was better than recall of the causal text: 58% versus 45%, respectively. For the two other groups, the recall of the causal text was better than the recall of the teleological text, an average of 40% versus 32%, respectively: $F(1, 114) = 19.57$, $p < .01$. The recall of causal compared with teleological text did not significantly differ between the beginners and intermediates: $F < 1$ (see Fig. 6.1).

Discussion

Our objective in this experiment was to study the interaction between the semantic coherence of texts and prior knowledge regarding the comprehension of a complex functional system. This was accomplished using a free

---

[1]We are indebted to Hervé Thomas for his help in administering this experiment to the intermediate learners.

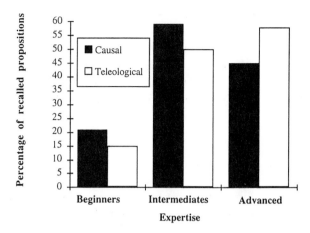

FIG. 6.1. Average percentages of recalled propositions as a function of the level of expertise and the semantic structure of the texts. Experiment 1.

recall task dealing with memory retrieval activities. Analysis showed a significant effect of the level of expertise: the recall performance of the advanced and intermediate groups was significantly better than that of the beginners. The advanced and intermediate groups differed in the type of coherence established between the information units, but not in the amount of information in memory. Indeed, the difference in the average recall performance was not significant between the two groups. Most importantly, the interaction between text structure and the level of expertise indicated that: (a) for beginner and intermediate learners, recall of the causal text was better than that of the teleological text, and (b) for advanced learners, recall of the teleological text was better than that of the causal text.

When a text is organized in a teleological semantic structure, it is similar to the organization of the representation in long-term memory of advanced learners. This facilitates the construction of an efficient macrostructure for retrieving information in memory more than a text organized causally, leading to better retrieval of information. We can assume that to acquire this functional organization, beginner and intermediate learners must first pass through a necessary stage—that of acquiring a causal structure—and then, the intermediate group becomes progressively able to reorganize information from a causal path as a hierarchical structure of goal and subgoals. The cognitive cost of this operation appears to be quite high for these learners, hence their preference for retrieving information governed by causal relations.

The comprehension of a text describing the functioning of a starter with an electromagnetic switch resulted in the construction of a coherent representation similar to the representation of the system. What about the comprehension of another functional system? If textual semantic coherence is a determining factor of the mental representations constructed by learners from different levels of expertise after reading texts explaining the functioning of a system, we should be able to reproduce the results using a different functional system. This was the main goal of Experiment 2.

EXPERIMENT 2

The second experiment studied the effect of semantic coherence on the construction of mental representations of beginner, intermediate, and advanced learners while using a text editor. We tried to replicate the results obtained in Experiment 1, but in the computer domain and with a retrieval task that is less demanding than free recall—cued recall. We also studied more precisely the role of text structure in retrieving propositional units considered as more or less important (Kintsch & Franzke, 1995). In this experiment, we focused on the input activities as measured by the reading times, as well as the output as estimated by cued recall. A ratio between the proportion of correctly recalled propositions and the average reading times was computed and allowed us to estimate the cognitive efficiency of the knowledge groups. Our predictions were the following:

1. Interaction between Expertise and Textual Structure. The advanced learners were expected to have a mental representation similar to the teleological text structure, and the beginners and intermediates to have a representation similar to the causal text structure. Consequently, beginner and intermediate subjects were expected to perform better after reading the causal text, whereas advanced subjects were expected to do better with the teleological text. We predicted a greater performance difference between the causal and teleological texts for beginners and intermediates than for the advanced. This hypothesis was consistent with the pattern of results obtained in Experiment 1.

2. Effect of prior knowledge. Advanced subjects were expected to show cognitive efficiency higher than that of both the beginner and intermediate subjects. We expected the advanced subjects to have the shortest reading times and the highest proportion of propositions correctly recalled, and the beginners to have the longest reading times but the lowest proportion of propositions correctly recalled.

3. Effect of level of importance on reading times and recall. Sentences considered to be important would require shorter processing times contrary to narratives, and would be more frequently recalled than the other sentences (Denhière, 1982; Denhière & Deschênes, 1987; Tapiero, 1992). We assumed that this levels effect would be more prominent for advanced subjects than for intermediates, and least important for beginners.

Method

Material

Domain Structure. The domain of knowledge comprised the description of three procedures of Microsoft Word™: "Select," "Cut," and "Paste." We constructed two types of textual structure to explain the three procedures—one corresponding to the causal system (temporo, causal structure) and the other to the teleological system (hierarchical goal structure) (see Fig. 6.2).

Texts. We constructed a text corresponding to each type of semantic structure: a text with causal coherence, in which information was temporally and causally organized, and a text with teleological coherence, in which information was hierarchically organized in goal–subgoal relationships. The two texts presented the same content, that is, the same actions, events, and states, but differed in their mode of textual organization (see Table 6.3 for an example).

These texts and the recall protocols of subjects were subjected to a propositional analysis (where concepts have been considered as proposi-

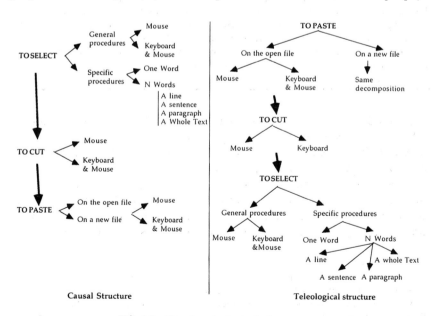

FIG. 6.2. Causal and teleological structures.

TABLE 6.3
Example of the Causal and the Teleological Texts

Excerpt of the Causal Text

... Then, you have to cut the word(s) selected:
either you simultaneously use the keyboard and the mouse, that is:
   you place the cursor on the "Edit" menu keeping the finger pressed on the mouse button,
   and you select the "Cut" command and release the mouse button,
or, you exclusively use the keyboard simultaneously pressing the "Pomme" and "X" keys.
Then, you have to paste word(s) cut into the file
by placing the cursor on insertion point chosen and pressing the mouse button,
then either, you exclusively use the mouse, that is:
placing the cursor on the "Edit" menu keeping the finger pressed on the mouse button,
   and select the "Paste" command and drop the mouse button;
or, you exclusively use the keyboard simultaneously pressing the "Pomme" and "V" keys.

Excerpt of the Teleological Text

To paste one or n words in a file,
place cursor on insertion point chosen by pressing the mouse button,
then either, you exclusively use the mouse, that is:
   you place the cursor on the "Edit" menu keeping the finger pressed on the mouse
   button,
   and you select the "Cut" command and release the mouse button;
or, you exclusively use the keyboard simultaneously pressing the "Pomme" and "V" keys.
To paste one or n words in a file, beforehand you have to cut them.
To this end, either you simultaneously use the keyboard and the mouse that is:
   placing the cursor on the "Edit" menu keeping the finger pressed on the mouse button,
   and select the "Paste" command and drop the mouse button;
or, you exclusively use the keyboard simultaneously pressing "Pomme" et "X" keys.
To cut one or n words, beforehand you have to select them,
To this end ...

---

tions and thus as nodes in the associative network; Denhière, 1984; Kintsch, 1988; Le Ny, 1989). Each recalled proposition, referring to the cue, was coded as either identical to the read text or as similar by acceptable variation of the predicate and argument.

Prior to this experiment, 30 other students judged the relative importance of the sentences of both texts on a 6-point scale. After examining the distributions, three levels of importance were distinguished: very important, moderately important, and less important sentences[2] (see Table 6.4).

---

[2]Each statement of experimental text was divided into segments corresponding to a minimal sentence. Subjects had to judge the relative importance of each sentence on a 6-point scale. These values were grouped into three importance levels as a function of the distribution. Each proposition belonging to a sentence inherited the relative judgment assigned to this sentence. In this way, a judgment value was assigned to each proposition of the causal and teleological texts.

TABLE 6.4
Number of Propositions of the Causal and Teleological Texts
for the Three Levels of Relative Importance

	Causal Text	Teleological Text
Very important	44	43
Moderately important	16	18
Less important	7	7
SUM	67	68

Apparatus

Texts were presented one sentence at a time on a Macintosh computer screen with RRR software (Reading, Recall, and Recognition) written by J. C. Verstiggel.[3]

Subjects

Ninety-six volunteer students from the University of Lyon II, France, participated in the experiment: 32 beginner subjects, 32 intermediate subjects, and 32 advanced subjects. They were assigned to one of the three groups according to their prior knowledge about the domain to be acquired, on the basis of oral questioning by the experimenter. This domain comprised three functions of Microsoft Word™ on the Macintosh: "Select," "Cut," and "Paste." The beginners had never used an Editor, the intermediates only knew Word Editor on an IBM-compatible PC, and the advanced used Microsoft Word™ on Macintosh every day. Each knowledge group was divided into two subgroups of eight subjects assigned to one of two experimental conditions: reading of the causal or teleological text.

Procedure

Subjects were tested individually. The subjects read one of the two types of text on the computer screen at an individually determined pace, sentence by sentence. Immediately after this task, they received a written cued recall task limited to 10 minutes.

Results

We were interested in:

---

[3] We are indebted to Jean-Claude Verstiggel, Research Engineer from the Textima team, ERS 139 at CNRS, University of Paris 8, for allowing us to use the software.

1. How the reading times per proposition for both types of text for the three prior knowledge groups interacted with the relative importance of the textual information; and

2. How the proportion of propositions, identical or similar, recalled by subjects in the three knowledge groups interacted with the textual structure and the relative importance of the information.

Reading Time

A 3 × 2 × 3 ANOVA on reading times per proposition was conducted with the factors Prior knowledge (beginners, intermediates, and advanced), Text (causal and teleological), and Importance level (very important, moderately important, and less important).

Consistent with our second hypothesis, Expertise was significant: $F(2, 90) = 6.39$, $p < .01$. The average reading time of the beginners was longer than that of the intermediates, which was longer than that of the advanced subjects, 1667.6 ms, 1449.4 ms, 1173.9 ms, respectively. The computation of contrasts showed a significant difference between beginners and other subjects, $F(1, 90) = 8.82$, $p < .01$, and also that advanced subjects read sentences significantly faster than intermediates: $F(1, 90) = 3.96$, $p < .05$.

The effect of relative importance of the information was also significant: $F(2, 180) = 72.01$, $p < .01$. The average reading time of the very important sentences (1369.5 ms) was significantly shorter than that of the other sentences (1460.6 ms): $F(1, 180) = 3.94$, $p < .05$, and the average reading time of the moderately important sentences (1146.8 ms) was significantly shorter than that of the less important sentences (1774.6 ms), $F(1, 180) = 140.6$, $p < .01$. These results confirmed our hypothesis 3.

Cued Recall

A 3 × 2 × 2 ANOVA with the factors Prior knowledge (beginners, intermediates, and advanced), Text (causal and teleological), Importance level (very important, moderately important, and less important) and Form of recalled proposition (identical, similar) was performed on the cued recall scores.

Consistent with our first prediction, the Expertise × Text interaction was significant: $F(2, 84) = 6.33$, $p < .01$ (see Fig. 6.3). The difference in proportion of recalled propositions between causal text and teleological text was greater for beginners than for the other subjects, $F(1, 84) = 3.79$, $p = .054$, and was greater for intermediates than for advanced subjects: $F(1, 84) = 8.87$, $p < .01$, with an inversion of these differences for the latter. The result for the causal text shows the same intermediate effect obtained in the research of Patel and Groen (1991a, 1991b) and Schmidt and Boshuizen (1993): the intermediate group (0.179) recalled more than the advanced subjects (0.155). The difference in the cognitive efficiency estimated by the ratio between the proportion of correctly recalled propositions and reading times multiplied by 100 between causal and teleological text was not significant between beginners (0.022) and the others (0.047) and was significantly greater for advanced (0.073) than for intermediate (0.034) subjects, $F(1, 90) = 8.36$, $p < .01$. As we also predicted, Expertise was significant: $F(2, 84) = 12.32$, $p < .01$. Beginners recalled a significantly lower proportion of propositions (0.092) than the other subjects (0.160), $F(1, 84) = 22.317$, $p < .01$, whereas intermediates (0.147) and advanced (0.173) did not significantly differ, $F(1, 84) = 2.332$, $p > .1$. Cognitive efficiency ratio significantly differed from one group to the next, $F(2, 90) = 20.25$, $p < .01$. The ratio of the beginners (0.068) was significantly lower than that of the two other groups (0.154), $F(1, 90) = 28.86$, $p < .01$, and intermediates (0.123) had a ratio significantly lower than that of advanced (0.186), $F(1, 90) = 11.66$, $p < .01$.

A significant difference was also observed in the recall of identical versus similar propositions: $F(1, 84) = 55.25$, $p < .01$. The recalled proportion of identical propositions (0.175) was significantly higher than of similar propositions (0.100). The interaction between form of the recalled proposition and expertise was also significant: $F(2, 84) = 6.71$, $p < .01$. Indeed, the difference in proportion of recalled propositions between both forms was significantly greater for advanced (0.127) than for intermediates (0.048), identical propositions being better recalled than similar propositions, $F(1, 84) = 10.27$, $p < .01$.

Relative importance of information was significant: $F(2, 168) = 211.59$, $p < .01$. The proportion of very important recalled propositions was significantly greater (0.267) than the proportions for other propositions, $F(1, 168) = 326.29$, $p < .01$, and the proportion of moderately important recalled propositions (0.134) was significantly greater than for less important propo-

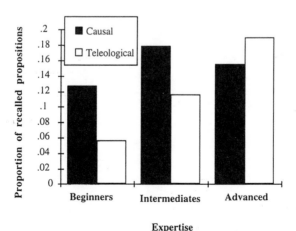

FIG. 6.3. Proportion of recalled propositions as a function of the level of expertise and the semantic structure of texts. Experiment 2.

sitions (0.011), $F(1, 168) = 96.89$, $p < .01$. Consistent with our third hypothesis, the probability of recalling a proposition varied as a function of its relative importance. The interaction of importance level and expertise was significant, $F(4, 168) = 5.6$, $p < .01$: the difference in the proportion of recalled propositions between the important statements and the others did not significantly differ between beginners and the other knowledge groups, and was greater for advanced (0.233) than for intermediates (0.186), $F(1, 168) = 10.93$, $p < .01$ (see Fig. 6.4). The difference in the cognitive efficiency ratio between the very important statements and the others and between moderately and less important sentences was significantly greater for advanced than for intermediate subjects, $F(1, 90) = 25.54$, $p < .01$; $F(1, 90) = 43.93$, $p < .01$.

Discussion

The analysis of the results showed that subjects with different levels of prior knowledge also differed regarding reading times and recall. Consistent with our second hypothesis, we observed a hierarchy in the reading and recall performance: advanced subjects had a higher cognitive efficiency ratio than the others, and intermediates had a higher ratio than the beginners. The results also indicated an effect of level of importance on reading times and recall that agree with our third prediction. Indeed, we observed that the subjects spent more time reading the unimportant statements than the very important, and that the probability of recalling a proposition varied as a function of its relative importance: the more important a proposition was considered, the better it was recalled.

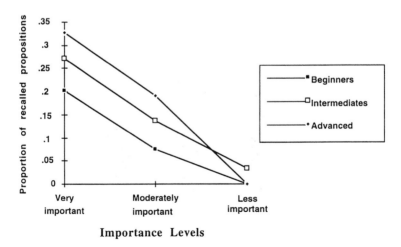

FIG. 6.4.   Proportion of recalled propositions as a function of the expertise level and the relative importance of information. Experiment 2.

The Expertise × Text interaction indicated that beginners recalled more information after reading the text with causal coherence, which supports the results obtained in Experiment 1. The advanced subjects recalled more information after reading the teleological text, their representations in long-term memory presumably being similar to the teleological structure. With experience, they had acquired knowledge about the functional system and had structured their representations into an autonomous system composed of subsystems linked to each other with goal–subgoals relations. Consistent with our expectations, intermediate subjects had knowledge structures closer to those of beginners and less elaborated than those of advanced subjects. They did not seem to have structured their representations in long-term memory into an autonomous functional system composed of subsystems. However, they had mastered the causal structure to such an extent that they recalled the causal text better than the advanced subjects did. Thus, we replicated the intermediate effect initially obtained by Patel and Groen (1991a, 1991b) and Schmidt and Boshuizen (1993) in domains other than medicine, and our explanation of this effect as the result of the interaction between textual structure and prior knowledge was confirmed.

The Relative Importance × Expertise interaction showed that the difference between the recall of important and nonimportant information (moderately and less) was greater for advanced than for intermediate subjects. Although the overall recall of advanced and intermediate subjects did not significantly differ, advanced subjects recalled relatively more important information than intermediates, indicating that they had constructed a more efficient macrostructure and/or retrieval structure (Ericsson & Kintsch, 1995).

The interaction of form of recalled proposition with expertise indicated that the advanced subjects recalled more information identical to the text than other subjects. This result does not support the interpretation of Schmidt and Boshuizen (1993) concerning the intermediate effect. Our results showed that the advanced subjects recalled more of the surface structure information but, given the length of the texts, it is difficult to imagine that they used a knowledge encapsulation module. Consequently, although the intermediate recalls were richer because they included more information, they nevertheless remained farther from the surface structure than those of the advanced subjects.

GENERAL CONCLUSION

The experiments showed that expertise involves difference in the organization of knowledge concerning a given domain. This difference is expressed as the structuring of a representation as an autonomous functional system composed of subsystems linked to each other into goal–subgoal relations, which leads to an increase in reading speed and greater facilitation in the recall of important information from the text. Our results also revealed that the semantic structure of the explanatory text is one of the determining factors of the learner's mental representation constructed after reading and that advanced subjects have a representation of the domain of knowledge similar to the teleological structure, contrary to beginner and intermediate subjects, who structure their knowledge in a causal way. Having constructed a temporocausal structure seems to be a necessary condition for constructing a hierarchical goal–subgoals structure. A beginner who is learning the functioning of a system memorizes the information in linear fashion and organizes it in a causal path. With further knowledge, the beginner will become intermediate, and will eventually progress to an advanced level. How does an individual with intermediate knowledge become advanced? We can assume that an intermediate subject who gathers information in a linear way will eventually face a problem of organization, which will lead him or her to macroprocessing and thus to the restructuring of the acquired knowledge. Indeed, it is this restructuring that defines the advanced level. An alternative interpretation is that students from all levels of expertise organize knowledge causally and that presenting text teleologically interferes with this organization: only advanced students are able to overcome this interference. This interpretation is nevertheless incompatible with the results that we obtained because: (a) the intermediates performed better than the advanced subjects for the recall of causal text, and (b) the advanced subjects recalled more after reading the teleological text.

Two implications, practical and theoretical, follow from these results. From a teaching point of view, it seems necessary to take into account the cognitive properties and, more precisely, to consider the prior knowledge structure of learners in the writing of explanatory or technical manuals. If the construction of a causal mental representation is a necessary condition for constructing a mental hierarchical representation, and if this prior knowledge restructuring defines the advanced level, as our results suggest, then the causal organization of the information in manuals will facilitate the learning of beginners and the teleological organization will facilitate that of advanced learners in the domain to be acquired.

From a theoretical point of view, if the origin of the interaction between the reader's prior knowledge and the textual structure is consistent with the interpretation we propose, that is to say, the similarity of structure between prior knowledge and texts—hierarchical for the advanced, linear for the intermediates and beginners—we should observe the same pattern of results with tasks other than free recall and cued recall. Walker and Kintsch (1985) assumed that the recall of a text is composed of an automatic and an intentional component of the search for information in memory. If this intentional component depends on prior knowledge organization (Kintsch, 1988), then a task such as primed recognition, which requires automatic processing, should allow us to observe the interaction again. More precisely, we assume that the difference between the prior knowledge organization of beginners and of the advanced subjects can be ascribed to the relation between the goal, the actions composing it, and the result obtained (Trabasso & van den Broek, 1985). Thus, our future research will investigate the effect of textual semantic coherence on the primed recognition performances of beginner, intermediate, and advanced learners after reading texts describing the use of a text editor and that of a spreadsheet (McKoon & Ratcliff, 1992; van den Broek & Lorch, 1993). We intend to explore further the mental relations that readers of different levels of knowledge establish between a goal and the actions composing it, and between the goal and the result of these actions while reading texts with causal and teleological structures, and second, the effect of these textual semantic structures on the automatic retrieval of these actions and their results (Ericsson & Kintsch, 1995).

ACKNOWLEDGMENTS

We thank Cathy Carmeni for her help regarding translation. We are indebted to Susan Goldman and Herre van Oostendorp and two anonymous reviewers for their comments on an earlier version of this chapter. We also gratefully acknowledge the thoughtful comments of Eileen Kintsch.

REFERENCES

Baudet, S., & Denhière, G. (1991). Mental models and acquisition of knowledge from text: Representation and acquisition of functional systems. In G. Denhière & J. P. Rossi (Eds.), *Text and text processing* (pp. 155–188). Amsterdam: North-Holland.

Chiesi, H. L., Spilich, G. J., & Voss, J. F. (1979). Acquisition of domain related information in relation to high and low domain knowledge. *Journal of Verbal Learning and Verbal Behavior, 18*, 257–273.

Denhière, G. (1982). Relative importance of semantic information in comprehension and recall. In F. Klix, J. Hoffmann, & E. van der Meer (Eds.), *Coding and knowledge representation: Processes and structures in human memory* (pp. 139–151). Amsterdam: North-Holland.

Denhière, G. (1984). *Il était une fois . . . Compréhension et souvenir de récits* [Once upon a time . . . Understanding and memorization of stories]. Lille, France: Presses Universitaires de Lille.

Denhière, G., & Deschênes, A. J. (1987). Please tell me what you know, I will tell you what you can learn. In E. De Corte, J. L. Lodewijks, R. Parmentier, & P. Span (Eds.), *Learning and instruction* (pp. 188–201). London: Pergamon Press.

Denhière, G., Legros, D., & Tapiero, I. (1993). Representation in memory and acquisition of knowledge from text and picture: Theoretical, methodological, and practical outcomes. *Educational Psychology Review, 5*(3), 311–324.

Denhière, G., & Mandl, H. (Eds.). (1988). Acquisition of knowledge from text and picture. *European Journal of Psychology of Education, 3*(2).

Denhière, G., & Rossi, J. P. (Eds.). (1991). *Text and text processing*. Amsterdam: North-Holland.

Ericsson, K. A., & Kintsch, W. (1995). Long-term working memory. *Psychological Review, 102*(2), 211–245.

Guindon, R., & Kintsch, W. (1984). Priming macropropositions: Evidence for the primacy of macropropositions in the memory for text. *Journal of Verbal Learning and Verbal Behavior, 23*, 508–518.

Jhean-Larose, S. (1991). L'apprentissage d'un système fonctionnel complexe [The learning of a complex functional system]. *Psychologie Française*, Tome 36-2, 167–177.

Kintsch, W. (1988). The role of knowledge in discourse comprehension: A construction integration model. *Psychological Review, 95*, 163–182.

Kintsch, W. (1994). Text comprehension, memory and learning. *American Psychologist, 49*(4), 294–303.

Kintsch, W., & Franzke, M. (1995). The role of prior knowledge in the recall of a new story. In R. F. Lorch & E. J. O'Brien (Eds.), *Sources of coherence in reading* (pp. 321–333). Hillsdale, NJ: Lawrence Erlbaum Associates.

Legros, D., Baudet, S., & Denhière, G. (1993). Analyse des représentations d'objets techniques complexes et production de textes. In G. Gagné (Ed.), *Papers in mother tongue education* (pp. 1–28). New York: Waxmann.

Le Ny, J. F. (1989). *Science cognitive et compréhension du langage* [Cognitive science and language comprehension]. Paris: Presses Universitaires de France.

McKoon, G., & Ratcliff, R. (1992). Inference during reading. *Psychological Review, 99*(3), 440–466.

McNamara, D. S., Kintsch, E., Songer, N. B., & Kintsch, W. (1996). Are good texts always better? Interactions of text coherence, prior knowledge knowledge, and levels of understanding in learning from text. *Cognition and Instruction, 14*(1), 1–43.

Means, M. L., & Voss, J. F. (1985). Star wars: A developmental study of expert and novice knowledge structures. *Journal of Memory and Language, 24*, 746–757.

Patel, V. L., & Groen, G. J. (1991a). The general and specific nature of medical expertise: A critical look. In K. A. Ericsson & J. Smith (Eds.), *Toward a general theory of expertise* (pp. 93–125). New York: Cambridge University Press.

Patel, V. L., & Groen, G. J. (1991b). Developmental accounts of the transition from medical student to doctor: Some problems and suggestions. *Medical Education, 25*, 527–535.

Schmidt, H. G., & Boshuizen, H. P. A. (1993). On the origin of intermediate effects in clinical case recall. *Memory and Cognition, 21*(3), 338–351.

Tapiero, I. (1992). *Traitement cognitif du texte narratif et expositif et connexionnisme: Expérimentations et simulations*. Thèse de Doctorat Nouveau Régime, Université de Paris VIII.

Trabasso, T., & Sperry, L. L. (1985). Causal relatedness and importance of story events. *Journal of Memory and Language, 24*, 595–611.

Trabasso, T., & van den Broek, P. (1985). Causal thinking and the representation of narrative events. *Journal of Memory and Language, 24*, 612–630.

van den Broek, P., & Lorch, R. F. (1993). Network representations of causal relations in memory for narrative texts: Evidence from primed recognition. *Discourse Processes, 16*, 75–98.

van Dijk, T. A., & Kintsch, W. (1983). *Strategies of discourse comprehension*. New York: Academic Press.

Voss, J. F., Vesonder, G. T., & Spilich, G. J. (1980). Text generation and recall by high-knowledge and low-knowledge individuals. *Journal of Verbal Learning and Verbal Behavior, 19*, 651–667.

Walker, W. H., & Kintsch, W. (1985). Automatic and strategic aspects of knowledge retrieval. *Cognitive Science, 9*, 261–283.

Chapter 7

Building Representations of Informational Text: Evidence From Children's Think-Aloud Protocols

Nathalie Coté
Susan R. Goldman
Vanderbilt University

Research during the past decade has revealed a wide range of strategies used by adults and children to comprehend what they read. For example, researchers using think-aloud methods have demonstrated that adults and children who explain and elaborate what they are reading to themselves and who have a flexible approach to solving comprehension problems (i.e., use a variety of strategies) remember text and solve problems better than those who do not (e.g., Chi, deLeeuw, Chiu, & LaVancher, 1994; Goldman, Coté, & Saul, 1994; Goldman & Saul, 1990a; Graesser, Singer, & Trabasso, 1994; Trabasso & Magliano, 1996). In fact, Pressley and Afflerbach (1995) were able to compile an impressive catalog of the wide range of comprehension, monitoring, and evaluation processes that researchers have found in think-aloud protocols of reading, usually in studies of highly skilled adult readers. However, our knowledge of the range of activities that skilled readers may engage in does not yet allow us to understand exactly how readers, especially children, construct coherent representations online as they process text, or which activities are related to constructing different types of representations. This information is particularly lacking for expository text from which readers are to learn and acquire new information, that is, informational or instructional text (e.g., Goldman, 1996; Goldman, Varma, & Coté, 1996; Lorch, 1995).

In common with contemporary discourse theories (e.g., W. Kintsch, 1988; W. Kintsch & van Dijk, 1978; van Dijk & W. Kintsch, 1983), the research reported here is based on several assumptions about the processing involved in constructing cognitive representations of text: (a) information from text is processed sequentially; (b) information from the text and information retrieved from long-term working memory is operated on in working memory and then stored as parts of an evolving representation; (c) readers construct different levels of representation online, such as a propositional representation of the text content as well as a representation of the situation being described by the text; (d) relationships between two units of text information, or between information from the text and information retrieved from long-term memory, can only be detected or generated if the pieces of information are active in working memory at the same time; and (e) the capacity of working memory is limited. (For further discussion of capacity limitations, see Goldman & Varma, 1995.)

It is well established that readers often do not construct coherent propositional or situational representations of text information. One reason for failures to detect or generate the connections necessary for coherent discourse representations is the unavailability of relevant information in working memory. In the process of reading a long text, keeping relevant information active in working memory often requires monitoring the coherence of the evolving representations and strategically using discourse and topic knowledge to identify relevant information in order to reinstate selectively previous text information, retrieve or reinstate information from long-term memory, or both (e.g., Ericsson & W. Kintsch, 1995; Fletcher, 1986; W. Kintsch, 1988; W. Kintsch & van Dijk, 1978).

Earlier work in our lab investigated several of these assumptions about the construction of coherent representations and failures to do so by assessing the reading behaviors and strategies of adult participants as they read difficult informational passages (Coté, Goldman, & Saul, 1993; Goldman & Saul, 1990a). By allowing readers to control the pace of their reading and the order in which they accessed the sentences of a text, Goldman and Saul (1990a) found differences both within and across adults in patterns of where and how much they chose to reread and in what order, indicating that the readers were very flexible in their backtracking or physical reinstatement of sentences. The adults seemed to be applying reading behaviors strategically. This research showed that characterizing readers' strategies based on their reading traces or patterns of movement through text predicted recall performance better than merely measuring the time adults spent processing the sentences. The high frequency with which Goldman and Saul's readers physically reinstated prior text led to a follow-up study to investigate adults' processing more directly by using a think-aloud methodology in conjunction with reading trace information (Goldman & Saul, 1990a, Experiment 3). The adults' verbalizations verified that their patterns of reading and reinstatement behavior were strategic and related to failures to establish local and global coherence as they constructed their mental representations of the text.

The research that we report in this chapter is part of a larger study extending our previous work to children. The issue of interest in the present context is how children attempt to generate and update coherent representations of the central concepts and relationships in instructional text. The relationships between children's reading behaviors, their difficulties in establishing and maintaining coherent conceptual understanding, and their choice of strategies were studied using think-aloud protocol methodology and a presentation format that allowed readers to control the pace and direction of their reading behaviors (Goldman & Saul, 1990b). In this chapter, we focus our discussion on the cognitive activities occurring during the online processing of the texts.

THINK-ALOUD PROTOCOL METHODOLOGY

The participants were 16 elementary school children in the sixth grade (ages 11 to 13) who were recruited to participate individually in two reading sessions. The children had the option of refusing to participate, although none did. As part of a larger study, the children whose data are discussed in the current chapter read four passages that contained material new to them. Two were on the more familiar topics of fat and sugar and two were on the less familiar topics of metabolism and hybrids. Students read two of the texts (on a more familiar topic and a less familiar topic) midway through the school year, and then read another two texts (on a more familiar topic and a less familiar topic) at the end of the school year. At each timepoint (midyear and end of year), the children began by reading a short training text to practice think-aloud and recall task procedures.

The data reported here focus on the children's processing of the two less familiar texts, Metabolism and Hybrids (see Appendix A and B), because these texts are the most revealing of the problems and processes involved in children's construction of a coherent representation. Also, it is commonly accepted that think-aloud protocols provide a more accurate picture of processing when the text being read is not so easy that reading activities are automatic and inaccessible to verbalization (Chi et al., 1994; Ericsson & Simon, 1984/1993; Trabasso, Suh, Payton, & Jain, 1995). Note that the texts were not unreasonably difficult; they were similar to material that children might encounter in school.

The texts were each presented on a computer screen in a format that exposed only one sentence at a time with the words of the other sentences masked. Information such as punctuation and paragraph indentation was not masked (Goldman & Saul, 1990b). This format allowed the students to read and reread sentences in any order for as long as they liked, leaving a computer record of their patterns of reading. The children were asked to verbalize what they were thinking as they tried to understand the passage, what they were doing to understand the passage, what they found easy or hard, and to describe any problems they had and what they were doing about them. The sessions were videotaped.

The students were instructed to read each passage in order to dictate a report on what they read for their peers, a form of recall task. After reading each passage, they dictated a report that the experimenter typed onto the computer.

ANALYSES AND RESULTS

The analyses of the children's efforts to build representations for the passages are based on transcripts of the videotapes of the students' verbalizations as well as the computer-recorded trace of their movement through the text. Ambiguities in the transcripts were resolved by consulting the actual videotapes.

Text Analysis

To provide a context for the analysis of the children's processing, it is informative to characterize the passages that they read. The Metabolism text is about factors that affect metabolism or metabolic rate (see Appendix A). The text gives some explicit information about metabolic rate in separate paragraphs about food, climate, activity, and genetic inheritance. However, to establish a coherent understanding of how metabolic rate is related to energy sources and energy requirements, the reader must integrate information from several text paragraphs as well as from general knowledge about the body. Readers who do not already know very much about the topic of metabolism are heavily dependent on the information explicitly available in the text for making the inferences and connections necessary for a coherent representation. Thus, we expected to find frequent reinstatement of information from the text and from long-term memory in the processing of children who attempted to construct a coherent representation of this text.

The second text was about hybrids and was titled "Improving Mother Nature" (see Appendix B). Whereas the Metabolism passage implicitly expressed, and thus required readers to infer, a complex relationship among a concept and the factors affecting it, the Hybrids text did not. Rather, the Hybrids passage contains a number of situations and examples of hybrids and how they are helpful. From these examples, readers (who in this case had little knowledge of the topic) must construct an understanding of the central concept, a hybrid. Most of the children found the central concepts of both of these texts to be new and relatively difficult to understand.

In this chapter, we report several aspects of our analyses of the think-aloud protocols to address the issue of what students do as they attempt to build representations of instructional texts. The think-aloud protocols were coded for number and type of events. Consistent with Coté, Goldman, and Saul (1998), an event was defined as a comment or set of comments on the same core sentence or group of sentences, as well as the reading behavior associated with those comments. Events can vary in length, ranging from a short utterance focused on one text sentence to several statements and some rereading behavior focused on the sentences of an entire paragraph. We categorized the events in terms of the types of reasoning that they reflected, as described in the next section. We also determined whether the reasoning on a particular focal sentence reflected use of information provided elsewhere in the text or in the student's comments given earlier in the think-aloud protocol.

Types of Events in the Think-Aloud Protocols

The categorical coding and analyses are of interest in terms of the kinds of comprehension and reasoning strategies and processes that they reveal.

Self-Explanations. Coded in this category were statements that elaborated on the focal sentence, interpretations of it in the student's own language, inferences, or implications of the text information, examples, analogies, cause–effect statements or questions about cause–effect. This kind of reasoning reveals students' efforts to create coherence within the text and with their prior knowledge by using logical relationships and content-relevant knowledge to build causal structures, draw out the implications of the information in focal sentences, make comparisons and contrasts with what they believe about the world, and so forth. Information in these protocol events came from prior knowledge, elsewhere in the text, or from the focal sentence.

Monitoring. Statements in this category confirmed comprehension (e.g., *I get it*), detected failures to understand (e.g., *I do not get it*), marked new knowledge (e.g., *I didn't know that*), or detected information inconsistent with known information or information that had been presented elsewhere in the text. Monitoring statements indicate evaluations of comprehension in that students are comparing their sense of understanding to some internal criterion of satisfactory meaning or coherence.

Evaluation statements form a subset of the monitoring category. They are similar to the first group of monitoring statements in that they reflect some evaluation of the text. Statements of this type commented on the organization of information in the passage (e.g., *That sentence belongs up there*), indicated affective responses (e.g., *That seems strange*), or suggested information that was missing from the text (e.g., *They should put in < >*).

Paraphrases. Protocol events were placed in this category if students merely reorganized the words in the sentence, repeated a phrase or clause, or substituted synonyms but otherwise preserved the text language. Trabasso et al. (1995) indicated that a primary function of paraphrases is to maintain information in working memory. The repeated processing of the meaning, perhaps with conversion into more familiar vocabulary, not only strengthens the memory trace through repetition but may make it more likely that the new information is connected to prior knowledge.

Predictions. These were statements that indicated what students expected to find in the next part of the text. In the context of story comprehension, predictions are referred to as forward inferences and have been shown to occur only under constrained circumstances (van den Broek, 1990, 1994). If they are confirmed, predictions are a mechanism for creating coherent connections. In general, due to a greater degree of uncertainty about the content and structure of expository texts, it is often the case that students are not very successful in predicting the information that will come next. In the context of the present study, predictions were infrequent, general, and only rarely confirmed. When they did occur, they were in response to the titles or to the topic sentences in the Metabolism and Hybrid passages. For example, the topic sentence *There are several factors that affect metabolic rate* sometimes led to a general prediction (e.g., " 'They' (the text) will go on to tell what those factors are") but rarely led to predictions of the specific content or identity of those factors.

Associations. In this category were statements of connections that seemed to have little bearing on the text (e.g., *I love carrots* when the word *carrots* appeared in the text). These events do not further understanding of the focal sentence but do provide a link between the focal sentence and some aspect of prior experience, albeit unrelated to the passage context.

The distributions of these five types of protocol events are presented in Table 7.1. Self-explanation and monitoring/evaluation accounted for the majority of the protocol events. The most frequent and universally used source of information for self-explanations was prior knowledge. The focal sentence was the locus of the self-explanation more often in the

TABLE 7.1
Mean Proportion of Protocol Events Observed in Think-Aloud Protocols

Category	Metabolism	Hybrids
Mean total events per protocol	26.13	25.13
Self-explanations	.41	.48
Monitoring/Evaluation	.44	.38
Predictions	.04	.07
Paraphrases	.10	.05
Associations	.03	.02

Hybrids than in the Metabolism passage. In the latter, other parts of the text were brought in more frequently in the self-explanations. Of the Monitoring statements, 16% for Metabolism and 33% for Hybrids were evaluative statements, primarily affective responses such as "That seems strange." Prediction, paraphrase, and association events were less frequent and tended to be localized in the protocols of smaller subsets of the children. Analyses of the correlations among the proportions of each type of protocol event for each passage showed few statistically reliable relationships. The only meaningful exception was that for both passages, there was a strong negative correlation between self-explanations and monitoring/evaluation events ($r = -.77$, $p < .01$ for Metabolism and $r = -.68$, $p < .05$ for Hybrids).

Reinstatement of Information

The analysis of types of protocol events was intended to capture the children's reasoning and comprehension strategies as they constructed a representation of the text. In a second analysis, we were interested in the degree to which children were making connections among elements in the text and between text elements and prior knowledge. To address this question, we examined the occurrence of reinstatements, which bring into working memory either previously processed text or knowledge elements previously retrieved or generated by the student. Because reinstatements bring elements into working memory cotemporaneously, they enable connections that would not be possible otherwise. Using the children's verbalizations as well as the computer record of their patterns of sentence accessing, we categorized reinstatements into three types according to the source of the reinstated information.

Physical Reinstatements. Because the computer presentation allowed us to record the order in which students accessed and read the sentences in the passage, we were able to distinguish between prior text that was physically reinstated as compared with mental reinstatement from memory without re-exposing the text information. Consistent with findings in our previous work with adults and children (e.g., Coté et al., 1998; Goldman

& Saul, 1990a; Saul, Coté, & Goldman, 1993), the reading traces showed that many of the children spontaneously and selectively reinstated previously read sentences by re-exposing them physically. As the data in Table 7.2 show, in processing the Hybrids text, 50% of the children physically reinstated sentences they had read earlier. In processing the Metabolism text, 37.5% of the children physically reinstated text information.

Mental Reinstatements. In addition to the physical reinstatements, there was evidence in the think-aloud protocols of two types of mental reinstatements. Mental–Text were reinstatements where the reader mentioned information previously presented in the text without physically uncovering the sentence. Mental–Student Generated were reinstatements of information known prior to reading the text, that is, prior knowledge of concepts and ideas related to the text information that the reader had verbalized on earlier focal sentences. When such reinstatements of text or student-generated information from memory are considered in addition to the physical reinstatements, the data in Table 7.2 show that almost all of the children (100% on Metabolism, 87.5% on Hybrids) engaged in at least one instance of reinstatement as they read.

Table 7.2 also shows the mean number of reinstatements of each type. In both passages, the most frequent type of reinstatement was of information previously provided in the text. In the Hybrids passage, reinstatements of information students had generated from prior knowledge and physical requirements occurred equally often, but in the Metabolism text, reinstatements of prior knowledge tended to occur more often than physical reinstatements of text information. In addition, somewhat more reinstatements occurred during the processing of the Metabolism passage ($M = 7.19$, $SD = 5.86$) than of the Hybrids passage ($M = 5.63$, $SD = 4.86$), although the variance among the readers was high and a paired t-test indicated that the difference between the means was not reliable, $t < 1$. The moderately higher total number of reinstatements in the Metabolism as compared to the Hybrids text indicates that children tried to make more connections

TABLE 7.2
Occurrence and Sources of Reinstatements of Information

Type of Information Reinstated	Metabolism		Hybrids	
	%Students[a]	Mean # Reinsts.	%Students[a]	Mean # Reinsts.
Physical–Text	37.50%	1.44	50%	1.63
Mental–Text	100%	3.69	75%	2.44
Mental–Student Generated from prior knowledge	68.75%	2.06	75%	1.56
(No reinstatements)	(0%)		(12.5%)	

[a]Percent who reinstated at least once, out of 16 students.

among the units of information in the former. We speculate that these data reflect the previously mentioned semantic and structural differences between the texts and suggest that the children were sensitive to them.

Relationships Between Protocol Events and Reinstatements

The process model we described earlier posits that reinstatements are related to attempts to make the connections necessary for constructing a coherent representation of text. As noted in the introduction, these connections may be among text elements themselves or between text elements and elements of prior knowledge. In examining the relationships between reinstatements and the different types of protocol events, we expected to find that children who often engaged in self-explanations were strategically reinstating information in their attempts to construct a coherent representation. Reinstatements were not expected to occur as often in the context of other types of protocol events such as monitoring/evaluation, association, or paraphrasing, which seemed to be tied more closely to processing single sentences.

These expectations were supported by positive (although not statistically reliable) correlations between total number of reinstatements and the proportion of protocol events coded as self-explanations ($r = .48$, $p < .07$ for Metabolism and $r = .32$, $p < .25$ for Hybrids). Also, the relationships between total reinstatements and the other types of protocol events were negative or near zero for both passages. A closer look at the relationship between reinstatements and self-explanations revealed a strong and reliable positive correlation between self-explanations and the subtype of reinstatements in which students mentally reinstated information that they had brought in earlier from prior knowledge ($r = .58$, $p < .05$ for Metabolism and $r = .50$, $p < .05$ for Hybrids). The correlations of prior knowledge reinstatement and self-explanations suggest that students were making sense of new information with respect to known information and were creating representations integrated with prior knowledge.

This pattern of correlations suggests that individuals might be differentiated on the basis of their active, constructive efforts after meaning (Bartlett, 1932; Scardamalia & Bereiter, 1991). We pursued this possibility by taking a more holistic approach to the protocols to capture individual differences in the students' general approach to processing each text.

General Approaches to Processing

The pattern of correlations between reinstatements and protocol events suggested that it would be fruitful to examine individual protocols to gain further understanding of the dynamic interplay of the various processing activities and students' attempts to establish coherent representations. Indeed, when we looked at individuals' protocols for a particular passage, it was clear that there were qualitative and emergent properties that were not captured by the correlations over the whole sample. These properties seemed to reflect differences in responding to difficulty establishing coherence, the types of events that co-occurred, the frequency of reinstatements and types of information reinstated, and how much of the passage was involved in a particular event. For example, some students adopted an approach of bringing in prior knowledge to self-explain individual sentences, whereas others made inferences connecting multiple sentences in their self-explanations. Such distinctions are not reflected in the previous correlations and frequency analyses.

To capture the nature of an individual student's processing activities over the whole passage, we developed a set of four categories. The first two categories, as compared to the third, reflect distinctions drawn by Bereiter and Scardamalia (1989) between reasoning that intentionally enhances understanding versus processing that "retells" the presented information.

Successful Knowledge-Building. Students who engaged in this type of processing put a lot of effort into their attempts to construct a coherent model of the central concepts and relations by engaging in a range of activities such as cause–effect explanations, elaborations, and cross-text integrative inferences that identified the macrostructure of the text.

Less Successful Knowledge-Building. These students also made an effort to understand the central concepts and relations expressed by the text, but their monitoring comments and requests for information indicated that they were less successful in constructing a coherent representation. Frequently, their self-explanations involved questions they wanted the text to answer but that it did not.

Text-Focused Processing. Students who engaged in text-focused processing demonstrated varying degrees of effort through paraphrasing, interpreting, questioning, bringing in examples, making affective evaluative comments, or monitoring, but their activities were primarily in reaction to single sentences rather than attempts to construct a global understanding of the text meaning.

Minimalists. These students gave verbalizations on approximately half or fewer of the text's sentences, resulting in protocols too poor to support a reliable analysis of their processing. For three of the five children in this category, the few comments that they made indicated that understanding

TABLE 7.3
Number of Children in Each General
Approach Protocol Category for Each Text[a]

Category	Metabolism	Hybrids
Successful Knowledge-Builder	4	2
Less Successful Knowledge-Builder	3	3
Text-Focused Processor	6	8
Minimalist	3	3

[a]Both texts were read by all 16 children. Note that these categories apply to individuals in interaction with particular texts. Eight of the 16 students were in the same category for both texts.

the text presented few problems for them and was largely automatic, perhaps because they were familiar with the content. Two others appeared to be rushed and unmotivated, possibly because they read the text in the last days of the school year.

The authors each sorted all 32 of the children's protocols and initially agreed on over 80% of the categorizations. Disagreements were resolved in discussion. The sorting was done holistically, that is, the authors did not categorize a protocol based on a "count" of types of events or reinstatements. Rather, each transcript was read in its entirety to determine the approach to processing reflected by the constellation and pattern of cognitive activities. The numbers of students in each category on each of the passages is provided in Table 7.3.[1] The protocols of 8 of the 16 students fell into the same general approach category on both passages. Generally speaking, more evidence of knowledge building was found in the Metabolism protocols as compared to the Hybrids protocols. Of the seven students who engaged in knowledge building (more or less successfully) while reading Metabolism, four also took a knowledge-building approach to Hybrids. The other three adopted a text-focused approach when they read Hybrids. One student engaged in text-focused processing on Metabolism but was categorized as a Less Successful Knowledge Builder on Hybrids. The remaining students were either categorized as Text-Focused Processors or Minimalists on both passages or moved between those two categories.

To verify that our holistic classification of the children's attempts to construct coherent representations of the texts was related to their strategic reinstatement of information and their attempts to explain the text to themselves, we looked at the distribution of protocol measures for the

---

[1]These results are consistent with the distribution we found in an earlier think-aloud protocol study with elementary students reading different expository texts (Goldman et al., 1994), in which about a third of the students took an explanation/reasoning approach, about half mainly paraphrased sentences, and the rest gave very limited protocols.

TABLE 7.4
Means (and Standard Deviations) of Protocol-Based Measures
for Each General Approach Category for Metabolism Text

Category	Total Reinstatements		Self-Explan.		Monitor/ Evaluate		Paraphrase	
Successful Knowledge-Builder ($n = 4$)	12.25	(8.54)	20.00	(9.35)	8.75	(2.99)	1.00	(.82)
Less Successful Knowledge-Builder ($n = 3$)	9.00	(5.00)	15.67	(6.81)	9.33	(4.73)	4.33	(3.51)
Text-Focused Processor ($n = 6$)	5.33	(2.88)	8.17	(4.45)	13.83	(7.08)	4.50	(5.86)
Minimalist ($n = 3$)	2.33	(.58)	2.67	(2.08)	7.33	(2.52)	.67	(1.15)

children in each of the general processing approach categories (see Tables 7.4 and 7.5). In both passages, self-explanation events and total number of reinstatements occurred more frequently among the children who took a knowledge-building approach to reading the texts. In contrast, monitoring/evaluation and paraphrase events have more inverted U-shaped distributions across the general approach categories. We followed up with correlation analyses.[2] For both the Hybrids text ($r = .58$, $p < .05$) and the Metabolism text ($r = .63$, $p < .01$), the correlations between the children's total number of reinstatements and the level of general processing approach evident in their protocols were positive and statistically reliable. Also, in both texts there was a positive relationship between the children's general processing approach levels and the proportion of their protocol events that were coded as self-explanations ($r = .71$, $p < .01$ for Metabolism and $r = .53$, $p < .05$ for Hybrids). A regression model with number of reinstatements and proportion of self-explanations as predictors of general processing approach level showed that the two variables, although intercorrelated, were independent and each was a strong predictor of the children's protocol category for both texts.

The patterns evident in Tables 7.4 and 7.5 and in the correlation analyses support the interpretation that the more "knowledge-building-like" children's general approach to constructing a representation of the text, the more likely they were to engage in frequent reinstatement and self-explanation. These reinstatements and self-explanations were often in the service of cognitive activities such as cause–effect reasoning, elaborating with prior knowledge or personal experiences, generating and testing hypotheses, requesting information, and interpreting sentences.

The data presented thus far reflect the types of things children did and, to some degree, the contexts in which they did them as they attempted

---

[2]For the correlation analysis, Minimalists were scored as 1, Text-Focused Processors as 2, Less Successful Knowledge-Builders as 3, and Successful Knowledge-Builders as 4.

TABLE 7.5
Means (and Standard Deviations) of Protocol-Based Measures
for Each General Approach Category for Hybrids Text

Category	Total Reinstatements		Self-Explan.		Monitor/ Evaluate		Paraphrase	
Successful Knowledge-Builder ($n = 2$)	20.50	(3.54)	11.00	(2.83)	0.00		6.00	(4.24)
Less Successful Knowledge-Builder ($n = 3$)	20.00	(2.65)	13.00	(6.25)	2.33	(1.53)	13.33	(4.93)
Text-Focused Processor ($n = 8$)	11.38	(4.00)	8.25	(5.06)	1.00	(1.85)	4.50	(1.77)
Minimalist ($n = 3$)	3.67	(2.89)	6.00	(2.65)	.33	(.58)	.67	(1.15)

to build coherent representations of the passages. However, the texture of the thinking and reasoning children were doing and the interplay between the text information and prior knowledge can only be fully appreciated by examining some of the individual think-aloud protocols. In the next section, we present excerpts from the protocols of three children who took different processing approaches: Successful Knowledge-Building, Less Successful Knowledge-Building, and Text-Focused Processing.

THINK-ALOUD PROTOCOLS ILLUSTRATIVE OF DIFFERENCES IN ONLINE PROCESSING

Student 3, Successful Knowledge-Building

Student 3 engaged in Successful Knowledge-Building in her reading of both texts. While reading Metabolism, for example, her protocol shows that she was determined to construct a coherent situational representation of the concepts and relationships presented in the text. She was very persistent, using strategies such as rereading the focal sentence, backtracking to reread previous sentences, making causal inferences, and elaborating the text with examples from prior knowledge until she was satisfied enough with her understanding of the relationship between each factor, energy, and metabolic rate to go to the next paragraph. In the process of reading Metabolism, she physically reinstated sentences she had already read 11 times, reinstated text information from memory 5 times, and reinstated student-generated information, such as concepts she earlier had brought in from prior knowledge, 9 times.

Table 7.6 contains excerpts from Student 3's Metabolism protocol. This excerpt shows her verbalizations as she read the first three paragraphs of the text. Note that at the very beginning she read the title and checked against her prior knowledge, commenting that she knew nothing about

TABLE 7.6
Excerpt From Think-Aloud Protocol of Student #3 Reading Metabolism
(student's comments are in boldface)

1	Metabolism. **I don't know anything about Metabolism.**
2	Customers in many pharmacies may soon be seeing the latest in new devices for the health con... sish.. ious [conscious]. **Con... I don't know that word. Con. . sish. . .ious. Con. . . I don't know.**
3	A sports physiologist is developing a Tab O Meter [metabometer], a device that he hopes will measure the human body's ability to produce energy efficiently. **O.K.**
2	[rereads] **O.K.**
3	**So the new device is the sports. . . Metab -O- Meter.**
4	The rate at which the body produces energy is called metabolism. **Ohh-K. So that's why. So he's going to make an invention that'll hopefully measure how much your body produces energy. O.K.**
5	Different people have different metabolic rates that indicate how easily they can produce energy. **O.K. That's sort of describing this sentence.** [returns to 4 briefly and then back to 5.] **Different people. . . Ur. . Helping it more. Not describing.**
6	The same person may have different metabolic rates depending on the circumstances. **The same person. . O.K. So if they're like in a game or something, they may have a higher metabolic rate, and if they're just sitting on a couch watching TV, they might not have as high cause they're not using as much energy.**
7	Different species of animals also have different metabolic rates. **O.K. So animals are different from humans, and I am thinking right now that the animals are going to have a little bit maybe higher metabolic rate, cause humans don't always have to run around watching out for predators.**
8	There are several factors that affect the metabolic rate. **O.K.**
9	One factor is the type of food a person or animal eats. **O.K. So like yesterday when we were talking about Coke, and it gives you sugar and energy** [referring to Sugar text]. **Coke would give you more. . . higher metabolic rate than like a vegetable without sugar or something. I'm not going to say anything, because, like name a certain vegetable, because I didn't know apples had sugar** [referring to Sugar text].
10	For example, some foods are hard to digest, such as complex carbohydrates like rice. **Ooohh. . . Processed sugar and carbohydrates** [referring to Sugar text]. **Processed sugar and rice are both carbohydrates, but that doesn't have anything to do. . . . O.K.**
9	[rereads 9, 10, 9, 8, back to 9] **O.K. the type of food a person eats. Like I just said,**
10	**if you eat Coke or something, it'll make you a little more hyper or something,**
11	**have a higher metabolic rate.** The body has to work harder to get energy from rice.
10	Some foods are hard to digest. **The body has to work hard to digest rice.**
11	Work harder to get energy. **Probably has to work harder because it's harder to digest.**
12	If a person ate a steady diet of rice, the result would be a higher metabolic rate. If a person ate a steady diet of rice, the result would be a higher metabolic rate.
11	**If they ate. . . The body has to work harder.**
12	**They would get a higher metabolic rate. Because the body is working up more energy maybe.**
11	**Because** the body has to work harder to get energy from rice.

(Continued)

TABLE 7.6
(Continued)

12	If a person ate a steady diet of rice, the result would be a higher metabolic. . . **But. . . . O.K. I don't really understand that. If the body has to work harder to get the energy.** . . . If a person ate a steady diet of rice, the result would be a higher metabolic rate.
11	**I'm thinking that maybe if the body has to work harder to get the energy from rice, if they kept eating it, the body might get used to having to work to get the energy.** [continues reading.]

metabolism. Line 4 in the passage gives a definition of metabolism, which she recognized and used as the basis for an inference that updated her understanding of the situation being described in the first few sentences. The child continued in this vein over the next few sentences, making connections among sentences and bringing in examples and inferences based on her general knowledge of when energy is required.

The next paragraph discusses the first factor that affects metabolic rate—food. Here the child engaged in extended effort after meaning that ranged far beyond the information that was explicitly in the text. She used words from the text, like *food* and *carbohydrates*, to activate some information she had learned the day before. She appeared to be using the information to update her evolving representation, as she realized that some of it might not be relevant to her understanding of the current text, but some of it was. As she said after reading lines 9 and 10 a few times, "Like I just said, if you eat Coke or something, it'll make you a little more hyper or something. Have a higher metabolic rate." We interpreted this statement as indicating that she understood that different foods have a different relationship with energy and metabolism. However, she apparently had a little trouble establishing a coherent understanding of the last two sentences in the paragraph. As she reinstated the information in them she made causal inferences until finally she was satisfied that she understood, and she went on to the next paragraph.

Student 2, Less Successful Knowledge-Building

Like Student 3, Student 2 also tried hard to construct a coherent understanding of Metabolism and Hybrids. As he read Hybrids, for example, he physically reinstated sentences he had already read 11 times, reinstated text information from memory 5 times, and reinstated student-generated information 3 times. However, this student met with less success than Student 3. As he tried to construct an understanding of the central concept of hybrid, which is crucial to building a coherent representation of the text information, he generated and abandoned a number of hypotheses.

He also at several points in the text appeared to be aware of gaps in his representation, as he asked questions looking for more information and he noted several vocabulary problems.

The excerpts in Table 7.7 show places in the text where Student 2 found information that he used to figure out what a hybrid is. His problems were evident early on in his response to line 4, which defines a hybrid. He said, "I don't get that sentence either. I didn't get this whole paragraph. I don't get this sentence. At all. I don't know what a hybrid is. That's why. It didn't tell you what it is." The next few sentences also contain the word "hybrid" and he repeated that he was still having trouble understanding what it meant.

When he reached lines 7 and 8 he generated a hypothesis: "I think a hybrid is something in a plant or a plant . . . I don't know what. Or something you can eat. It says it adds vitamins." However, subsequent sentences do not bear out this hypothesis, and so later, on line 17, he generated another one: "I think that hybrid is something in a plant that helps it grow and grow faster or something and makes it like stronger roots in a plant or something. I think that's a hybrid." But then he read on and again found information that challenged his hypothesis. Although this child tried very hard to generate and test hypotheses to construct a coherent understanding of the main concept in the text, the window onto his processing provided by his verbal protocol suggests that he did not succeed. Although he tried, failing to understand the central concept would make it very unlikely that he was able to generate a coherent representation.

Student 15, Text-Focused Processing

The knowledge-building approach taken by Students 3 and 2, even though they varied in how successful they seemed to be at building a coherent representation, can be contrasted with the text-focused processing of Student 15. This child had a standardized reading comprehension score

TABLE 7.7
Excerpt From Think-Aloud Protocol of Student #2 Reading Hybrids
(student's comments are in boldface)

---

1   Improving Mother Nature. **I think it's going to talk about how they keep the forest clean. No littering or something. And take care of animals and don't pollute and all that.**

2   Produce department and garden shops are brimming with odd new . . . **let's see. . what's that?. . . I don't know that word. . .**hybrids. . . of some familiar fruits and vegetables. **I'm thinking . . . . what . . .?. . What has that got to do with**

1   Mother Nature ?

2   **It's talking about the shops and all that.**

(Continued)

TABLE 7.7
(Continued)

3   This year the first genetical. . . genetically. . . . **what's that ?. . . I dunno that. . . .altered** tomato went on the market. . . and. . **what's that. . .** ushered?. . . **I dunno that. . .** in a new area [era]. . . **I don't know that one.** This era in growing crops for food. **I don't know some words in here. I still don't know what's. . . . . this don't make sense with this.** [returns to title]

3   **I think this should not. . this should make another title or something because this. . this sentence right here . . . I don't think goes with this.** [returns to title].

3   **This is talking about markets and foods, and this**

1   **is just Mother Nature.** [returns to 3]

4   A hybrid refers to a plant or animal that been created by crossing two different plants. **I don't get that sentence either. I didn't get this whole paragraph.** [points to first paragraph]. **I don't get this sentence. At all. I don't know what a hybrid is. That's why. It didn't tell you what it is.**

[reads a few more sentences]

7   Hybrids are helpful for several reasons. **I'm thinking like. . like. . I still don't know what hybrids is. That's why I don't know. . . .**

8   For one thing, plants can be altered so that the hybrid has more vitamins than the original plant did. **I think a hybrid is some sort of plant of some. . . I think it's like, uh, something in a plant or a plant. . . I don't know what. Or something you can eat. It says it adds vitamins. Than the original plant did.**

9   Or if the original plant is high in some un. .de. .sirable substance such as fat or sugar, the amount may be reduced in the hybrid. **Wait a second. I think. . I don't get this sentence. Well, because it doesn't make sense because it's talking about. . see it says. . uh. . let's see. . .** [clicks on 8 and returns to 9] **I get it. . . Why they. . . I. . See. . . I don't know. I don't get this. Because they just talk about plants, and the thing about sugar. . and they have sugar. Why'd they tell us that for?**

10   This type of hybrid is helpful for people who may only have access to a small amount of food such as the people living on a sub. . . submarine. . . Is that submarine? **See. . . wait. . I'm thinking like. . I think. . I think that a hybrid is like some sort of vitamin or something. And it keeps you healthy and if you don't get a lot amount of food, you eat 'em or something. I think that's what they're talking about.**

11   Another reason that hybrids are helpful is that they may make a plant stronger and better able to resist environmental threats such as insects or frost. **Now I don't know, because it says hybrids are helpful to make the plant stronger. And to protect. . .See - it says. . now it says uh. . uh. . . that it can resist. . it can make plants resist threats such as insects or frost. And I thought it was a vitamin or something. Now I don't know what it is. Because first I thought it was a vitamin because it said all that stuff about it being vitamins. . . had vitamins and all that. Now. . now it says it can plants resist insects and frost. So I don't know what it is now.**

[reads a few more sentences]

17   Finally, hybrids may change the appearance of a plant in some way, perhaps making it easier to grow. **I think hybrid is something in a plant that helps it grow and grow faster and makes it like stronger roots in a plant or something. I think that's a hybrid.**

[continues reading].

slightly higher than Student 2, a less-successful knowledge builder. In the sample as a whole, the standardized reading scores did not predict the children's general approach to reading as identified by their protocol category ($r = .25$, $p > .05$ for Metabolism; $r = .15$, $p > .05$ for Hybrids), as illustrated by the differences between Students 2 and 15.

Student 15 read straight through the sentences sequentially, with no physical reinstatements of prior sentences, only 2 reinstatements of text information from memory, and 3 reinstatements of student-generated information. Table 7.8 provides excerpts from Student 15's protocol. His verbalizations were short, and most of them were focused on the sentence level. For example, in response to line 3, he pointed to several words and said, "I don't understand that word [genetically], that word [altered], that word [era], and that word [ushered]" but he made no further attempt to address the problems. He paraphrased or interpreted several sentences; for example, his response to line 5 was "They mixed up broccoli and cauliflower." These brief comments continued throughout, with little evidence that the child was making connections among text segments or trying to construct, monitor, and update a coherent situational representation of the text.

Our quantitative and qualitative analyses of the strategies and reasoning processes used to build coherent representations of instructional text reveal that rather than restricting themselves to a very narrow range of operations, most students are quite flexible in how they use text information and their existing knowledge as they proceed through an informational text. However, when reading material of this type, readers (and especially children)

TABLE 7.8

Excerpt From Think-Aloud Protocol of Student #15 Reading Hybrids
(student's comments are in boldface)

---

1   Improving Mother Nature. **It's gonna talk about how you can help the world.**

2   Produce departments and garden shops are brimming with odd new hybrids of some familiar fruits and vegetables. **This new hybrids. . .**

3   This year the first gen. . .genet. . . .genetically altered . . .altered tomato went to the market and un. . . .ushered in a new era in growing crops for food. **I don't understand that word [genetically], that word [altered], and that word [era] and that word [ushered].**

4   A hybrid refers to a plant or animal that has been created by crossing two different plants. [experimenter gives neutral prompt] **Like, cross breeding.**

5   For example, the broccoflower is a hybrid of broccoli and cauliflower. **They mixed up broccoli and cauliflower.**

6   Hybrids such as the broccoflower are being created by scientists through a process known as genetic engineering. **It don't make sense. . .to me.**

7   Hybrids are helpful for several reasons. **They'll tell the reasons what they are.**

[continues reading].

are often in knowledge-lean situations (Coté et al., 1998) and limited in the kind of inferences they can make. The representational coherence that results from the use of strategies such as self-explaining, including cause–effect reasoning and reasoning by analogy, is constrained by both the topic and discourse knowledge the reader brings to the task and by the content and structure of the passage. For example, the self-explanations in the Metabolism and Hybrids passages differed, with those in the Hybrids passage more frequently restricted to thinking just about the focal sentence. This may have been a reflection of the passage differences in that the Hybrids text deals with relatively encapsulated examples of how hybrids are helpful, whereas the Metabolism text deals throughout with relationships among energy needs and energy sources. As well, twice as many self-explanation questions occurred in the Hybrids (31%) as compared to the Metabolism (16%) passage, which reflected students' desires to better understand the reasons why hybrids are helpful. Because instructional texts such as the ones examined here may be structured in a variety of ways (cf. Beck & McKeown, 1992; Britton, 1994; Meyer, 1985), readers need to be sensitive to such differences and appropriately adapt their strategies for achieving coherent representations.

CONCLUSIONS AND DISCUSSION

Although researchers have identified many strategies in which readers engage, identifying them is not enough; we need to know about relationships between strategies and online processes of representation construction. In the research reported here, reading traces and think-aloud protocols of reading showed a wide range in the approaches of elementary students to reading difficult informational text. The strategies and meaning construction efforts we have reported are similar to those found when children process story texts (cf. Trabasso et al., 1995). However, the dominant mode of explanation appropriate to understanding stories is causal inferencing; here, prior knowledge limitations and a greater variety of expository content structures constrain the success of efforts to understand not only underlying causal mechanisms but also other types of relationships among concepts in instructional texts.

    Indeed, children often find themselves reading in areas where they know little about the topic and where the discourse structure is unfamiliar. One strategic adaptation to this situation is to devote processing resources to the information in the text and relevant prior knowledge for purposes of creating connections among seemingly disparate pieces of information (cf. Chi et al., 1994). Our knowledge builders provide examples of this type of approach. In about a third of the students, the pattern of online processes seemed to be aimed at knowledge building, where students often reinstated information, both physically and mentally, as they carried out a variety of processing strategies. These students did not always succeed in constructing a coherent situational representation, but they exhibited a wide range of strategies in their attempts. For example, they made relevant connections to examples from their prior knowledge, generated and checked hypotheses, made inferences to interpret the text and create new knowledge, monitored the mapping between text information and their existing knowledge, monitored the coherence of their evolving representations, and persisted in their attempts to resolve difficulties. These students appeared to be attempting to construct rich situation models for the material. Situation models for expository material reflect the underlying structure of the content domain and are important for performance on reasoning and problem-solving tasks (cf. McNamara, E. Kintsch, Songer, & W. Kintsch, 1996; van Dijk & W. Kintsch, 1983; Zwaan & Brown, 1996). In the two-dimensional framework discussed by Coté et al. (1998; see also Goldman & van Oostendorp, this volume), the representations of the successful knowledge builders would be placed high on the dimension of integration with prior knowledge as well as high on the dimension of textbase quality.

Another adaptation to coping with a text presenting new information on an unfamiliar topic, especially when the purpose for reading is to provide a report from memory, is to focus on the text and create as strong a "veridical" trace as possible. Our text-focused processors took this approach. They tended to direct their processing resources to achieving local understanding of the focal sentence by paraphrasing and bringing in examples or associations from prior knowledge and to monitoring comprehension problems, although they did not persist in attempts to resolve them. They did not attempt to create a coherent, interconnected representation of the underlying message of the text. The pattern of processing strategies in text-focused processing was related to a low level of reinstatement activity. About half of the students were classified as engaging in this type of processing. Text-focused processing can produce a reasonably solid textbase, that is, a representation of the information explicitly presented in the text. There are many tasks for which a strong textbase is all that is needed for good performance (e.g., E. Kintsch, 1990; McNamara et al., 1996; Zwaan & Brown, 1996). Thus, as an adaptation to difficult and new material, the strategy of focusing on the text per se can produce a representation that allows adequate performance on at least some tasks. In the two-dimensional framework discussed by Coté et al. (1998), the representations of the text-focused processors might be placed high on the dimension of textbase quality, like those of the successful knowledge builders. However, their representations would place low on the dimension of integration with prior knowledge.

The children's think-aloud protocols revealed some interesting aspects of monitoring, a skill that is often cited as very important to good comprehension (e.g., Baker & Brown, 1984). Our data indicate that although monitoring is important, unless readers actively apply strategies to resolve the problems they identify, they are likely to end up with fragmentary representations. For example, some students showed evidence of comprehension monitoring by pointing out words they did not know, but their protocols showed no evidence of a strategic response such as attempting to understand the words from the context. In contrast, the students who engaged in knowledge building often attempted to resolve difficulties by selectively reinstating information and engaging in various strategic activities like rereading and hypothesis checking. In related work (Coté et al., 1998), we reported positive correlations between problem *resolution* and comprehension, with the strongest correlations occurring in more difficult passages, but no correlation between problem *identification* and comprehension. In the process of constructing a coherent representation of a text, readers must not only be aware of gaps and problems in their understanding, but must also bring to bear strategies to resolve the problems in order to build coherent representations.

In accord with several recent publications on think-aloud protocols and comprehension strategies (e.g., Chi et al., 1994; Coté et al., 1998; Long & Bourg, 1996; Pressley & Afflerbach, 1995; Trabasso & Magliano, 1996; Trabasso et al., 1995; Trabasso & Suh, 1993; Zwaan & Brown, 1996), the work reported in this chapter supports the utility of think-aloud methodology for studying online processing activities. It extends what we know about the construction of coherent representations by examining comprehension in reading-to-learn situations where students are faced with texts of unpredictable structure containing new concepts and ideas. Focusing on how readers adapt to these kinds of learning situations constitutes an important research area (Coté et al., 1998; Goldman et al., 1996; W. Kintsch et al., 1993; Lorch, 1995). Strategies learners use to capitalize on whatever relevant prior knowledge they do have, how they reason with it and the information in the text, and how they determine what they do and do not understand are all aspects of the online construction of meaning and knowledge acquisition. The patterns of correlations among protocol events and reinstatements plus the illustrative cases suggest that there are prior knowledge and processing constraints that may limit the success of strategies used in online construction of discourse representations. To understand how readers overcome such constraints we need to examine how they allocate resources to different processing strategies and how they capitalize on resources in their learning environments (cf. Goldman, 1997).

ACKNOWLEDGMENTS

This chapter is based on papers presented at the annual meeting of the Society for Text and Discourse, Albuquerque, New Mexico, July 1995, and at the conference of the European Association for Research on Learning and Instruction, Nijmegen, the Netherlands, August 1995.

APPENDIX A: METABOLISM TEXT*

1. Metabolism
2. Customers in many pharmacies may soon be seeing the latest in new devices for the health conscious.
3. A sports physiologist is developing the metabometer, a device that he hopes will measure the human body's ability to produce energy efficiently.
4. The rate at which the body produces energy is called metabolism.
5. Different people have different metabolic rates that indicate how easily they can produce energy.
6. The same person may have different metabolic rates, depending on the circumstances.
7. Different species of animals also have different metabolic rates.
8. There are several factors that affect metabolic rate.
9. One factor is the type of food a person or animal eats.
10. For example, some foods are hard to digest, such as complex carbohydrates like rice.
11. The body has to work harder to get energy from rice.
12. If a person ate a steady diet of rice, the result would be a higher metabolic rate.
13. Another factor affecting metabolism is the climate of the environment.
14. Temperature may cause the metabolism to change.
15. People and animals that live in cold environments need to produce more energy in order to keep warm.
16. Most animals that live in polar regions have high metabolisms.
17. If people move from a warm to a cold climate, their metabolic rates will increase.
18. Metabolic rate also differs depending on activity level.
19. Changing the level of activity may cause the body to change its metabolism because different activities require different amounts of energy.
20. For example, basketball players use more energy than golfers so their metabolic rates are generally higher.
21. To some degree, metabolic rate is influenced by genetic inheritance.
22. Children of parents who have high metabolic rates tend to have high metabolic rates also.
23. This is because the body chemistry of the children is a combination of the body chemistry of the parents.
24. Metabolism is regulated by hormones produced by the thyroid gland, a tiny gland located at the base of the neck.

25. These hormones regulate the behavior of all the cells in the body so that enough energy is produced.
26. The metabometer will work by measuring hormone levels in the blood.

Note. The sentences are on separate numbered lines here for clarity. In the actual experimental text, the sentences ran consecutively within paragraphs and were not numbered.

APPENDIX B: HYBRIDS TEXT*

1. Improving Mother Nature
2. Produce departments and garden shops are brimming with odd new hybrids of some familiar fruits and vegetables.
3. This year, the first genetically altered tomato went on the market, and ushered in a new era in growing crops for food.
4. A hybrid refers to a plant or animal that has been created by crossing two different parents.
5. For example, the "broccoflower" is a hybrid of broccoli and cauliflower.
6. Hybrids such as the broccoflower are being created by scientists through a process known as genetic engineering.
7. Hybrids are helpful for several reasons.
8. For one thing, plants can be altered so that the hybrid has more vitamins than the original plant did.
9. Or, if the original plant is high in some undesirable substance, such as fat or sugar, the amount may be reduced in the hybrid.
10. This type of hybrid is helpful to people who may only have access to a small amount of food, such as those people living on a submarine.
11. Another reason that hybrids are helpful is that they may make a plant stronger and better able to resist environmental threats, such as insects or frost.
12. Raising stronger plants helps farmers be assured of a good crop.
13. Hybrids help farmers in another way as well.
14. They allow farmers to adapt plants to new environments.
15. For example, some tomatoes have been designed to grow in unusual environments such as styrofoam containers, or even in space.
16. Plants that would normally only grow in very warm weather may be changed to allow them to grow year-round.
17. Finally, hybrids may change the appearance of a plant in some way, perhaps making it easier to grow.
18. For example, scientists have developed a tiny version of the carrot.
19. The hybrid carrot's smaller size makes it possible to grow it in window boxes in the city, or other places where space is limited.
20. Genetic engineering involves taking the genes of one plant and adding on, or splicing, the genes from another so that the new plant has characteristics of both plants.
21. Scientists can examine the parent plants and decide what traits they wish for the plant to have from each parent.
22. It is a bit like being able to design a human baby so that it has the father's nose, but the mother's eyes, and so on.

Note. The sentences are on separate numbered lines here for clarity. In the actual experimental text, the sentences ran consecutively within paragraphs and were not numbered.

REFERENCES

Baker, L., & Brown, A. L. (1984). Metacognitive skills and reading. In P. D. Pearson (Ed.), *Handbook of reading research* (pp. 353–392). New York: Longman.

Bartlett, F. C. (1932). *Remembering: A study in experimental and social psychology.* Cambridge, England: Cambridge University Press.

Beck, I. L., & McKeown, M. G. (1992). Young students' social studies learning: Going for depth. In J. J. Dreher & W. H. Slater (Eds.), *Elementary school literacy: Critical issues* (pp. 133–156). Norwood, MA: Christopher-Gordon.

Bereiter, C., & Scardamalia, M. (1989). Intentional learning as a goal of instruction. In L. B. Resnick (Ed.), *Knowing, learning, and understanding: Essays in honor of Robert Glaser* (pp. 361–392). Hillsdale, NJ: Lawrence Erlbaum Associates.

Britton, B. K. (1994). Understanding expository text: Building mental structures to induce insights. In M. A. Gernsbacher (Ed.), *Handbook of psycholinguistics* (pp. 641–674). San Diego: Academic Press.

Chi, M. T. H., deLeeuw, N., Chiu, M., & LaVancher, C. (1994). Eliciting self-explanations improves understanding. *Cognitive Science, 18,* 439–477.

Coté, N., Goldman, S. R., & Saul, E. U. (1993, November). *Do kids read like adults? A qualitative comparison of the reading behaviors of college and elementary school students.* Invited address to the Vanderbilt University Department of Psychology and Human Development Developmental and Cognitive Psychology Brown Bag Series.

Coté, N., Goldman, S. R., & Saul, E. U. (1998). Students making sense of informational text: Relations between processing and representation. *Discourse Processes, 25,* 1–53.

Ericsson, K. A., & Kintsch, W. (1995). Long-term working memory. *Psychological Review, 102,* 211–245.

Ericsson, K. A., & Simon, H. A. (1984/1993). *Protocol analysis: Verbal reports as data.* Cambridge, MA: MIT Press.

Fletcher, C. R. (1986). Strategies for the allocation of short-term memory during comprehension. *Journal of Memory and Language, 25,* 43–58.

Goldman, S. R. (1996). Reading, writing, and learning in hypermedia environments. In H. van Oostendorp (Ed.), *Cognitive aspects of electronic text processing* (pp. 7–42). Norwood, NJ: Ablex.

Goldman, S. R. (1997). Learning from text: Reflections on the past and suggestions for the future. *Discourse Processes, 23,* 357–398.

Goldman, S. R., Coté, N., & Saul, E. U. (1994, January). *Children's strategies for making sense of informational text.* Paper presented at the fifth annual Winter Text Conference, Jackson Hole, WY.

Goldman, S. R., & Saul, E. U. (1990a). Flexibility in text processing: A strategy competition model. *Learning and Individual Differences, 2,* 181–219.

Goldman, S. R., & Saul, E. U. (1990b). Applications for tracking reading behavior on the Macintosh. *Behavior Research Methods, Instruments, and Computers, 22,* 526–532.

Goldman, S. R., & Varma, S. (1995). CAPping the construction-integration model of discourse comprehension. In C. A. Weaver, III, S. Mannes, & C. R. Fletcher (Eds.), *Discourse comprehension: Essays in honor of Walter Kintsch* (pp. 337–358). Hillsdale, NJ: Lawrence Erlbaum Associates.

Goldman, S. R., Varma, S., & Coté, N. (1996). Extending capacity-constrained construction integration: Toward "smarter" and flexible models of text comprehension. In B. K. Britton & A. C. Graesser (Eds.), *Models of understanding text* (pp. 73–113). Mahwah, NJ: Lawrence Erlbaum Associates.

Graesser, A. C., Singer, M., & Trabasso, T. (1994). Constructing inferences during narrative text comprehension. *Psychological Review, 101,* 371–395.

Kintsch, E. (1990). Macroprocesses and microprocesses in the development of summarization skill. *Cognition and Instruction, 7*(3), 161–195.

Kintsch, W. (1988). The role of knowledge in discourse comprehension: A construction-integration model. *Psychological Review, 95*, 163–182.

Kintsch, W., Britton, B. K., Fletcher, C. R., Kintsch, E., Mannes, S. M., & Nathan, M. J. (1993). A comprehension-based approach to learning and understanding. In D. L. Medin (Ed.), *The psychology of learning and motivation: Advances in research and theory* (Vol. 30, pp. 165–214). San Diego: Academic Press.

Kintsch, W., & van Dijk, T. A. (1978). Toward a model of text comprehension and production. *Psychological Review, 85*, 363–394.

Long, D. L., & Bourg, T. (1996). Thinking aloud: "Telling a story about a story." *Discourse Processes, 21*, 329–339.

Lorch, R. F., Jr. (1995). Integration of topic information during reading. In R. Lorch & E. O'Brien (Eds.), *Sources of coherence in text comprehension* (pp. 279–294). Hillsdale, NJ: Lawrence Erlbaum Associates.

McNamara, D. S., Kintsch, E., Songer, N. B., & Kintsch, W. (1996). Are good texts always better? Interactions of text coherence, background knowledge, and levels of understanding in learning from text. *Cognition and Instruction, 14*, 1–43.

Meyer, B. J. F. (1985). Prose analysis: Purposes, procedures, and problems. In B. K. Britton & J. B. Black (Eds.), *Understanding expository text: A theoretical and practical handbook for analyzing explanatory text* (pp. 11–64). Hillsdale, NJ: Lawrence Erlbaum Associates.

Pressley, M., & Afflerbach, P. (1995). *Verbal protocols of reading.* Hillsdale, NJ: Lawrence Erlbaum Associates.

Saul, E. U., Coté, N., & Goldman, S. R. (1993, April). *Students' strategies for making text make sense.* Paper presented at the annual meeting of the American Education Research Association, Atlanta, GA.

Scardamalia, M., & Bereiter, C. (1991). Literate expertise. In K. A. Ericsson & J. Smith (Eds.), *Toward a general theory of expertise* (pp. 172–194). Cambridge, England: Cambridge University Press.

Trabasso, T., & Magliano, J. P. (1996). Conscious understanding during comprehension. *Discourse Processes, 21*, 255–287.

Trabasso, T., & Suh, S. (1993). Understanding text: Achieving explanatory coherence through on-line inferences and mental operations in working memory. *Discourse Processes, 16*, 3–34.

Trabasso, T., Suh, S., Payton, P., & Jain, R. (1995). Explanatory inferences and other strategies during comprehension: Encoding effects on recall. In R. Lorch & E. O'Brien (Eds.), *Sources of coherence in text comprehension* (pp. 219–239). Hillsdale, NJ: Lawrence Erlbaum Associates.

van den Broek, P. (1990). The causal inference maker: Toward a process model of inference generation in text comprehension. In D. A. Balota, G. B. Flores d'Arcais, & K. Rayner (Eds.), *Comprehension processes in reading* (pp. 423–445). Hillsdale, NJ: Lawrence Erlbaum Associates.

van den Broek, P. (1994). Comprehension and memory of narrative texts: Inferences and coherence. In M. A. Gernsbacher (Ed.), *Handbook of psycholinguistics* (pp. 539–588). San Diego: Academic Press.

van Dijk, T. A., & Kintsch, W. (1983). *Strategies for discourse comprehension.* New York: Academic Press.

Zwaan, R. A., & Brown, C. A. (1996). The influence of language proficiency and comprehension skill on situation-model construction. *Discourse Processes, 21*, 289–327.

Chapter 8

The Role of Illustrations
in Text Comprehension:
What, When, for Whom, and Why?

Valérie Gyselinck
Hubert Tardieu
Université René Descartes

"A picture is worth a thousand words" is a widely used proverb in our culture. Instructional texts often include a variety of illustrations, which are thought to promote learning. However, the choice of the type, number, and location of illustrations in a text or in a textbook is often made on the basis of intuition. There have been quite a few studies on the kinds of illustrations that benefit learning and memory.[1] There has been less work, however, on the processes by which these effects come about. The important question at this point in the history of research on illustrations is what precisely is the processes involved when illustrations and graphics (are utilized to) facilitate memory and comprehension. In other words, we know that graphics in text can be effective for learning, but we need to know more about the processes involved in text and graphics comprehension that contributes to the formation of an elaborated representation. This chapter focuses on research that contributes to our understanding of the circumstances and processes whereby illustrations and text interact so that the result is an elaborated representation.

In research on the role of illustrations, several authors have attempted to explain the facilitative effect of illustrations on memory. Probably the most notable and most widely known is Paivio (1971, 1986) and his dual-code

---

[1]Some studies deal with the role of illustrations in the acquisition of reading (see, for a review, Lemmonier-Schallert, 1980), but we only focus on studies dealing with the role of illustrations in the acquisition of information from text.

theory. According to this theory, at least two coding systems are available: a verbal system and a nonverbal system. These two systems are independent although interconnected. Pictures are automatically stored both in the nonverbal system and in the verbal system, whereas the reverse would not be as systematic. As a result, pictures would be memorized as such by the reader who would benefit from two memory traces, one in a verbal form and one in a nonverbal form. This theory has proved very useful to explain many memory effects, such as the image-superiority effect and the concreteness effect. At first glance, Paivio's theory could also interpret the role of text illustrations on memory. However, it is not clear how the dual-code theory would account for text comprehension per se. Indeed, no assumption is made about the construction of mental representations during the reading process, nor about the levels of representations in which the interaction between text and illustrations takes place.

Contemporary theories of language comprehension commonly assume that texts are represented at three levels (Johnson-Laird, 1980, 1983; Kintsch, 1988; van Dijk & Kintsch, 1983). For van Dijk and Kintsch (1983), a verbatim representation is derived from the surface structure of the text at the first level. At the second level, a propositional textbase is derived, which is a representation reflecting the microstructure and the macro-structure of the text. Finally, at the third level, a situation model is built. It features the information that is implicit in the text. The situation model reflects the domain structure, that is a fragment of the world (van Dijk, 1987). The model is the product of the interaction between information provided by the text and world knowledge, including the goals and attitudes of the reader. Thus, understanding a text requires the representation of the meaning of the text, which adds to the literal meaning of the text by incorporating relevant world knowledge.

Similarly, Johnson-Laird (1983) considered that comprehension involves three levels of representation: a graphemic (or phonemic) representation, a propositional representation, and a mental model. He regarded the second stage of text comprehension as the automatic construction of a propositional or linguistic representation of the text that is close to the surface form of the text. In the third stage of comprehension, a procedural semantics acts on the propositional representation to construct a mental model. It is a mental representation that integrates both the text and the world denoted by this text. A mental model is an internal model of a state of affairs, and its structure is analogical to the state of affairs it represents. Viewed as a dynamic representation, the mental model reflects the reader's current under-standing of the text, and the model is updated as reading progresses.

A specific element of Johnson-Laird's theory is the notion of homomor-phism to the world: a mental model has a structure analogical to that of the situation it represents, and its content corresponds to the objects and events of the world. Therefore, because of its analogical structure, a mental model is close to a mental image of this world (see Denis, 1991, for a review of studies on the role of imagery in language processing). These two kinds of representations provide readers with a nonlinguistic equivalent of the world, and allow for a kind of computation close to the computation one may apply to the world itself. However, a mental image and a mental model are not to be confused. In particular, whereas a mental image is a representation of a situation from a certain point of view, a mental model would allow several points of view on the situation (e.g., Franklin & Tversky, 1990).[2]

An illustration is also an analogical representation, although an external one. It closely mirrors the situation described in the text. Thus, a picture can be viewed as one possible expression of a mental model. Hence, presenting pictures that depict the content of the text they accompany may facilitate the construction of a mental model. We propose that the beneficial effect of illustrations takes place during the construction of a mental model.

According to the views of Johnson-Laird and Kintsch, both explicit information in the text and readers' inferences based on world knowledge contribute to text representations. Hence, inference processes play a central role in the construction of a mental model (or situation model), which is both the byproduct and the source for inferences. The acceptance of such a proposal leads to assessing subjects' comprehension of a text via their ability to generate elaborative inferences (e.g., Kintsch, Welsch, Schmalhofer, & Zimny, 1990; Perrig & Kintsch, 1985; Tardieu, Ehrlich, & Gyselinck, 1992; Taylor & Tversky, 1992). By contrast, using tasks that involve literal sentences or paraphrases would address the linguistic representation. Thus, the quality and/or the speed of responses to such tests should reflect the quality of the representation built. According to the view we defend, the beneficial effect of illustrations in text comprehension should therefore be preferentially observed in performance on tasks involving inferences.

To answer some of the various questions one could ask about the effect of illustrations on text comprehension, four main points are now discussed. In the first section, we present some studies that attempt to determine what should be illustrated in a text to improve the outcomes of memory and understanding. We briefly survey studies conducted in an educational or instructional perspective, whose authors were mainly interested in finding means to enhance subjects' learning from texts, and who did not relate their findings to any cognitive theoretical framework.

---

[2]The situation model and the mental model concepts share many properties and are often used synonymously. However, the propositional representation of Johnson-Laird (1983) is not identical to the propositional textbase in the model of van Dijk and Kintsch (1983). Furthermore, a mental model is necessarily nonpropositional, whereas a situation model is mostly propositional (see Kintsch, 1988; Kintsch, Welsch, Schmalhofer, & Zimny, 1990).

In the next sections, we present some empirical evidence that allows us to suggest when and what illustrations modify in text processing. In the second section, we report studies related to when an illustration should be presented to facilitate understanding. In the third section, studies concerned with individual differences observed in the beneficial effect of illustrations are presented. In the fourth section, we discuss the mechanisms that could be responsible for the beneficial effect of illustrations on text comprehension. We propose that illustrations promote text understanding because they facilitate the construction of a mental model that is the source for inferences. The way illustrations may facilitate such construction is discussed.

WHAT KINDS OF ILLUSTRATIONS BENEFIT MEMORY AND COMPREHENSION?

Illustrations and Memory

The literature is overflowing with work investigating the facilitative effect of pictures on text processing. Many studies, mainly conducted in the educational field, are concerned with the effectiveness of pictures in promoting memory for factual information. In most of them, memory performance is compared when a text is presented (orally or visually) without pictures and when it is presented with pictures. Whereas it seems widely accepted that pictures in text facilitate memory, the research has not focused on how or why they do so. However, efforts have been made to classify the functions of pictures. For example, Levie and Lentz (1982), and Levin, Anglin, and Carney (1987), made distinctions among five main functions of illustrations. The illustration can serve a *representation* function when it repeats the content of the text or overlaps substantially with the text (the use of a photograph, often found in narratives, is a typical instance of this kind of illustration). The illustration can serve an *organization* function when it gives a text greater coherence (e.g., maps that make geographical relationships more transparent or diagrams embedded in procedural texts). When graphic displays illustrate the content of texts that are abstract or difficult to comprehend, providing concrete examples, then the illustrations serve an *interpretation* function (see, e.g., the pictures used by Bransford & Johnson, 1972). Less conventional in textbooks, illustrations that target the critical information to be learned and give a way to recode it in a more memorable form serve a *transformation* function. Finally, illustrations may serve a *decoration* function when they are not directly related to the text. They are added to the text for their aesthetic properties or to increase the interest of the learner. Levin et al. (1987) conducted a meta-analysis of the effects of illustrations, and showed that all functions but the decorative function facilitate memory. Those that allow recoding or greater coherence benefit memory the most. More precisely, when the text is presented visually or orally (though the benefit is of lesser importance in the latter case), illustrations that lead to the greatest benefit are, in order of importance, transformational, interpretational, organizational, and representational pictures.

One problem for the classification scheme just presented is that transformational, organizational, and interpretational pictures are also representational because some information can be presented both textually and graphically. Moreover, the classification of an illustration depends partly on the kind of text it accompanies, and partly on the task demands. For example, Waddill and McDaniel (1992) studied the role of pictures depicting details of an expository text about glaciers compared to pictures depicting the relationships expressed in the text. In this experiment, subjects were asked to recall the content of the text. Both types of pictures were representational because they repeated part of the content of the text—either the details or the relationships. However, from the perspective of the formation of an elaborated representation of the meaning of the text, the pictures depicting the relationships could easily be classified as transformational, whereas the pictures of the details would only serve a representational function.

Waddill and McDaniel's (1992) results showed that both types of pictures had a beneficial effect on recall of the respective target information. Presentation of pictures did not benefit recall of nontarget information, except for the highly skilled comprehenders. In that case, presentation of relational pictures increased recall of both the relations and the details expressed in the text. It seems then that illustrations may facilitate the memorization of both target information and nontarget information. This result is confirmed by Small, Lovett, and Scher (1993), who showed that pictures facilitate children's recall of both illustrated and nonillustrated information in expository prose. These two sets of results suggest that illustrations may not only serve a repetition function, but also help the reader construct a more elaborated representation of the text content, and as such, could be classified as transformational or even interpretational pictures.

Illustrations and Comprehension

In recent years, researchers have more directly attempted to explore the role of illustrations on text comprehension rather than memory (see, e.g., the edited volumes by Mandl & Levin, 1989; Schnotz, 1993; Schnotz & Kulhavy, 1994; Willows & Houghton, 1987).

Glenberg and Langston (1992) conducted a study focused on the role of pictures in the processing of texts describing four-step procedures, such as the procedure for writing a paper. The two middle steps were explicitly stated to be performed at the same time, but because of its linear structure, the text describes the four steps one after the other. In their first experiment, Glenberg and Langston (1992) presented texts either with pictures that highlighted the simultaneity of some steps (picture group) or without pictures (no-picture group). Results showed that subjects in the picture group were more accurate at verifying the sequence of steps than subjects in the no-picture group. In a second experiment, Glenberg and Langston (1992) showed that pictures that maintained the linear ordering of the text did not improve performance. Thus, presenting pictures that emphasized the temporal relationships between the steps enhanced subjects' processing of procedural texts, whereas pictures that did not emphasize such relationships appeared to be of no help.

Concerned with the comprehension of explanative texts, Mayer and Gallini (1990) conducted a series of three experiments in which various pictures were contrasted. Subjects read texts concerning how scientific devices such as braking systems or pumps work. The texts contained either no illustration (control), static illustrations of the device with labels for each part (parts), static illustrations of the device with labels for each major action (steps), or dynamic illustrations showing the off and on states of the device along with the corresponding labels (parts and steps). Then, just after reading, subjects completed the three following tests: a recall task, a questionnaire in which subjects had to answer open-ended transfer questions that required elaborative inferences, and a verbatim recognition task. Results showed that only the parts-and-steps illustrations improved performance (a) on recall of conceptual information, but not on the other type of information, and (b) on answers to transfer questions, but not on verbatim recognition. These results suggest that parts-and-steps illustrations helped the readers build internal connections to draw elaborative inferences and guide selective attention on explanative information. In addition, providing static illustrations with labels for parts of the device or even labels for the actions did not benefit comprehension when compared to a text without pictures.

The results of these two studies suggest that the type of illustrations that improve text comprehension highlight the temporal or causal relations between the objects or events described in the text. These pictures help subjects construct a more elaborated representation of the text content. By contrast, pictures that only repeat the elements described in the text do not seem to help the reader. It should be noted, however, that in Mayer's work, labels that consisted of a whole sentence could play a central role in directing subjects' attention to the explanative information. This might then help them draw elaborative inferences (see also Mayer, 1989).

Thus, it is clear that illustrations supplementing a text can promote the memorization of the content of the text and its comprehension. The more elaborate and coherent the representation, the better the memory and the comprehension. We know that illustrations in texts can be effective for learning, but we do not have much knowledge about the way text comprehension interacts with graphics comprehension. The question is, what are the processes involved in text and graphics comprehension that contribute to the formation of an elaborated representation. A number of researchers have called for investigations of the processes whereby illustrations have such effects (e.g., Peeck, 1987; Pressley & Miller, 1987). For example, Peeck (1987) pointed out that the effect of illustrations should not only be explored right after reading, but also during reading, and over delays. The aim of the following sections is to survey some empirical data that may provide answers to how illustrations improve understanding.

WHEN AND WHAT DO ILLUSTRATIONS CHANGE IN TEXT PROCESSING?

The question we wish to address is the following: When is a picture worth a thousand words? Three aspects of this question are discussed. First, when should an illustration be presented to facilitate understanding? Is an illustration more beneficial when the subjects can explore it before reading, after reading, or when they can navigate from one source of information to the other? Second, when does an illustration facilitate understanding? Can the beneficial effect of illustrations be observed during the course of reading, or is it noticeable only once the whole content of the text has been processed? Third, is this beneficial effect only transient, fading rapidly after reading, or does the beneficial effect of illustrations last even after a long delay?

When Should Illustrations Be Presented?

Mayer and Anderson (1991) compared the effect of animation depicting the operation of a bicycle pump that was presented after (words-before-pictures) or during (words-with-pictures) a verbal description. Immediately after the study stage, low-knowledge students completed a free recall test, and had to answer transfer questions that required elaborative inferences. Results showed that the words-with-pictures group outperformed the words-before-pictures group on transfer questions (experiments 1 & 2), but not on recall (experiment 2a). In addition, performance of the words-with-pictures group on the transfer test was higher than performance of both a words-only group and a pictures-only group, and these last two did not differ from one another. Regarding verbal recall performance, the words-with-pictures group and the words-only group outperformed the control group (who did not participate to the study stage), but did not differ from each other (experiment 2b). In another study by Mayer and Sims (1994), subjects were presented with a picture animation and listened to an explanative text dealing with the workings of either a bicycle tire pump or the human respiratory system. The authors compared the benefit of presenting the picture and the text concurrently to the successive presentation of the two sources of information (the picture animation could be presented either before or after the text). Results on transfer questions requiring elaborative inferences showed that the concurrent group outperformed the successive groups.

These findings may be related to the conclusions drawn by Hegarty and Just (1993). In one experiment, subjects either studied texts alone, diagrams alone, or texts and diagrams conjointly. Both texts and diagrams described the configuration and kinematics of pulley systems. Concurrent presentation of the diagram and the text allowed subjects more accurately to answer questions involving elaborative inferences about the system kinematics than when the diagram or the text was presented alone. In a second experiment, readers' eye fixations were recorded. A close analysis of the numerous data collected (gaze duration, regressions, numbers of graphics inspections, etc.) suggested that readers integrated the information from the diagram and the text. In addition, subjects inspected the diagram to encode the relations between the components rather than the characteristics of individual components. Hegarty and Just (1993) suggested that readers integrate information in text and graphics in local units that are manageable within the capacity of working memory. Later, they combine these local units at a more global level.

It seems then that pictures help subjects to construct an elaborated representation of the text content when the text and the pictures are presented simultaneously. This conjoint presentation may allow subjects to navigate between the two sources of information and help them build connections between the sentences of the text and the pictures.

At What Time in the Process Do Illustrations Have an Effect?

As regards the second aspect of the when question, the second experiment of Hegarty and Just (1993), in which readers' eye movements were recorded, provides evidence that the picture is actually processed during reading, and that this processing has an effect on the subsequent off-line comprehension test. At least, this indicates that the beneficial effect of illustration can be observed during retrieval time. One possibility is that the pictures can have a beneficial effect only after the representation has been stabilized in a schematic form that is independent of the sensory input on which it was based. Another interpretation is that the presentation of an illustration, which appears to help subjects process the content of the text more deeply, could have an effect during the construction of the mental representation. In this case, the beneficial effect should be observed during the process of comprehension.

Gyselinck (1995) attempted to study the effect of pictures on the course of comprehension by means of questions that interrupted reading. In her second experiment (see also Gyselinck & Tardieu, 1994), participants who had little knowledge of physics and chemistry read four short texts nine sentences long dealing with basic notions of physics and chemistry in two conditions. They read texts without illustrations and texts in which each sentence was illustrated. Each illustration was designed to overlap with the content of the corresponding sentence. Subjects' comprehension was tested during reading by the means of two multiple-choice questions that interrupted reading, and their comprehension was also tested immediately after reading by means of four statements the subjects had to verify. Two types of questions or statements were designed: one type involved a paraphrase of a sentence of the text, and the other type involved an elaborative inference that could be drawn from several sentences of the text. Results showed that the presentation of illustrations improved subjects' correct response times on paraphrase and inference questions during reading. After reading, illustrations improved accuracy on inference statements, but not on paraphrase statements.

In the third experiment (Gyselinck, 1995), the content depicted by the illustrations was detailed and fine grained. Under these circumstances, the beneficial effect of pictures occurred on accuracy and on correct response times during the course of reading (Gyselinck, 1995). In that experiment, subjects had to read four texts dealing with basic notions of physics and chemistry, which could be either presented without illustration (no picture), with an illustration of each sentence that depicted only the elements mentioned in the corresponding sentence (elements), or with an illustration of each sentence that depicted the elements mentioned and their relations (relations). Subjects were administered an online test, consisting of two three-choice questions that interrupted reading. Immediately after the presentation of each text, the subjects were administered an off-line test that consisted of four new questions. As in Experiment 2, two types of questions were designed: one type involved a paraphrase of a sentence of the text, and the other type involved an elaborative inference that could be drawn from several sentences of the text. A part of an illustrated text is presented in Fig. 8.1. A paraphrase question and an inference question are illustrated in Table 8.1.

Results of the online test showed that the pictures conditions led to higher percentages of correct responses and shorter correct response times than the no-picture condition on inference questions, but not on para-

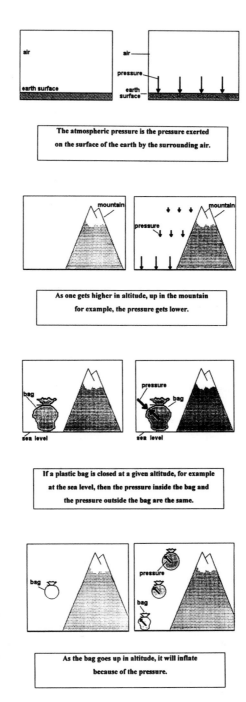

FIG. 8.1. The first four illustrated sentences of the text "The Gas Pressure," used by Gyselinck (1995). The elements pictured are presented on the left side and the relations are pictured on the right side, with the corresponding sentence below.

TABLE 8.1
Example of Paraphrase and Inference Question
for the Passage Illustrated in Fig. 8.1

Paraphrase Question	*Inference Question*
The ascent of the mountain leads to a. a decrease in the atmospheric pressure b. an increase in the atmospheric pressure c. no change in the atmospheric pressure	The bag inflates with altitude because its pressure, compared to the pressure outside, is a. superior b. inferior c. equal

phrase questions. Regarding the off-line test, this superiority of the pictures condition was observed on accuracy and response times for paraphrase and inference questions. In addition, relations pictures led to faster correct responses than elements pictures in the online test. After reading, this superiority was observed both on accuracy and response times.

These results give evidence that online comprehension is modified by the presentation of pictures, and that the beneficial effect of pictures can be observed during reading. In addition, even in the case of pictures depicting only the elements described, a beneficial effect of illustrations is observed over the presentation of the text alone, although the benefit is lower than with relation pictures.

In these experiments, however, online comprehension was evaluated by means of questions that interrupted reading, a technique that is intrusive and might have an effect on the processing strategies of the readers. Converging evidence using various techniques is thus necessary to study precisely the integration of information from text and pictures, as well as the updating of the representation that is in progress. In this respect, a study such as the one reported by Hegarty and Just (1993), who measured participants' eye-movement behavior while reading, appears very fruitful and provides evidence for the course of processing texts and pictures.

When Does the Beneficial Effect of Illustrations Stop?

Finally, we asked whether the beneficial effect of illustrations on text comprehension was a transient one. This issue is important, as regards the acquisition of knowledge and the nature of the representations held in long-term memory. Does presenting an illustration allow readers to build more-permanent representations of the text content, thus helping them acquire new knowledge? Or does this presentation simply allow them to process the text more easily, thus assisting them in answering questions about the content of the text after reading (and even during reading) without helping construct a more elaborated representation of the text content? In the fourth experiment conducted by Gyselinck (1995), subjects were presented with texts dealing with basic notions of physics and chemistry either alone or together with a picture illustrating each sentence of the text. As in experiment 3, two pictures conditions were compared to a no-picture condition: the relations pictures condition and the elements pictures condition. Comprehension was tested at three different times. The online test consisted of paraphrase and inference questions that interrupted reading, and the immediate off-line test consisted of new paraphrase and inference questions subjects had to answer. In addition, subjects had to come back 1 day after reading to explore the time course of the representations. First, they had to answer a series of paraphrase questions and inference questions about the texts they had read the day before. Second, subjects were presented with some sentences of the texts they had read, and were instructed to fill in words or groups of words that had been removed from the sentences. Half of these words referred to an element named in the text and illustrated in both types of pictures. The other half correspond to a relationship described in the sentences and illustrated only in the relations pictures.

Results of the online and the immediate off-line test show that presenting illustrations leads to better accuracy and shorter correct response times than presenting no picture. Moreover, as in experiment 3, relation pictures proved more beneficial than elements pictures, but in this experiment this effect was observed on accuracy and response times during the course of reading, whereas it was only observed on response times in the off-line test.

One day after reading, results on paraphrase and inference questions show that the beneficial effect of pictures could last even after a long delay. The rich representation built a day before seemed to allow the subjects to develop retrieval cues that helped them perform well on the retrieval task. This was confirmed by the results showing that recall was higher in the picture conditions than in the no-picture condition, and that the relations picture condition led to greater recall than did the elements picture condition. Moreover, the relations picture condition led to greater recall than the elements picture conditions only for relations missing words.

The various data reported here indicate that the presentation of pictures—especially those highlighting relations together with the text—helps the readers process the text more deeply, and assists them in building connections that allow them to answer inference questions quite readily. This beneficial effect can be observed during the course of reading, and it lasts even after a delay. Therefore, it appears that the presentation of pictures has not only a superficial and transient effect on the processing of the text, but that it also leads to an elaborated and long-lasting representation.

FOR WHOM DO ILLUSTRATIONS IMPROVE COMPREHENSION?

Thus far, we have focused on the impact of different presentation configurations of text and picture. We now examine who benefits from the presentation of illustrations. Does it depend on one's knowledge? Do some readers have specific abilities that make them good picture users?

Illustrations and Domain Knowledge

In most of the studies we have presented so far, the effect of illustrations on text comprehension has been examined for subjects with low prior knowledge in the domain of the texts (Gyselinck, 1995; Hegarty & Just, 1993; Mayer, 1989; Mayer & Anderson, 1991; Mayer & Sims, 1994). However, Mayer and Gallini (1990) did contrast low prior knowledge with high prior knowledge students. Results showed that the beneficial effect of parts-and-steps illustrations was observed mainly for the low prior knowledge subjects. Presenting pictures may help subjects who cannot use their domain knowledge to focus on explanative information that builds the appropriate connections in a representation of how the system works.

Illustrations and Knowledge of Picture Unity

A prerequisite for a picture to have an effect on the mental representation is that the reader recognize the utility of the picture and spend sufficient time processing it. Even if readers realize the utility of pictures, they may underestimate the amount of processing time needed for the picture to have a beneficial impact on their representation (Weidenmann, 1989). Another reason a reader may not spend sufficient time processing a picture is that the additional cognitive load associated with integrating text and picture may exceed available attentional resources (e.g., Sweller, Chandler, Tierney, & Cooper, 1990).

Two sets of empirical data indicate a clear relationship between allocating sufficient processing time to illustrations and whether they have a beneficial effect. In Gyselinck's (1995) second experiment, a subsidiary analysis was run on the data, using reading times to divide subjects into those assumed to have processed the pictures and those who had not. Results showed that the beneficial effect of illustrations on answers to inference questions was restricted to subjects who took more time to read illustrated texts than nonillustrated texts. In the same vein, Glenberg and Langston (1992) showed in their first experiment that subjects benefited from pictures highlighting the temporal links between the steps of the procedures described in the corresponding texts. In their second experiment, however, they were not able to replicate their results entirely. The authors split their sample into slow and fast readers, and were then able to show that only slow readers benefited from the presentation of pictures. Thus, it appears that the first condition for illustrations to be effective is that subjects must process the pictures and/or must be able to do so. Learners may have erroneous knowledge about the usefulness of pictures, and the use of pictures while reading is a skill that might be learned. This is consistent with Waddill and McDaniel's (1992) work that showed a beneficial effect of relations pictures on recall as well as for target information and nontarget information for highly skilled comprehenders but not for low ones. This suggests that the beneficial effect of illustrations on text processing may also depend on the comprehension skill of the learner. Then, a question that would be worth exploring further is whether comprehension skill is related to a picture-using skill. Results of studies concerned with the influence of spatial and visual ability may give us some elements of answer.

Illustrations and Spatial or Visual Ability

The effectiveness of pictures could also depend on a specific ability of learners to process graphical material. In the study of Mayer and Sims (1994), the authors took a step further in the attempt to clarify the internal conditions for illustrations to be an aid to comprehension. Recall that low-knowledge students listened to an explanative text that was either presented simultaneously with a picture animation (concurrent condition) or presented successively (successive condition). On the basis of results on tests of spatial visualization that emphasize mental manipulation of objects, subjects were placed into a high- or low-spatial ability group. Results on transfer questions requiring elaborative inferences show that the participants in the concurrent condition outperformed the participants in the successive condition, and that this effect is stronger for the high spatial ability subjects than for low spatial ability subjects.

Hegarty and Sims (1994) also explored individual differences relative to spatial visualization ability. The authors studied how people infer the motion of a component in a mechanical system, that is, how they mentally animate the component when they are given a static display of the system. In experiments 1 and 2, subjects' task was to verify whether a sentence was true or false with respect to the depicted pulley system. The sentences could describe either static relations between components or kinematic relations. In addition, the components described in the sentences could be involved in interactions toward the beginning, the middle, or the end of the causal chain of events in the system. In experiment 3, an additional task was designed to explore the influence of the sentence comprehension phase as well as the sentence and diagram integration phase in the process of reasoning. Subjects had to verify whether an arrow showing the motion of the components showed the correct direction of motion. Moreover, in addition to spatial ability tests, subjects also took a verbal ability test.

Correlation measures show that although verbal ability contributed to performance on the motion-verification task, spatial ability made a unique contribution to performance that was not related to verbal ability. The authors suggested that this result was primarily due to the mental animation component of the task. In addition, whereas a different pattern of errors was found for low- and high-spatial ability subjects, reaction patterns are similar in the two groups. In particular, errors increased with the distance of the component to be animated from the beginning of the causal chain in the system for low-spatial ability subjects, but not for high-spatial ability subjects. In addition, experiment 3 showed that the sentence comprehension and text diagram integration processes are independent of mental animation, for they affect neither accuracy nor speed of mental animation.

As reaction time and eye-fixations patterns (experiment 2) were not different between high- and low-spatial ability subjects, this result indicated that both groups animated the pulley system in a piecemeal way and followed the order of the causal chain of events. It seems then that the differences concern how accurately they carry out this piecemeal strategy. However, the question of why such differences are observed remains unanswered by this study. Did the high- and low-spatial ability subjects differ in the accuracy of the spatial transformation processes they used or in the capacity of their spatial working memory? Moreover, do people infer the notion of mechanical systems by transforming mental images or by applying rules of mechanical reasoning? Hegarty and Sims (1994) suggested that measuring the effects of spatial and verbal interference tasks on the process of inferring motion in machines could address this issue.

The beginnings of an answer can be found in a series of experiments conducted by Kruley, Sciama, and Glenberg (1994). Using a concurrent tasks methodology, their results suggest that the integration of text and pictures is processed in the visuospatial sketchpad of working memory (Baddeley, 1986). In their experiment, subjects had to listen to texts describing natural phenomena or mechanical systems that were illustrated or not. Comprehension was assessed with questions involving elaborative inferences. Results showed that the processing of illustrated texts interfered with the performance of a concurrent spatial task more than the processing of texts without pictures. This interference was not found when subjects were not required to comprehend the texts, or when the concurrent task was verbal. This set of results indicates that the comprehension of illustrated texts makes use of the visuospatial sketchpad component of working memory. However, we do not know the extent of the involvement of the visuospatial sketchpad in constructing a mental representation and drawing inferences from it.

In summary, the studies reviewed here suggest that individual differences in cognitive capacities and knowledge, especially differences in spatial and/or visualization ability, should be more fully examined in future research. Variations in spatial or visualization abilities, whether due to different spatial working memory capacities or to the use of different spatial transformation processes, should be taken into account when the events or the physical systems described (in texts and illustrations) involve "running" the representation to draw inferences. Understanding how these abilities play a role in comprehension should help us grasp more thoroughly the comprehension process itself, whether comprehension involves the integration of pictures or not.

WHY DO ILLUSTRATIONS IMPROVE TEXT COMPREHENSION?

In the preceding sections, we have briefly reported results obtained in some of the experiments that were concerned with the role of illustrations in text comprehension. Yet one crucial question about the conditions under which illustrations facilitate comprehension remains to be answered: Why does an illustration facilitate text comprehension, and particularly answers to inference questions?

Text illustrations can be defined as any graphical display that portrays more or less directly the content or a part of the text it accompanies. Illustrations and texts are both external representation that convey information about the world from a certain point of view. As such, text and illustrations may be informationally equivalent, for each could be constructed from the information in the other. However, their computational efficiency may not be equivalent: inferences drawn easily from the information given explicitly in one type of representation may not be drawn as easily and quickly from the information given explicitly in the other type of representation (Larkin & Simon, 1987). In this section, we discuss why pictures and texts have a differential computational efficiency, and why illustrations can be used as a device to build an elaborated representation of the text content, thus allowing the readers to generate elaborative inferences easily.

Illustrations and Dual-Coding Theory

In the experiments we report in this chapter, pictures depict the content or some aspects of the text they accompany, and comprehension performance has been compared mainly when texts were presented with pictures, and when they were presented alone. Thus, we could argue that comprehension was enhanced simply because of a repetition effect. Indeed, the integration of both the linguistic information from the texts and the information stemming from illustrations could just have acted as if the information was presented twice, thus enhancing performance. The facilitative effect of illustrations could also be explained because of dual coding, one in a verbal form and one in a nonverbal form.

The repetition hypothesis and the dual-code hypothesis both predict that pictures should facilitate performance in tests tackling information explicitly portrayed in the picture (that is, information repeated or double coded), but that pictures should have relatively little effect on information not represented in the picture. These hypotheses could then well account for part of the results observed. However, a beneficial effect of pictures has been observed in most of the studies in performance on tests involving elaborative inferences. Because information conveyed by these inferences is by definition neither stated explicitly in texts nor portrayed in illustrations, it cannot be repeated in any form. Consequently, these results cannot be accounted for by the repetition hypothesis or the simple version of the dual-code theory.

Nevertheless, Paivio (1986; see also Clark & Paivio, 1991; Sadoski, Paivio, & Goetz, 1991) claimed that dual-code theory is a theory of cognition that can account for text comprehension as well as for other cognitive articles. He considers that it is not necessary to postulate an integrated symbolic representation, and that the verbal and nonverbal systems can account for the results generally observed. Yet it is not clear how dual-code theory can explain the inferences a subject can draw from the information he or she is given. In this respect, the integrated dual coding hypothesis of Mayer and colleagues (Mayer & Anderson, 1991; Mayer & Sims, 1994), derived from Paivio's dual-code theory, seems very reasonable at first glance. They proposed a framework to account for how visually and verbally presented materials are integrated within the learner's working memory during learning. When readers are presented with a text, they would build a verbal representational connection, corresponding to the verbal encoding. As they are presented with material such as a picture, they would build a visual representational connection, corresponding to a verbal encoding. The learner could build referential connections between the verbal and the visual representations, and all three connections would be necessary for the learner to solve transfer problems that involve elaborative inferences. However, it is not clear how these referential connections are made. The establishment of these referential connections seems to correspond only to associating verbal and visual information. This would surely result in a greater memorization of explicit information, but tell us little about the new relations. Therefore, it seems that the multiple codes lead to a unified abstract representation that is richer than the simple juxtaposition of the byproducts of the processing of the codes. This view is compatible with the position of Marschark (1985), who acknowledged the validity of a form of dual coding in a variety of tasks involving lists of words or unrelated sentences. However, in the light of empirical evidence, he argued that in the case of connected prose, we need theoretical mechanisms beyond those currently provided by memory models emphasizing the availability of modality-specific codes.

Illustrations and Mental Model Theory

The beneficial effect of illustrations in comprehension, when not explained by a dual-coding view, is often interpreted through the properties of graphics that have an effect on working memory. For some authors, illustrations act as an external memory (e.g., Larkin & Simon, 1987). For others, because diagrams are usually more concise than equivalent textual statements and because the essential information tends to be perceptually clear, illustrations can reduce the cognitive load associated with complex reasoning tasks (e.g., Marcus, Cooper, & Sweller, 1996). In other words, the advantage of illustrations, as well as other iconic modes of representation, is that they make structural relations more transparent. As such, illustrations are easier to process than the corresponding statements, thus facilitating the understanding of the situation described (and depicted). However, nothing is said about the representations constructed. It is worth noting that Marcus et al. (1996) stated that one advantage of illustrations is that they make spatial relations explicit, "whereas a textual format requires the reader to construct a mental representation of these relations" (p. 52). But what is this mental representation? Recall that a mental model is an analogical representation and that an illustration is also an analogical representation that closely mirrors the situation described in the text. Thus, a picture can be viewed as one possible expression of a mental model, and presenting pictures may facilitate the construction of a mental model. Illustrations would provide support for the model by concretely illustrating the entities and the relations, and perceiving the picture may well serve to instantiate the model (Kruley et al., 1994). This view is shared by Denis and de Vega (1993), who proposed that a mental image should be considered as a device to instantiate a mental model from a certain point of view, when the model includes spatial or quasispatial data (for a related view, see also Seel & Strittmatter, 1989).

There could be at least two ways for pictures to facilitate mental model building. First, "the entities in the encoded picture would serve as referent for the words in the text, and the encoded picture would become a mental model" (Glenberg, Kruley, & Langston, 1994, p. 616). Therefore, from this point of view, pictures would act as a transitory step in the process of transforming prose into mental images that would become a mental model afterward. Secondly, because pictures could suggest an appropriate model for a text, they would be used as a guide to construct the model. That is, they would be employed as a scaffolding and readers would then easily encode entities and relations from both the text and the picture.[3]

For Glenberg and Langston (1992), a mental model consists of representational elements arrayed in the spatial medium of the visuospatial scratchpad. These elements represent objects or events described in the text and depicted in the pictures. They would point to both propositional and pictorial information. During comprehension, the mental model is updated by adding, deleting, and changing the locations of the representational elements. Whenever a mental model is updated, attention would be focused on the updated element, which is then *noticed* along with the neighboring elements. The implicit relations between the elements are encoded in the mental model. Thus, presenting illustrations that closely mirror the structure of the required mental model would facilitate the noticing process and the construction of this representation.

Glenberg and Langston (1992) assumed therefore that the drawing of inferences occurs during encoding and storage. This view is, however, highly controversial, especially with respect to the elaborative inferences such as those studied in most of the experiments we reviewed. In those experiments, it is unlikely that subjects would make and store such inferences spontaneously during reading. We think that subjects draw inferences because they manipulate the representation they have built by relocating, combining, or modifying the encoded representational elements. This can occur during reading, but only if subjects have been encouraged to draw the inference, for example, with a question interrupting reading.

Let us take an example of how a reader would build and manipulate a mental model. For example, one of the paragraphs presented to participants in Gyselinck's (1995) experiments described the phenomena of atmospheric gas pressure (see Fig. 8.1). As the second sentence states that the higher the altitude, the lower the pressure, the mental model built by the reader would take the form of an analogical representation where the variation of pressure with altitude could be represented on a vertical axis. The mental model is probably not an exact analogue of the real situation.

---

[3]Many studies concerned with spatial representations are consistent with this view. Subjects are presented a text that describes the actions of a protagonist inside a spatial environment together with a map of this environment (e.g., Bower & Morrow, 1990; Gray-Wilson, Rinck, McNamara, Bower, & Morrow, 1993). Results suggest that subjects build a model of the situation, whose elements would be activated or deactivated depending on the spatial relations they have with the actions of the protagonist that are described in the text. The map then serves as a frame in which a spatial mental model is built.

It consists of entities representing the objects and, depending on the context, some salient features. The relations between the objects, whether they are spatial, temporal, or even in some cases causal, would be represented by spatial relations in the model. Next, the third sentence states that when a plastic bag is closed at sea level, the pressure inside the bag and the atmospheric pressure are the same. Consequently, the mental model is updated and the representational element of the bag located along the vertical axis (at the bottom in this example). As the fourth sentence states that the plastic bag will inflate with altitude, again the mental model is updated: The bag is relocated on the axis and its features are modified. If pictures are presented with the sentences, then the reader would have a frame available to construct this mental model more easily. From our point of view, it is unlikely that most of the subjects would spontaneously infer that the bag is going to inflate because the pressure inside the bag is higher than the pressure outside the bag. However, if a question is asked, then the subjects would manipulate their model, allowing them to relate the content evoked by the various sentences to find the answer.

The aim of this section was to discuss why a difference in the computational efficiency of text and illustrations could occur. It appears that explanations in terms of repetition or dual coding of information cannot account well for the beneficial effect of illustrations when readers answer questions that involve elaborative inferences. We proposed that the pictures help the readers build a mental model, and we described, in a very speculative way, the processes that could account for this beneficial effect. Finally, we suggested that information in a mental model is manipulated for purposes of drawing elaborative inferences, although this manipulation is not necessarily automatic.

SUMMARY AND CONCLUSION

This chapter presented a number of recent studies concerned with the role of text illustrations on comprehension, and more specifically their role on inference making. We attempted to address questions about the conditions for illustrations to improve comprehension. We argued that to understand the role of illustrations in text processing, it is more useful to focus on the processes by which the beneficial effects of illustrations come about than to focus on the description of illustrations per se, given that this description is in most cases highly dependent on the processes involved in the formation of the reader's representation. Various types of illustrations may be designed. The results reported indicate that pictures that highlight the relationships between the objects being described in the text are the most beneficial for readers, allowing them to build connections in order to draw inferences. Moreover, the presentation of illustrations seems to be most effective when pictures are presented simultaneously with the text, thus permitting readers to navigate between the two sources of information. In addition, results indicate that the beneficial effect of illustrations can be observed during the course of reading itself, although methodological problems have been raised regarding the technique used to assess online comprehension. It can also be noted that this beneficial effect lasts even after a long delay. Finally, an important issue that bears emphasizing relates to what we named the internal conditions for illustrations to improve comprehension. It appears that mainly low-knowledge subjects benefit from the presentation of illustrations. The use of illustrations could in addition be a skill that has to be learned, and it could also depend on some specific abilities of the readers, such as spatial ability. We think that further research should be devoted to individual differences and to cognitive constraints imposed by the processing of illustrations, especially as regards working memory capacities.

The last question we examined was why illustrations improve comprehension. The dual coding theory was presented, and we argued that it could not fully explain the role of illustrations in inference making. We suggested that mental model theory provides a better account of the beneficial effect of illustrations in text comprehension. The main advantage of iconic modes of representations is that they make structural relations more transparent, thus allowing readers to build a mental model that can be manipulated afterward to draw inferences. However, many questions about the involvement of pictures in the representation and about the form of the representations remain to be answered. Whether readers encode the picture, which then becomes a mental model, or whether they use the picture as a frame would allow us to comprehend the nature and the content of the representations built. Do readers separately build the linguistic representation, the pictorial representation, and then the mental model as a combination? This would amount to a kind of multiple codes representation. In addition, do readers keep traces of both the linguistic and the pictorial representations as separate entities and access them separately? If not, do readers construct a unique representation right from the beginning of the comprehension process? Research such as that conducted by Hegarty and Just (1993) gives us some of the elements of answers. We believe that research using concurrent methodology tasks could prove very useful to a more precise understanding of how pictures and texts are integrated by readers in working memory. We also need to know whether readers, even when they are not presented with pictures, make use of their visuospatial working memory. This could tell us if an analogical representation is built during understanding. In addition, more research should be devoted to the use of representations built with text and pictures after long delays, which could give us an idea of the characteristics of the representations held in long-term memory.

REFERENCES

Baddeley, A. D. (1986). *Working memory.* Oxford, England: Oxford University Press.

Bower, G. H., & Morrow, D. G. (1990). Mental models in narrative comprehension. *Science, 247,* 44–48.

Bransford, J. D., & Johnson, M. K. (1972). Contextual prerequisites for understanding: Some investigations of comprehension and recall. *Journal of Verbal Learning and Verbal Behaviour, 11,* 717–726.

Clark, J. M., & Paivio, A. (1991). Dual coding theory and education. *Educational Psychology Review, 3,* 149–210.

Denis, M. (1991). *Image and cognition.* New York: Harvester-Wheatsheaf.

Denis, M., & de Vega, M. (1993). Modèles mentaux et imagerie mentale [Mental models and mental imagery]. In M.-F. Ehrlich, H. Tardieu, & M. Cavazza (Eds.), *Les modèles mentaux: Approche cognitive des représentations* (pp. 79–100). Paris: Masson.

Franklin, N., & Tversky, B. (1990). Searching imagined environments. *Journal of Experimental Psychology: General, 119,* 63–76.

Glenberg, A. M., Kruley, P., & Langston, W. E. (1994). Analogical processes in comprehension: Simulation of a mental model. In M. A. Gernsbacher (Ed.), *Handbook of psycholinguistics* (pp. 609–640). San Diego, CA: Academic Press.

Glenberg, A. M., & Langston, W. E. (1992). Comprehension of illustrated text: Pictures help to build mental models. *Journal of Memory and Language, 31,* 129–151.

Gray-Wilson, S., Rinck, M., McNamara, T. P., Bower, G. H., & Morrow, D. G. (1993). Mental models and narrative comprehension: Some qualifications. *Journal of Memory and Language, 32,* 141–154.

Gyselinck, V. (1995). *Les modèles mentaux dans la compréhension de textes: Le rôle des illustrations* [Mental models in text comprehension: The role of illustrations]. Unpublished doctoral thesis, University of Paris V.

Gyselinck, V., & Tardieu, H. (1994). The role of text illustrations in the construction of non-spatial mental models. In F. De Jong & B. van Hout-Wolters (Eds.), *Process-oriented instruction and learning from texts* (pp. 175–181). Amsterdam: VU University Press.

Hegarty, M., & Just, M. A. (1993). Constructing mental models of machines from texts and diagrams. *Journal of Memory and Language, 32,* 717–742.

Hegarty, M., & Sims, V. K. (1994). Individual differences in mental animation during mechanical reasoning. *Memory & Cognition, 22,* 411–430.

Johnson-Laird, P. N. (1980). Mental models in cognitive science. *Cognitive Science, 4,* 71–115.

Johnson-Laird, P. N. (1983). *Mental models.* Cambridge, England: Cambridge University Press.

Kintsch, W. (1988). The use of knowledge in discourse processing: A construction-integration model. *Psychological Review, 95,* 163–182.

Kintsch, W., Welsch, D., Schmalhofer, F., & Zimny, S. (1990). Sentence memory: A theoretical analysis. *Journal of Memory and Language, 29,* 133–159.

Kruley, P., Sciama, S. C., & Glenberg, A. M. (1994). On-line processing of textual illustrations in the visuospatial sketchpad: Evidence from dual-task studies. *Memory & Cognition, 22,* 261–272.

Larkin, J. H., & Simon, H. A. (1987). Why a diagram is (sometimes) worth ten thousand words. *Cognitive Science, 11,* 65–99.

Lemmonier-Schallert, D. (1980). The role of illustrations in reading comprehension. In R. J. Spiro, B. C. Bruce, & W. F. Brewer (Eds.), *Theoretical issues in reading comprehension* (pp. 503–524). Hillsdale, NJ: Lawrence Erlbaum Associates.

Levie, W. H., & Lentz, R. (1982). Effects of text illustrations: A review of research. *Education Communication and Technology Journal, 30*, 195–232.

Levin, J. R., Anglin, G. J., & Carney, R. N. (1987). On empirically validating functions of pictures in prose. In D. M. Willows & H. Houghton (Eds.), *The psychology of illustration: Volume 1. Basic research* (pp. 51–86). New York: Springer-Verlag.

Mandl, H., & Levin, J. R. (Eds.). (1989). *Knowledge acquisition from text and pictures.* Amsterdam: Elsevier, North-Holland.

Marcus, N., Cooper, M., & Sweller, J. (1996). Understanding instructions. *Journal of Educational Psychology, 88*, 49–63.

Marschark, M. (1985). Imagery and organization in the recall of prose. *Journal of Memory and Language, 24*, 734–745.

Mayer, R. E. (1989). Systematic thinking fostered by illustrations in scientific texts. *Journal of Educational Psychology, 81*, 240–246.

Mayer, R. E., & Anderson, R. B. (1991). Animations need narrations: An experimental test of a dual-coding hypothesis. *Journal of Educational Psychology, 83*, 484–490.

Mayer, R. E., & Gallini, J. K. (1990). When is an illustration worth ten thousand words? *Journal of Educational Psychology, 82*, 715–726.

Mayer, R. E., & Sims, V. K. (1994). For whom is a picture worth a thousand words? Extensions of a dual-coding theory of multimedia learning. *Journal of Educational Psychology, 86*, 389–401.

Paivio, A. (1971). *Imagery and verbal processes.* New York: Holt, Rinehart & Winston.

Paivio, A. (1986). *Mental representations: A dual coding approach.* New York: Oxford University Press.

Peeck, J. (1987). The role of illustrations in processing and remembering illustrated text. In D. M. Willows & H. A. Houghton (Eds.), *The psychology of illustration: Volume 1. Basic research* (pp. 115–151). New York: Springer-Verlag.

Perrig, W. J., & Kintsch, W. (1985). Propositional and situational representations of text. *Journal of Memory Language, 24*, 503–518.

Pressley, M., & Miller, G. E. (1987). Effects of illustrations on children's listening comprehension and oral prose memory. In D. M. Willows & H. A. Houghton (Eds.), *The psychology of illustration: Volume 1. Basic research* (pp. 87–114). New York: Springer-Verlag.

Sadoski, M., Paivio, A., & Goetz, E. T. (1991). A critique of schema theory in reading and a dual coding alternative. *Reading Research Quarterly, 26*, 463–484.

Schnotz, W. (Ed.). (1993). *Comprehension of graphics in texts.* Oxford, England: Pergamon Press.

Schnotz, W., & Kulhavy, R. W. (Eds.). (1994). *Comprehension of graphics.* Amsterdam: North-Holland.

Seel, N. M., & Strittmatter, P. (1989). Presentation of information by media and its effect on mental models. In H. Mandl & J. R. Levin (Eds.), *Knowledge acquisition from text and pictures* (pp. 37–84). Amsterdam: North-Holland.

Small, M. Y., Lovett, S. B., & Scher, M. S. (1993). Pictures facilitates children's recall of unillustrated expository prose. *Journal of Educational Psychology, 85*, 520–528.

Sweller, J., Chandler, P., Tierney, P., & Cooper, M. (1990). Cognitive load as a factor in the structuring of technical material. *Journal of Experimental Psychology: General, 119*, 176–192.

Tardieu, H., Ehrlich, M.-F., & Gyselinck, V. (1992). Levels of representation and domain-specific knowledge in comprehension of scientific texts. *Language and Cognitive Processes, 7*, 335–352.

Taylor, H. A., & Tversky, B. (1992). Spatial mental models derived from survey and route descriptions. *Journal of Memory and Language, 31*, 261–292.

van Dijk, T. A. (1987). Episodic models in discourse processing. In R. Horowitz & S. J. Samuels (Eds.), *Comprehending oral and written language* (pp. 161–196). New York: Academic Press.

van Dijk, T. A., & Kintsch, W. (1983). *Strategies of discourse comprehension.* New York: Academic Press.

Waddill, P. J., & McDaniel, M. A. (1992). Pictorial enhancement of text memory: Limitations imposed by picture type and comprehension skill. *Memory & Cognition, 20,* 472–482.

Weidenmann, B. (1989). When good pictures fail: An information-processing approach to the effect of illustration. In H. Mandl & J. R. Levin (Eds.), *Knowledge acquisition from text and pictures* (pp. 157–170). Amsterdam: Elsevier, North-Holland.

Willows, D. H., & Houghton, H. A. (Eds.). (1987). *The psychology of illustrations: Volume 1. Basic research.* New York: Springer-Verlag.

Chapter 9

The Role of Situational Continuity in Narrative Understanding

Joseph P. Magliano
Northern Illinois University

Rolf A. Zwaan
Florida State University

Art Graesser
The University of Memphis

Since the early 1980s, there has been a considerable amount of theoretical conjecture and empirical research regarding the construction of situation models during the comprehension of narrative texts. This interest in situation models was largely influenced by the seminal book by van Dijk and Kintsch (1983). van Dijk and Kintsch argued that readers not only construct a representation for the gist of the explicit text, but also a representation for the situation described in the text. An underlying assumption of van Dijk and Kintsch's thesis is that there is a verisimilitude between the real world and the story world. Readers presumably use their general knowledge of the real world to construct a mental model of the events depicted in the narrative world. As an example of this verisimilitude, narrative events are understood as being causally linked within a narrative time and space, much like the manner in which we understand events in the real world. Thus, the situation model provides an index of narrative events along a number of dimensions, such as characters and objects, temporality, spatiality, causality, and intentionality (Magliano, Trabasso, & Langston, 1995; Zwaan, Langston, & Graesser, 1995; Zwaan, Magliano, & Graesser, 1995).

Most of the research on situation-model construction has focused on one dimension of a situation model. There has been considerable research on the construction of spatial (Glenberg, Meyer, & Lindem, 1987; Morrow, Bower, & Greenspan, 1989; Morrow, Greenspan, & Bower, 1987; Zwaan & van Oostendorp, 1993), temporal (Anderson, Garrod, & Sanford, 1983; Ohtsuka & Brewer, 1992; Zwaan, in press), causal (Graesser & Clark, 1985;

Magliano, Baggett, Johnson, & Graesser, 1993; Myers, Shinjo, & Duffy, 1987; Trabasso, Secco, & van den Broek, 1984; Trabasso & Sperry, 1985; Trabasso, van den Broek, & Suh, 1989), and motivational (Dopkins, 1996; Dopkins, Klin, & Myers, 1993; Graesser & Clark, 1985; Long & Golding, 1993; Long, Golding, & Graesser, 1993; Lutz & Radvansky, 1997; Suh & Trabasso, 1993; Trabasso & Suh, 1993; van den Broek & Lorch, 1993) dimensions in isolation from one another. Although this research has been very informative, it does not provide insights into the relative function of these dimensions in story understanding. Recently, we have begun to investigate the extent to which readers construct multidimensional situation models (Magliano et al., 1995; Zwaan, Langston, & Graesser, 1995; Zwaan, Magliano, & Graesser, 1995). We believed that specifying the relative impact of the different dimensions (i.e., characters and objects, time, space, causality, intentionality) in situation-model construction will provide a more comprehensive view of the nature of a situation model and its role in story understanding.

Zwaan, Langston, and Graesser (1995) proposed an event indexing model of situation-model construction that specifies the nature in which the situational dimensions are monitored and updated. A central assumption of this model is that the main purpose of constructing a situation model is to monitor what characters are involved in a story, what is happening to them, what their goals are, and how they are achieving those goals, all within a narrative time and space. As each story event and action is comprehended, readers monitor changes in continuity in characters and objects, time, space, causality, and intentionality. Changes along these dimensions cue the reader that the mental representation for a story must be updated. In the present chapter, we first describe the event indexing model and specify the manner in which situational continuities along the characters and objects, temporal, spatial, causal, and motivational dimensions are monitored and updated. We then present evidence that the model accounts for fit judgments for story sentences, sentence processing time, online inference generation, and long-term representation for stories.

THE EVENT-INDEXING MODEL
AND SITUATIONAL CONTINUITIES

As mentioned, there is an assumed verisimilitude between the real world and a narrative story world (Segal, 1995). For example, the rules that govern our perception of causality between real-world events also govern our perception of causality between story-world events (Trabasso et al., 1989; van den Broek, 1990). A cause must occur prior to the onset of its effect. A cause typically occurs in close spatial proximity to its effect (although this is not a necessary condition of causality). Establishing continuities in time, space, and causality is critical for the coherent understanding of real-world events (Collingwood, 1938; Mackie, 1980) and story-world events (Dahlgren, 1988; Gernsbacher, 1990; Gernsbacher & Givon, 1995; Givon, 1995; Magliano et al., 1995; Zwaan, Langston, & Graesser, 1995; Zwaan, Magliano, & Graesser, 1995).

However, there are nontrivial differences between the manner in which we experience real-world and story-world events. Temporality, spatiality, and causality are closely linked when we experience real-world events. For example, movement in space is not possible without movement in time. There are inextricable links between time and causality with respect to the order and duration in which events must occur for causality to be perceived. In contrast, the narration of a story is not constrained by the laws of nature. In literary theory, there is a long-standing distinction between the story and discourse structures (see Brewer & Lichtenstein, 1982, for discussion). The story structure refers to a hypothetical representation of what characters are involved in a story, the events that are happening to them, and their goals and actions, all within a narrative time and space. Thus, the story structure is essentially a model of the situation. The discourse structure refers to the order and manner in which events and actions are presented in the explicit text. In literary texts, there is not always a direct correspondence between the story structure and the discourse structure. For example, through conventions of flashbacks and flashforwards, the order in which events are conveyed in a narrative is not constrained by the order in which they are supposed to occur within the story world. Furthermore, the narrator can describe events that occur at the same time but at different locations in the story world. Similarly, a narrator can describe events that take place over large spans of time but occur at the same location.

While comprehending a story, a reader must derive the story structure (or situation model) from the discourse structure. That is, a reader must construct a representation of the story events and actions as they occur within the story time and space. We believe that one of the primary functions of monitoring situational continuities is to derive a model of the story structure from the discourse structure.

The "event indexing" model proposed by Zwaan, Langston, and Graesser (1995) describes how readers construct a coherent representation of the story structure. The model assumes that readers simultaneously monitor continuities in story characters and objects, time, space, causality, and intentionality. When a focal sentence describes an event that is continuous with respect to these situational dimensions, there is a high correspondence between the discourse structure and the story structure. However, discontinuities along these dimensions often occur when there are discrepancies between the discourse and story structures. It is under these conditions that readers must engage in effortful processing to construct a representation of the story structure.

To illustrate how the model identifies continuities and discontinuities along these situational dimensions, consider the narrative "Ivan the Warrior" shown in Table 9.1. Continuity in characters and objects occurs when a sentence contains objects and characters that were introduced in the prior context. Discontinuity in characters and objects occurs when a new character or object is introduced. For example, sentence 2 is continuous with sentence 1 on this dimension, because sentence 2 does not introduce any new characters or objects. However, sentence 3 is partially discontinuous on this dimension because two new characters are introduced, namely the giant and the villagers.

Temporal continuity occurs when an incoming sentence in a story describes an event, state, or action that (a) occurs within the same time interval as the previous story event, state, or action, or (b) immediately follows the previous story event or action in the narrative timeline. A sentence is temporally discontinuous with the prior context when there is a time shift. A time shift occurs when (a) a large amount of story time must elapse between the immediately prior context and the current story event, action, or state, (b) the current sentence contains a distant "flash-forward" in the narrative timeline, or (c) the current sentence contains a

TABLE 9.1
Ivan the Warrior

Story Sentence	Episodic Category
1. Ivan was a great warrior.	Setting
2. He was the best archer in his village.	Setting
3. One day, Ivan heard that a giant had been terrifying people in his village.	Initiating Event
4. They said that the giant came to the village at night and hurt people.	Initiating Event
5. Ivan was determined to kill the giant.	Goal
6. He waited until dark.	Attempt
7. When the giant came, Ivan shot an arrow at him.	Attempt
8. Ivan hit him but the arrow could not hurt the giant.	Outcome
9. The people were disappointed.	Reaction
10. One day, a famous swordsman came to a nearby village.	Initiating Event
11. Ivan decided to learn how to fight with a sword.	Goal
12. He went to the swordsman.	Attempt
13. Ivan studied very hard for several weeks.	Attempt
14. He became a very skilled swordsman.	Outcome
15. Ivan got a powerful sword from his teacher.	Outcome
16. That night, Ivan returned back to his village with his mighty sword.	Attempt
17. He finally killed the giant with his sword.	Outcome
18. The people thanked Ivan a hundred times.	Reaction

"flashback" to a past story event in the narrative timeline. Of course, a flashback or flashforward would require the narrator to return to the current point on the narrative timeline, which would also involve a temporal shift. Temporal continuities and discontinuities can be explicitly cued in the text through tense and aspect markers and temporal adverbial phrases, such as "shortly afterward" and "the next day" (Givon, 1995). Temporal shifts can also be implied by general knowledge about the duration of events (Anderson et al., 1983). For example, if one sentence describes a character going to a movie and the next sentence describes the character discussing the movie after it is over, the reader can use his or her general knowledge about the length of a movie to infer that at least 2 hours have elapsed in story time. Anderson et al. (1983) found that such temporal inferences influence the availability of anaphoric references. In the example story in Table 9.1, sentences 3 and 4 are temporally continuous because they depict successive narrative events (Ivan is being told about the giant), whereas sentences 12 and 13 are temporally discontinuous.

Spatial continuity occurs when a narrative event, action, or state takes place in the same story region described in the immediately prior context. A narrative location is a region of narrative space that has distinctive features that are discriminable from other locations. A spatial discontinuity occurs when a story event, action, or state occurs in a different story region from the immediate context. Spatial discontinuities shift the narrative "here" to new locations (Morrow et al., 1989). Changes and spatial locations can be cued by deictic verbs, such as *go* and *come* (see Duchan, Bruder, & Hewitt, 1995), tense and aspect makers, and prepositional phrases (Morrow, 1985). For example, the sentence "John WAS WALKING from the kitchen TOWARD the bedroom" places John somewhere along the path between the kitchen and the bedroom, whereas the sentence "John WALKED from the kitchen INTO the bedroom" places John in the bedroom. Despite the fact that these sentences contain essentially the same content words, Morrow (1985) showed that they evoke different situation models in a reader. In Table 9.1, sentences 3 and 4 are spatially continuous because they describe events that take place in Ivan's village, whereas sentences 9 and 10 are not spatially continuous because they take place in Ivan's village and another village, respectively.

Causal continuities occur between story events if one story event is the cause of another. These causal relationships are both immediate and distal in the representation of the text. The causal network model proposed by Trabasso et al. (1989) provides a basis for determining causal relationships between sentences in stories. According to the causal-network model, story sentences can be classified according to how they fit into an episodic structure. Episodes consist of a set of categories of story units (cf. Stein & Glenn, 1979). These categories consist of settings (S), events (E), goals

(G), attempts (A), outcomes (O), and reactions (R). Table 9.1 shows the episodic categories of each sentence in "Ivan the Warrior." The causal-network model specifies the types of causal relationships that can occur between these categories. Settings enable all other categories. Events can cause events, goals, and reactions. Goals can motivate other goals and attempts. Attempts can enable attempts and cause outcomes. Outcomes, as well as events, can cause reactions and goals. Outcomes can also enable attempts. The causal relationships specified by the model for a particular story are based on criteria of necessity and weak sufficiency in the circumstances (Mackie, 1980). According to the necessity criterion, an event A is necessary for an event B if event B will not occur in the story without event A. For example, Ivan would not have wanted to kill the giant if he had not heard that the giant was hurting the villagers. According to the sufficiency criterion, if event A occurs in the story, then event B is likely to follow. For example, given that Ivan heard about the giant, it is likely that he would want to do something about it. Therefore, sentence 5 is causally connected to sentences 3 and 4. In contrast, sentences 9 and 10 are causally discontinuous, because the disappointment of the villagers does not provide a necessary and sufficient condition for the swordsman's arrival in the nearby village.

Finally, there is continuity in the intentionality dimension when a protagonist's goals, actions, or the outcomes of actions are consistent with an explicit or inferred goal plan. Again, the Causal Network Model provides a basis for determining if an action is part of an existing goal plan. That is, if an explicit or inferred goal provides a necessary and sufficient condition for a protagonist's goals, actions, or outcomes of actions, then that action is part of an existing goal plan. For example, sentences 6, 7, 8, 11, 16, and 17 are all part of Ivan's goal to kill the giant. In contrast, sentence 10 describes a character's action that is not part of an established goal plan, and is thus not continuous with respect to the intentionality dimension.

What Is the Relationship Between Situational Continuities and Online Processing Time?

The event-indexing model assumes that readers construct a mental representation of the situation while reading a text, such that incoming information is mapped onto the evolving structure. Continuities along the situational dimension aid in the mapping process. That is, continuities cue the reader that the focal information can be readily understood in terms of the prior story context. When the reader encounters a discontinuity in any of these dimensions, he or she must update the index for that particular dimension. For example, if there is a break in temporal cohesion but not in spatial or causal cohesion, then the temporal but not the spatial or causal index must be updated. Breaks in one or two dimensions may not require that readers abandon the model of the current situation. However, when there are breaks in several dimensions, as is the case when a new episode starts (Chafe, 1979), readers must construct a model for the new situation. Sentences 3 and 4 contain the initiating event for the first episode. At these sentences, readers must construct an initial representation of the unfolding situation (containing Ivan and his attributes, as well as where Ivan is located in story space and time). This initial construction should be effortful and time-consuming. Sentences 5 through 9 are continuous on one or more situational dimensions, and therefore, should be readily mapped onto the evolving mental model of the situation. In sentence 10, however, a new character is introduced who is in a new time and space with respect to the prior episode. As consistent with Gernbacher's (1990) structure-building model, the event-indexing model assumes that shifts in multiple dimensions of situational continuity, such as this, cue the reader that the prior situation should be wrapped up and a model for a new situation must be constructed. Again, this should be relatively time-consuming.

From the event-indexing model, it is possible to derive a general principle regarding the relationship between situational continuity and processing time:

Principle 1. If a focal sentence is continuous with the prior situational context, then processing time is facilitated. If a focal sentence is discontinuous on any dimension with respect to the prior situational context, then processing time slows down compared to when it is continuous.

It is important to reiterate that the event-indexing model assumes that readers simultaneously monitor continuity along multiple situational dimensions. Consequently, continuities and discontinuities in time, space, causality, and intentionality should each have unique impacts on processing time. There is, in fact, ample evidence that breaks in temporality (Magliano et al., 1995; Mandler, 1986; Ohtsuka & Brewer, 1992; Zwaan, in press; Zwaan, Magliano, & Graesser, 1995), causality (Fletcher & Bloom, 1988; Graesser, 1981; Magliano et al., 1995; Singer, Halldorson, Lear, & Andrusiak, 1992; Trabasso & Sperry, 1985; Zwaan, Magliano, & Graesser, 1995), and intentionality (Dopkins, 1996; Dopkins et al., 1993; Magliano et al., 1995; Suh & Trabasso, 1993; Trabasso & Suh, 1993) slow down processing time during the comprehension of narrative text.

What Is the Relationship Between Situational Continuities and Inference Generation?

The event-indexing model, as articulated by Zwaan, Langston, and Graesser (1995), does not explicitly specify the relationship between situational continuities and discontinuities and inference generation. However, it is possible to derive general principles regarding this relationship within the framework of the event-indexing model. As stated previously, situational continuity cues the reader that the focal sentence is connected to the prior story context. As such, the prior context can be readily used to help interpret and understand the focal sentence within the framework of the evolving story. For example, continuity in the causal and intentional dimensions indicates that a causal antecedent can be found in the explicit prior context. Consider sentence 16 in the story in Table 9.1. The causal network analysis of this story indicates that this sentence has a direct causal connection with Ivan's goal to kill the giant. As such, one would expect that readers inferentially connect sentence 16 with the superordinate goal statement (sentence 5). Suh and Trabasso (1993) and Trabasso and Suh (1993) investigated the extent to which readers generate goal-based, text-connecting inferences while reading stories such as "Ivan the Warrior." They showed evidence from think-aloud protocols and online priming that readers generate goal-based inferences when a focal sentence is continuous with the previous text along the intentionality dimension.

When breaks in continuity occur in several dimensions, then the focal sentence cannot be understood in terms of the prior context. When this occurs, readers must rely on their general world knowledge and the explicit context to resolve these breaks in coherence. For example, sentence 10 in Table 9.1 is not continuous on any of the situational dimensions, and so there is nothing in the prior context to which it can be inferentially connected. We believe that breaks in continuity, such as this, serve as a kind of heuristic indicating that a reader must rely more heavily on world knowledge, rather than on the prior context, to interpret and understand a focal sentence.

From the event-indexing model, it is possible to derive two general principles regarding the relationship between situational continuity and inference processing:

> *Principle 2.* If a focal sentence is continuous with the prior situational context, then readers should generate backward text-connecting inferences in order to connect the focal sentence with the prior context.

> *Principle 3.* If a focal sentence is discontinuous with the prior situational context, then readers should generate new knowledge-based inferences in order to understand the sentence in the context of the story.

In support of these principles, Graesser (1981) reported that readers generate more knowledge-based inferences at the beginning of story episodes than during the middle. The inferences generated during the beginning of the episode lay the groundwork by which the subsequent sentences can be understood. A study conducted by Goldman and Varnhagen (1986) also provided support for these principles. They had children and adults read a series of stories in which a character's goal plan either succeeded or failed. The goal-failure stories provided a situation in which there was a break in the causal continuity dimension within a story context. They found that on recalling the stories, both children and adults included more temporal connectives (then, when, after) between story events, goals, and actions in the goal-success stories than in the goal-failure stories. This increase in temporal connectives is most likely the result of the causally continuous situations inherent in the goal-success stories. Interestingly, there were more inferences in the recall protocols for the goal-failure stories than the goal-success stories. Furthermore, more causal explanations as marked by causal connectives (e.g., because, so, since) occurred in the recall protocols for the goal-failure stories than for the goal-success stories. These two results indicate that the breaks in causal continuity within the goal-failure stories triggered causal inferences in both children and adults.

The inference-processing principles (2 and 3) are related to the processing-time principle (1). Specifically, text-connecting inferences facilitate integration into the prior context and therefore are associated with a decrease in processing time. In contrast, new knowledge-based inferences require effortful processing and therefore are associated with an increase in processing time.

What Is the Relationship Between Situational Continuities and Long-Term Memory for a Text?

A final set of principles involves the relationship between situational continuity and the long-term memory representation for a story. The event-indexing model assumes two events are more strongly related in a long-term memory representation to the extent that they share situational indices (Zwaan, Langston, & Graesser, 1995). For example, sentences 6 and 7 should be highly connected in the memory representation because they share continuities along character, temporal, spatial, causal, and intentional dimensions. In contrast, sentences 6 and 12 are not continuous on temporal, spatial, causal, or intentional dimensions (although they are continuous on the character dimension), so they should be weakly connected in the memory representation. The implications of this assumption extend beyond the dyadic relationships between sentences. Specifically, the event-indexing model assumes that the overall structure of the memory representation for the situation is mediated by the number of shared situational indices. There is evidence that the causal index, for example, has an impact on overall long-term memory for a story. Specifically, events that are highly causally integrated in the story structure are remembered better (Fletcher & Bloom, 1988; Goldman & Varnhagen, 1986; Graesser

& Clark, 1985; Trabasso & van den Broek, 1985), included more often in summaries (Trabasso & van den Broek, 1985), and rated as more important and central to a story (Graesser & Clark, 1985; Trabasso & Sperry, 1985). A major claim of the event-indexing model is that the other situational dimensions also have an impact on the overall structure of a memory representation for a story.

From the event-indexing model, it is possible to derive a general principle regarding the relationship between situational continuity and memory representation:

> *Principle 4.* If story events share situational indices, then they should be highly associated in the long-term memory representation. If story events do not share situational indices, then they should be relatively unassociated in the long-term memory representation.

There is evidence for this principle with respect to the causal and temporal dimensions. If one event that is either temporally close in narrative time (Zwaan, in press) or causally connected (Myers et al., 1987) with a second event, then the first event provides a sufficient cue for the recall of the second event. However, there has been very little research investigating the role that multiple situational dimensions play in the association of story events in memory. Zwaan, Langston, and Graesser (1995) did, however, investigate the impact of multiple situational dimensions on the memory for a story. They showed evidence for this principle with a word-clustering task. We discuss this study in detail in the next section.

In summary, we have described the event-indexing model, which assumes that readers construct a representation that indexes connections between story events and actions along multiple situational dimensions (i.e., characters and objects, time, space, causality, intentionality). From the event-indexing model, we have derived principles regarding the relationship among situational continuities and processing time, online inference generation, and long-term memory representation. In the next section, we describe a set of recent studies that provide evidence for each of these principles.

STUDIES THAT HAVE INVESTIGATED THE EVENT-INDEXING MODEL

In this section, we describe four studies conducted in our laboratories, along with our respective collaborators, that provide evidence in favor of the event-indexing model. We first describe two studies that investigated the processing-time principles (Magliano et al., 1995; Zwaan, Magliano, &

Graesser, 1995). We subsequently present a study conducted by the first and third authors, in collaboration with Tom Trabasso, that examined the inference-processing principles. Finally, we describe the Zwaan, Langston, and Graesser (1995) study that investigated the memory-representation principles.

Principle 1: Situational Continuities Facilitate Sentence Processing

We conducted two studies that provide evidence for Principle 1 of the event indexing model. A study by Magliano et al. (1995) examined the contribution of multiple sources of situational continuity to sentence integration and story understanding. They had participants read a series of short narratives, such as "Ivan the Warrior" presented in Table 9.1. These stories were constructed by Suh (1988) to test assumptions of the causal network model (Trabasso et al., 1989). There were two versions of each story. In a goal-failure version, the main protagonist fails to achieve a goal introduced in the first episode of a story. A subsequent goal introduced in the second episode can be understood as subordinate to the first in a goal-plan hierarchy. The story in Table 9.1 is the goal-failure version of "Ivan the Warrior." Ivan was unable to kill the giant in the first episode; his goal of wanting to learn how to fight with a sword can be interpreted as a subgoal in a plan to kill the giant. In a goal-success version, the main protagonist is able to achieve the goal in the first episode. Therefore, the goal introduced in the second episode is a new, unrelated goal. In the goal-success version of "Ivan the Warrior," Ivan is able to kill the giant in the first episode and therefore, his goal of wanting to learn how to fight with a sword cannot be interpreted as a subgoal for the purpose of killing the giant.

Story sentences were analyzed to determine if they were continuous with the prior context along the temporal, spatial, causal, and intentional dimensions. Temporal and spatial continuities were determined using the aforementioned criteria. Continuities along the causal and intentional dimensions were identified via causal network analyses (Trabasso et al., 1989), as also discussed previously. The causal network analyses allowed us to distinguish between local and distal causal connections. Local causal connections occurred between adjacent sentences, whereas distal causal connections occurred between sentences that were a distance of two or more sentences in the surface structure. With respect to the intentionality dimension, we determined if a sentence was causally connected to either goal 1 from the first episode (e.g., Ivan's desire to kill the giant) and/or goal 2 from the second episode (e.g., Ivan's desire to learn to fight with a sword). This distinction was made in order to test assumptions made by the constructionist position (Graesser, Singer, & Trabasso, 1994) regarding the construction of global coherence, which is, however, beyond the scope of this chapter. Temporal, spatial, local causal, goal 1, and goal 2 connections were scored on a dichotomous scale (continuous sentences = 1 and discontinuous sentences = 0). The distal causal variable, was, however, scored on a continuous scale and involved the total number of distal causal connections for each story sentence.

In Experiment 1, readers judged online how well sentences fit into the context of a story. These fit judgments were made on a six-point scale (1 = does not fit in at all, 6 = fits in very well). There were two groups of participants. One group read and made fit judgments on each story sentence only once. A second group read and made the same fit judgments twice. This second group allowed us to assess how fit judgments changed when readers knew the entire story. With the initial reading of a story, it was predicted that the sentence fit scores would increase as a function of spatial, temporal, and causal continuity with the immediately preceding sentence. Furthermore, fit scores would also increase as a function of the availability of goals and other distal causal antecedents from nonadjacent sentences.

In experiment 2, sentence reading times were collected to assess the impact of situational continuity on online processing time. It was predicted that sentences would be processed faster when more cues of situational continuity are available. It was also predicted that there would be convergence between the first reading fit scores and sentence reading times. More specifically, those factors that contribute to an increase in fit scores should also be associated with a decrease in processing time.

First and second reading fit scores and reading times were analyzed in a series of multiple regression analyses. Table 9.2 reports the b-weights and variance explained for each of the variables of interest from these analyses. A positive b-weight indicates that the dependent variable increases as a function of the presence of the independent variable, whereas a negative b-weight indicates it decreases as a function of the presence of the independent variable.

As can be seen in Table 9.2, there was convergence between the initial fit judgments and sentence reading times. Initial fit judgments increased and reading times decreased when a sentence was continuous with the prior context on the causal and intentional dimensions. There was not, however, convergence between the temporal and spatial dimensions. Fit judgments did not change as a function of temporal and spatial dimensions, although the spatial dimension was significant in a subject analysis and approached significance in an item analysis ($p < .10$). In contrast, reading times did decrease as a function of temporal continuities, but not as a function of spatial continuities. This convergence on the causal and inten-

TABLE 9.2
b-Weights and Variance Explained by the Regression Analysis
of Fit Judgments for the First and Rereading of the Stories
and Sentence Reading Times From Magliano et al. (1995)

	DEPENDENT MEASURE					
	First Reading		*Re-reading*		*Reading Times*	
PREDICTOR VARIABLES	*b-Weights*	*Variance Explained*	*b-Weights*	*Variance Explained*	*b-Weights*	*Variance Explained*
Time	.15	NS	−.20s	NS	−215is	2%
Space	.11s	NS	.19s	NS	77	NS
Local Causal	.24is	2%	−.08	NS	−231is	2%
Distal Causal	−.01s	NS	.18is	4%	−51	NS
Goal 1	.54is	8%	.30is	2%	−200is	2%
Goal 2	.88is	14%	.42is	3%	−396is	3%

Note. An *s* indicates that a variable was significant in a subject analysis and an *i* indicates that a variable was significant in an item analysis. NS indicates that a variable did not predict a significant amount of unique variance.

tional dimensions but not on the temporal and spatial dimensions suggests that monitoring the casual and intentional dimensions may be more central to story understanding than monitoring time and space. The lack of convergence between time and space could have resulted from task demands (cf. van den Broek, 1994, for a discussion of how task demands might operate online). Specifically, the monitoring of spatial continuity may have required more strategic processing (Zwaan & van Oostendorp, 1993) than did temporal continuity.

As expected, fit judgments made during rereading were based on distal causal and intentional dimensions, rather than local temporal, spatial, and causal dimensions. That is, these fit judgments were based on the extent to which a sentence was already integrated into a global representation of the story. This representation is globally structured both in terms of a goal-plan hierarchy and other distal causal relationships (e.g., Trabasso et al., 1989).

Magliano et al. (1995) provided clear evidence in support of the processing-time principles derived from the event-indexing model. Furthermore, their data indicated that readers monitor multiple dimensions of situational continuity when making fit judgments and during silent reading. Convergence across these two measures suggests that an increased perception of fit as a function of situational continuities is associated with a decrease in processing time. This convergence is consistent with Gernsbacher's (1990) structure-building framework. The structure-building model assumes that sentences that are coherently related to the prior story context are readily mapped onto an existing representation, and thus, are processed relatively more quickly. On the other hand, comprehension may be effortful when sentences are not perceived as being coherently related to the prior context. Readers must update the current representation of a text in order to resolve such breaks, which requires more processing time.

A second study that provides evidence for the processing time principles was conducted by Zwaan, Magliano, and Graesser (1995). In fact, these researchers developed the analyses of temporal and spatial continuities that were used by Magliano et al. (1995). They had participants read actual short stories, such as Edgar Allan Poe's "The Tell-Tale Heart." These stories were analyzed for temporal, spatial, and causal continuities. Unlike Magliano et al. (1995), causal continuities were not based on a causal-network analysis of the stories. They were, however, based on criteria of necessity and sufficiency (Mackie, 1980; Trabasso et al., 1989; van den Broek, 1990). It is also important to note that Zwaan et al. coded for discontinuity (i.e., continuous sentences = 0 and discontinuous sentences = 1), whereas Magliano et al. coded for continuity. Therefore, in the Zwaan et al. study, it was expected that reading times would increase, rather than decrease, if a situational dimension was monitored.

Zwaan, Magliano, and Graesser (1995) manipulated reading instruction. In the first experiment, half of the participants were instructed to read for pleasure and the other half were instructed to read for memory. These reading instructions allowed Zwaan, Magliano, and Graesser to assess the impact of reading goals on situation-model construction. Sentence reading times were collected. Table 9.3 shows the b-weight for the situational variables. The pattern in the reading times for the normal reading condition was consistent with Magliano et al. (1995). Specifically, reading times increased when there were temporal and causal discontinuities, but did not change as a function of spatial discontinuities. In contrast, reading times

TABLE 9.3
b-Weights From the Regression Analyses of Sentence Reading Times for
Experiments 1 and 2 from Zwaan, Magliano, and Graesser (1995)

| | EXPERIMENT 1 | | EXPERIMENT 2 | | | |
| | | | 1st Reading | | 2nd Reading | |
PREDICTOR VARIABLES	Normal Condition	Memory Condition	Normal Condition	Memory Condition	Normal Condition	Memory Condition
Time	297is	187s	189is	172s	141is	150is
Space	120	234s	107s	−18	166is	128s
Causality	201is	34	216is	163s	83	154is

Note. An s indicates that a variable was significant in a subject analysis and an i indicates that a variable was significant in an item analysis.

did not change as a function of situational discontinuities in the memory condition. Apparently, participants reading for memory focused their attention on encoding the explicit textbase at the expense of monitoring situational continuities.

A second experiment was designed, in part, to determine if readers monitor situational continuities differently when rereading a text. In this experiment, participants read each story twice. Again, participants were either instructed to read normally or to read for memory. The pattern of results for first reading replicated that of the first experiment for both the normal and memory reading conditions. For the normal condition, reading times increased when there were temporal and causal discontinuities, but did not change as a function of spatial continuities. For the memory condition, reading times did not change as a function of situational discontinuities. However, the pattern of results for rereading was different than that of the first reading for both instruction conditions. In the normal condition, reading times changed as a function of spatial continuities. Apparently, when rereading a story, readers monitored those dimensions that were not monitored during the first reading. In support of this claim, reading times varied as a function of temporal and causal continuity during rereading for the memory. Rereading allowed the participants reading for the memory to construct a situation model that was not constructed during the first reading.

In summary, unlike much of the prior research on situational model construction, Magliano et al. (1995) and Zwaan, Magliano, and Graesser (1995) investigated the impact of multiple situational dimensions on online processing. Consistent with the event-indexing model, both studies found evidence that readers monitor multiple dimensions of a situation model. Furthermore, they found evidence in favor of the online processing principle that states that sentence processing time should be mediated by the perception of fit with the prior situational context. The consistency in findings between Magliano et al. (1995) and Zwaan, Magliano, and Graesser (1995) is not trivial because they used experimenter-generated and literary texts, respectively. Such consistency across a wide range of text indicates that these results are generalizable across different reading circumstances.

Principles 2 and 3: Situational Continuities Have an Impact on Online Inference Processes

Magliano, Trabasso, and Graesser recently conducted a study to investigate the role of strategic processing in inference generation. They had participants read story sentences, one at a time, at their own pace. These were the same stories that were investigated by Graesser and Clark (1985). Participants were instructed to report their thoughts as they understood each story sentence. This section presents analyses of the think-aloud data, which directly test the inference-generation principles of the event-indexing model.

The think-aloud protocol analysis developed by Trabasso and Magliano (1996) was adopted to analyze the inferential content of the protocols collected by Magliano, Trabasso, and Graesser. The Trabasso and Magliano analysis identifies the kinds of inferences that are made during thinking aloud, as well as the information sources for these inferences. This analysis distinguishes between three general categories of inferences: explanations, predictions, and associations. Explanations are backward oriented in narrative time with respect to a focal sentence and provide reasons why a story event or action has occurred within the narrative context. Predictions are forward oriented in narrative time with respect to the focal sentence and provide the consequences of narrative events and actions. Associations are concurrent in time with respect to the focal sentence and typically provide elaborative and descriptive detail (e.g., the age of a character, the size or color of an object, or an instrument used to accomplish an action). These inferences are based on three information sources: the prior text, world knowledge, or a previously generated knowledge-base of inferences from the long-term memory representation for the text.

Trabasso and Magliano (1996) found that explanations predominate thinking aloud, comprising nearly 70% of the inferences. Furthermore, they found that prior text information, world knowledge, and prior inferences are primarily activated to generate explanations. However, associative inferences tended to be based on world knowledge rather than prior text or inferences. Consistent with Trabasso and Magliano (1996), Magliano, Trabasso, and Graesser found that explanations predominated understanding, followed by associations and predictions. Explanations constituted 55% of the inferences, 24% of the inferences were associations, and 22% of the inferences were predictions (see Trabasso & Magliano, in press, and Zwaan & Brown, 1996, for similar findings).

In order to determine the relationship between the thoughts produced during thinking aloud and situational continuities, Magliano, Trabasso, and Graesser analyzed story sentences to determine if they were continuous with the prior context along the character and object, temporal, spatial, and causal dimensions. Continuity in characters and objects was scaled by counting the number of new concrete nouns in each sentence. New concrete nouns were not mentioned anywhere in the prior text. Magliano, Trabasso, and Graesser used the criteria for determining temporal and spatial continuities that were described previously and used by Magliano et al. (1995). Again, time and space were scored on a dichotomous scale, but unlike Magliano et al. (1995) the scale marked discontinuities rather than continuities (i.e., continuities = 0 and discontinuities = 1). Causal continuity was determined by counting the number of direct causal connections between a sentence and the prior text, as identified by a causal network analysis. These stories contained very few explicit goals of characters. Therefore, they were not analyzed for continuities along the intentional dimension.

The inference-processing principle specifies the conditions for generating text-connecting and new knowledge-based inferences, respectively. In order to address this principle, Magliano, Trabasso, and Graesser identified the number of new explanations, predictions, and associations that occurred at each sentence. An inference was considered new if it was not generated in any of the prior sentences by any participant. There were 4.27 new explanations, 1.75 new predictions, and 2.23 new associations generated for each sentence. Thus, as is consistent with Trabasso and Magliano (1996), explanations predominate new knowledge-based inferences. Magliano, Trabasso, and Graesser also identified those inferences that were text-connecting inferences. Text-connecting inferences contained information that was mentioned in a prior sentence. Text-connecting inferences were almost exclusively explanations. There were .86 text-connecting inferences generated per sentence.

Magliano, Trabasso, and Graesser then calculated bivariate correlations between the breaks in situational continuity and the number of new explanations, associations, predictions, and text-connecting inferences that occurred at each story sentence. Table 9.4 contains these correlations. The correlations support Principle 2, which states that text-connecting inferences occur when the focal sentence is situationally connected with the prior context. Specifically, text-connecting inferences occur when there is an explicit cause(s) in the prior context, as identified through a causal-network analysis. Furthermore, these inferences do not occur when new characters and objects are mentioned (i.e., there is a break in the character

TABLE 9.4
The Correlations Between Character and Object, Temporal, Spatial,
and Causal Continuities and the Occurrence of New Explanations,
Association, Predictions, and Text-Connecting Inferences

INFERENCE CATEGORY	SITUATIONAL DIMENSION			
	Number of Concrete Nouns	Temporal Discontinuity	Spatial Discontinuity	Number to Text-Based Antecedents
New explanation	.20*	.22**	.12	−.24**
New associations	.23**	.13	.22**	−.34**
New predictions	−.15	−.18	−.19	−.14
Text connecting	−.30**	.03	.11	.27**

Note. ** = correlation is significant ($p < .05$) and * = correlation is significant ($p < .10$).

and object dimension). The correlations, with respect to new explanations and associations, also show support for Principle 3, which states that new knowledge-based inferences are generated when there are breaks in situational continuity. New explanations occur when there are breaks in temporal continuity and when new characters and objects are introduced. Furthermore, new explanations and associations do not occur when there is an explicit cause(s) in the prior story context (i.e., there is causal continuity). Thus, text-connecting inferences occur when there is continuity in the character and object and causal dimensions, whereas new explanations and associations occur when new characters and objects are introduced and when there are breaks in temporal, spatial, and causal continuities. Apparently, the occurrence of new predictions was not associated with situational continuities and discontinuities. Predictive inferences most likely occur when they are highly sufficient, given the prior context (van den Broek, 1990).

What impact does the number of breaks in situational continuity have on inference generation? Magliano, Trabasso, and Graesser determined the number of breaks in situational continuity for each sentence. The number of breaks ranged from zero (i.e., a sentence was continuous with the prior context on all four dimensions) to four (i.e., a sentence was discontinuous on all four dimensions). They then calculated the correlations between the number of breaks in situational continuity and the number of new explanations, associations, predictions, and text-connecting inferences. Figure 9.1 shows these relationships. There was a fairly steady increase in the number of new explanations generated as a function of the number of breaks in continuity ($r = .30$, $p < .05$), ranging from about three new explanations when there were no breaks to about seven new explanations when there were breaks in all four dimensions.

The number of new associations also increased as a function of the number of breaks in continuity ($r = .30$, $p < .05$). Unlike explanations, however, the number of new associations did not increase until there were breaks in three or more dimensions. Apparently, new associations primarily occur when the focal sentence is highly discontinuous with the prior context. For example, new associations are likely to occur most often at the beginning of new episodes, when readers are constructing indices for new characters, time, and space. These associations serve an important function of elaborating on the features of the newly constructed situation model. These data are consistent with Gernsbacher's (1990) structure-building framework, which assumes that the bulk of the knowledge-based inferences are generated in the initial stages of constructing a new framework.

The number of new predictions appeared to decrease as a function of the number of breaks in continuity, although this correlation only approached significance at a one-tailed test ($r = -.18$, $p = .12$). It is possible

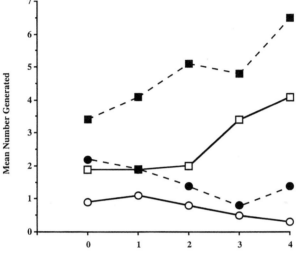

The Number of Breaks in Situational Indicies

FIG. 9.1. The mean number of new explanations, associations, predictions, and text-connecting inferences as a function of the number of breaks in situational continuity.

that there is a relationship between breaks in continuity and the sufficiency of a predicted event. That is, the sufficiency of a predicted event most likely increases when the focal event is situationally continuous with the prior context.

Finally, there was a tendency for breaks in continuity to be related to the occurrence of text-connecting inferences ($r = -.20$, $p = .10$). The number of text-connecting inferences decreased as a function of the number of breaks in situational continuity.

The inference-processing principles (i.e., Principles 2 and 3) should be related to the processing-time principle (i.e., Principle 1). More specifically, text-connecting inferences should facilitate processing, whereas new knowledge-based inferences should slow down processing. A series of two-step hierarchical multiple regression analyses were conducted to test this prediction. Sentence reading time was the dependent measure. In the first step of each analysis, a set of auxiliary variables were force-entered into the equation. These variables were the number of syllables in a sentence, mean word frequency of usage, and story coherence ranking. In the second step, the variable of interest was entered into the equations (e.g., new explanations). This procedure yielded an estimate of the unique variance accounted for by the variable of interest while partialing out the variance accounted for by the auxiliary variables. It also yielded a b-weight that indicated the direction of the relationship between the variable of interest and reading time. Table 9.5 contains the directional b-weights and variance explained by each of the predictor variables. As predicted, reading times increased as a function of new explanations and new associations, and decreased as a function of text-connecting inferences.

These data appear to be inconsistent with a claim made by Graesser (Graesser, Bertus, & Magliano, 1995; Graesser et al., 1994) that text-connecting inferences should be more time consuming to generate than knowledge-based inferences. The basis of this claim is that text-connecting inferences require a relatively effortful search through a long-term memory representation for a text, whereas knowledge-based inferences are based on the information that is activated through passive, associative mechanisms. Therefore, generating text-connecting inferences places more constraints on working memory than generating knowledge-based inferences. However, when unpacking the processes that contribute to sentence reading times, these data may not be as damaging to this claim as they may appear to be. In a simplistic view, there are two processes that may contribute to reading time: (a) the activation and search for relevant information in general knowledge or in a specific memory representation, and (b) the constructive and interpretive processes involved in incorporating that activated information into a coherent text representation (Kintsch, 1988). The impact of these two processes on reading time may differ. Specifically, it is possible that integrative processes may have a greater impact on reading time than activation processes. Although the activation of text-based information may be relatively time consuming when compared to the activation of knowledge-based information, text-based infor-

TABLE 9.5
b-weights and Variance Explained by the
Regression Analyses of Sentence Reading Times

PREDICTOR VARIABLES	b-Weights	Variance Explained
New explanation	25*	2%
New associations	67**	7%
New predictions	−.21	0%
Text connecting	−107*	3%

Note. ** = b-weight is significant ($p < .05$) and * = b-weight is significant ($p < .10$).

mation may aid in the integration of the focal sentence with the prior context. On the other hand, an interpretation of a focal sentence based primarily on new knowledge-based inferences may require relatively more effort to integrate into the existing structure.

In summary, we have again shown support for the event-indexing model. Specifically, we have shown that situational continuity is related to online inference processes. Thus, we extend Magliano et al. (1995) and Zwaan, Magliano, and Graesser (1995) by indicating the kinds of inferences that occur as a function of situational continuities and discontinuities. Breaks in continuity are resolved through new knowledge-based inferences, which are time consuming to generate. Continuity in the causal dimension facilitates the generation of text-connecting inferences, which, in turn, facilitates sentence processing.

Principle 4: Situational Continuities Influence the Long-Term Memory Representation for a Text

Zwaan, Langston, and Graesser (1995) conducted a study that provided direct evidence in favor of the memory principles of the event-indexing model. They developed a verb-clustering analysis to assess the role of the situation model in the organization of a text representation in long-term memory. They had subjects read the Graesser and Clark (1985) corpus of stories. After each narrative, the participants were presented with 10 verbs from that narrative. Participants were instructed to group verbs that they considered related in the context of the story. Zwaan, Langston, and Graesser (1995) used verbs in the clustering task because they are rich in semantic content (Miller & Johnson-Laird, 1976), are representative of the events depicted in simple sentences (Fillmore, 1968) and indicate changes in story elements. The dependent measure was the likelihood that two verbs would be grouped together in the verb-clustering task.

Zwaan and his colleagues were interested in three sources of potential influence on the verb-clustering task: the lexicon, the textual representation, and the situation model. The lexicon would have influence in the verb-clustering task if participants grouped verbs according to their relatedness in the lexicon in long-term memory, independent of their relatedness in the story context (both at the textual and situational levels). The textual representation would have an influence if participants grouped verbs according to their relatedness in the surface structure and propositional textbase representation. Finally, the situation model would have an influence if, as according to Principle 4, verb clustering is mediated by the degree of shared situational indices in long-term memory. That is, verbs that share situational indices (e.g., events that are causally connected and occurred in the same story time and space) should have a higher likelihood of being grouped together than verbs that do not share situational indices.

Zwaan and colleagues analyzed each possible verb pair on a number of variables representing relatedness along the lexical, textual, and situational dimensions. Relatedness in the lexicon was determined by having a group of participants group the verbs without reading the stories. The degree of relatedness between two verbs in the lexicon was operationalized as the likelihood that verbs were grouped together in this clustering task. Three variables captured textual relationships. Surface distance coded the distance between the two verbs, in number of words, in the surface structure of the text. Sentence connections coded whether two verbs were in the same sentence or not. And finally, argument overlap (Kintsch & van Dijk, 1978) coded whether two verbs share an argument and co-occur in working memory. The situational relationships were captured by determining if verbs were related along the protagonist, temporal, spatial, causal, and intentional dimensions. Two action verbs were considered related on the protagonist dimension if they were performed by the same character. Two verbs were related on the temporal dimension if they occurred within the same narrative time. Two verbs were related on the spatial dimension if they occurred within the same narrative space. Two verbs were related on the causal dimension if one verb described an event that provided a necessary and sufficient condition for the other. Finally, two verbs were related on the intentionality dimension if they described actions that were part of the same goal plan.

Participants performed the clustering task twice. On the first occasion, participants read a story, turned the page, and then performed the clustering task for that particular story. Participants were required to group verbs based on their memory for a story. This was called the memory condition. After all the stories were read and the initial clustering tasks were performed, participants were presented with the stories again. This time the verb clustering was performed with the stories present. This was called the text-present condition.

In the memory condition, the likelihood that verbs were grouped together significantly increased as a function of shared indices in the protagonist (Beta weight = .30), temporal (Beta weight = .16), spatial (Beta weight = .24), causal (Beta weight = .17), and intentional (Beta weight = .20) dimensions. Thus, these data clearly support the memory principle of the event-indexing model. The mental lexicon was also a significant predictor of verb clustering (Beta weight = .39). This suggests that the subjects' situational representations were not sufficiently strong during the clustering task, so that they partly had to rely on their mental lexicon. Interestingly, the likelihood that verbs were grouped together did not increase as a function of the textual variables. This counterintuitive finding suggests that subjects did not have the textual representations available during the clustering task.

In the text-present condition, all five situational variables were significant; the likelihood that verbs were grouped together significantly increased as a function of shared indices in the protagonist (Beta weight = .38), temporal (Beta weight = .12), spatial (Beta weight = .34), causal (Beta weight = .19), and intentional (Beta weight = .10) dimensions. Thus, again, there is clear support for the memory principle. The lexicon was also again significant, but made a much smaller contribution toward explaining variance than in the memory condition (Beta weight = .11). Interestingly, two surface-structure variables were significant in this condition. Specifically, the likelihood of grouping verbs decreased as a function of distance in the surface structure (Beta weight = −.15) and increased as a function of being in the same sentence (Beta weight = .11). These results suggest that the text must be present for textual relations to have an impact on verb clustering. In a second experiment, Zwaan, Langston, and Graesser (1995) reversed the order of the memory and text-present condition and replicated the first experiment. This showed that the pattern observed in their first experiment was not due to a dual-test effect.

In summary, Zwaan, Langston, and Graesser (1995) showed strong evidence that the memory for a story is structured by the situational indices specified by the event-indexing model. Their clustering analysis also provides an extremely useful task for determining the impact of multiple factors (e.g., lexical, textual, and situational factors) on the memory for a story. With this task, they showed evidence that each of the situational indices has a unique impact on the memory for a text. This clearly demonstrates that situational models provide multidimensional representations of a story. The relationships among situational dimensions need to be investigated and there are, to our knowledge, no models currently available that make specific predictions about these relationships. The event-indexing model is a step in this direction.

CONCLUSIONS

In this chapter, we described the event-indexing model (Zwaan, Langston, & Graesser, 1995) of situation-model construction. The model assumes that readers monitor changes in characters and objects, time, space, causality, and intentionality that occur within a story. In support of the event-indexing model, the research presented in this chapter suggests that situation models are multidimensional, rather than unidimensional. Readers monitor what characters are involved in a story, what events are happening to them, what goals they have in light of those events, and what they are doing to achieve those goals, all within narrative time and space.

We presented studies that indicate that changes in these situational dimensions have an impact on online processing time, inference generation, and the long-term memory for a story.

Most theories of situation-model construction focus on one dimension of a situation model (e.g., Trabasso et al., 1989; Glenberg, Kruley, & Langston, 1995). One exception is Gernsbacher's (1990) structure-building framework. This framework assumes that situational discontinuities prompt readers to shift from building a main mental structure to building a substructure. This shift is resource consuming. The studies testing the processing-time principle (Principle 1) provide clear evidence for this assumption. We view the event-indexing model as an extension of Gernsbacher's framework. Specifically, the event-indexing model makes specific assumptions regarding the role that situational continuities play in online inference processing and memory for a text.

Can we make any conclusions regarding the relative importance of the different dimensions in narrative comprehension? Although the research presented here did not directly test this, it does suggest that the causal and intentional dimensions are most central to narrative comprehension. These two dimensions were significant predictors of virtually all of the dependent measures in the four studies. This finding suggests that events and intentional actions of characters are central to situation models. These causal and motivational inferences provide the foundations of situational coherence in story understanding. There are, however, conditions in which monitoring temporality and spatiality are important for establishing text coherence (Zwaan, van den Broek, Truitt, & Sunder-Meir, 1996). Future research should further specify the circumstances that influence the monitoring of the different dimensions of situational continuity. Such endeavors will undoubtedly lead to a more complete understanding of the nature of narrative comprehension.

REFERENCES

Anderson, A., Garrod, S. C., & Sanford, A. J. (1983). The accessibility of pronominal antecedents as a function of episode shifts in narrative text. *Quarterly Journal of Experimental Psychology, 36A*, 1–12.

Brewer, W. F., & Lichtenstein, E. H. (1982). Stories are to entertain: A structural-affect theory of stories. *Journal of Pragmatics, 6*, 473–486.

Chafe, W. L. (1979). The flow of thought and the flow of language. In T. Givon (Ed.), *Syntax and semantics, Vol. 12: Discourse and syntax* (pp. 159–181). New York: Academic Press.

Collingwood, R. G. (1938). On the so-called idea of causation. *Proceedings of the Aristotelian Society, XXXVIII*, 85–108.

Dahlgren, K. (1988). *Naive semantics for natural language understanding.* Boston: Kluwer Academic.

Dopkins, S. (1996). Representation of superordinate goal inferences in memory. *Discourse Processes, 21*, 85–104.

Dopkins, S., Klin, C., & Myers, J. L. (1993). The accessibility of information about goals during the processing of narrative texts. *Journal of Experimental Psychology: Learning, Memory, and Cognition, 19*, 70–80.

Duchan, J. F., Bruder, G. A., & Hewitt, L. E. (Eds.). (1995). *Deixis in narrative: A cognitive science perspective.* Hillsdale, NJ: Lawrence Erlbaum Associates.

Fillmore, C. J. (1968). Toward a modern theory of case. In D. A. Reibel & S. A. Schano (Eds.), *Modern studies in English* (pp. 361–375). Englewood Cliffs, NJ: Prentice-Hall.

Fletcher, C. R., & Bloom, C. P. (1988). Causal reasoning in the comprehension of simple narrative texts. *Journal of Memory and Language, 27*, 235–244.

Gernsbacher, M. A. (1990). *Language comprehension as structure building.* Hillsdale, NJ: Lawrence Erlbaum Associates.

Gernsbacher, M. A., & Givon, T. (Eds.). (1995). *Coherence in spontaneous text.* Philadelphia, PA: John Benjamins.

Givon, T. (1995). Coherence in text vs. coherence in mind. In M. A. Gernsbacher & T. Givon (Eds.), *Coherence in spontaneous text* (pp. 189–214). Philadelphia, PA: John Benjamins.

Glenberg, A. M., Kruley, P., & Langston, W. E. (1995). Analogical processes in comprehension: Simulation of mental model. In M. A. Gernsbacher (Ed.), *Handbook of psycholinguistics* (pp. 609–640). San Diego, CA: Academic Press.

Glenberg, A. M., Meyer, M., & Lindem, K. (1987). Mental models contribute to foregrounding during text comprehension. *Journal of Memory and Language, 26*, 69–83.

Goldman, S. R., & Varnhagen, C. K. (1986). Memory for embedded and sequential story structures. *Journal of Memory and Language, 25*, 401–418.

Graesser, A. C. (1981). *Prose comprehension beyond the word.* New York: Springer-Verlag.

Graesser, A. C., Bertus, E. L., & Magliano, J. P. (1995). Inference generation during the comprehension of narrative text. In E. J. O'Brien & R. F. Lorch (Eds.), *Sources of coherence in text comprehension* (pp. 295–319). Hillsdale, NJ: Lawrence Erlbaum Associates.

Graesser, A. C., & Clark, L. F. (1985). *Structures and procedures of implicit knowledge.* Norwood, NJ: Ablex.

Graesser, A. C., Singer, M., & Trabasso, T. (1994). Constructing inferences during narrative text comprehension. *Psychological Review, 101*, 371–395.

Kintsch, W. (1988). The role of knowledge in discourse comprehension: A construction-integration model. *Psychological Review, 95*, 163–182.

Kintsch, W., & van Dijk, T. A. (1978). Toward a model of text comprehension and production. *Psychological Review, 85*, 363–394.

Long, D. L., & Golding, J. M. (1993). Superordinate goal inferences: Are they automatically generated during comprehension. *Discourse Processes, 16*, 55–73.

Long, D. L., Golding, J. M., & Graesser, A. C. (1993). A test of on-line status of goal-related inferences. *Journal of Memory and Language, 31*, 634–647.

Lutz, M. F., & Radvansky, G. A. (1997). The fate of completed goal information. *Journal of Memory and Language, 36*, 293–310.

Mackie, J. L. (1980). *The cement of the universe.* Oxford, England: Clarendon.

Magliano, J. P., Baggett, W. B., Johnson, B. K., & Graesser, A. C. (1993). The time course in which causal antecedent and causal consequence inferences are generated. *Discourse Processes, 16*, 35–53.

Magliano, J. P., Trabasso, T., & Langston, M. C. (1995). *Cohesion and coherence in sentence and story understanding.* Unpublished manuscript.

Mandler, J. M. (1986). On the comprehension of temporal order. *Language and Cognitive Processes, 1*, 309–320.

Miller, G. A., & Johnson-Laird, P. N. (1976). *The perception of language.* Cambridge, England: Cambridge University Press.

Morrow, D. G. (1985). Prominent characters and events organize narrative understanding. *Journal of Memory and Language, 24,* 304–319.

Morrow, D. G., Bower, G. H., & Greenspan, S. L. (1989). Updating situation models during comprehension. *Journal of Memory and Language, 23,* 441–469.

Morrow, D. G., Greenspan, S. L., & Bower, G. H. (1987). Accessibility and situation models during comprehension. *Journal of Memory and Language, 26,* 165–187.

Myers, J. L., Shinjo, M., & Duffy, S. A. (1987). Degree of causal relatedness and memory. *Journal of Memory and Language, 26,* 453–465.

Ohtsuka, K., & Brewer, W. F. (1992). Discourse organization in the comprehension of temporal order in narrative texts. *Discourse Processes, 15,* 317–336.

Segal, E. M. (1995). A cognitive-phenomenological theory of fictional narrative. In J. F. Duchan, G. A. Bruder, & L. E. Hewitt (Eds.), *Deixis in narrative: A cognitive science perspective* (pp. 61–78). Hillsdale, NJ: Lawrence Erlbaum Associates.

Singer, M., Halldorson, M., Lear, J. C., & Andrusiak, P. (1992). Validation of causal bridging inferences in discourse understanding. *Journal of Memory and Language, 31,* 543–572.

Stein, N. L., & Glenn, C. G. (1979). An analysis of story comprehension in elementary school children. In R. O. Freedle (Ed.), *New directions in discourse processing.* Hillsdale, NJ: Lawrence Erlbaum Associates.

Suh, S. (1988). *Converging evidence for causal inferences during comprehension.* Unpublished doctoral dissertation, The University of Chicago.

Suh, S., & Trabasso, T. (1993). Inferences during reading: Converging evidence from discourse analysis, talk-aloud protocols, and recognition priming. *Journal of Memory and Language, 32,* 279–301.

Trabasso, T., & Magliano, P. A. (in press). How do children understand what they read and what can we do to help them? In M. Graves, P. van den Broek, & B. Taylor (Eds.), *The first R: A right of all children.* New York: Teachers College, Columbia University Press.

Trabasso, T., & Magliano, J. P. (1996). Conscious understanding during comprehension. *Discourse Processes, 21,* 255–287.

Trabasso, T., Secco, S., & van den Broek, P. (1984). Causal cohesion and story coherence. In H. Mandl, N. L. Stein, & T. Trabasso (Eds.), *Learning and comprehension of text* (pp. 83–111). Hillsdale, NJ: Lawrence Erlbaum Associates.

Trabasso, T., & Sperry, L. (1985). Causal relatedness and importance of story events. *Journal of Memory and Language, 24,* 595–611.

Trabasso, T., & Suh, S. (1993). Understanding text: Achieving explanatory coherence through on-line inferences and mental operations in working memory. *Discourse Processes, 16,* 3–34.

Trabasso, T., & van den Broek, P. (1985). Causal thinking and the representation of narrative events. *Journal of Memory and Language, 24,* 612–630.

Trabasso, T., van den Broek, P., & Suh, S. (1989). Logical necessity and transitivity of causal relations in the representation of stories. *Discourse Processes, 12,* 1–25.

van den Broek, P. (1990). Causal inferences and the comprehension of narrative texts. In A. C. Graesser & G. H. Bower (Eds.), *Inferences and text comprehension.* New York: Academic Press.

van den Broek, P. (1994). Comprehension and memory of narrative texts: Inferences and coherence. In M. A. Gernsbacher (Ed.), *Handbook of psycholinguistics* (pp. 539–588). San Diego, CA: Academic Press.

van den Broek, P., & Lorch, R. F. (1993). Network representations of causal relations in memory for narrative texts: Evidence from primed recognition. *Discourse Processes, 16,* 75–98.

van Dijk, T. A., & Kintsch, W. (1983). *Strategies of discourse comprehension.* New York: Academic Press.

Zwaan, R. A. (in press). Processing narrative time shifts. *Journal of Experimental Psychology: Learning, Memory, and Cognition.*

Zwaan, R. A., & Brown, C. M. (1996). The influence of language proficiency and comprehension skill on situation-model construction. *Discourse Processes, 21,* 289–328.

Zwaan, R. A., Langston, M. C., & Graesser, A. C. (1995). The construction of situation models in narrative comprehension: An event-indexing model. *Psychological Science, 6,* 292–297.

Zwaan, R. A., Magliano, J. P., & Graesser, A. C. (1995). Dimensions of situation model construction in narrative comprehension. *Journal of Experimental Psychology: Learning, Memory, and Cognition, 21,* 386–397.

Zwaan, R. A., van den Broek, P., Truitt, T. L., & Sunder-Meier, B. (1996, November). *Causal coherence and the accessibility of object location in narrative comprehension.* Paper presented at the 37th annual meeting of the Psychonomic Society, Chicago, IL.

Zwaan, R. A., & van Oostendorp, H. (1993). Do readers construct spatial representations in naturalistic story comprehension? *Discourse Processes, 16,* 125–143.

Chapter 10

Learning From Text: Structural Knowledge Assessment in the Study of Discourse Comprehension

Evelyn C. Ferstl
Walter Kintsch
University of Colorado at Boulder

Domain knowledge is an important factor in discourse comprehension (for reviews of this literature, see Schneider, Körkel, & Weinert, 1990; Voss, Fincher-Kiefer, Greene, & Post, 1986). In general, readers with high domain knowledge perform better than readers with low domain knowledge on a variety of comprehension tasks. Knowledge effects have been demonstrated by manipulating subjects' expertise (e.g., Spilich, Vesonder, Chiesi, & Voss, 1979), or by providing subjects with different amounts of prior knowledge (e.g., Bransford & Johnson, 1972).

However, not only does background knowledge facilitate reading comprehension, reading a text also involves the formation of episodic representations of the text. Most current discourse processing theories postulate that these representations occur on different levels. One level encodes the semantic content and structure of the text (the textbase, in the terminology of van Dijk & Kintsch, 1983), while a second level encodes a more general understanding of what the text is about. This level of representation has variously been called the mental model of the text (Johnson-Laird, 1983), the text model (Perfetti, 1985), discourse model (Altmann & Steedman, 1988), or situation model (van Dijk & Kintsch, 1983). The situation model is defined as the integration of the episodic text memory with prior domain knowledge. Both background knowledge and text information determine the contents of the situation model. Studying how readers construct a textbase representation corresponds to investigating how readers learn a text, that is, how they memorize the text in order to reproduce it.

Studying how readers construct a situation model, on the other hand, corresponds to investigating how they learn *from* text. Thus, if we are not only interested in comprehension, but also in how readers acquire knowledge from text, we need to study how situation models are constructed. Although there is empirical evidence for the psychological reality of a situational representation (e.g., Fletcher & Chrysler, 1990; Kintsch, Welsch, Schmalhofer, & Zimny, 1990; Perrig & Kintsch, 1985; Schmalhofer & Glavanov, 1986; Speelman & Kirsner, 1990), many of these studies used texts that are specifically designed to elicit a known situational representation, for instance, a spatial description. If we want to study learning from texts occurring in the real world, a more general description of the situation model is desirable. Furthermore, a prerequisite for studying whether and how situation models are constructed online is an accurate and complete description of the result of this online processing.

The goal of this chapter is to present an empirical methodology that permits such a general description. In order to be useful as a tool in both text comprehension research and educational applications, this methodology was developed to be efficient and objective. In addition, the method was intended to be independent of the specific text and knowledge domain, so that it could be adopted to study the situation model and learning from text in a wide variety of contexts.

The most promising approach to studying the situation model seems to be the assessment of its structure, because learning involves more than the acquisition of new concepts and facts. Learning often consists of updating previous knowledge by changing associative relationships between already-known concepts. Because the situation model depends on individuals' background knowledge and may contain elements that were not explicitly mentioned in the text, an accurate description must include an assessment of both the text memory and the reader's background knowledge.

The issue of how knowledge is represented has been influential in cognitive psychology and artificial intelligence research (for a review, see Rumelhart & Norman, 1988). A variety of empirical paradigms have been developed to assess knowledge structures (Gammack, 1987; Olson & Biolsi, 1991). These methodologies have been mainly applied to assess stable, long-term memory structures, in particular the organizations of semantic domains (e.g., Fillenbaum & Rapoport, 1971; Rips, Shoben, & Smith, 1973) and expert knowledge (Adelson, 1981; Chi, Feltovich, & Glaser, 1981; Murphy & Wright, 1984). In contrast, changes in knowledge structures have not been in the focus of this research. As Goldsmith and Johnson (1990) pointed out, few applications of structural assessment are available that address the question of how knowledge is updated over time (e.g., Ballstaedt & Mandl, 1991; Chi & Koeske, 1983; Graesser & Clark, 1985).

Similarly, few empirical studies assessed the structure of episodic memory, in particular the structure of text memory (e.g., Britton & Gulgöz, 1991; Graesser, Robertson, & Anderson, 1981; McNamara, Kintsch, Songer, & Kintsch, 1996; Zwaan, Langston, & Graesser, 1995).

That structural assessment is a relatively rare tool for text comprehension research is somewhat surprising, given that there is a small, but interesting literature on the use of multidimensional scaling techniques from the late 1970s. Bisanz, LaPorte, Vesonder, and Voss (1978) and Gliner, Goldman, and Hubert (1983) used similarity judgments and a sorting task to assess the semantic space of animals. Although the MDS structures before reading reflected the dimensions size and predativity (Henley, 1969), the structures after reading a narrative reflected two dimensions induced by specific text information. Using more naturalistic texts, Stanners, Price, and Painton (1982) and LaPorte and Voss (1979) conducted relatedness rating tasks and found that the temporal order of selected concepts was reflected in the MDS solutions. Whereas in the former study no other results were readily interpretable, the latter showed that the solutions after reading were sensitive to variations in the text information. The themes of the stories appeared as central items, and clusters represented episodes within the texts. Even though these results seemed promising, the approach was not pursued further.

One reason for this was that the assumptions necessary for multidimensional scaling are too restrictive. The psychological proximities between items are assumed to be distances in a geometric space, which excludes, for instance, the use of asymmetric proximities. Furthermore, the resulting dimensions should be interpretable in a meaningful way. Thus, the method is only applicable if both the knowledge domain and the text information have a clear-cut dimensional structure.

A second reason might have been that the statistical methods for data analysis were not sufficient. The comparisons of the empirical structures were based on the MDS solutions, but not on raw data. In most cases, these solutions were derived from data aggregated across subjects. The question of how the response patterns change for individual subjects, as a function of test time and experimental condition, was not specifically tested with traditional inferential statistics (cf. Zwaan, Langston, & Graesser, 1995).

Third, and most importantly, the studies were not based on a text comprehension theory. To be able to formulate specific predictions about the structural representations, we need to understand *how* text information and background knowledge are combined.

More recent studies have avoided these problems. For instance, Britton and Gulgöz (1991) used relatedness ratings to study the efficacy of theoretically motivated text revisions. Correlations of readers' ratings with experts' structures were higher after reading the revised versions than after reading the original text. In contrast, McNamara et al. (1996) showed that the coherence of a text improved readers' representations only if they did not have the relevant background knowledge. In this latter study, a sorting task was used to assess readers' knowledge structures before and after reading, and the dependent variable was the similarity of the resulting representations to an ideal categorical structure.

These two studies illustrate that knowledge assessment paradigms can be used to test theoretical predictions, and that they are not restricted to an interpretation of aggregated data. However, the tasks used in these and the previously described studies have some features that limit their applicability.

In a similarity rating task, subjects are presented with a pair of words. On a rating scale, they estimate how similar, or how related, the words are to each other. This procedure has the advantage of providing rich knowledge structures specifying a relationship for each pair of concepts. The cost for this completeness is that the task is feasible only for a small number of items. For any knowledge domain of even moderate size, paired comparisons are simply too numerous. With a set of 10 words, for instance, 45 comparisons are sufficient, whereas for a set of 30 words, several hundred comparisons are needed. If the knowledge assessment is time-consuming and effortful, though, it is likely to interfere with eventual effects of text information.

In a sorting task, the trade-off between feasibility of the task and richness of the resulting structures is reversed. Subjects are presented with a pile of cards, each containing one keyword. They then sort the cards into groups, based on any criterion they wish to adopt. If two items were sorted into the same group, they are assumed to be related. This task is straightforward even with a larger number of items. However, the resulting structures for each individual are relatively sparse. All relationships are assumed to have equal strength, and items in the same group are not differentiated at all.

In this chapter, we propose a knowledge assessment paradigm for text comprehension research without these limitations. In a cued association task, subjects are presented with a word, and they are asked to provide an association to it. A relationship between the cue and the response is then assumed. Two experiments document the practicability of the task even with a larger number of items, while yielding structures rich enough to allow analysis of individual data. The goal is to show that the results can be used to describe the structure of episodic text memory as a function of structural properties of both text information and the background knowledge of the reader.

THE CUED ASSOCIATION PARADIGM

In this section, we describe in detail the building blocks for the studies. We summarize our theoretical framework that specifies an appropriate knowledge representation scheme. This representation allows us to capture background knowledge, text information, and episodic text memory in the same format. After providing the necessary notation, we describe how the theory yields a description of the text's structure, and how empirical assessment yields comparable background knowledge and text memory structures.

Text Comprehension Theory and Knowledge Representation

The framework used for this work is the discourse theory of Kintsch and van Dijk (1978; van Dijk & Kintsch, 1983). This theory provides a method for analyzing the structure of a text, as well as a psychologically relevant knowledge representation scheme. Text information is assumed to be encoded in the form of propositions, which are connected according to argument overlap. Thus, a theoretically motivated analysis of the ideal text structure is possible. In addition, the theory specifies a mechanism for how background knowledge is used in comprehension, and how a text representation is constructed.

Following Kintsch (1988, 1989), the background knowledge, as well as the text memory, is represented in the form of associative networks. The nodes in these networks correspond to concepts or propositions, whereas the associative links connecting them are directed and unlabeled. Describing the structure of text memory in this framework corresponds to identifying the nodes in the network, and estimating the association strengths of the links. Gammack (1987) called these two steps *concept elicitation* and *structure elicitation*, respectively.

Domain and Text

We wanted to use a general knowledge domain with a relatively stable, well-known structure, which would nevertheless be sufficiently flexible for allowing at least transient changes. We chose the script of a children's birthday party. A script's general representation is commonly shared, but it can also be newly instantiated depending on current information (Schank & Abelson, 1977).

The text consisted of a simple narrative about a little boy's birthday. Although the events described contain many script-relevant elements, the party itself is not described. The text was written in the style of a children's story, and is therefore easily comprehensible. The story, which is provided in Appendix A, is about 600 words long.

Concept Elicitation

Because we wanted to capture effects of both background knowledge and text information, the concept elicitation involved two steps. First, we used a Free Association task to elicit words related to the domain of the story, *Children's Birthday Party*. Seventeen subjects were asked to write down as many words as they could think of when hearing this cue. From the 418 different responses, the 30 concepts were selected which more than 35% of the subjects had provided. Twenty of these high-frequency associations were mentioned in the story about Tim's birthday, but some of them in a rather unusual context.

The second step consisted of identifying additional key concepts in the story. Thirty words were selected. Twelve of these were low-frequency associations in the birthday party script, and 18 had not been associated to the script at all. Taking these two sets together yielded a list of 60 selected keywords, denoted the *List*.

For a rough measure of how important each of the 60 words was to the script, we used the frequency with which it was mentioned. This measure is referred to as *Script Frequency* in the remainder of the chapter. For a rough approximation of how important each word was in the text, we counted how often it occurred in the text. This measure is referred to as *Text Frequency*. The List is shown in Appendix B, together with the script frequency and the text frequency for each word.

Notation

The psychological terminology of an associative network consisting of nodes and links is easily translated into a mathematical notation. If the network contains n nodes, its structure is fully described by the $n \times n$ matrix $A = (a_{i,j})_{i,j=1 \ldots n}$ of association strength values. These values are assumed to be proximities; that is, a larger coefficient $a_{i,j}$ indicates a stronger associative link from the node i to the node j. If $a_{i,j} = 0$, no associative relationship between i and j holds.

For our study, the nodes of the network consisted of the 60 selected keywords. Thus, all associative structures considered are equivalent to a 60 $\times$ 60 matrix containing the non-negative association strength values for each pair of words from the List. In the following section, we define such a structure to capture the text information. Then, we describe the structure-elicitation paradigm for the empirical networks, and define assocation matrices based on the resulting data.

Definition of the Text Structure

For defining an associative network approximating the text structure, the story about Tim's birthday was first propositionalized (e.g., Turner & Greene, 1978). The text consisted of about 200 propositions, not counting single concepts. Connections between propositions were defined according to argument overlap. Of course, this principle provides only a minimal structure, because other coherence relations, such as causal, temporal, or spatial relations, also contribute to the structure of text information (e.g., Trabasso & Sperry, 1985; Gernsbacher, 1990; Zwaan, Magliano, & Graesser, 1995). However, argument overlap is an objective criterion based on the wording of a text only. It is applicable to any type of text—be it narrative or expository—independent of its specific contents.

The resulting propositional structure was then used to define connections between keywords on the List. If two concepts were arguments of the same proposition, of neighboring propositions, or of propositions two steps apart in the structure, a text connection between the two concepts was assumed. We opted to include these latter connections because they provided a richer structure that seemed to capture the content-based relationships more clearly.

For example, the sentence " 'You have to give party favors to your friends,' the clown said." is represented by the three propositions

(P1) say [clown, P2]

(P2) have-to [Tim, P3]

(P3) give [Tim, party favors, friends].

Using the stronger requirement of connecting only concepts from adjacent propositions would link CLOWN to only one other word, TIM. Including connections from propositions two steps apart provides additional connections to PARTY FAVORS and FRIENDS. To illustrate the text network resulting from the propositional structure, Fig. 10.1 shows a section of it. To make the graph more easily readable, this figure shows the nodes and links from the third paragraph of the story only. In addition, the numerous links to TIM are omitted.

The 60×60 – matrix $T = (t_{i,j})_{i,j = 1 \ldots 60}$ defining the Text Structure was obtained from this network by assigning the coefficient $t_{i,j} = 1$ to a pair of concepts if there was a text connection between them, and the coefficient $t_{i,j} = 0$ otherwise.

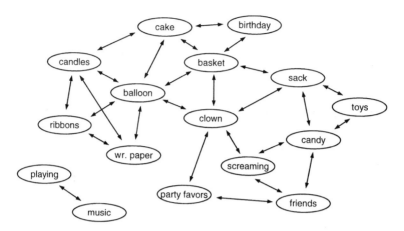

FIG. 10.1. The text structure representing the third paragraph of the story.
Links are defined according to propositional overlap in the text, and links
to and from TIM are omitted.

Empirical Structure Elicitation

For an estimation of readers' knowledge structures, a Cued Association
paradigm is proposed. As described previously, this task involves the presentation of a cue, and requires subjects to respond with the first word
that comes to mind. An associative link from the cue to the response is
then assumed. In order to obtain richer structures containing more links,
we chose to modify this basic paradigm slightly and allow subjects to provide
up to three answers to each of the 60 words on the List.

Based on the results of this task, asymmetric proximity matrices A can
be calculated. Taking into account the order of the responses to a given
cue, a coefficient $a_{i,j} = 1$ is assigned to a pair of nodes (i, j) if j is the first
answer to the cue i. If it is the second, a weaker connection strength $a_{i,j}$
$= 1/2$ is assigned, and $a_{i,j} = 1/3$ if it is the third. All other connections are
set to 0, that is, $a_{i,k} = 0$ if k is not an answer to the cue i. Answers that do
not come from the List are ignored, because they do not define relationships between the selected keywords.

EXPERIMENT 1

The first experiment was conducted to see whether the Cued Association
paradigm was indeed applicable to the study of learning from text. We
assessed subjects' knowledge structures before reading to obtain a description of their background knowledge structures. After reading, the same
assessment was repeated to obtain a description of their episodic text

memory. The question of interest was whether the changes in response patterns could be attributed to the use of text information.

Participants and Procedure

Forty-two undergraduate students at the University of Colorado at Boulder participated in the experiment as part of a course requirement. To avoid order effects in the Cued Association task, and to familiarize the subjects with the domain, the first task was to read through the List. For this familiarization task, a computer presented each of the 60 keywords twice, at a rate of 1.25 sec per word. The order was randomized.

After viewing the List, a response sheet for the Cued Association task was handed to the subject. On this sheet, the 60 words from the List were typed in random order. Next to each word were three blank lines for the responses. The written instructions asked the subject to write down next to each word the one, two, or three words that first came to mind. Subjects were told to use words from the List presented before. The instructions stressed that it was important to respond spontaneously and that there were no correct answers. The task was completed in about 10 minutes.

For the subsequent reading task, the instructions were to read the story carefully, at normal reading speed, and to try to understand the contents. In addition, one group of subjects was instructed to memorize the text, whereas another group was instructed to relate the contents to their own experience. The computer then presented the story one sentence at a time, and subjects controlled the presentation rate. Reading of the story took about 3 to 4 minutes.

After reading, the Cued Association task was repeated. Each subject received an answer sheet with the cues printed in a different random order than before reading. The instructions were identical to those used before, that is, subjects were *not* explicitly told to use the text information for their answers.[1]

Results

Reading instructions did not influence the results of the Cued Association task, and the data are thus collapsed across conditions. For each subject and each test time, association matrices were derived as described.

Feasibility of the Cued Association Task. The Cued Association task was selected because it was hypothesized to be less tedious than relatedness ratings, and thus an appropriate task for the assessment of large network

---

[1]Several other subtasks were part of this experiment (Ferstl, 1991). Only those that pertain to the Cued Association paradigm are described here.

structures. After conducting the experiment, it was clear that subjects did not have difficulties understanding the instructions. The average number of answers given was 116 (sd = 36.1) before reading the text, and 118 (sd = 37.0) after reading. These numbers show that subjects did give a response to most items, and that they took advantage of the possibility to provide more than one association to each cue. Furthermore, there was no difference between the number of answers given before and after reading ($F(1, 40) < 1$), indicating that subjects did not change their response strategies. Because the task took only about 10 minutes, the number of concepts could easily be extended beyond the already large number of 60 keywords.

The second open question was whether the individuals' network structures would be rich enough to allow analyses by subjects. Defining the associative matrices requires a relatively large number of answers from the List, because all the other answers are excluded. The majority of the responses were from the List of selected keywords. Only 30% of the answers had to be excluded for the definition of the connection matrices. For a test of whether the number of answers changed as a function of test time, we defined the *network size* as the sum of all the link strengths in the matrix A representing the network

$$\text{netsize}(A) = \Sigma_{i,j} \, a_{i,j} \qquad (10.1)$$

This score roughly represents the number of answers given that were from the selected List. However, it is more differentiated because it takes into account whether a word was the first, second, or third answer to a cue. Before reading, the mean network size was 54.3 (sd = 25.6), which increased significantly to 66.4 (sd = 22.3) after reading ($F(1, 40) = 27.9$, $p < 0.01$). More answers from the List were given after reading than before. At this point, we cannot decide whether this is due to repeated exposure to the keywords or to text influences.

Text Similarity. To assess the influence of the text information on the answers directly, we used the propositional Text Structure T as described previously. For each subject and each test time, a text similarity score was defined by calculating the proportion of subjects' links that were also present in T. Formally defined in Equation 10.1, these scores are obtained by adding up the link strength values for only those connections that were included in the Text Structure, and dividing the result by the sum of all links.

$$\text{text similarity} \, (A,T) = 1/\text{netsize}(A) \times (\Sigma_{i,j}(t_{i,j} \times a_{i,j})) \qquad (10.2)$$

These scores increased dramatically after reading ($F(1, 40) = 168.5$, $p < 0.01$). Before reading, the proportion of text links in the association matrices was 0.15 on average ($sd = 0.06$). After reading, it more than doubled to 0.36 ($sd = 0.10$). This result shows that the networks after reading contained links directly corresponding to text information. Because the text structure was derived using only propositional overlap, the influence of the text is even underestimated.

Centrality of Concepts. The respective influence of background knowledge and text information can also be evaluated using an item analysis. Specifically, we hypothesized that the centrality of a word, that is, how strongly the word was connected to other words in the structure, would depend on the script frequency before reading, and on the text frequency after reading.

For this item analysis, data were first aggregated across subjects. Group matrices were obtained for both test times by adding up all the individuals' matrices. As a measure of centrality, we then borrowed the concept of the *degree of a node* from graph theory (e.g., Ore, 1963). Specifically the in-degree was defined as the sum of all the links going into the node, and the out-degree as the sum of all the links going out of the node.

$$\text{in-degree}(k) = \Sigma_i \, a_{i,k}, \text{ out-degree}(k) = \Sigma_j \, a_{k,j} \qquad (10.3)$$

The in-degree corresponds roughly to a measure of how often a word was mentioned as an answer to any cue. The out-degree of a word reflects the number of answers to this word that were from the List of selected keywords. For each word and each of the two test times, the in-degree and the out-degree were calculated. Spearman rank-order correlations were calculated between the two degree measures at both test times and the script frequency and text frequency. The results are shown in Table 10.1.

Two correlations were significant. Before reading, the out-degree of a node was correlated with the script frequency. When a cue was important in the birthday party script, it was more likely to elicit responses from the List.

TABLE 10.1
Spearman Correlations ($n = 60$) of the Degrees of the Nodes
(Experiment 1) With Script Frequency and Text Frequency

	In-Degree	*Out-Degree*
Script Frequency		
Before Reading	.23	.37*
After Reading	−.08	.07
Text Frequency		
Before Reading	.12	−.01
After Reading	.46**	.17

Note. *$p < .05$. **$p < 0.01$.

After reading the text, the in-degree of a node was highly correlated with the text frequency. When a word was mentioned more often in the text, it was more likely to be used as a response in the Cued Association task.

Pathfinder Analysis. In addition to these quantitative measures of text influence, a content-based interpretation of the resulting structures is desirable. Only an inspection of the networks can provide information about the consistency of text information or background knowledge. In a network containing 60 nodes and a correspondingly large number of connections, this can be a difficult task. Thus, we are looking for a method that highlights the structural properties and provides the means for a graphical depiction.

Because the proximity matrices from the Cued Association task are asymmetric, hierarchical clustering and multidimensional scaling algorithms are not applicable. The network algorithm Pathfinder (Schvaneveldt, 1990), in contrast, allows directed links. The algorithm systematically reduces the links in the network, while preserving coherence. This is accomplished by omitting direct links between two nodes if there exists a shorter, indirect path connecting the two nodes. Two parameters guide the amount of reduction and the distance metric used. We chose parameter values so that maximal reduction of the networks was achieved, and no additional assumptions about the proximities were necessary ($q = 59$, $r =$ infinite).

Pathfinder was applied to the aggregated data both before and after reading. For a comparison of the resulting networks, Fig. 10.2 presents the links that were only present in the Before structure, but lost after reading of the text. As expected, links contained in this network include general knowledge associations that were not reinforced in the story, such as DECORATION–BALLOON and LUNCH–SACK. However, there are also some text links contained in this structure (e.g., TIM–CHARLIE or BIRTHDAY–CAKE). Moreover, the structure contains subnetworks corresponding to general world knowledge categories. For example, there is a small subnetwork around CHILDREN containing activities, and a subnetwork around KITCHEN containing words related to the house.

Figure 10.3 shows links that were included in the Pathfinder solutions Before as well as After. Solid lines indicate stronger associations after reading the story, and dotted lines indicate stronger associations before reading the story. Although most of the associations that gained strength are text links, there are also associations involving words that were not mentioned in the story (e.g., PARTY HATS–PARTY, PLAYING–GAMES), and connections that were not directly given by the text (e.g., TOYS–PRESENTS, CONFETTI–PARTY). The weaker links, on the other hand, include not only general world knowledge associations, which might have been replaced by text-related ones (e.g., HOT DOG–HAMBURGER, FUN–GAMES), but also asso-

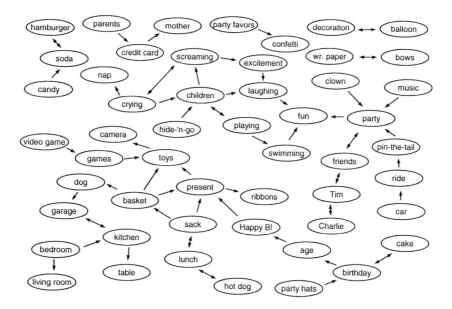

FIG. 10.2. Subnetwork for the Cued Association task from Experiment 1. Shown are only the links included in the Pathfinder solution *before* reading the story but not after reading.

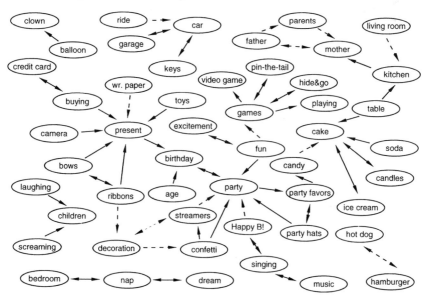

FIG. 10.3. Subnetwork for the Cued Association task from Experiment 1. Shown are the links common to both Pathfinder solutions, before *and* after reading. Broken lines are links that were stronger before reading; solid lines are links that were stronger after reading.

ciations that were reinforced in the text (e.g., MOTHER–FATHER, DECO-
RATIONS–STREAMERS).

Figure 10.4, finally, depicts the links that were newly established after
reading the text. This graph contains text links that might also be part of the
general world knowledge of our subjects (e.g., LUNCH–SODA, LAUGH-
ING–CRYING), and therefore are probably due to random variation between the two test times. However, more text specific associations, such as
CHARLIE–DOG and CLOWN–DREAM, and the apparent representation
of text episodes (see the subnetwork around LUNCH, and around BAL-
LOON) illustrate the direct effect of the story information on the associative
structure.

This short description was intended to illustrate that the links in these
Pathfinder solutions do reflect the trade-off between certain associations.
Although some links were reinforced by the story, they nevertheless are
lost in the Pathfinder solution after reading. This may be because a stronger
indirect link has been found by the algorithm, or because subjects abandoned the association in favor of a more crucial one. However, as Goldsmith, Johnson, and Acton (1991) argued, it is more informative to look
at the internal structure, such as clusters around a node, than at individual
links. In our solutions, clusters before reading included some world knowledge categories, whereas clusters after reading reflected text episodes.
Thus, the network algorithm facilitated data interpretation and showed

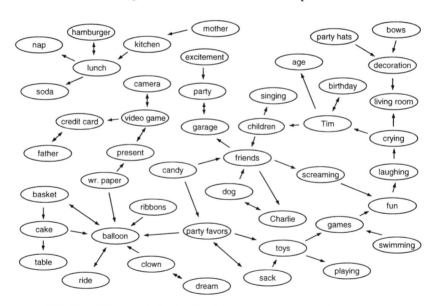

FIG. 10.4. Subnetwork for the Cued Association task from Experiment 1.
Shown are the links that were added to the structure *after* reading, but were
not included before reading.

that the results of the Cued Association task reflected both background knowledge and text information.

EXPERIMENT 2

Experiment 1 established clearly that the Cued Association paradigm was appropriate for assessing background knowledge and text memory. In the analysis by subjects, the influence of text information was indicated by an increase in text similarity scores. In the analysis by items, background knowledge had an effect on the centrality of a node before reading, and text information influenced it after reading. Furthermore, we illustrated the applicability of the network algorithm Pathfinder by interpreting the resulting group data in a meaningful way.

To extend these results, we conducted a second experiment with two goals. First, we wanted to dissociate the effects of repeated exposure to the word list from the effects caused directly by text information. To this end, we added a control condition in which subjects read an unrelated text. Second, we wanted to show that the observed text effects were not merely a reflection of the textbase that is still available immediately after reading. Thus, a third Cued Association task was added to test whether the birthday party story would play a role even after a delay of 1 week.

Method

Twenty-three undergraduate students at the University of Colorado participated in the experiment for course credit. They were randomly assigned to conditions, with 11 subjects in the experimental group and 12 in the control group. The experiment was conducted in small groups.

Using the same materials as in Experiment 1, we employed a paper-and-pencil version. A booklet contained the List of keywords, response sheets for the Cued Association tasks, and one of two texts. In the first session, subjects read the List of 60 keywords twice, and performed the Cued Association task before and after reading. The instructions for these tasks were identical to those in Experiment 1. While subjects in the experimental group read the birthday party story, subjects in the control group read an unrelated history text of similar length. This text did not contain any of the keywords. Subjects were instructed to read the text carefully and to memorize the contents.

After a week of delay, the participants performed the familiarization task by reading through the List twice, followed by one Cued Association task.

Results and Discussion

The Cued Association responses were scored in the same way as in Experiment 1, yielding associative networks for each subject at each of three different test times: before reading, immediately after reading, and after a delay of 1 week. Due to a technical error, however, one of the 60 concepts (the word "dog") was omitted on the answer sheets, so that the networks contained only 59 concepts.

Unless specified otherwise, the analyses conducted were mixed factorial analyses of variance (ANOVAs) with the between-subjects factor Condition (with two levels: Experimental and Control), and the within-subjects factor Test Time (with three levels: Before, After-Immediate, and After-Delay). The analyses were performed using two contrast codes for the factor test time. The first contrast code compared the results before reading to that of after-immediate and after-delay, and the second contrast code compared the results of the Cued Association task after-immediate to those of after-delay. Because these two comparisons are sufficient to test the main hypotheses of the experiment, no omnibus tests for the within-subjects factor test time and its interaction with condition are reported (Judd & McClelland, 1989).

Network Size. In Experiment 1, subjects provided more answers from the List after reading than before. It was not possible to distinguish whether this increase in netsize was due to repeated exposure to the List, or to the additional use of text information. If repeated exposure facilitated the selection of answers from the List, an increase in netsize is expected across the course of Experiment 2, independent of condition. On the other hand, if the text information led to more answers from the List, the netsize scores for the control condition should remain stable across the three test times.

The means of the network size scores (defined as in Experiment 1) are shown in Fig. 10.5. There was no main effect of Condition ($F(1, 21) < 1$). For both subject groups, however, the network sizes increased during the course of the experiment. The networks before reading were smaller than the networks assessed later in the experiment ($F(1, 21) = 10.8$, $p < 0.01$), and the networks assessed immediately after reading were somewhat smaller than the networks from the delayed test ($F(1, 21) = 3.98$, $p < 0.06$). Neither of the corresponding interaction terms was significant ($F(1, 21) = 1.8$ and $F(1, 21) = 1.7$, respectively).

The increase in network size can therefore be attributed to repeated exposure to the word list, rather than to reading the related story. Thus, a purely quantitative explanation of eventual text effects is not warranted. If the network size had been larger for the experimental group, it could have been argued that text effects might have emerged after reading by

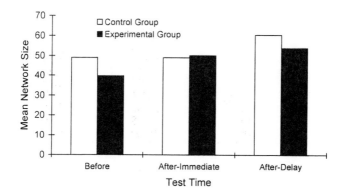

FIG. 10.5. Mean network size in Experiment 2 as a function of test time and reading condition. Network size is defined as the sum of all the link strength values in the network.

merely adding more links to the network before reading. Given the comparable network sizes for the two conditions, this explanation can be ruled out.

Text Similarity. Experiment 1 had shown that the propositional structure of the text was used in subjects' Cued Association responses immediately after reading. Although this suggests that subjects accessed their episodic text memory, it was not clear whether the textbase or the situation model was tapped. Because the textbase decays more quickly than the situation model (e.g., van Dijk & Kintsch, 1983), cued associations immediately after reading are more likely to depend on the textbase, whereas associations at the delayed test are more likely to depend on the situation model. We expected that for the experimental group after a delay of 1 week, the text similarity scores would be smaller than immediately after reading, but still larger than before reading. For the control group, text similarity scores were expected to remain stable across the course of the experiment.

Text similarity scores were calculated as before, and their means are shown in Fig. 10.6. The main effect of Condition was highly significant ($F(1, 21) = 46.8$, $p < 0.01$), indicating that across all test times, subjects in the experimental condition provided more text associations than subjects in the control condition. Moreover, the proportion of text links in the After-Immediate and After-Delay networks was higher than in the Before networks ($F(1, 21) = 34.3$, $p < 0.01$). Because it was mainly due to changes for the experimental group, this effect depended highly on Condition ($F(1, 21) = 35.3$, $p < 0.01$). The same pattern of results was obtained for the difference between After-Immediate and After-Delay. The text propor-

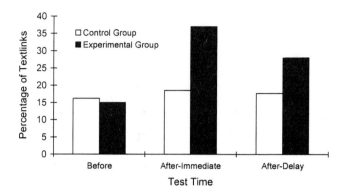

FIG. 10.6. Mean percentage of text links from Experiment 2, shown as a
function of test time and reading condition.

tions were higher immediately after reading than after a week delay (F(1,
21) = 13.3, p < 0.01), and this effect was again due to changes for the
experimental group only (F(1, 21) = 7.2, p < 0.05).

Thus, the Cued Association task yields results that are consistent with
findings from other paradigms. After the week of delay, text information
was still retained, but to a lesser degree than immediately after reading.
Moreover, for the control group, no text effects were observed.

Reliability of Cued Association Data. In this section, we address the reliability of the Cued Association task. Even in the absence of any additional
information, subjects will not provide the same responses when they repeat
the task. If we want to argue that the networks reflect the relatively stable
background knowledge of the subjects, we need to show that there is
considerable within-subjects consistency. The control group allows us to
estimate this baseline for the overlap of the networks at different test times.
We expected that the networks assessed in the first session would be more
similar to each other than to the network assessed after 1 week.

For the experimental group, we expected the opposite pattern. If the
network immediately after reading reflects the text information, the difference to the network before reading should be more pronounced. In
addition, the similarity of the network assessed after a delay to those from
the first session estimates the relative contribution of background knowledge and text information. If at the delayed test, subjects still retained
their text memory, the overlap for the two test times after reading should
be considerable. In contrast, if subjects forgot most of the text infomation
and fall back on their script knowledge, the overlap between the structures
before reading and after the delay is expected to be larger.

To test these hypotheses, overlap scores were calculated for each subject
and each pair of test times (Before/After-Immediate, Before/After-Delay,

and After-Immediate/After-Delay). These overlap scores were defined as the inner product between two matrices A and B, and normalized so that their range fell between 0 (for networks not sharing any links), and 1 (for identical networks; see Goldsmith & Davenport, 1990, for a discussion of various similarity measures between matrices).

$$\text{overlap } (A, B) = \frac{\Sigma \, a_{i,j} \times b_{i,j}}{\frac{1}{2} \times (\Sigma \, a_{i,j}^2 + \Sigma \, b_{i,j}^2)} \qquad (10.4)$$

The means of the resulting overlap scores are shown in Fig. 10.7.

One contrast code was defined to compare the overlap score from the two test times in the first session (Before/After-Immediate) to the other two overlap scores (Before/After-Delay and After-Immediate/After-Delay). The interaction of this contrast with group tests the hypothesis that the overlap between Before and After-Immediate is large for the control group, but small for the experimental group.

The second, orthogonal contrast code, consequently compared the overlap scores for Before/After-Delay to those for After-Immediate/After-Delay. There were two significant effects in these analyses. The interaction term for the first contrast showed that for the control condition, the overlap scores for the two test times in the first session (Before/After-Immediate) were higher than the other two overlap scores. The opposite was the case for the experimental condition ($F(1, 21) = 4.4$, $p < 0.05$). The results for the second contrast did not vary with Condition, but the overlap between After-Immediate and After-Delay was higher for both groups of subjects than the overlap between Before and After-Delay ($F(1, 21) = 4.3$, $p = 0.05$; all other F's < 1).

Although the magnitude of the overlap between the After-Immediate and After-Delay networks was equal for the two conditions, the source of the overlap was hypothesized to be different. For subjects in the experimental group, a higher portion of the overlap was assumed to be due to

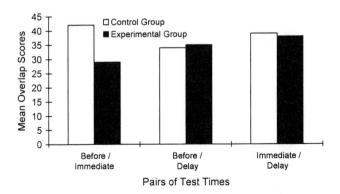

FIG. 10.7. Mean overlap scores for each pair of test times, shown as a function of reading condition.

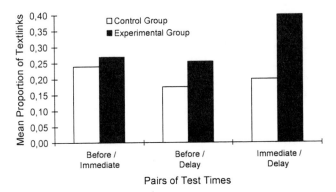

FIG. 10.8. Mean proportion of text links in the overlap networks for each pair of test times, shown as a function of reading condition.

text links included in both networks. To test this hypothesis, the proportion of text links in the overlap networks was calculated for each subject and each of the pairs of test times. The means are displayed in Fig. 10.8.[2]

An ANOVA using the same contrast codes as in the analysis of the overlap scores confirmed the hypothesis. Consistent with the finding that subjects in the Experimental group provided more text associations, the proportion of text links in the overlap networks was also higher for this group ($F(1, 20) = 9.7$, $p < 0.01$). There was no overall difference for the first contrast ($F(1, 20) < 1$), and the interaction term only approached significance ($F(1, 20) = 4.2$, $p = 0.06$). However, the proportion of text links was higher for After-Immediate/After-Delay than for Before/After-Delay ($F(1, 20) = 10.5$, $p < 0.01$), and the interaction term for this second contrast code demonstrated clearly that this effect was more pronounced for the Experimental group than for the Control group ($F(1, 20) = 4.8$, $p < 0.05$).

Centrality of Concepts. The analyses by subjects showed clear-cut text effects for all measures considered. For an item analysis, we made corresponding predictions. Specifically, we expected that the results of Experiment 1 would be replicated for the experimental group, and that no influence of text frequency would be observed for the control group. An open question was whether text information would be retained sufficiently to influence the in-degree of the nodes after a delay.

---

[2]Data from one subject in the Experimental condition had to be excluded. For this subject, the networks from Before and After-Delay did not have any links in common, and thus the text proportion was not well defined.

TABLE 10.2

Spearman Correlations ($n = 59$) of the Degrees of the Nodes
(Experiment 2) With Script Frequency and Text Frequency

	In-Degree		Out-Degree	
	Control	Experimental	Control	Experimental
Script Frequency				
Before	.21	.35**	.29*	.26*
After-Immediate	.20	.13	.27*	−.07
After-Delay	.17	.25	.20	.11
Text Frequency				
Before	.20	.00	−.03	.00
After-Immediate	.12	.42**	.08	.15
After-Delay	.11	.21	.03	.11

Note. *$p < 0.05$. **$p < 0.01$.

For each of the three test times, the association data was aggregated across subjects in each group. As described for Experiment 1, in-degrees and out-degrees were then calculated for each word. Spearman rank-order correlations with the variables script frequency and text frequency are presented in Table 10.2. For the control group, the only significant correlations were between script frequency and out-degree in the first session. Thus, as in Experiment 1, words were more likely to elicit a response from the List if they were important to the birthday party script.

For the experimental group, script frequency was positively related to both the in- and out-degree before reading. Consistent with the results of Experiment 1, text frequency was highly correlated with the in-degree immediately after reading. Once more, words mentioned more often in the text were used more often as responses in the association task.

At the delayed test, no significant correlations were obtained. This suggests that text information had less influence for the experimental group, and script frequency became less important for the subjects in the control group.

Summary. The results of Experiment 1 were replicated and extended. By adding a control group, we demonstrated the applicability of inferential statistics to Cued Association data. All measures considered clearly differentiated between the two conditions. Text information influenced the responses in the experimental group over and above changes due to repeated exposure to the task. Moreover, the delayed test showed that text information was retained and used in the Cued Association task even after a week, although the influence of the text was not as strong as immediately after reading. Thus, the paradigm is useful not only to study the textbase, but also to assess the situation model.

GENERAL DISCUSSION

Two experiments illustrated a new approach to discourse comprehension research. A cued association paradigm was applied to study comprehension and learning from a simple narrative. The resulting associative networks described the structural relationships among 60 text-related concepts, both before and after reading.

Methodological Implications

Despite the relatively large number of items, most subjects perceived the Cued Association task as meaningful and straightforward. In contrast to rating tasks, in which the number of required comparisons prohibits the use of such a large set of items, the short amount of time required to perform the task indicates that using an even larger set of concepts is feasible. In contrast to recall scores or summarization data, scoring is objectively determined. Whereas scoring of recall data often requires the definition of scoring units, and the agreement of several scorers, the knowledge assessment data are unambiguously defined. Moreover, the method does not require a priori assumptions about specifically what subjects are expected to learn. The Cued Association task (in contrast to recall or comprehension questions) does not have predefined answers, so that it is more suitable for capturing an individual's situational representation of the text.

Knowledge assessment paradigms can only be used widely if the data allow fine-grained analyses, comparable to those of traditional comprehension data. In fact, the lack of powerful statistical methods for the comparison of network structures has been noted (Olson & Biolsi, 1991). A direct comparison of entire networks is only feasible when the networks contain a moderate number of nodes. For larger networks, the number of coefficients that are expected to remain stable despite the text information is far greater than the number of connections that are predicted to change. Correlation measures or the method of quadratic assignment (Hubert & Schulz, 1976) will yield highly significant relationships between the networks. Therefore they are not sensitive enough to capture differences between the matrices.

As an alternative, we used different types of analyses to demonstrate that the data are as informative as other comprehension data. Because the primary goal of the structural assessment was to provide means for qualitatively describing the relations among text relevant concepts, the use of graphical methods (Pathfinder) was illustrated in Experiment 1. In order to evaluate the reliability of these graphical results (which were based on group data), comparative statistics were used in Experiment 2 on appropriately defined dependent variables. Overlap scores provided the means to measure the changes in response patterns for each subject. More importantly, the assumption of a propositional representation of text enabled us to compare the empirical networks to a theoretically based text structure.

These measures illustrate a statistical approach to analyzing proximity data. As related studies show, it can be extended in various ways, depending on the issue at hand. For instance, McNamara et al. (1996) used a harmony measure (similar to our overlap scores) between an ideal knowledge structure and proximity data from a sorting task. They found that this measure varied with reader's background knowledge as well as with the coherence of the text. Ferstl and Franzke (1993) studied the extent to which the macro- and microstructures of a newspaper article were reflected in Cued Association responses of subjects with various levels of background knowledge. The overlap between the subjects' networks with the propositional structure of the text (as described in this chapter) did not differ as a function of background knowledge. However, comparisons of the subjects' answers to a text network representing the macrostructure showed that the overlap was larger for subjects who had read appropriate background information.

These examples suggest that knowledge assessment is sufficiently sensitive for capturing even subtle comprehension effects. Moreover, both studies used expository texts and complex knowledge domains. The set of keywords included low-frequency words as well as abstract concepts. Thus, the applicability of knowledge assessment paradigms extends beyond simple narratives and highly overlearned knowledge domains.

Theoretical Considerations

We designed this study within the framework of the construction-integration model of discourse comprehension (Kintsch, 1988, 1998). This model specifies a mechanism for how general world knowledge is used in comprehension, and describes a representation of the resulting episodic text memory. In this section, we outline in more detail the relationship between the empirically assessed associative networks and the text comprehension theory.

The construction-integration model contains two stages. In the construction phase, a network is formed consisting of text concepts and text propositions (which are connected according to argument overlap). In addition, elaborations to these text propositions are retrieved from long-term memory. These elaborations correspond to associations in the general world knowledge, and they are connected to the text propositions with a link strength corresponding to the long-term memory association strength. For example, reading about a birthday cake would lead to the retrieval of an association to the word *candles*. The model can accurately describe the reading process only if an empirical assessment of these associations is available. The associative networks before reading of the relevant text, as assessed in this study, provide these empirical estimates of association strength values.

In the second stage, the integration phase, a spreading activation process integrates the text propositions (which in the case of ambiguities can also include contextually inconsistent propositions) with the general world knowledge elaborations. The resulting activation pattern is the reader's representation of the text. This so-called textbase can contain elements that were not explicitly mentioned in the text, and irrelevant text propositions can be deactivated. Probing a text concept in the text representation network activates related concepts, in part through direct associations, in part through indirect paths across several nodes. The response pattern in the Cued Association task after reading is assumed to correspond to the activation pattern after probing with a concept cue. In particular, if a proposition containing two concepts as arguments is part of the text representation, an association between the two concepts is predicted. That the network structures after reading the text are in fact approximations of this text representation was confirmed by using the text structure as a predictor for changes in the associative networks. However, there were also associations that could not be accounted for by the text structure. Thus, a more comprehensive analysis of the text representation, including, for instance, macropropositions, is needed to account for the full range of text effects.

Can the networks assessed after reading be interpreted as a *representation* of the textbase or the situation model? The only claim that is warranted is that the observed text effects do *reflect* the episodic text memory. Of course, the text memory also contains elements that are not captured in the empirical networks. For instance, the text representation contains proposition nodes, as well as nodes for concepts that were not included in the list of selected words. Because subjects are encouraged to use concepts from the List for their answers, and because exposure to the List activates related knowledge, the selection of words influences the results.

Furthermore, the response patterns cannot be used to distinguish between a compartmentalized and an integrated text representation (Potts, St. John, & Kirson, 1989). Although the networks after reading contained associations from both the text structure and the background knowledge, it is not clear if this combination truly reflects an integration of the text information into the background knowledge. As Reder (1980) showed, subjects can either retrieve text information directly from memory, or they can use their general world knowledge to answer comprehension questions. Similarly, in the knowledge assessment tasks presented here, if subjects provide an association that is part of their background knowledge, it is not clear whether this association became part of the situation model. It might also be the case that subjects access their (compartmentalized) text memory for some of their answers, while relying on their background knowledge for others. In our framework, however, this distinction is not crucial. What Reder called strategic differences (and Potts et al., 1989, attentional shifts) is in the associative memory representation a matter of activation levels. The episodic text memory is considered a subnetwork of the general world knowledge, which is initially connected to a context node (cf. Anderson, 1983; Potts et al., 1989; Raaijmakers & Shiffrin, 1981). If a text-related cue is presented, the strongest association is retrieved, no matter if it is directly linked to the context node. As long as the context node is strongly activated (or retrieval cues are available), the associations to a text-related cue are most likely from the text representation, and text information is more easily accessible within the appropriate context. If the cue is not strongly linked to the context node, or to other nodes within the text representation, an association from the general world knowledge is retrieved.

This description of the relationship between knowledge assessment and comprehension directly leads to a conceptualization of learning within our framework. Learning from text, as contrasted with learning of text, takes place when text information is permanently added to the general world knowledge network. As outlined here, the nodes representing text information are initially connected to a context node that allows their retrieval within the text context. Once the context node has decayed and context-specific retrieval cues are no longer available, the episodic text memory seems to be forgotten. However, the text nodes, and their associations to related concepts, are still part of the general knowledge net and can be retrieved via activation of connected concepts. Thus, the text permanently modifies the reader's world knowledge, however minute and local these modifications might be. Learning from text can therefore be operationalized as the change of association patterns in the empirically estimated networks. How stable these changes are, and under which circumstances they have a long-term effect, is an empirical question.

CONCLUSIONS

In this chapter, we presented structural knowledge assessment as a fruitful methodology for text comprehension research. In contrast to previous research, we utilized a well-developed theory of text comprehension to guide our search for an appropriate knowledge representation scheme and a corresponding knowledge assessment paradigm. We showed that the method was useful for measuring domain knowledge, as well as episodic text memory structures. Comparative statistics and graphical analyses complemented each other in providing evidence for text effects. In contrast to previous research, the paradigm can be applied to a wide range of domains and texts. Thus, we are confident that the method will be useful in further research and that it will be beneficial for studying how readers acquire knowledge from text. Specifically, we hope that knowledge assessment methodologies will bring us closer to a characterization of readers' learning from text.

ACKNOWLEDGMENTS

This research was supported by Project MDA903-86-C0143 from the Army Research Institute. Experiment 1 was performed as the master's thesis of E. Ferstl. We are grateful to Nancy Pennington and Mike Mozer for their comments on this work. We would also like to thank Susan Goldman and Art Graesser for their careful reviews of an earlier draft. E. Ferstl is now at the Max-Planck-Institute of Cognitive Neuroscience, Leipzig, Germany.

APPENDIX A

TIM'S BIRTHDAY

Today was Tim's birthday. Tim's mother had fed him hamburgers for lunch and although it was a special day for Tim, she had insisted that he take a nap after lunch. He reluctantly went up to his bedroom. As Tim began to drift off to sleep, he was full of thoughts about the party and all the presents he would get. Suddenly he thought he heard his father laughing and calling out to him, "Tim, get up! Come with me!" When he opened his eyes, not his father but a big beautiful clown with red fuzzy hair was standing next to the bed.

"Come on," the clown said, "let's go for a balloon ride!" Tim jumped out of bed and together they went. When they got outside, they climbed into the basket of a big balloon parked next to the porch. They rose up in the balloon and flew over Tim's neighborhood, where Tim could see all of his friends waving and singing "Happy Birthday to Tim."

"You have to give party favors to your friends," the clown said and showed Tim a big sack hanging on the outside of the basket. Tim reached into the sack filled with little toys and candies and threw them down to his screaming friends. After a while, the balloon came down and landed in a park. Music was playing. Tim and the clown jumped out of the basket. When Tim turned around to catch a look at the big balloon, the basket had turned into a tremendous birthday cake! The six candles on the cake heated the balloon which was now made of colorful wrapping paper and had red ribbons tied around it.

"Blow out the candles, Tim!" the clown told Tim. Tim closed his eyes, made a wish, took a deep breath, and blew as hard as he could at the candles on the cake. When he opened his eyes, Tim was back in his bedroom. The ride had just been a dream! But it really was his birthday today!

Tim ran downstairs to the kitchen where he thought his mother and father were busy preparing for his big party. He kicked the kitchen door open. He couldn't wait to see the presents he was going to get. As he burst through the door, his mother was nowhere in sight. Not even Charlie, his dog, was waiting for him. The kitchen was cleaned up. Tim's parents were probably in the living room putting up the streamers and decorating the table with nicely wrapped presents. Tim ran to the living room and found it empty, just like the kitchen had been. He sat down and started crying. Not because his parents were gone, but because they had forgotten to buy him presents.

Suddenly Tim had an idea. He would go and buy the birthday presents himself! He would buy the camera and video game he had been wanting for so long. After all, he was already six years old, and it was time to show his parents that he was not a little child any more. He grabbed his mother's car keys and his father's credit card and went to the garage. When he stepped into the garage, confetti filled the air, children screamed, and a table with a big birthday cake on it sat where the car should have been. His friends and his parents were there and sang "Happy Birthday" to a surprised Tim. He gave his mother a hug and said: "Why didn't you wait for me to play hide-and-go-seek?"

APPENDIX B

The following are the set of words used in the Cued Association task. The first column shows the frequency of the word in the birthday party script. The second column shows the number of times the word was mentioned in the text.

	frequency			*frequency*	
	script	*text*		*script*	*text*
age	7	0	hot dogs	7	0
balloon	15	6	ice cream	15	0
basket	0	4	keys	0	1
bedroom	0	2	kitchen	0	4
birthday	0	6	laughing	12	1
bows	7	0	living room	0	2
buying	0	3	lunch	0	2
cake	17	4	mother	7	5
camera	8	1	music	8	1
candles	17	3	nap	0	1
candy	11	1	parents	14	4
car	1	2	party	3	2
Charlie	0	1	party favors	7	1
children	9	1	party hats	14	0
clown	13	4	pin tail on donkey	13	0
confetti	5	1	playing	5	2
credit card	0	1	presents	17	5
crying	6	1	ribbons	9	1
decorations	7	1	ride	0	2
dog	0	1	sack	0	2
dream	0	1	screaming	1	2
excitement	5	1	singing	9	2
father	4	4	soda	7	0
friends	8	4	streamers	12	1
fun	7	0	swimming	8	0
games	14	0	table	0	2
garage	0	2	Tim	0	24
hamburger	5	1	toys	12	1
Happy Birthday	2	2	video games	5	1
hide-and-go-seek	6	1	wrapping paper	7	1

REFERENCES

Adelson, B. (1981). Problem solving and the development of abstract categories in programming languages. *Memory & Cognition, 9,* 422–433.

Altmann G. T. M., & Steedman, M. (1988). Interaction with context during human sentence processing. *Cognition, 30,* 191–238.

Anderson, J. R. (1983). *The architecture of cognition.* Cambridge, MA: Harvard University Press.

Ballstaedt, S. P., & Mandl, H. (1991). Knowledge modification during reading. In G. Denhière & J.-P. Rossi (Eds.), *Text and text processing* (pp. 189–204). Amsterdam: North-Holland.

Bisanz, G. L., LaPorte, R. E., Vesonder, G. T., & Voss, J. F. (1978). On the representation of prose: New dimensions. *Journal of Verbal Learning and Verbal Behavior, 17,* 337–357.

Bransford, J. D., & Johnson, M. K. (1972). Contextual prerequisites for understanding: Some investigations of comprehension and recall. *Journal of Verbal Learning and Verbal Behavior, 11,* 717–726.

Britton, B. K., & Gulgöz, S. (1991). Using Kintsch's computational model to improve instructional text: Effects of repairing inference calls on recall and cognitive structures. *Journal of Educational Psychology, 83*, 329–345.

Chi, M. T. H., Feltovich, P. J., & Glaser, R. (1981). Categorization and representation of phsyics problems by experts and novices. *Cognitive Science, 5*, 121–152.

Chi, M. T. H., & Koeske, R. D. (1983). Network representation of a child's dinosaur knowledge. *Developmental Psychology, 19*, 29–39.

Ferstl, E. C. (1991). *Assessment of knowledge structures before and after reading of a text.* Unpublished master's thesis, University of Colorado at Boulder, Boulder, CO.

Ferstl, E. C., & Franzke, M. (1993, June). *Understanding newspaper articles: Structural knowledge assessment in the study of discourse comprehension.* Paper presented at the third annual meeting of the Society of Text and Discourse, Boulder, CO.

Fillenbaum, S., & Rapoport, A. (1971). *Structures in the subjective lexicon.* New York: Academic Press.

Fletcher, C. R., & Chrysler, S. T. (1990). Surface forms, textbases, and situation models: Recognition memory for three types of textual information. *Discourse Processes, 13*, 175–190.

Gammack, J. G. (1987). Different techniques and different aspects on declarative knowledge. In A. L. Kidd (Ed.), *Knowledge acquisition for expert systems: A practical handbook* (pp. 137–163). New York: Plenum Press.

Gernsbacher, M. A. (1990). *Language comprehension as structure building.* Hillsdale, NJ: Lawrence Erlbaum Associates.

Gliner, G., Goldman, S. R., & Hubert, L. J. (1983). A methodological study on the evaluation of learning from story narratives. *Multivariate Behavioral Research, 18*, 9–36.

Goldsmith, T. E., & Davenport, D. M. (1990). Assessing structural similarity of graphs. In R. Schvaneveldt (Ed.), *Pathfinder associative networks: Studies in knowledge organization* (pp. 75–88). Norwood, NJ: Ablex.

Goldsmith, T. E., & Johnson, P. J. (1990). A structural assessment of classroom learning. In R. Schvaneveldt (Ed.), *Pathfinder associative networks: Studies in knowledge organization* (pp. 241–254). Norwood, NJ: Ablex.

Goldsmith, T. E., Johnson, P. J., & Acton, W. H. (1991). Assessing structural knowledge. *Journal of Educational Psychology, 83*, 88–96.

Graesser, A. C., & Clark, L. F. (1985). *Structures and procedures of implicit knowledge: Advances in discourse processes* (Vol. XVII). Norwood, NJ: Ablex.

Graesser, A. C., Robertson, S. P., & Anderson, P. A. (1981). Incorporation of inferences in narrative representations: A study of how and why. *Cognitive Psychology, 13*, 1–26.

Henley, N. M. (1969). A psychological study of the semantics of animal terms. *Journal of Verbal Learning and Verbal Behavior, 8*, 176–184.

Hubert, L., & Schulz, J. (1976). Quadratic assignment as a general data analysis strategy. *British Journal of Mathematical and Statistical Psychology, 26*, 190–241.

Johnson-Laird, P. N. (1983). *Mental models.* Cambridge, MA: Harvard University Press.

Judd, C. M., & McClelland, G. H. (1989). *Data analysis: A model comparison approach.* San Diego: Harcourt Brace Jovanovich.

Kintsch, W. (1988). The role of knowledge in discourse comprehension: A construction-integration model. *Psychological Review, 95*, 163–182.

Kintsch, W. (1989). The representation of knowledge and the use of knowledge in discourse comprehension. In R. Dietrich & C. F. Graumann (Eds.), *Language processing in social context* (pp. 159–209). Amsterdam: North-Holland.

Kintsch, W. (1998). *Comprehension: A paradigm for cognition.* New York: Cambridge University Press.

Kintsch, W., & van Dijk, T. (1978). Toward a model of discourse comprehension and production. *Psychological Review, 85*, 363–394.

Kintsch, W., Welsch, D., Schmalhofer, F., & Zimny, S. (1990). Sentence memory: A theoretical analysis. *Journal of Memory and Language, 29,* 133–159.

LaPorte, R. E., & Voss, J. F. (1979). Prose representation: A multidimensional scaling approach. *Multivariate Behavioral Research, 14,* 39–56.

McNamara, D. S., Kintsch, E., Songer, N. B., & Kintsch, W. (1996). Are good texts always better? Interactions of text coherence, background knowledge, and levels of understanding in learning from text. *Cognition and Instruction, 14,* 1–43.

Murphy, G. L., & Wright, J. C. (1984). Changes in conceptual structure with expertise: Differences between real-world experts and novices. *Journal of Experimental Psychology: Learning, Memory, and Cognition, 10,* 144–155.

Olson, J. R., & Biolsi, K. J. (1991). Techniques for representing expert knowledge. In K. A. Ericsson & J. Smith (Eds.), *Toward a general theory of expertise* (pp. 240–285). Cambridge, England: Cambridge University Press.

Ore, O. (1963). *Graphs and their uses.* New York: Random House.

Perfetti, C. A. (1985). *Reading ability.* New York: Oxford University Press.

Perrig, W., & Kintsch, W. (1985). Propositional and situational representations of text. *Journal of Memory and Language, 24,* 503–518.

Potts, G. R., St. John, M. F., & Kirson, D. (1989). Incorporating new information into existing world knowledge. *Cognitive Psychology, 21,* 303–333.

Raaijmakers, J. G., & Shiffrin, R. M. (1981). A theory of probabilistic search of associative memory. *Psychological Review, 88,* 93–134.

Reder, L. M. (1980). The role of elaboration in the comprehension and retention of prose. *Review of Educational Research, 50,* 5–53.

Rips, L. J., Shoben, E. J., & Smith, E. E. (1973). Semantic distance and the verification of semantic relations. *Journal of Verbal Learning and Verbal Behavior, 12,* 1–20.

Rumelhart, D. E., & Norman, D. A. (1988). Representation in memory. In R. C. Atkinson, R. J. Herrnstein, G. Lindzey, & R. C. Luce (Eds.), *Stevens' handbook of experimental psychology* (pp. 511–588). New York: Wiley.

Schank, R. C., & Abelson, R. P. (1977). *Scripts, plans, goals and understanding: An inquiry into human knowledge structures.* Hillsdale, NJ: Lawrence Erlbaum Associates.

Schmalhofer, F., & Glavanov, D. (1986). Three components of understanding a programmer's manual: Verbatim, propositional, and situational representations. *Journal of Memory and Language, 25,* 279–294.

Schneider, W., Körkel, J., & Weinert, F. E. (1990). Expert knowledge, general abilities, and text processing. In W. Schneider & F. E. Weinert (Eds.), *Interactions among aptitudes, strategies, and knowledge in cognitive performance* (pp. 235–251). New York: Springer.

Schvaneveldt, R. W. (Ed.) (1990). *Pathfinder associative networks: Studies in knowledge organization.* Norwood, NJ: Ablex.

Speelman, C. P., & Kirsner, K. (1990). The representation of text-based and situation-based information in discourse comprehension. *Journal of Memory and Language, 29,* 119–132.

Spilich, G. J., Vesonder, G. T., Chiesi, H. L., & Voss, J. F. (1979). Text processing of domain-related information for individuals with high and low domain knowledge. *Journal of Verbal Learning and Verbal Behavior, 18,* 275–290.

Stanners, R. F., Price, J. M., & Painton, S. (1982). Interrelationships among text elements in fictional prose. *Applied Psycholinguistics, 3,* 95–107.

Trabasso, T., & Sperry, L. L. (1985). Causal relatedness and importance of story events. *Journal of Memory and Language, 24,* 595–611.

Turner, A. A., & Greene, E. (1978). *Construction and use of a propositional textbase.* JSAS Catalogue of selected documents in psychology, MS 1713.

van Dijk, T., & Kintsch, W. (1983). *Strategies of discourse comprehension.* New York: Academic Press.

Voss, J. F., Fincher-Kiefer, R. H., Greene, T. R., & Post, T. A. (1986). Individual differences in performance: The contrastive approach to knowledge. In R. J. Sternberg (Ed.), *Advances in the psychology of human intelligence* (Vol. 3, pp. 297–334). Hillsdale, NJ: Lawrence Erlbaum Associates.

Zwaan, R. A., Langston, M. C., & Graesser, A. C. (1995). The construction of situation models in narrative comprehension: An event-indexing model. *Psychological Science, 6,* 292–297.

Zwaan, R. A., Magliano, J. P., & Graesser, A. C. (1995). Dimensions of situation model construction in narrative comprehension. *Journal of Experimental Psychology: Learning, Memory, and Cognition, 21,* 386–397.

Part III

MONITORING AND UPDATING REPRESENTATIONS

Chapter 11

Metacognitive Monitoring
of Text Cohesion in Children

Marie-France Ehrlich
EPHE, Université René Descartes, CNRS, Paris

Do children control the coherence of the mental representation they build when reading a text? Such a question is very complex. The present chapter focuses on the control of the processing of anaphoric devices that ensure local textual cohesion. Several experiments are summarized investigating metacognitive monitoring (self-evaluation and revision) in the processing of anaphors in children classified as skilled versus less-skilled comprehenders.

Anaphoric devices are linguistic markers that contribute to the local cohesion of the text (Halliday & Hasan, 1976). Along with other markers (e.g., connectives), these devices are used by writers to signal relations among text units. They belong to what Lorch and O'Brien (1995) named "text-based sources" of coherence in contrast to "reader-based sources" of coherence. The online processing of anaphoric devices, which involves searching for and identifying referents, is an important component of the process of building a coherent mental representation of the content of texts.

It has been shown that this processing depends on complex factors and that it is sometimes performed in an incomplete way. In addition, the resolution of anaphors is a source of difficulty for less-skilled children. Such findings raise the question of the role of control processes in the building of a coherent representation, and more specifically in the processing of anaphoric devices. Control processes have received little attention in the literature devoted to cognitive models of text comprehension. However, they play an important role in studies of reading comprehension using a metacognitive approach. Thus, along the lines suggested in Flavell's (1981) model, I propose to study metacognitive monitoring in the processing of anaphors. Metacognitive monitoring is viewed as involving three main components: planning prior to reading, self-evaluation, and revision linked to cognitive processes underlying text comprehension. More specifically, it is assumed that self-evaluation and revision activities control the resolution of anaphors.

The present chapter is organized as follows. The first section is devoted to the processing of anaphoric devices, especially in children. The second section focuses on comprehension monitoring, with particular attention to methodological issues. The third and fourth sections summarize experiments investigating self-evaluation and revision linked to the processing of anaphors in children classified as skilled versus less-skilled comprehenders (young children in the third section, adolescents in the fourth). Whereas most investigations on anaphor resolution have been conducted with very short texts, the experiments reported here investigate anaphor processing in the case of rather long written texts similar to those encountered in natural reading situations.

PROCESSING OF ANAPHORIC DEVICES

Anaphoric devices denote a referent that has been mentioned in a previous part of the text by means of another referring expression—the antecedent—thereby ensuring the referential continuity of text. Several classes of anaphors can be distinguished. Among them, definite noun phrases and pronouns are frequently used. A lot of investigations have been devoted to the processing of anaphors in adults (see Ehrlich & Charolles, 1991; Garnham, 1987; Garrod & Sanford, 1994). Different factors—morphological, syntactic, and semantic—affect the resolution of anaphors. For example, pronoun resolution depends on syntactic matching (based on gender and number cues) between the pronoun and its potential antecedents. It also depends on the implicit causality of the verb that links the potential antecedents. Other factors, such as the role of the antecedent with regard to the theme of the text and the distance between an anaphor and its antecedent, contribute to processing difficulty. The question of the immediacy of the resolution is still in debate. With definite noun anaphors, there seems to be good evidence for immediate resolution. With pronouns, the time course of the resolution seems to be dependent on several factors, in particular the thematic role of the antecedent (Sanford, 1989; Sanford & Garrod, 1989) and explicitness of pronouns (Gernsbacher, 1989).

Indeed, the main factor to be considered in the processing of anaphoric devices is the relative accessibility of potential antecedents in the mental representation of the text's content built during the course of reading. Usually, this accessibility will lead to an automatic and rapid identification of a unique antecedent. In some other conditions, this automatic process will fail and the interpretation will remain incomplete if the subject does not use some strategic process (Greene, McKoon, & Ratcliff, 1992; Oakhill, Garnham, & Vonk, 1989). It is interesting to note that most investigations in adults have examined anaphor processing in very short texts containing two or three short sentences involving only two protagonists. In longer natural texts that have many protagonists, it can be expected that anaphoric expressions will be often interpreted in an incomplete way if the subject does not use any control procedure.

In children, it has been shown that 7-year-olds process anaphoric devices as efficiently as adults in oral comprehension situations. However, in reading long texts, less-skilled children often fail to resolve anaphors. Tyler (1983) investigated the processing of three types of anaphoric devices—repeated definite noun phrase, more general noun phrase, and pronoun—using short texts presented orally and an online phonological error detection task (*leffer* replaced *letter*). Several experiments were conducted with four age groups: 5-, 7-, and 10-year-old children and adults. For all age groups, general noun phrases tended to be more difficult to interpret, although in some conditions the processing of pronouns was slower than the processing of general nouns, due to the number of potential antecedents. By the age of 7, children were able to process pronouns efficiently, by relying on different sources of information: the lexical properties of pronouns, the pragmatic plausibility of potential antecedents, and the thematic structure of the text. Five-year-old children relied more on the thematic structure of the text and on the pragmatic plausibility of the antecedents. There was no evidence of any developmental change in anaphor processing after the age of 7.

However, other studies indicate that processing of anaphoric devices is a major source of difficulty for children with comprehension problems (Oakhill & Yuill, 1986; Yuill & Oakhill, 1988, 1991). Moreover, less-skilled children make inappropriate use of anaphoric ties in their written productions (Cox, Shanahan, & Sulzby, 1990). Yuill and Oakhill's (1988) investigation was particularly interesting in that it studied the processing of different types of anaphoric devices (reference, ellipsis, substitution, and lexical, according to Halliday & Hasan's, 1976, classification) that appeared in a long natural text (a 700-word story). The distance between the anaphors and antecedents was very close, intermediate, or far. Processing was tested in a natural situation: The text was visually presented with the target anaphors underlined and the experimenter read the story aloud. As each target anaphor was encountered, the experimenter asked children what this anaphor pointed back to or stood for (e.g., "*what does 'he' stand for here?"*). If children gave a wrong answer, they were asked another question that aimed at checking the implicit resolution of the anaphor. Two groups of 8-year-old children participated in the experiments: Children were matched on vocabulary and reading accuracy scores but contrasted on comprehension scores. Results clearly showed that less-skilled comprehenders performed less well than their skilled peers both in identifying the correct antecedents of the anaphors and in answering questions tapping anaphor resolution. The differences between the two groups were significant for all anaphor types, but they appeared stronger for references that included personal and demonstrative pronouns. In addition, both groups performed more poorly as distance between anaphor and antecedent increased, this effect being stronger for less-skilled comprehenders than for skilled ones in the case of ellipsis.

Considering convergent results from several experiments showing that skilled and less-skilled comprehenders differ markedly in their ability to process anaphoric devices efficiently, Yuill and Oakhill (1991) suggested that the two groups differ in the strategies they use to monitor their own comprehension during reading. Such a suggestion leads to assume that deficiencies in metacognitive monitoring could partially account for the incomplete processing of anaphoric devices shown by less-skilled comprehenders. Before summarizing the experiments designed to test this interpretation, the following section briefly describes the metacognitive approach of comprehension monitoring.

METACOGNITIVE APPROACH OF COMPREHENSION MONITORING

In the reading comprehension area, the metacognitive approach has been very popular, because of its instructional implications (see Baker, 1989; Baker & Brown, 1984; Garner, 1987). In line with the seminal work of Flavell (1976, 1981) and Brown (1980), empirical studies have investigated the two components of metacognition: verbalizable knowledge about reading comprehension and active monitoring of comprehension including self-evaluation and revision. Results are usually interpreted as providing evidence that younger and poorer readers have lower reading awareness than older and better readers and fail to monitor successfully their own understanding in the course of reading (see Garner's, 1987, review). However, these studies raise some serious problems. At the theoretical level, most of them have tended to ignore models of reading comprehension or have made only brief reference to them. Therefore, the psycholinguistic processes for which monitoring might fail have not been clearly identified. At the methodological level, a central issue concerns the paradigms and variables appropriate to reveal comprehension monitoring.

A frequently used paradigm has been error detection inspired by Markman's (1977, 1979) oral communication research. Children were asked to answer questions such as "Did the passage make sense?" or to indicate any problem by underlining words, clauses, or sentences in the text. Detecting errors is considered to indicate that subjects are evaluating their own understanding in the course of reading. Results have shown that although poor readers could detect a high proportion of nonsense words, they had marked difficulties in detecting sentences that contradicted previous sentences, thus violating the coherence of the text (Baker, 1984; Zabrucky & Moore, 1989, using fourth- and sixth-grade children differing in reading ability). Such data suggest that less-skilled comprehenders do not efficiently monitor the coherence of the representation they build in the course of reading.

However, also interested in the control of text coherence, Zabrucky and Ratner (1986) showed that even young children are able to monitor their own comprehension to some extent, although this monitoring is not revealed by verbal responses. In their study, third- and sixth-grade children read a series of stories, some of which contained a sentence that contradicted a previous sentence. They used both online and off-line variables to assess self-evaluation and revision during reading comprehension. Longer reading times were assumed to reveal implicit detection of inconsistencies; look-backs assessed explicit revision in order to resolve comprehension difficulties. In addition, after reading a story, children were asked to recall it and answer several questions. The first question, "Did the story make sense?", was assumed to assess children's explicit detection of inconsistencies. In agreement with previous studies, third graders detected far fewer inconsistencies than sixth graders in the classical off-line verbal reports. However, both third and sixth graders spent more time reading inconsistent sentences than consistent ones, with a similar increase in the two groups. Sixth graders had more look-backs throughout the text than third graders, particularly in the case of inconsistent sentences. According to Zabrucky and Ratner, younger readers might have generated an internal signal of comprehension failure, but this signal might not result in conscious awareness of noncomprehension.

Results from Zabrucky and Ratner (1986), as well as from Yuill and Oakhill (1991), illustrate why it is interesting to analyze different kinds of indicators revealing self-evaluation and revision in order better to characterize comprehension monitoring. Nevertheless, the difficulties raised by the error-detection paradigm should not be neglected. In fact, most researchers have noted that error-detection data require careful interpretation. In a natural-reading task, subjects follow Grice's (1975) maxim of relevance and assume that the text is coherent. Therefore, searching for and detecting errors is an unnatural task that violates this maxim. In such a task, detection depends on the implicit standards the subject adopts for "what makes sense"; performance is very dependent on instructions, on reading purpose, and on the number of errors inserted in text. Even skilled, mature readers show low rates of error detection in particular conditions.

The paradigm of error detection can be viewed as an indirect means to study how subjects evaluate and revise their comprehension. Another paradigm provides a direct self-evaluation of comprehension. It has been used in a set of studies conducted with adults and initiated by Glenberg and Epstein (1985, 1987). These authors were interested in the "calibration of comprehension," a notion coming from the feeling-of-knowing literature. Calibration of comprehension refers to subjects' accuracy in self-evaluation in comparison to their performance with an objective test of comprehension. In this paradigm, texts were normal and did not incorporate any errors. Subjects were asked to rate their confidence in understanding with a six-point scale and to perform a verification task. These studies have been developed within a different framework than the one used by research on metacognitive monitoring in reading comprehension. However, confidence ratings on comprehension can be viewed as indicators of the explicit self-evaluation of comprehension. Thus, the direct self-evaluation task allows the investigation of comprehension monitoring in a natural reading situation using normal texts (see Baker, 1989).

In the experiments reported next, metacognitive monitoring of anaphor processing was investigated by means of two tasks: a direct self-evaluation task derived from Glenberg's paradigm and an inconsistency detection task. The first task was carried out with normal texts in which target anaphors were either repeated noun phrases or pronouns. The second task was carried out with texts in which target anaphors were either repeated noun phrases or inconsistent noun phrases.

Experiments I and II: Metacognitive Monitoring
in Anaphor Processing in 9- and 10-Year-Old Skilled
and Less-Skilled Comprehenders

Experiment I was designed to show that young, less-skilled comprehenders have specific difficulties in processing anaphors (see Ehrlich & Rémond, 1997). Experiment II was conducted 1 year later with the same children. It was designed to investigate the two components of monitoring—self-evaluation of comprehension and revision—in the processing of different types of anaphors in skilled and less-skilled comprehenders. It was assumed that less-skilled comprehenders would show deficiencies in the two components of monitoring (see Ehrlich, Rémond, & Tardieu, 1993, 1998).

Experiment I was conducted with two groups of 9-year-old children, matched in decoding and vocabulary skills but contrasted in reading comprehension ability. Children read two long natural stories (688 and 773 words) and the resolution of anaphors was tested in the course of reading. The experimenter stopped the child after an anaphor and asked him a question: "What does this word point back to?" (procedure similar to Yuill & Oakhill's, 1988). Three properties of anaphors were manipulated: type of anaphor (personal pronoun or general noun), syntactic function (subject or object), and distance in relation to antecedents (near or far). The number of antecedents correctly produced on questions was computed and the incorrect responses were analyzed.

In agreement with our hypotheses, in both stories, less-skilled comprehenders produced less correct antecedents than skilled comprehenders. Type and syntactic function affected anaphor resolution: Pronouns were more difficult to resolve than general nouns, objects more difficult than subjects. In one story, far antecedents were more difficult to identify than near antecedents, but the opposite effect was observed in the other story. The interactions between comprehension skill and the three manipulated factors suggested a specific deficit in the processing of anaphors in less-skilled comprehenders, who had particular difficulties with object pronouns. The analysis of incorrect responses confirmed the weight of such difficulties.

To what extent do deficiencies in metacognitive monitoring contribute to explain the poor performance observed in less-skilled comprehenders? Experiment II was designed to answer this question. Monitoring was investigated by means of two tasks. For the direct self-evaluation task, children read normal expository texts in which target anaphors were either repeated noun phrases or pronouns. They self-evaluated their own comprehension on a 6-point scale after sentences containing target anaphors. Reading times and look-backs were registered. For the inconsistency detection task, children read texts containing some inconsistent anaphors. They were asked to detect these inconsistencies. Reading times and look-backs were also registered. In both tasks, actual comprehension was assessed after reading each text by means of multiple-choice questions designed to test the processing of target anaphors. Several indicators of evaluation and revision components of metacognitive monitoring could be analyzed. In both tasks, it was assumed that an increase in reading times with critical clauses (containing the target anaphors) would reflect implicit evaluation and revision, that look-backs would assess explicit revision, and that performance on multiple-choice questions would measure actual comprehension. In addition, it was considered that verbal comprehension ratings collected in the self-evaluation task would assess subjects' explicit evaluation of their own comprehension, whereas verbal reports of detection of inconsistencies would provide another measure of explicit evaluation of comprehension. An analysis of responses to multiple-choice questions should assess the efficiency of revision activities.

The same eight texts dealing with various topics (the seaside, wolf hunting, holidays in the mountains, etc.) were used in the two tasks. The mean number of words per text was 187. Each text was composed of four paragraphs. In each paragraph, the processing of one target anaphor was examined. This anaphor was located in a critical sentence that followed one or two introductory sentences. This critical sentence could be divided into several meaning units: One critical unit (U1), which was always a full main clause, contained the target anaphor and two immediately successive units (U2 and U3) provided further information related to the denoted referent. The antecedent of the target anaphor was always a subject noun in the preceding sentence. The mean distance between anaphors and their antecedent was 18.4 words (range 8–28).

For the direct self-evaluation task, target anaphors varied along two factors: type of anaphor (repetition of the noun preceded by a demonstrative determinant or personal pronoun) and syntactic function (subject or object). In the preceding sentence, another noun phrase bearing the same gender and number cues as the antecedent could be considered as a potential antecedent in processing the pronouns. The combination of the two factors produced four kinds of target: Subject Noun (SN), Object Noun (ON), Subject Pronoun (SP), and Object Pronoun (OP).

For the inconsistency detection task, the target anaphors varied along two factors. The first one was the consistency of the anaphor, that is, a demonstrative nominal either repeated the same lexical content or changed this content to a different one, involving the same gender and number cues, but a meaning discontinuity in the text. The second factor was the syntactic function of the anaphor, subject, or object. The combination of the two factors produced four kinds of target anaphors.

For both tasks, the four kinds of anaphors occurred in the four paragraphs of each text. For each of the eight basic texts, four versions were prepared in which the occurrence of the four kinds of anaphors in the four successive paragraphs was counterbalanced. One of the versions of the text "La mer" and its English translation used in the self-evaluation task are shown in Table 11.1. In the inconsistency detection task, two target anaphors were replaced by inconsistent noun phrases.

Texts were presented on a computer screen and a self-paced procedure was used. In addition, from any unit in the critical sentence, children could re-read the previously presented parts of the text. The self-evaluation task involved three phases: (a) reading the whole text; (b) reading the same text after it had been segmented into sentences and into meaning units in the case of critical sentence and self-evaluating one's own comprehension on a 6-point scale from 1 (*I understood very poorly*) to 6 (*I understood very well*) after each paragraph; (c) answering four multiple-choice questions testing the processing of target anaphors. Each child carried out this

TABLE 11.1
One of the Versions of the Text "La Mer" and Its
English Translation, Used in Experiment II

Text: La mer

Chaque été, on constate combien la mer fascine les enfants, soumis toute l'année au rythme et à la pollution de la ville. / Les médecins *la* recommandent / pour ses effets favorables sur la santé, / mais, de plus, elle offre de nombreuses activités. / (OP).

La découverte des animaux marins présente des surprises souvent renouvelées. Les coquillages amenés par les vagues se trouvent en abondance sur la plupart des rivages. Après la marée, / *ces coquillages* peuvent être ramassés / dans les flaques d'eau laissées au creux des rochers / ou plus simplement dans le sable recouvert d'algues. / (SN).

Souvent peuplées d'oiseaux, les grottes sont des lieux où les enfants imaginent plein d'aventures et jouent aux explorateurs. / *Elles* ont été creusées / dans les falaises de roches tendres / petit à petit, au cours des siècles passés. / La légende racote que les corsaires disparus y ont caché de fabuleux trésors, rapportés du bout du monde, à l'époque où la technique des voiliers permettait de parcourir les mers. (SP).

De nos jours, la voile est devenue un sport et une activité de loisirs, accessible à tous. A la belle saison, / les amateurs pratiquent *la voile* / soit sur l'océan soit sur des eaux plus calmes, / après quelques séances d'initiation et d'apprentissage des règles de sécurité. / Les grands voiliers sont, maintenant, admirés comme des objets de musée chargés d'une fabuleuse histoire. (ON).

In the inconsistency detection task, two paragraphs contained inconsistent anaphors. For example: "Les médecins recommandent *l'usine*" (paragraph 1) and *"Ces boutiques* ont été creusés" (paragraph 3).

Text: The seaside

Every summer, we see how much the seaside fascinates children who are all year round submitted to the rhythm and pollution of city life. / Doctors recommend *it* / for its favorable effects on health, / but furthermore, it allows numerous activities. / (OP).

Discovering sea animals is a constant source of surprises. Shells, brought by the waves, are plentiful on most shores. After the tide, / *these shells* can be picked up / in the puddles left in the holes of rocks / or even more easily in the sand covered by sea weeds. / (SN).

Often inhabited by birds, the caves are places where children imagine numerous adventures and pretend to be explorers. / *They* have been dug / into tender rock cliffs / little by little, during past centuries. / The legend says that lost pirates have hidden in them the fabulous treasures, they brought from the other end of the world, in the days when sailing ships allowed to plough the seas. (SP).

Nowadays, sailing has become a sport and a leisurely activity, accessible to everyone. In fair weather, / amateurs practice *sailing* / either on the ocean or on quieter waters, / after a few sessions of training and of learning safety rules. / Big sailing ships are, now, admired like museum pieces loaded with fabulous stories. (ON).

In the inconsistency detection task, two paragraphs contained inconsistent anaphors. For example: "Doctors recommend *factory*" (paragraph 1) and *"These shops* have been dug" (paragraph 3).

Note. The symbol / signals the boundaries of the critical units.

289

task with a list of four different texts. For the inconsistency detection task, the basic procedure was the same. The main difference concerned the second phase. After reading the first paragraph, the experimenter asked the child, "Have you found a word that does not fit the text?" In the case of a positive response, the paragraph was presented again and the child was asked to indicate the erroneous word and the other word in the paragraph with which it did not fit. Children did not receive any feedback about the accuracy of their response. Instructions specified what kind of inconsistent words could be inserted in the text by providing examples. Each child carried out the inconsistency detection task with a list of four texts that was different from the list read in the self-evaluation task.

In both tasks, as expected, results converged to show different patterns of monitoring in skilled and less-skilled comprehenders. Clearly, less-skilled comprehenders showed deficiencies in monitoring activities linked to the processing of anaphors.

In the direct self-evaluation task, skilled comprehenders spent significantly more time on the critical clause (U1) when the target anaphor was a pronoun rather than a repeated noun. In addition, they sometimes read the preceding part of the text over again. When they were asked to rate their own comprehension, skilled children asserted that they had understood well or very well. They were able to modulate their ratings depending on the syntactic function of the target anaphors (they reported understanding object anaphors less well than subject ones) and also depending on the type of anaphors in the case of objects (they reported understanding pronouns less well than nouns). Regarding actual comprehension, skilled comprehenders got high mean scores (86.56%) in response to multiple-choice questions that tested the processing of target anaphors.[2] In the case of object anaphors, scores were significantly lower for pronouns than for nouns. The partial interactions observed both in self-evaluation of comprehension and actual comprehension indicated that skilled comprehenders were able to modulate their evaluation in accordance with their actual comprehension.

Results were different in less-skilled comprehenders. Their reading times were globally longer than those observed in skilled comprehenders. They spent more time on the critical clause (U1) when it contained a pronoun, but this increase was only marginally significant. They nearly never read the preceding part of the text over again. When they rated their own comprehension, less-skilled children reported understanding less well than skilled ones. When they answered multiple-choice questions that tested their actual

---

[1]On a preliminary session, children were submitted to a test aiming at assessing their pre-reading level for the multiple-choice questions. The percentages of correct responses were 48% and 40% for skilled and less-skilled comprehenders, respectively, whereas chance predicted only 20%. The pre-reading scores were used as a covariate in the analysis of actual comprehension.

comprehension, their scores were lower than those of skilled comprehenders. Thus, to some extent, less-skilled comprehenders seemed aware of their difficulties in understanding texts. However, in comparison to skilled comprehenders, they tended to overestimate their own comprehension. In addition, they were not able to modulate their evaluation depending on the properties of anaphors, whereas skilled comprehenders did so. In other words, less-skilled children were clearly not aware of their difficulties in processing anaphoric pronouns to the same extent as were skilled ones.

In the inconsistency detection task, skilled comprehenders showed reading times much longer than those observed in the self-evaluation task. Such an increase revealed an adaptation to the requirements of the task. These children spent significantly more time on the critical clause (U1) when the target anaphor was an inconsistent noun rather than a repeated one, as well as on the following unit (U2), which facilitated the resolution of the inconsistency. They tended to read the preceding part of the text over again, especially when they met an inconsistent anaphor. They explicitly detected many inconsistent anaphors and could very often identify the source of the inconsistency. In answer to multiple-choice questions that tested the processing of target anaphors, skilled comprehenders reached a high performance. Performance was significantly lower for inconsistent anaphors as compared to consistent ones. When they detected an inconsistent anaphor, they could resolve it and give a correct response on the multiple-choice questions. When they did not detect the inconsistency, their performance on multiple-choice questions was not better than their pre-reading score. Thus, analyses of indicators of implicit and explicit evaluation and revision clearly show that skilled comprehenders engage in active monitoring during the processing of anaphors.

In less-skilled comprehenders, the reading times observed in the detection task were longer than those observed in the self-evaluation task. However, this increase was of lesser magnitude than with skilled comprehenders. Less-skilled comprehenders spent more time on the critical clause (U1) when the target anaphor was an inconsistent noun, but this increase was not significant. No increase was observed on the subsequent unit (U2). Children sometimes read the preceding part of the text over again, but these look-backs were not a function of the presence of an inconsistency. They detected few inconsistent anaphors and in a large number of these detections they could not specify the source of the inconsistency. In addition, they tended to make false detections. With multiple-choice questions, the performance of less-skilled comprehenders was lower than the one displayed by skilled comprehenders. Performance was lower for inconsistent anaphors than for consistent ones; when children were able to detect inconsistent anaphors, they could respond correctly to multiple-choice questions, but otherwise their performance was equal to their pre-reading score.

Thus, in both tasks, on measures assessing implicit and explicit evaluation and revision, less-skilled comprehenders showed deficiencies in monitoring activities. The observed increase in reading times with pronouns or with inconsistent anaphors revealed that less-skilled children were sensitive to the text cohesion. However, this sensitivity was weak (the increase was not statistically significant) and did not trigger explicit activities. Altogether, these results show that metacognitive monitoring is an important aspect of the processing of anaphors, and partially account for the individual differences in young children.

**Experiments III and IV: Metacognitive Monitoring
in Anaphor Processing and Domain-Specific Knowledge
in 13- and 15-Year-Old Skilled and Less-Skilled Comprehenders**

In the same line as the previous experiment, Experiments III and IV were designed to investigate how adolescent skilled and less-skilled comprehenders monitor their own comprehension while reading expository texts containing different types of anaphors (see Ehrlich, 1996). Experiment III was conducted with two groups of 15-year-old subjects, matched in decoding skill, but contrasted in reading comprehension ability. Subjects in two groups were also matched on scores assessing the prereading level of domain-specific knowledge. This prereading test was a necessary control, given that the texts were expository ones implying domain-specific knowledge. In this prereading test, subjects completed 24 multiple-choice questions (3 questions for each of the 8 texts) that were identical to the questions assessing comprehension after reading the experimental texts. On this test, subjects in both groups showed 48% correct responses although chance predicted only 20%. In order to study the role played by prior knowledge, Experiment IV was conducted with two groups of 13-year-old skilled and less-skilled comprehenders, for which the prereading score was lower than in the previous experiment (35% correct responses).

As in Experiment II, children carried out a direct self-evaluation task and an inconsistency detection task. However, methodology was different on two points: First, the target anaphors present in a text belonged all to the same type, in such a way that three different versions of each text could be compared (nominal, pronominal, and inconsistent). Second, only indicators of explicit evaluation and revision (verbal comprehension ratings and verbal detection of inconsistencies) were collected, technical constraints preventing the recording of reading times and look-backs. As previously, actual comprehension was assessed by means of multiple-choice questions testing the processing of target anaphors.

The same materials and the same procedure were used in the two experiments. Eight expository texts, two series of four texts about Canada and China (agriculture, industry, transportation, etc.) were prepared. The mean number of words per text was 93. Each text was composed of three sequences of two sentences. In each sequence, the second sentence began with a subject anaphor for which the antecedent was the noun phrase subject of the first sentence. For each of the eight texts, three versions were constructed with different subject anaphors. In the *nominal version,* the three anaphoric devices were the repetitions of the noun phrases preceded by demonstrative determinants. In the *pronominal version,* the three anaphoric devices were pronouns. On the basis of gender and number cues, each pronoun had two potential antecedents. In the *inconsistent nominal version,* the three anaphoric nouns were replaced by nouns whose meaning tended to be contrary. Thus, the continuity of the two sentences of the sequence was disrupted, although the second sentence itself was consistent. By contrast with this inconsistent nominal version, the nominal version could be named a *consistent nominal version* when used in the detection task. An example of a text with its three versions is shown in Table 11.2.

Texts were printed in a booklet. For the direct self-evaluation task, the booklet included three pages for each text. The first page displayed one whole text in a nominal or pronominal version preceded by a title. The second page displayed the same text segmented into three sequences of two sentences. Subjects self-evaluate their own comprehension on a 6-point scale after each sequence. The third page contained the three multiple-choice questions testing the processing of target anaphors.

For the inconsistency detection task, the basic procedure was the same. Subjects were asked to detect errors when the text was segmented into three sequences: "In each part, if you detect some errors, that is, a word or a group of words that does not fit with the text, you underline it and you indicate the other word in the text with which it is inconsistent by means of an arrow."

Subjects completed first the direct self-evaluation task with two different consistent texts, one in a nominal version and the other in a pronominal version. Then they completed the inconsistency detection task with two other texts, one in a consistent nominal version and the other in an inconsistent nominal version. This procedure, applying the same order (self-evaluation before detection task) was repeated with different texts such that a trial factor with two levels could be examined.

For both tasks, data were analyzed in taking into consideration comprehension skill (2), text version (2), trial (2), and sequence of the text (3) factors. For purposes of characterizing the differences between skilled and less-skilled comprehenders, special attention was paid to the interactions between comprehension skill and the other factors.

In Experiment III, results from the two tasks were convergent. They clearly indicated that the processing of anaphoric devices was not submitted

TABLE 11.2
The Text "Les Ressources Naturelles" and Its
English Translation, Used in Experiments III and IV

"Les ressources naturelles"

Nominal version
La richesse du Canada en tant que nation aux ressources naturelles abondantes est connue. *Cette richesse* est menacée par les effets d'une exploitation intense et par ceux de la pollution./L'exploitation des ressources, au rythme actuel, conduit à prévoir leur disparition prochaine. *Cette exploitation* est pourtant plus facile à contrôler que les productions de déchets qui nuisent à l'environnement./La protection des réserves existantes doit être assurée par les entreprises qui profitent de la richesse du pays. *Cette protection* doit être accompagnée d'une augmentation du budget que les entreprises consacrent à combattre la pollution.

Pronominal version
1) *Elle* est menacée . . . 2) *Elle* est pourtant . . . 3) *Elle* doit être accompagnée . . .

Inconsistent nominal version
1) *Cette pauvreté* est menacée . . . 2) *Cette non utilisation* est pourtant . . . 3) *Cette dilapidation* doit accompagnée . . .

"Natural resources"

Nominal version
It is well known that the wealth of Canada is a nation with plentiful natural resources. *This wealth* is endangered by the effects of pollution and an intense exploitation of the resources./ The present rate of this exploitation will lead to extinction in the future. Nevertheless *this exploitation* is easier to control than the production of wastes which damages the environment./ The protection of the existing reserves have to be controlled by the firms which make a profit from the wealth of the country. *This protection* must be accompanied by an increase in the budget that firms devote to control pollution.

Pronominal version
1) *It* is endangered . . . 2) Nevertheless *it* is . . . 3) *It* must be accompanied . . .

Inconsistent nominal version
1) *This poverty* is endangered . . . 2) Nevertheless *this absence of use* . . . 3) *This wastage* must be accompanied . . .

Note. The symbol / signals the boundaries of the sequences.

---

to efficient metacognitive monitoring, either in the skilled or the less-skilled comprehenders. Thus in the direct self-evaluation task, skilled and less-skilled comprehenders evaluated their own understanding to the same level in pronominal and nominal versions (asserting they had understood well or very well), but showed lower actual comprehension scores in pronominal versions. Both groups seemed unaware of the difficulties of the pronouns and they did not process them in a complete way. No interaction was observed between comprehension skill and the factors that affected or did not affect self-evaluation: The text version and the trial factors did not affect the self-evaluation of comprehension either in the skilled or the less-skilled group; the sequence factor affected it similarly in both groups.

In the inconsistency-detection task, detection was poor in both groups, and it tended to be lower for less-skilled comprehenders than for skilled comprehenders. Detection did not vary as a function of trials, but it tended to decrease from the first to the third sequence of the text. No interaction was observed between comprehension skill and the trial or the sequence factor. Actual comprehension scores were lower for less-skilled than for skilled comprehenders. They also were much lower for the inconsistent version than for the consistent version, this negative effect being similar for both groups. The analysis of responses on multiple-choice questions showed that less-skilled comprehenders had more difficulties than skilled comprehenders in engaging in revision actions to solve inconsistencies even when they were correctly detected.

In Experiment IV, results were different from those in Experiment III. Data from both skilled and less-skilled comprehenders tended to show that processing of anaphoric devices involved metacognitive monitoring.

In the direct self-evaluation task, both skilled and less-skilled comprehenders modulated their evaluations as a function of anaphoric devices and showed similar comprehension performance for nominal and pronominal versions. Less-skilled comprehenders asserted that they understood less well than skilled comprehenders, in agreement with their actual comprehension. Thus, less-skilled comprehenders seemed aware of their difficulties. However, the examination of the relationship between self-evaluation and actual comprehension showed that compared to skilled comprehenders, less-skilled subjects tended to overestimate their own understanding. Additionally, the three-way interaction between comprehension skill, trial, and text version showed that less-skilled comprehenders modulated their evaluation of their own understanding as a function of text version only in the second trial, whereas this modulation appeared even on the first trial in skilled comprehenders.

In the inconsistency detection task, some findings were similar to those observed in Experiment III: Less-skilled comprehenders showed lower detection performance than skilled comprehenders and no interaction was observed between comprehension skill and trial and sequence factors. Less-skilled comprehenders again showed more difficulties in solving the inconsistencies that were correctly detected. However, new findings emerged. Both groups provided false detections for the inconsistent and consistent versions as well. These results reflected more active processing than in the first experiment. Moreover, skilled comprehenders seemed to conduct revision actions in the absence of an explicit detection of the inconsistency. Their level of actual comprehension reached the same values as in older skilled comprehenders who participated in the first experiment.

Overall, data from these two experiments do not support the hypothesis that less-skilled adolescent comprehenders suffer deficiencies in metacognitive monitoring while processing anaphoric devices in expository texts. Data show that monitoring is affected by the same variables in skilled and less-skilled comprehenders. In particular, monitoring seems to be dependent on the level of domain-specific knowledge: It is more efficient when domain-specific knowledge is low.

CONCLUSION

Processing of anaphoric devices is one of the central components in the building of a coherent mental representation of the text's content. In reading long natural texts, anaphor resolution involves complex subprocesses that depend on several factors. Some studies conducted with English and French children have shown that anaphor processing in written texts is a major source of difficulty for children with comprehension problems. Skilled and less-skilled comprehenders differ widely in their ability efficiently to process different kinds of anaphors. The present chapter summarized several experiments designed to test the hypothesis that the difficulties observed in less-skilled comprehenders might be related to deficiencies in metacognitive monitoring.

This hypothesis was confirmed for 10-year-old children, but not for 13- or 15-year-olds. In younger children, skilled comprehenders were able to engage in active monitoring in relation to the processing of anaphors. Less-skilled comprehenders seemed to be sensitive to some extent to the text cohesion, but they were unable to use efficient monitoring. In older children, no marked difference was observed between skilled and less-skilled comprehenders. Both groups engaged in efficient monitoring depending on their prior knowledge in the text domain.

Considering the inconsistency detection task, inconsistencies localized on anaphors constitute a particular form of violation of internal text consistency. To our knowledge, the effect of such inconsistencies had still not been investigated in children. Results from the younger children are in agreement with previous results reported in the literature, in particular with Yuill and Oakhill's (1991) data showing that less-skilled comprehenders have strong difficulties in detecting errors that violate the internal coherence of the text. Results from older children, at first glance, seem to be discrepant from previous ones. However, a close examination of the expository texts used in several experiments shows that the role of the difficulty of the texts has not been taken into account. For example, Garner (1980) and Zabrucky and Moore (1989) used expository texts whose readability level was appropriate for children younger than the adolescents participating in their experiments. They did not control the level of prior domain knowledge. In reading texts that they perceive as easy to understand, children might minimize the need for monitoring.

In addition to the inconsistency detection task, children carried out a direct self-evaluation task, a paradigm used to investigate comprehension monitoring in adults. One of the main interests of this task is to place children in a natural reading situation. Overall, the results regarding the differences between skilled and less-skilled comprehenders were similar to those observed with the inconsistency detection task. Moreover, new findings emerged showing that young and older less-skilled comprehenders were aware of their difficulties (they asserted that they understood less well than skilled comprehenders), even if they tended to overestimate their own comprehension. The basis used by subjects to provide verbal ratings of comprehension needs clarification (see Glenberg, Sanocki, Epstein, & Morris, 1987; Maki & Serra, 1992). However, the self-evaluation task appears relevant to study comprehension monitoring in children.

As has been stressed by Baker (1994), many studies document the existence of developmental differences in metacognition, but do not offer explanations as to how metacognition develops. Such a remark is especially valid for metacognitive monitoring in reading comprehension. Our results showing that 13-year-old skilled and less-skilled comprehenders are able to use efficient monitoring in reading comprehension, whereas only skilled comprehenders among younger children do so, raise the problem as to the development of such monitoring capacities. Karmiloff-Smith's (1986) model could offer an interesting theoretical framework. This model assumed two kinds of metaprocesses, some of which are unconscious, and others of which are accessible to consciousness and verbalization. Studying oral comprehension and production tasks, Karmiloff-Smith showed an important developmental gap between spontaneous repairs (assumed to reveal unconscious metaprocesses) and verbal metalinguistic comments (see also Hickman & Schneider, 1993; Karmiloff-Smith et al., 1993). In reading comprehension, reading times can be considered as revealing unconscious metaprocesses, whereas explicit detection of inconsistencies or verbal ratings of comprehension correspond to conscious metalinguistic comments. Such investigations, taking unconscious and conscious metaprocesses into account, and conducted with children varying in age and reading ability, should lead to a better understanding of development of cohesion monitoring.

Adolescents are able to engage in efficient cohesion monitoring while reading expository texts. However, reliance on monitoring activities is not systematic. Our data show that monitoring is dependent on the subjects' prior knowledge of the content of texts in particular domains: Self-evaluation and revision are more efficient when their level of prior knowledge is low. At first glance, such a result is counterintuitive, given that domain-specific knowledge has been shown to be a powerful factor affecting the construction of situation models with expository texts (Tardieu, Ehrlich, & Gyselinck, 1992). However, this result is in agreement with data showing

that experts (adults) in a particular domain do not know how to evaluate
their own comprehension when they read a text dealing with this domain
(Glenberg et al., 1987). Flavell (1987) suggested that subjects' high familiarity with particular domains can lead them to view text understanding as
an easy task that prevents the use of control mechanisms. In other words,
high familiarity can influence the subjects' perception of the cognitive
requirements of the reading task and more specifically what van den Broek,
Risden, and Husebye-Hartmann (1995) called the readers' standards for
coherence. Studying the generation of inferences and the establishment
of referential coherence during reading, these authors argued that "readers
maintain standards of coherence that determine at each point in the text
whether they have adequately understood what they are reading and
whether they need to engage in further inference generation in order to
achieve complete understanding" (p. 367). Thus, standards of coherence
drive inference generation and anaphor processing. They vary as a function
of subjects' motivation and goals when reading, as well as with their reading
ability: Poor readers are likely to adopt lower standards for coherence and
may be satisfied more easily than good readers. Such an account, which
views readers' standards for coherence as a central notion, is in agreement
with Sanford's position (Sanford & Garrod, 1994; Sanford, Barton, Moxey,
& Patterson, 1995), according to which processing in the service of coherence establishment is both selective and incomplete, implying some sort
of criterion of satisfaction for coherence. In particular, these authors assume that global cohesion dominates and inhibits local cohesion processes.
The finding that the detection of inconsistencies tended to decrease from
the first to the third sequence of the text in Experiments III and IV support
this hypothesis. It can therefore also be assumed that high familiarity with
a particular text domain enhances the establishment of global cohesion
and inhibits the processing of anaphors that ensures local cohesion. Thus,
van den Broek and Sanford both attribute to metacognitive monitoring
an important role in the building of the mental representation, even if
the metacognitive approach is not explicitly taken into consideration. Monitoring processes are in fact included in the recent model of text comprehension proposed by Goldman, Varma, and Coté (1996). Such processes
are components of a Strategy Competition module that acts as a general
executor, in addition to four language-processing modules.

REFERENCES

Baker, L. (1984). Spontaneous versus instructed use of multiple standards for evaluating
    comprehension: Effects of age, reading proficiency and type of standard. *Journal of
    Experimental Child Psychology, 38*, 289–311.

Baker, L. (1989). Metacognition, comprehension monitoring, and the adult reader. *Educational Psychology Review, 1,* 3–38.

Baker, L. (1994). Fostering metacognitive development. In H. W. Reese (Ed.), *Advances in child development and behavior* (Vol. 25, pp. 201–239). San Diego: Academic Press.

Baker, L., & Brown, A. L. (1984). Metacognitive skills and reading. In P. D. Pearson, M. Kamil, R. Barr, & P. Mosenthal (Eds.), *Handbook of reading research* (pp. 353–394). New York: Longman.

Brown, A. L. (1980). Metacognitive development in reading. In R. J. Spiro, B. Bruce, & W. Brewer (Eds.), *Theoretical issues in reading comprehension* (pp. 453–481). Hillsdale, NJ: Lawrence Erlbaum Associates.

Cox, B. E., Shanahan, T., & Sulzby, E. (1990). Good and poor elementary readers' use of cohesion in writing. *Reading Research Quarterly, 25,* 47–64.

Ehrlich, M.-F. (1996). Metacognitive monitoring in the processing of anaphoric devices in skilled and less skilled comprehenders. In C. Cornoldi & J. Oakhill (Eds.), *Reading comprehension difficulties. Processes and intervention* (pp. 221–249). Mahwah, NJ: Lawrence Erlbaum Associates.

Ehrlich, M.-F., & Charolles, M. (1991). Aspects of textual continuity: Psycholinguistic approaches. In G. Denhière & J.-P. Rossi (Eds.), *Text and text processing* (pp. 269–284). Amsterdam: Elsevier Science Publishers.

Ehrlich, M.-F., & Rémond, M. (1997). Skilled and less skilled comprehenders: French children's processing of anaphoric devices in written texts. *British Journal of Developmental Psychology, 15,* 291–309.

Ehrlich, M.-F., Rémond, M., & Tardieu, H. (1993). Composantes cognitives et métacognitives de la lecture: le traitement des marques anaphoriques par des bons et mauvais compreneurs [Cognitive and metacognitive components of reading: The processing of anaphoric devices in skilled and less-skilled comprehenders]. In J.-P. Jaffre, L. Sprenger-Charolles, & M. Fayol (Eds.), *Les actes de la Villette. Lecture-écriture: acquisition* (pp. 279–298). Paris: Nathan.

Ehrlich, M.-F., Rémond, M., & Tardieu, H. (1998). Processing of anaphoric devices in young skilled and less skilled comprehenders: Differences in metacognitive monitoring. *Reading and Writing, 10.*

Flavell, J. H. (1976). Metacognitive aspects of problem solving. In L. B. Resnick (Ed.), *The nature of intelligence* (pp. 231–235). Hillsdale, NJ: Lawrence Erlbaum Associates.

Flavell, J. H. (1981). Cognitive monitoring. In P. Dickson (Ed.), *Children's oral communication skills* (pp. 35–60). New York: Academic Press.

Flavell, J. H. (1987). Speculations about the nature and development of metacognition. In F. E. Weinert &. R. H. Kluwe (Eds.), *Metacognition, motivation and understanding* (pp. 21–29). Hillsdale, NJ: Lawrence Eribaum Associates.

Garner, R. (1980). Monitoring of understanding: An investigation of good and poor readers' awareness of induced miscomprehension of text. *Journal of Reading Behavior, 12,* 55–63.

Garner, R. (1987). *Metacognition and reading comprehension.* Norwood, NJ: Ablex.

Garnham, A. (1987). Understanding anaphora. In A. W. Ellis (Ed.), *Progress in the psychology of language* (Vol. 3, pp. 253–300). Hillsdale, NJ: Lawrence Erlbaum Associates.

Garrod, S. C., & Sanford, A. J. (1994). Resolving sentences in a discourse context. In M.-A. Gernsbacher (Ed.), *Handbook of psycholinguistics* (pp. 675–698). New York: Academic Press.

Gernsbacher, M. A. (1989). Mechanisms that improve referential access. *Cognition, 32,* 99–156.

Glenberg, A. M., & Epstein, W. (1985). Calibration of comprehension. *Journal of Experimental Psychology: Learning, Memory, and Cognition, 11,* 702–718.

Glenberg, A. M., & Epstein, W. (1987). Inexpert calibration of comprehension. *Memory and Cognition, 15,* 84–93.

Glenberg, A. M., Sanocki, T., Epstein, W., & Morris, C. (1987). Enhancing calibration of comprehension. *Journal of Experimental Psychology: General, 116,* 119–136.

Goldman, S. R., Varma, S., & Coté, N. (1996). Extending capacity-constrained construction integration: Toward "smarter" and flexible models of text comprehension. In B. K. Britton & A. C. Graesser (Eds.), *Models of understanding text* (pp. 73–113). Mahwah, NJ: Lawrence Erlbaum Associates.

Greene, S. B., McKoon, G., & Ratcliff, R. (1992). Pronoun resolution and discourse models. *Journal of Experimental Psychology: Learning, Memory and Cognition, 18*, 266–283.

Grice, H. P. (1975). Logic and conversation. In P. Cole & J. L. Morgan (Eds.), *Syntax and semantics, Vol. 7: Speech acts* (pp. 41–58). New York: Academic Press.

Halliday, M. A. K., & Hasan, R. (1976). *Cohesion in English*. London: Longman.

Hickmann, M., & Schneider, P. (1993). Children's ability to restore the referential cohesion of stories. *First Language, 13*, 169–202.

Karmiloff-Smith, A. (1986). From meta-processes to conscious access: Evidence from children's metalinguistic and repair data. *Cognition, 23*, 95–147.

Karmiloff-Smith, A., Johnson, H., Grant, J., Jones M.-C., Karmiloff, Y.-N., Bartrip, J., & Cuckle, P. (1993). From sentential to discourse functions: Detection and explanation of speech repairs by children and adults. *Discourse Processes, 16*, 565–589.

Lorch, R. F., Jr., & O'Brien, E. J. (1995). Introduction: Sources of coherence in reading. In R. F. Lorch, Jr., & E. J. O'Brien (Eds.), *Sources of coherence in reading* (pp. 1–8). Mahwah, NJ: Lawrence Erlbaum Associates.

Maki, R. H., & Serra, M. (1992). The basis of test predictions for text material. *Journal of Experimental Psychology: Learning, Memory, and Cognition, 18*, 116–126.

Markman, E. M. (1977). Realizing that you don't understand: A preliminary investigation. *Child Development, 48*, 986–992.

Markman, E. M. (1979). Realizing that you don't understand: Elementary school children's awareness of inconsistencies. *Child Development, 50*, 643–655.

Oakhill, J., Garnham, A., & Vonk, W. (1989). The on-line construction of discourse models. *Language and Cognitive Processes, 4*, 263–286.

Oakhill, J., & Yuill, N. (1986). Pronoun resolution in skilled and less-skilled comprehenders: Effects of memory load and inferential complexity. *Language and Speech, 29*, 25–37.

Sanford, A. J. (1989). Component processes of reference resolution in discourse. In N. E. Sharkey (Ed.), *Models of cognition* (pp. 113–140). Norwood, NJ: Ablex.

Sanford, A. J., Barton, S. B., Moxey, L. M., & Paterson, K. (1995). Cohesion processes, coherence and anomaly detection. In G. Rickheit & C. Habel (Eds.), *Focus and processing in discourse coherence* (pp. 201–211). Berlin: de Gruyter.

Sanford, A. J., & Garrod, S. C. (1989). What, when, and how? Questions of immediacy in anaphoric reference resolution. *Language and Cognitive Processes, 4*, 235–262.

Sanford, A. J., & Garrod, S. C. (1994). Selective processing in text understanding. In M. A. Gernsbacher (Ed.), *Handbook of psycholinguistics* (pp. 699–720). New York: Academic Press.

Tardieu, H., Ehrlich, M.-F., & Gyselinck, V. (1992). Levels of representation and domain-specific knowledge in comprehension of scientific texts. *Language and Cognitive Processes, 7*, 335–351.

Tyler, L. K. (1983). The development of discourse mapping processes: The on-line interpretation of anaphoric expressions. *Cognition, 13*, 309–341.

Van den Broek, P., Risden, K., & Husebye-Hartmann, E. (1995). The role of readers' standards for coherence in the generation of inferences during reading. In R. F. Lorch, Jr., & E. J. O'Brien (Eds.), *Sources of coherence in reading* (pp. 353–373). Mahwah, NJ: Lawrence Erlbaum Associates.

Yuill, N., & Oakhill, J. (1988). Understanding of anaphoric relations in skilled and less-skilled comprehenders. *British Journal of Psychology, 79*, 173–186.

Yuill, N., & Oakhill, J. (1991). *Children's problems in text comprehension.* Cambridge, England: Cambridge University Press.

Zabrucky, K., & Moore, D. (1989). Children's ability to use three standards to evaluate their comprehension of text. *Reading Research Quarterly, 24,* 336–352.

Zabrucky, K., & Ratner, H. H. (1986). Children's comprehension monitoring and recall of inconsistent stories. *Child Development, 57,* 1401–1418.

Chapter 12

Modifying Mental Representations: Comprehending Corrections

Hollyn M. Johnson
Washington State University at TriCities

Colleen M. Seifert
University of Michigan

At times, people are exposed to initial misinformation that is corrected later. For example, suppose a newspaper initially reports that a family died of food poisoning after eating at a Chinese restaurant. If it turned out that the restaurant was not responsible for the deaths, the newspaper would typically print a retraction or correction. Ideally perhaps, the misinformation should not influence people's final understanding of that event because the newspaper should not have presented the misinformation in the first place. People who continued to rely on the misinformation could misunderstand the event's true causes, make biased evaluations of the dangers of eating Chinese food, and take actions with unfair consequences for the restaurant's innocent owners. However, a number of studies in text comprehension (Johnson & Seifert, 1994; Wilkes & Leatherbarrow, 1988) and studies of social judgments (Anderson, Lepper, & Ross, 1980; Ross, Lepper, & Hubbard, 1975; Wyer & Unverzagt, 1985) found that corrected misinformation can continue to influence people's reasoning. This chapter reviews evidence on possible reasons why people have difficulty in comprehending corrections, and then presents some new data on updating situation models after a correction.

Comprehending a correction, and thereby limiting influence from misinformation, may be broken down into phases of surface updating and global updating. *Surface updating* entails noticing the correcting information, incorporating its text within a representation, and detecting that it has a correcting relationship with a specific piece of prior information. In the previous example, a correction could explicitly state that medical tests ruled out food poisoning as the cause of death. People who have done surface updating would realize that the correction indicates that the initial information about the occurrence of food poisoning was wrong.

On the other hand, *global updating* entails realizing the implications that a correction has for one's situation model and making appropriate inferences to update it. Thus, to go beyond mere surface updating, people would also have to evaluate the validity of other aspects of the situation model, such as assumptions about the restaurant's culpability. People might also attempt to generate alternate inferences about the cause of the event. Presumably, people who encounter a correction would need to do surface updating before they would make alterations to their situation models; however, people could potentially do surface updating yet have situation models that are still influenced by misinformation. The next section reviews evidence on factors that could contribute to surface and global updating following a correction, and examines the extent to which problems in local understanding account for continued influence from misinformation.

SOURCES OF DIFFICULTY IN CORRECTION COMPREHENSION

Influences on Surface Understanding

People may show influence from corrected misinformation because they do not understand the correction in a superficial sense. Potentially, this could occur if people fail to notice the correcting information in the first place, or if they forget it later. It could also occur if people notice the correcting information but fail to detect that it is inconsistent with earlier information. Finally, people may notice a discrepancy between two pieces of information, but they might not accept that the later information completely invalidates the former. Instead, they may reject the intended correction, or maintain both pieces of information as contradictory but competing hypotheses. If influence from misinformation arises due to problems with surface updating, providing stronger or clearer corrections should improve comprehension. This section argues that problems in surface updating contribute to, but do not completely account for, continued influence from misinformation.

A number of studies suggest that people can notice or remember a correction but still show influence from misinformation. Prior work on correction comprehension (Johnson & Seifert, 1994; Wilkes & Leatherbarrow, 1988) found that people consistently report correcting information in recall protocols and when directly asked about corrections within the text. However, they answer inference questions differently when a story contains corrected misinformation than when the story does not mention the misinformation. Johnson and Seifert (1994) also found that 75–90% of participants in correction conditions showed influence, and influence occurred whether people explicitly acknowledged the correction or not. Evidence from social judgment studies involving corrected misinformation also finds that people can show influence despite being able to recall correcting information spontaneously (Schul & Burnstein, 1985; Wyer & Unverzagt, 1985). These findings suggest that continued influence cannot always be attributed to failure to notice or remember a correction.

Evidence also suggests that people can fail to detect discrepancies in a text in some situations, but influence can occur even when conditions favor detection. Markman (1979) had children listen to statements such as "Ants have no noses. They use their sense of smell to find food." She found that the children could repeat the statements accurately, but they did not indicate that they found the statements confusing or contradictory. They were also unable to explain the discrepancy when confronted with it directly.[1] Other studies (Glenberg, Wilkinson, & Epstein, 1982; Otero & Kintsch, 1992) also found that college-age adults have difficulty detecting the contradiction between antonymic statements embedded within a text (e.g., "the procedure increases turbulence," followed later by "following the procedure, turbulence is decreased"). If people fail to detect a discrepancy, they would be unlikely to re-evaluate and potentially revise the earlier information.

Other work has found conditions in which people are more successful in detecting discrepancies. First, people detect contradictions better when the discrepant statements are closer together within a text, and when their literal forms have a high degree of overlap (Epstein, Glenberg, & Bradley, 1984). People also show better detection in shorter texts, even with distance between statements held constant (Glenberg et al., 1982). Baker and Wagner (1987) found that people detected contradictions better when the information was presented in main clauses, rather than embedded in subordinate clauses. On the other hand, people are more likely to miss contradictions that are syntactically marked as new (Glenberg et al., 1982).

A number of studies of correction comprehension, however, found influence even when conditions favored detection of the discrepancy between initial and correction information. Johnson and Seifert (1994) found influence despite using a correction with a simple clause structure and a form that literally negated earlier information. They also found influence even when a correction occurred immediately after the information it was

---

[1]An adult might resolve the apparent discrepancy by presuming that an ant's sense of smell has a different anatomical location, so it does not need a nose to smell. However, children rarely used this sort of "repair strategy" to make sense of the discrepant statements.

intended to correct. Similarly, van Oostendorp (1996) found that present-ing an initial and a subsequent text back-to-back did not improve people's updating performance. Repeating a correction for emphasis also failed to eliminate influence from initial information (van Oostendorp & Bonebak-ker, this volume), although this manipulation would presumably help any-one who had not detected the correction before. These results suggest that people may detect a correction yet still not completely update their model of the event.

However, detection failure may contribute to updating difficulty in some cases. Van Oostendorp (1996) had people read news reports about a mili-tary intervention in Somalia. For example, an initial text stated that "op-eration Restore Hope started under American control," whereas a sub-sequent text stated that "the United Nations took over the command in Somalia." If understood as intended, these statements would mean that a change in command had occurred; however, performance on a later in-ferencing task showed that little updating occurred. In this case, people may have failed to notice that the later statement contradicted the former because the statements had little overlap in literal wording. Instead, many people may have simply encoded both statements without establishing the relation between them. Johnson and Seifert (1994) also found more in-fluence from misinformation when using a correction in which a subordi-nate clause contained key information. As with other work on discrepancy detection (Baker & Wagner, 1987), a complex clause structure may have made it harder for people to detect what was being corrected. Thus, it is possible that some influence from initial information arises through this source.

Finally, a number of studies have found that influence occurs despite few overt indications that people have rejected the correcting information. Over time, research on persuasion (Abelson, 1959; Steiner & Rogers, 1963) and belief revision (Chinn & Brewer, 1993) has proposed a number of strategies that people can adopt to avoid changing their beliefs. People can ignore or reject new information outright, explain away discrepancies with prior beliefs, or discount the new information's source or value. If people use such processes when they encounter correcting information, it would be no surprise to find that they continue to rely on initial infor-mation. Presumably, then, all people would need is a more convincing correction that they will believe instead of reject.

However, it is unclear that rejection accounts for all the influence ob-served in correction studies. Johnson and Seifert (1994) presented stories that contained corrections about the cause of a warehouse fire, and directly asked participants what they thought caused the fire. People rarely men-tioned the misinformation in response to this direct question. Furthermore, they produced correct answers to direct questions about the content of the message containing the correction. Thus, people had the opportunity to indicate that they did not believe the correction, if that was the case. It also seems unlikely that people would feel pressure to answer direct questions "correctly" yet be careless when answering inference questions, on which influence effects more typically occur. Although these results do not rule out the possibility that people are rejecting the correction, they do not show overt evidence of this. Such disbelief would need to be subtle not to show up in direct measures.

In summary, misinformation can potentially influence people's judgments because they fail to do surface updating following a correction, but this does not account for all the influence observed. First, people show influence even when conditions are optimal for detecting the correction, and when they acknowledge that the correction occurred. This suggests that detection failure does not sufficiently explain the source of influence. People can also show influence even when they produce the correction as part of their recall of an event, which suggests that mere memory failure does not account for all cases of influence. Finally, people can show influence despite no other overt indications that they have rejected the correction. Although disbelief cannot be ruled out completely, it must be a subtle form if it cannot be assessed through direct questions about what people believe. Alternatively, people may have done appropriate surface updating, in the sense of establishing a relationship between initial and correcting propositions in the textbase, but they may fail to completely update their situation model of the event. The next sections discuss issues of global updating following a correction and present some data on model revision.

Factors in Global Updating

To do global updating after a correction, people would need to go beyond surface updating and consider the correction's implications for their situation model of the account. First, people may have used initial information to generate inferences. People are most likely to make online inferences about causal explanations, motives and goals, and actors' feelings (Graesser, Singer, & Trabasso, 1994). When initial information is corrected, people would need to evaluate any such inferences, and ignore or revise them if invalid. For example, if a correction indicates that a child was kidnapped by her father, not a neighbor, people might want to revise inferences they have made about the kidnapper's motive. Second, to understand information provided after a correction, people would need to integrate it within the current story structure by establishing links with the valid information, not the misinformation. In the prior example, information that the child was seen in a blue car may follow the correction.

It would be appropriate to infer that the child's father was the car's driver; people should not generate further inferences about the neighbor.

Some evidence suggests that people can have difficulty in updating their situation model when a correction has occurred. First, as just discussed, several studies (Johnson & Seifert, 1994; Wilkes & Leatherbarrow, 1988) found that people remember, acknowledge, and accurately answer direct questions about a correction. This suggests that people have the correcting information as part of the text representation that they have constructed. These studies also found that people who had read a corrected story version could recall as many story facts as people who had read a version that did not contain misinformation. This suggests that people in both conditions had a similar quantity of valid information as part of their representation. Given similar contents in memory, people who received a correction could potentially generate (or regenerate) answers to inference questions without relying on misinformation. However, people who received a correction of misinformation answered inference questions differently than those not exposed to the misinformation. Because people could not answer inference questions directly from the information presented, they would presumably base their answers on a situation model of the event.

Some evidence suggests that misinformation can influence how people construct a representation, even after a correction occurs. With a delay between initial and correcting information, people would have opportunity to learn additional facts and relate them to the initial information. At the point of correction, they would need to re-evaluate the validity of these inferences, which may prove difficult and effortful. In contrast, an immediate correction would give people less opportunity to make inferences involving the initial information because they would have learned fewer facts that the initial information could potentially explain. Furthermore, they would not be expected to generate such inferences spontaneously, simply based on the initial information (van den Broek, 1990). In this case, people should show less influence when a correction immediately follows misinformation, because they would have made fewer inferences potentially needing revision. However, Johnson and Seifert (1994) found similar levels of influence, regardless of how soon the correction was presented. This suggests that people may continue to use misinformation in constructing a situation model even after a correction has occurred.

Studies have also found evidence that people update a representation more easily when a correction provides positive content, as well as indicating that prior information is invalid. In a story about a warehouse fire, Wilkes and Leatherbarrow (1988) presented initial information that a closet in the building was empty, and later corrected this by indicating that the closet had contained volatile materials instead. They found that people made inferences based on the correcting information and showed little influence from the initial information. Similarly, Johnson and Seifert (1994) found less influence when a correction provided a concrete alternative to misinformation, rather than simply negating it; however, this did not eliminate all influence. On the one hand, providing positive content may help people detect a correction and thus facilitate surface updating; however, it may also help people construct an alternative representation and attain a more accurate global understanding. First, the newer alternative may suggest implications that contradict those of the initial information, and thus may stimulate people to consider which implications are correct. This could help people revise inferences they have made prior to the correction. Second, people could use the positive content when making new inferences. This would allow them to create a model that was potentially as coherent as that based on the initial information. When people do not receive such content, they would need either to generate their own alternatives or to maintain a representation in which some factors are unexplained.

Reader variables could also potentially influence people's success in updating a representation of an event, although prior results have been mixed. Simply detecting the correction and adding it to a textbase would not necessarily result in updating aspects of a complex internal model. Rather, people may expend the effort to consider their inferences carefully only when motivated by particular reading goals. However, studies have found influence from misinformation when people expect to have to answer comprehension questions (van Oostendorp & Bonebakker, this volume), as well as when they only expect to have to recall a text (Johnson & Seifert, 1994; Wilkes & Leatherbarrow, 1988). An additional study (van Oostendorp, 1996) found that instructions to read "normally" or "for comprehension" did not have a significant effect on people's updating performance. These results suggest either that comprehension instructions do not sufficiently motivate people to expend the effort to update a situation model, or that people may not know how to update a model fully. However, improved updating occurred when people had a strong situation model of the initial event. Again, having a strong model may help people notice that new information is discrepant with it; it may also help people recognize the implications of the updating information and stimulate inference revision.

In summary, some evidence suggests that difficulty in updating a representation may extend beyond that of merely establishing a superficial understanding of the correction. First, people use correcting information in free recall and direct questions about its content, which suggests that they have incorporated it into their representation and are not overtly rejecting it. However, their answers to inference questions, which cannot be answered directly from the textbase, show influence from misinformation. Second, people show influence, even when a correction occurs immediately following the misinformation. In this case, detecting it should not be a problem, and people would not have reason to disbelieve it. This suggests that the effect occurs as people try to incorporate subsequent information into their representation. Lastly, providing a correction with positive content tends to improve updating performance. Again, this content may improve correction detection, but would also provide people with information that would allow them to construct an alternate representation. However, further work is needed to understand how people construct these alternate representations when initial information is corrected, and what kinds of instructions or conditions can induce people to make these efforts.

GENERATION OF ALTERNATE MODELS
AFTER CORRECTION

The evidence just discussed, as well as studies of social judgments (Anderson, 1982; Anderson, New, & Speer, 1985), suggests that providing an alternative to misinformation reduces its influence on later judgments and inferences. When misinformation is merely negated, however, people show more difficulty in constructing a situation model that does not involve the misinformation. This could occur for a number of reasons: First, of course, they might not believe the correction. However, mere belief in the correction would not guarantee that people could update their models appropriately. They would also need to become aware that the correction has more global implications for their representations. Finally, they would need to know how to make appropriate adjustments. These latter stages may be particularly difficult when a correction does not provide alternate content. Alternate content may suggest how to construct a coherent situation model that does not involve misinformation; it may also suggest alternate implications that contradict those stemming from the misinformation, and thereby stimulate people to re-examine earlier inferences they may have made. However, people may not spontaneously think of alternatives when they are not provided. Research on social theories has found that people rarely generate alternatives spontaneously when initial information is discredited (Anderson, 1982); however, they show less influence from discredited information when they are explicitly asked to consider alternatives (Anderson, 1982; Anderson et al., 1985).

On the other hand, people may have potentially relevant information available but not use it. Johnson and Seifert (1994) tested the hypothesis that the mere mention of discredited information made it more available, and thus more likely to be reported in inferences. People read a series of reports about a warehouse fire, with the reports containing either discredited information about volatile materials stored in the warehouse, an incidental mention of volatile materials across the street from the warehouse, or no mention of volatile materials. A final group did a distractor task after reading the reports, which involved generating associates to the volatile-material words used in the discrediting message. Validation tasks showed that information was available when presented incidentally or in the distractor task; however, people did not use that information to make inferences. People did make volatile-materials inferences when the reports stated that such materials were inside the warehouse, whether this was discredited later or not. This suggests that people may need to see available alternatives as explicit potential causes before they will use them to generate an alternate scenario.

To investigate whether instructions to consider alternate causes can mitigate continued influence from misinformation, the present study used an account containing a series of reports on a fire investigation, taken from a paradigm developed by Wilkes and Leatherbarrow (1988). The experiment manipulated whether participants were asked to generate alternative causal explanations for the fire after they had read the story. Participants who generated alternatives should show fewer influenced inferences if the alternatives provide causal activation of concepts other than those that are discredited. On the other hand, people may need to have an alternative explanation actually instantiated within the particular story context, rather than generated without clear ties to the event. In this case, mere activation of alternate causes would not be sufficient to mitigate continued influence from the misinformation, and one would expect little effect from merely generating alternatives.

Method

We had 46 University of Michigan undergraduates participate in single sessions lasting approximately 50 minutes. Participants read a series of 13 reports describing the investigation of a warehouse fire (see Wilkes & Leatherbarrow, 1988, or Johnson & Seifert, 1994, for complete materials). The design included three groups: In the correction-only and correction-generate groups, the fifth message stated that a particular closet on the premises contained cans of oil paint and pressurized gas cylinders (volatile materials), and the eleventh message stated the correction: that the closet had not contained such materials before the fire. In the control-generate group, misinformation was not presented. Instead, the fifth message in the series stated that a particular closet in the warehouse was empty, and this was not corrected later. For this group, Message 11 was instead a notice that several firefighters had been released from the hospital. In each condition, the other messages describe features of the fire, such as the presence of toxic fumes, but do not explicitly provide further information about potential causes of the fire.

Participants were told to read each message at their own pace and not to look back at prior messages. They were also told that they would be asked to recall the reports at a later time. When each individual participant had finished reading, the experimenter collected his or her booklet of reports. Each participant then received a summary sheet and wrote a free recall of the reports' contents. For participants in the control-generate and the correction-generate groups, this sheet also asked them to generate four or five possible causes for a fire of the type they had just read about. Participants in the correction-only group were simply asked what was responsible for the fire and did not generate a set of possible alternatives. When everyone had finished the recall test, all participants worked on a distractor task for 10 minutes. After this time had elapsed, participants received a memory questionnaire and were instructed to answer each question based on their understanding of the reports. This questionnaire included 10 questions on facts directly presented in the messages (e.g., what type of business was the warehouse involved in), 10 other questions requiring the participants to make inferences about the event (e.g., what might be responsible for the toxic fumes), and 2 final questions assessing whether participants were aware of any correction or contradiction in the series.

Results

First, a coder who was blind to the experimental conditions scored the responses to the inference questions for "negligence" theme inferences. These were responses consistent with believing that the warehouse contained carelessly stored volatile materials that caused or contributed to the fire, as would be reasonable if the information about the volatile materials had not been discredited. This theme encompassed references using key words from the discredited message (e.g., oil, paint, gas(es), cans or cylinders thereof), mentions of the closet itself without indications that it was empty, and attributions of carelessness or negligence. Second, the entire protocol (i.e., recall sheet, fact questions, and inference questions) was scored for the number of direct and uncontroverted references to the volatile materials.

A participant was scored as noticing the correction if the participant referred to it accurately on either the summary or the memory questionnaire. Both the correction groups showed high levels of recall of the correction, with only 5 of 30 failing to acknowledge it. The free recall summaries were scored for presence of thought units (Kintsch, 1974) that were common to all three conditions; thus, the summary recall scores do not reflect participants' recall of the message about the closet's contents (empty or storing volatile materials). Fact questions from the memory questionnaire were also scored for accurate content. There were no group differences in summary recall or in fact recall ($F < 1$ for each). The overall mean for summary recall was 9.6 units; participants recalled a mean of 9.0 facts correctly.

The number of alternatives each participant generated, either in response to the generation question or the fire's cause question, were tallied. Participants in the control-generate condition provided a mean of 4.7 alternatives, and those in the correction-generate condition had a mean of 4.5 alternatives. Participants who were only asked about the fire's cause (correction-only group) averaged 1.5 alternatives in response to that question. The difference among the groups was significant ($p < .0001$). Table 12.1 shows how often volatile materials and arson were generated as alternatives, in each of the conditions.

If generating possible alternatives helps people avoid falling back on earlier misinformation, the correction-generate group should show fewer inferences involving this information. However, that is not what we found. Instead, Table 12.2 shows the mean number of direct references to the stored volatile materials, and the number of negligence-theme inferences, for each group. Analyses of variance showed a significant difference among groups on both variables ($ps < .001$). For both variables, planned contrasts found that the two correction groups were significantly different from the control-generate condition ($ps < .0001$), but the two correction groups did not differ from each other ($Fs < 1.4$). Overall, only 4 out of 30 participants

TABLE 12.1
Proportion of People Who Generated Volatile
Materials and Arson as Alternatives, by Group

	Control-Generate	Correction-Generate	Correction-Only
Volatile materials	.07	.60	.20
Arson	.87	.73	.33

Note. The proportions within a single condition reflect the fact that people were asked to generate multiple alternatives.

TABLE 12.2
Number of Negligence Inferences and Direct
References to Volatile Materials, by Group

	Control-Generate	Correction-Generate	Correction-Only
Negligence inferences	.73	2.73	3.33
References to volatile materials	.80	3.73	3.40

in the correction groups failed to make at least one direct and uncontroverted reference to the volatile materials. In contrast, however, only 4 of the 30 participants from the correction groups spontaneously reported the volatile materials as a cause when directly asked what was responsible for the fire.

Discussion

The results show that having people generate alternatives does not necessarily lead them to revise their situation models. People in the two correction conditions did not differ in amount of influence from misinformation. However, people in the correction-generate condition reported a similar number of possible causes as those in the control-generate condition. Furthermore, 73% generated arson as an alternative cause. On one hand, this suggests that the misinformation did not inhibit generation of strong causal alternatives that could form a basis for revising situation models. On the other hand, activating these potential causes did not lead people to alter their situation models substantially. Johnson and Seifert (1994) found that presenting arson as an alternative within the story led to less influence from misinformation. This suggests that people may need to have an alternate cause instantiated within the story context before they will construct a situation model that shows less influence from misinformation.

As in prior studies (Johnson & Seifert, 1994), this study's participants show little overt rejection of the correction. On one hand, people in the correction-generate condition still generated "volatile materials" as a salient possible cause of "this type" of fire; few people in the control-generate condition (under 8%) reported this alternative spontaneously. Certainly, the correction did not lead people to forget the misinformation's possible causal relevance. However, few people endorsed the volatile materials as the cause of the particular fire described in the reports after the correction. Again, this suggests that people acknowledge the correction on one level but may not appreciate its more global implications for their representations.

The current results conflict with previous work (Anderson, 1983), which found that participants showed less influence from discredited information when asked to generate alternative explanations. Anderson (1983) had participants learn a positive or negative relationship between firefighting success and risk preference, and then told them that the experimenter had contrived the data presented. People who then generated reasons why the opposite relationship could be true (e.g., explained a negative relationship when they had originally learned a positive one) showed less influence from the discredited information than those who did not consider the alternative. The current study differs from this work in two important ways. First, the current study merely manipulated activation of alternative causes, rather than having participants create elaborated explanations based on what they had generated, as in Anderson (1983). Second, participants in the current study were told to generate items as alternative explanations for "this type" of fire, rather than explicitly told to consider alternative explanations for the particular event they had read about. They may not have evaluated whether their generated alternatives "did" cause the particular fire they read about. The differences between the current work and previous findings (Anderson, 1983) support the claim that mere causal activation, without further elaboration in the particular context, is insufficient to mitigate continued influence from misinformation. These results suggest that people may need to have an alternative explanation instantiated within a particular context before it will mitigate influence from misinformation. If people do not incorporate these alternatives into their story representation, the alternatives do not appear to affect people's later inferences.

GENERAL CONCLUSIONS

In this chapter, we have argued for a distinction between surface and global updating following a correction. On one hand, people may show influence from misinformation because they have not established a local understanding. Certainly, people may fail to notice the correcting information, not detect its discrepancy with earlier information, or not believe that it invalidates earlier information. In each of these cases, people would be unlikely to alter a situation model that features the initial information. On the other hand, engaging in global updating would involve recognizing the correction's implications for one's model of the event. People may need to re-evaluate and possibly revise any prior inferences they have made on the basis of misinformation. Furthermore, they would need to understand information presented after the correction in terms of valid facts and avoid linking it to the misinformation. A correction may not directly address more global aspects of people's representations, so comprehenders themselves may need to make additional updating efforts.

Some studies show that influence can occur, even when people have apparently done surface updating. First, people may show influence from misinformation despite being able to recall the correction, and even when conditions favor detecting the discrepancy between initial and correcting information. Furthermore, people may show influence on inference questions, despite using correcting information appropriately when asked direct questions about an event's cause and about the correction itself. This suggests that people do not overtly reject correcting information, although this cannot be ruled out completely.

In addition, manipulations that would presumably facilitate surface updating occasionally reduce but do not eliminate influence from misinformation. Some research (Johnson & Seifert, 1994; van Oostendorp, 1996) found that decreasing the delay between initial and updating information did not affect the amount of influence, although this could presumably help people detect the discrepancy between statements. Repeating a correction for emphasis also did not decrease the amount of influence (see van Oostendorp & Bonebakker, this volume). People did show less influence when a correction used a simple clause structure and had high literal overlap with the phrasing of the initial information, but this did not eliminate the effect (Johnson & Seifert, 1994). This suggests that combating influence from misinformation may not be just a matter of providing a clear correction statement.

Some evidence suggests that people may have difficulty in knowing how to revise a situation model, rather than in knowing that they should. Most of the studies that have found influence have used corrections that negate earlier material. People may accept that the initial information is false but not know how else to create a coherent account. In contrast, providing positive content tends to decrease or even eliminate influence effects (Johnson & Seifert, 1994; Wilkes & Leatherbarrow, 1988). Such information may provide a basis that allows people to generate a coherent alternative representation. However, as in the study reported here, people may need such information instantiated in a causal context within the story; people may not spontaneously generate alternatives (Anderson, 1982), or use alternatives that have been activated outside the story's causal context (Johnson & Seifert, 1994).

One direction for further work is to extend what we know about when influence from misinformation occurs. On one hand, researchers have found such effects in a wide variety of situations, ranging from social judgments (Ross et al., 1975; Schul & Burnstein, 1985) to event (Massad, Hubbard, & Newtson, 1979) and person perception (Wyer & Budesheim, 1987; Wyer & Unverzagt, 1985) to juror decision-making (Thompson, Fong, & Rosenhan, 1981). On the other hand, misinformation effects have been tested in only a small number of different texts, and at times the effects, although reliable, are small. Larger influence effects may occur when people attempt to comprehend complex information on unfamiliar topics, such as technical issues introduced in court or counterintuitive findings in science. In these cases, people may learn correcting information but show influence because they do not appreciate the correction's implications.

Another direction is to shift from sources of misinformation influence to processes of correction comprehension. We know little about how updating proceeds when people do it successfully. Some important issues are how people evaluate correcting information when they read it, what (if any) prior inferences people revise and when, and how they might avoid using corrected misinformation as they continue constructing their representations. Corrections may add a special spin to the more general problem of updating because people would need to deal with the additional implications of having learned false information.

In conclusion, how people comprehend corrections and deal with misinformation may have implications for their understanding of an event, as well as affecting judgments they make based on the event. People would need to realize that a particular piece of earlier information is false and do surface updating. However, people may also need to alter more global aspects of their representation of the event in order to have a complete and accurate understanding of what has occurred. Evidence on correction comprehension suggests that people may have difficulty with both surface and global updating. Further research is needed to determine what processes people use when successfully comprehending corrections, and how their failure contributes to continuing influence from misinformation.

REFERENCES

Abelson, R. P. (1959). Modes of resolution of belief dilemmas. *Journal of Conflict Resolution, 3*, 343–352.

Anderson, C. A. (1982). Inoculation and counterexplanation: Debiasing techniques in the perseverance of social theories. *Social Cognition, 1*, 126–139.

Anderson, C. A. (1983). Abstract and concrete data in the perseverance of social theories: When weak data lead to unshakeable beliefs. *Journal of Experimental Social Psychology, 19*, 93–108.

Anderson, C. A., Lepper, M. R., & Ross, L. (1980). Perseverance of social theories: The role of explanation in the persistence of discredited information. *Journal of Personality and Social Psychology, 39*, 1037–1049.

Anderson, C. A., New, B. L., & Speer, J. R. (1985). Argument availability as a mediator of social theory perseverance. *Social Cognition, 3*, 235–249.

Baker, L., & Wagner, J. (1987). Evaluating information for truthfulness: The effects of logical subordination. *Memory & Cognition, 15*, 247–255.

Chinn, C. A., & Brewer, W. F. (1993). The role of anomalous data in knowledge acquisition: Theoretical framework and implications for science instruction. *Review of Educational Research, 63*, 1–49.

Epstein, W., Glenberg, A. M., & Bradley, M. M. (1984). Coactivation and comprehension: Contribution of text variables to the illusion of knowing. *Memory & Cognition, 12*, 355–360.

Glenberg, A. M., Wilkinson, A. C., & Epstein, W. (1982). The illusion of knowing: Failure in the self-assessment of comprehension. *Memory & Cognition, 10*, 597–602.

Graesser, A. C., Singer, M., & Trabasso, T. (1994). Constructing inferences during narrative text comprehension. *Psychological Review, 101*, 371–395.

Johnson, H. M., & Seifert, C. M. (1994). Sources of the continued influence effect: When misinformation in memory affects later inferences. *Journal of Experimental Psychology: Learning, Memory, and Cognition, 20*, 1420–1436.

Kintsch, W. (1974). *The representation of meaning in memory.* Hillsdale, NJ: Lawrence Erlbaum Associates.

Markman, E. (1979). Realizing that you don't understand: Elementary school children's awareness of inconsistencies. *Child Development, 50,* 643–655.

Massad, C. M., Hubbard, M., & Newtson, D. (1979). Selective perception of events. *Journal of Experimental Social Psychology, 15,* 513–532.

Otero, J., & Kintsch, W. (1992). Failures to detect contradictions in a text: What readers believe versus what they read. *Psychological Science, 3,* 229–235.

Ross, L., Lepper, M. A., & Hubbard, M. (1975). Perseverance in self-perception and social perception: Biased attributional processes in the debriefing paradigm. *Journal of Personality and Social Psychology, 32,* 880–892.

Schul, Y., & Burnstein, E. (1985). When discounting fails: Conditions under which individuals use discredited information in making a judgment. *Journal of Personality and Social Psychology, 49,* 894–903.

Steiner, I. D., & Rogers, E. D. (1963). Alternative responses to dissonance. *Journal of Abnormal and Social Psychology, 66,* 128–136.

Thompson, W. C., Fong, G. T., & Rosenhan, D. L. (1981). Inadmissible evidence and juror verdicts. *Journal of Personality and Social Psychology, 40,* 453–463.

van den Broek, P. (1990). Causal inferences and the comprehension of narrative texts. In A. C. Graesser & G. Bower (Eds.), *The psychology of learning and motivation: Inferences and text comprehension* (Vol. 25, pp. 175–196). San Diego, CA: Academic Press.

van Oostendorp, H. (1996). Updating situation models derived from newspaper articles. *Medienpsychologie, 8,* 21–33.

Wilkes, A. L., & Leatherbarrow, M. (1988). Editing episodic memory following the identification of error. *Quarterly Journal of Experimental Psychology: Human Experimental Psychology, 40A,* 361–387.

Wyer, R. S., & Budesheim, T. L. (1987). Person memory and judgments: The impact of information that one is told to disregard. *Journal of Personality and Social Psychology, 53,* 14–29.

Wyer, R. S., & Unverzagt, W. H. (1985). Effects of instructions to disregard information on its subsequent recall and use in making judgments. *Journal of Personality and Social Psychology, 48,* 533–549.

Chapter 13

Difficulties in Updating Mental Representations During Reading News Reports

Herre van Oostendorp
Christiaan Bonebakker
Utrecht University, The Netherlands

In news, understanding previously stored knowledge is of crucial importance: One can fully understand news only if one can accurately recall and use information from previously read news reports. This is how situation models, the representations of what the text is about, develop and get updated (see Van Dijk & Kintsch, 1983). But unfortunately, in practice this activation and updating process does not operate as smoothly as the theory suggests it might (Findahl & Höijer, 1981; Larsen, 1983). The two studies presented in this chapter examine this updating process.

There is now considerable evidence that under certain circumstances readers develop several levels of representation during the processing of a text: a representation of the surface structure; a semantic representation of the input discourse in the form of a propositional textbase; and a representation of what the text is about, namely a situation model (Fletcher & Chrysler, 1990; Gray-Wilson, Rinck, McNamara, Bower, & Morrow, 1993; Kintsch, Welsch, Schmalhofer, & Zimny, 1990; Morrow, 1994; Schmalhofer & Glavanov, 1986; Van Dijk & Kintsch, 1983; Zwaan & van Oostendorp, 1993).

It can be expected that the construction and updating of a situation model is particularly important for reading newspaper articles. In general, the primary goals of reading this kind of text are to understand the world and to accommodate this understanding to changes that happened in the world, rather than understanding the text itself or remembering the exact surface structure.

However, a recurring finding of studies on the way readers process news stories is the fact that they process these texts very superficially (Bell, 1991; Graber, 1988; Gunter, 1987). For instance, the extensive, qualitative study of Bell (1991) showed that factually correct information in the media is often misunderstood. He did his research in New Zealand, where he catalogued all media messages concerning climate change over 6 months. These messages were compared with the ideas of a sample of subjects representative of the New Zealand population. Although daily media were almost the only source of information about this issue, many people had dissenting ideas. Of course, it is quite possible that these findings reflect the negative influence of hearsay. Several subjects thought the ozone hole was located right over New Zealand, which had never been suggested in the media. Hardly anybody could recall the correct time in which the hole occurs, whereas the media provided the correct information. Figures in the media were often exaggerated by the public. For example, the rise of the sea level as a result of the greenhouse effect was often estimated many times higher than was (correctly) reported in the media. Furthermore, the greenhouse effect and the ozone hole were mixed up. These outcomes may be caused by the blurring of the distinction between events belonging to similar mental models or situation models.

More specifically, it seems that readers (or listeners) really have trouble updating their situation model when they read (or hear) a news text, and more importantly, it is unclear what factors do affect this process of updating. It is worthwhile to note here that we use the term *updating* in a strict sense. We denote with it the transformation or replacement of knowledge already represented in subjects' memory. We want to distinguish it from, for instance, extending a model, that is, adding or elaborating a model with new knowledge that had no predecessor in subjects' representation.

In a series of experiments, van Oostendorp (1996a) explored the importance of a number of factors for an effective updating of situation models derived from newspaper articles. Subjects were presented with a text about the situation in Somalia at the time of the U.S. operation "Restore Hope," followed by a second related text some time later. This second text contained transformations of facts mentioned in the first text. For example, the first text reported "operation Restore Hope started under American control," and in the second text it was reported that the command structure of the operation had been transformed into "the United Nations took over the command in Somalia." Please note that the current command is in hands of the UN, and no longer in the hands of the United States. A correct updating of the situation model implies that the old information is replaced by the new information. It is important to note that the main reason for presenting the first text is to control for original model strength of subjects, and to be able to manipulate the situation model by adding transformations in the second text.

The main questions of these experiments were whether the transformations are incorporated in the reader's situation model after they read the second text, and which factors were involved. Several variables were included in these experiments. First, the instruction was varied; that is, subjects were instructed to read "carefully" or to read "normally." Second, the delay of the presentation of the second text was varied: immediately, or 1 day after reading the first text. A third variable was the strength of the original situation model. The strength of the original situation model established after reading the first text was measured by an inference judgment task that was presented after subjects had read the first text. On the basis of the median score on this test subjects with a "weak" or "strong" model were distinguished. Fourth, interest in the situation in Somalia was measured on the basis of rating scales that resulted in groups of low- versus high-interest subjects. Fifth, the relevance of items on the inference judgment task was also assessed. The information involved in the items of this task was not equal in its relevance to the situation described by the text. Some verified only details of the situation, others were highly relevant. On the basis of rating by subjects of the relevance of the items to the situation, items were divided into low- versus high-relevant by using the median relevance score. This was done in a separate norming study.

The main dependent variable was the performance of subjects on an inference judgment task presented after reading the second text. They had to judge the correctness of the presented statements in view of the second text. For instance, a test item was "The USA troops operate under the UN flag" (True/False?) in the previous example. This inference judgment task was used because the interest was in the subjects' situational representation rather than in their textbase representation. In order to judge the inferences accurately, subjects cannot rely solely on their textbase representation. Also, after reading the first text, subjects received an inference judgment task. The text had a rather factual character in order to avoid effects regarding attitudes. Each text was about 1,000 words. The nature of the transformations was one of describing changes to the situation in the world (e.g., first the command by the United States, next by the UN) rather than of introducing logical inconsistencies or contradictions.

Very briefly (for details see van Oostendorp, 1996a), the main results were, first, that the updating performance was, in general, very low: Only approximately 70% of the true/false items on the judgment inference test were answered correctly. This is considered low, given that 50% correct would be expected by chance. It appeared that instruction, delay, and interest had no significant effects.

Furthermore, model strength had a significant influence on updating, that is, updating was facilitated when the old, to-be-modified information was correctly represented in memory. In particular, a strong influence of prior knowledge was found in a conditional analysis. In this analysis, the performance of subjects on the second test was analyzed, given that they correctly knew the corresponding information in the first text. This analysis was performed because one could say that real or strict updating only occurs if subjects correctly knew the original facts of the first text and could correctly substitute these with the corresponding transformed, new facts in the second text. Subjects who had initially constructed a strong situation model and knew the related information in the first text—assessed by means of an inference judgment task presented directly after reading the first text—judged inferences concerning the transformations in the second text better and faster than subjects with a weak model. This result extends findings of Kintsch and Franzke (1995), who reported that the availability of an appropriate situation model influences the extension of it when reading new information. The study by van Oostendorp (1996a) showed that an appropriate model also leads to a higher degree of updating of a situation model when the representation had to be transformed.

In addition, an effect of relevance of information to the situation model was found. Remarkably, transformations of low-relevant information were much better updated than those of high-relevant information. Changes of minor importance were better encoded than major changes. This effect was found for subjects with an originally weak situation model as well as for subjects with an originally strong model. We elaborate on this finding somewhat.

Several interpretations for this effect of relevance are possible; one interpretation is that the distinction between low- and high-relevant items may not be reliable. However, the agreement between subjects in rating was high, and it appeared to be the case in two experiments with different items. Alternatively, there might be a "Von Restorff"-like effect, such as low-relevant items are "funnier." Carefully inspecting the items does not make this interpretation very plausible.

Another, more plausible interpretation is based on a kind of rejection process, that is, readers refuse to make changes in their situation model on important points. This kind of reaction from readers is what Chinn and Brewer (1993) called peripheral theory change. Hardcore propositions cannot easily be altered without scrapping the entire theory (or situation model), but peripheral propositions can be altered while preserving the kernel of the theory (or situation model).

The most plausible interpretation, however, is a kind of sloppy encoding, that is, subjects encode the changed information superficially because they erroneously think that they already know the transformations. This may be true in the case of high-relevant information. This interpretation is more or less similar to one of the responses individuals typically make integrating anomalous data in an existing theory (or situation model). Chinn and Brewer (1993) called it "ignoring anomalous data." That is, one way to dispose of anomalous data is simply to ignore it.

In a follow-up study (van Oostendorp, 1996b), we tried to get direct evidence about the occurrence of skipping or rejection processes by using the think-aloud method as used by Trabasso and Suh (1993). The focus of this study was on the processing of the transformations in the second text of the two Somalia texts described previously. The results showed that skipping could be the main cause of failing to update. Multiple linear regression analyses showed that test performance (on the inference judgment task) could be best explained by activities of readers that pointed to skipping the transformations, which was indicated, for instance, by careless metacomments during processing of the transformations. Further research and more converging evidence is needed to support the plausibility of this interpretation, and also to examine what causes a reader to show one or the other response to changes in the described situation.

Difficulties in updating situation models were also the focus of a series of experiments by Wilkes and Leatherbarrow (1988) and by Johnson and Seifert (1993, 1994b, this volume). Both research teams made use of fictional news events consisting of brief, single messages. In the experimental conditions a correction was inserted, which denied a fact reported earlier. Ideally the subjects should not only integrate these corrections in their situation model, but also re-interpret all intermediate messages, which were given after the misinformation and before the correction.

Wilkes and Leatherbarrow, for instance, presented subjects with a story on a fire in a warehouse. Subjects in the experimental condition read that "inflammable materials were carelessly stored in a side room." Later in the story they read that "the side room happened to be empty." And the explicit information was added that no storage of inflammable materials had occurred. At the same time the control condition first read the sentence, "the side room happened to be empty." and later some neutral, irrelevant message on "how the fire brigade's investigation was progressing."

The most obvious conclusion was that the influence of old, obsolete information (something like "inflammable, carelessly stored materials in room" in the example story) could not be fully eradicated by new, discrediting information (something like "no inflammable, carelessly stored materials"). Answers to questions (e.g., "What was the cause of the explosions?") were frequently based on the old information, even when subjects were aware of the fact that certain information was discredited. Recall and direct questions showed that almost all readers had the correction available but still did not use it during processing of the text (Johnson & Seifert, 1994; Wilkes & Leatherbarrow, 1988).

Johnson and Seifert also showed that the correction of an incorrect fact reported earlier was processed substantially more successfully if the correction contained an alternative causal explanation of the event. Alternative explanations were provided through insertions in the story of a sentence like, "Firefighters have found evidence of gasoline-soaked rags." This sentence indicates evidence that the fire was started deliberately. Nevertheless, some influence of the discredited information remained noticeable.

Johnson and Seifert therefore concluded that the influence of old information cannot be fully eradicated. The relationship between these experiments and the experiments with the Somalia texts is clear. Both lines of research show that updating is difficult and that new information is incompletely represented. Furthermore, the work by Johnson and Seifert, and Wilkes and Leatherbarrow adds the idea that the existing old model constitutes a negative factor for updating. However, it is not clear from Johnson and Seifert's experiments what the exact cause is of the incomplete updating: Is it a rejection process, that is, actively holding on to the old information, or is it merely superficial encoding of the new information, which seemed to be the case in the Somalia experiments? These questions concern the first point of attention in the current experiments. A single revocation or replacement of previously given information perhaps does not have enough impact on readers to result in updating their situation model. However, the possibility of loose processing is less plausible, if even after confirmation of the correction—by a repetition—the misinformation continues to play a part. Instead, in that case we may assume that people actively refuse to update their situation model. In other words, they reject the correction.

The second point of consideration concerns the control condition in Wilkes and Leatherbarrow's and Johnson and Seifert's experiments. There can be some doubt as to its adequacy. In their control condition, the correct information was given in an earlier stage than in the experimental condition. Therefore, in the control condition, many messages could immediately be interpreted from the right perspective, whereas subjects in the experimental condition had to re-interpret these messages in retrospect. It would be more adequate if in all conditions the correct information was provided in the same (late) stage, so that the right interpretation always must be made in retrospect.

The third point of attention in the experiment is that we wanted to replicate the results of Johnson and Seifert concerning the influence of the alternative causal explanation: Is there less influence of discredited information when an alternative causal explanation has been provided?

EXPERIMENT 1

To investigate these issues, we did an experiment with a structure similar to Wilkes and Leatherbarrow's and Johnson and Seifert's, but with some important adaptations. First, the adequacy of the control condition (Condition 0) is increased. Second, we used three experimental conditions: one with a single correction (Condition 1); one with a repeated correction, in order to examine the question of rejection versus loose encoding (Condition 2); and one with a correction plus causal alternative, in order to replicate the findings of Johnson and Seifert (Condition 3). Third, we used four different news stories in order to be able to generalize over more than one specific situation.

Method

Materials. Each story consisted of a series of 13 messages, all referring to one fictional event. These stories were very comparable to the stories used by Wilkes and Leatherbarrow, and Johnson and Seifert. Two stories were even (almost) identical. The structure of the four stories we used was as similar as possible (see Table 13.1). In the three experimental conditions, the text mentions a possible cause of the event at issue in stage I, which in stage II turns out to be incorrect. There were, as stated, three versions of this correction: a preclusion or single negation of the cause mentioned (Condition 1), a preclusion of the cause mentioned followed by a confirmation of that correction (i.e., a repeated correction; Condition 2), and a preclusion of the cause mentioned immediately followed by an alternative explanation (Condition 3). The control condition (Condition 0) makes no reference to any possible cause of the news event.

For instance, the story about the fire in a warehouse, adapted from Wilkes and Leatherbarrow, is provided in the Appendix. In the experi-

TABLE 13.1
Structure of Experimental Stories (Experiment 1)

	Condition 0	*Condition 1*	*Condition 2*	*Condition 3*
Stage I: Message 5	Neutral; nothing about cause	Possible cause	Possible cause	Possible cause
Stage II: Message 10	Preclusion of cause	Preclusion of cause	Preclusion of cause	Preclusion of cause; alternative
Stage III: Message 13	Neutral	Neutral	Repeated preclusion of cause	Neutral

mental conditions, message 5 mentions the presence of carelessly stored lightly inflammable materials in the side room where the fire started. In the control condition, message 5 consists of the neutral information that both police and firemen are involved in the investigation. In all conditions, message 10 states that the side room happened to be empty; in the three experimental conditions this is augmented by the explicit information that the previous message was incorrect. On top of this, condition 3 provides an alternative explanation of the fire, indicating that the fire may have been started deliberately: "Fire men have found evidence of gasoline-soaked rags." In condition 2, message 13 contains a confirmation from another source, "The fire officer confirms that there were no lightly inflammable materials in the side room." The other conditions state that the fire has been brought under control.

An important difference with Johnson and Seifert and Wilkes and Leatherbarrow is the timing of the message that the side room was empty in the control condition. They presented this information at the moment that the other conditions received the possible cause, the "lightly inflammable materials" scenario. In our text, the mention of the side room being empty is made at the same stage in all conditions.

The second story was about a fight between the janitor of a nightclub and a guest, which might have had a racist background. Later in the story, it appeared to have no racist background. Story 3 was about world-cup swimming. The Brazilian team set a new world record, but there was the suspicion of narcotics usage. Later, it appeared that no team had used narcotics. The fourth story was about a jewelry theft in a house. The son of the family living in that house is suspected. Later, this appeared to be incorrect because he was abroad during the time of the theft.

Subjects. Fifty-one students took part in this experiment, randomly assigned to the four conditions.

Procedure. The subjects received a booklet with a series of messages referring to one event. Every message was on a separate page. They read them at their own pace, and they were not allowed to turn back and reread the messages. Every subject was presented with four stories, each in a different condition, in such a way that each story was presented 12 or 13 times in each condition.

Scoring. The questionnaire contained six factual questions and eight inference questions for every story. The factual questions referred to information explicitly stated in the texts, and gave some insight into the subjects' textbase. The inference questions were focused directly or indirectly on the cause of the event at issue, and stimulated the subjects to speculate about this. For instance, in the warehouse fire example, "What could have been the cause of the explosions?" or "For what reason might an insurance claim be refused?" The responses to the inference questions are supposed to shed light on the scenario that must have been at the basis of it. Four possible scenarios were distinguished:

1. Old: a response on the basis of information that in a later stage turned out to be incorrect (the corrected information).
2. New: a response on the basis of information that eventually turned out to be correct (the correction). A response was judged as *new* not only if it explicitly stated that the previously mentioned cause was incorrect, but also if it provided a plausible explanation that was not incompatible with the correction.
3. Alternative: a response on the basis of the alternative causal explanation mentioned in the text.
4. Non-responses: questions that were not responded to at all, as well as responses like "don't know" and "?".

For each question, lists of key words corresponding to each of the four scenarios were constructed, on the basis of which the judgments of the answers were made. This method resulted in an interjudge reliability of .95.

Results

There were no significant differences between conditions in performance on the factual questions. Consequently, we may assume that subjects in all conditions have similar textbases, so that possible differences in results on the inference questions are to be attributed to differences in situational representations.

Table 13.2 shows the major results, which concern the performance on the inference questions (averaged over subjects and stories). The maximum

TABLE 13.2
Mean Score on the Inference Questions (Experiment 1)

Scenario	Condition			
	0	*1*	*2*	*3*
old	0.20	0.84	0.57	0.57
new	7.57	6.94	7.02	5.45
alternative	0.06	0.04	0.16	1.92
nonresponses	0.18	0.18	0.26	0.06

score per condition is 8, the number of inference questions. In this table, each column sums to 8. The most important results concern the old and new responses. Though the means are low, analysis of variance showed that Conditions 1, 2, and 3 generate significantly ($p < .05$) more old information than control Condition 0 does (see Table 13.2). The results showed no significant difference between Conditions 1 and 2 concerning old information.

Furthermore, Conditions 0, 1, and 2 produce more new information than Condition 3 does, and Condition 0 produces more new information than Conditions 1 and 2 do. There is no significant difference concerning new information between Condition 1 and 2.

The results also showed that Condition 3 produces more alternative information than Conditions 0, 1, and 2 do. However, these differences in the production of alternative information do not result in any significant differences in the production of old information between Condition 3 on the one hand and Conditions 1 and 2 on the other. Also there is still more production of old information in Condition 3 than in Condition 0.

Discussion

Briefly, the main conclusion based on these results is that the influence of old information is hard to neutralize (Condition 1), also with an improved control condition, replicating the results of Johnson and Seifert (1993, 1994): Subjects in Condition 1 more strongly used the old scenario and, at the same time, use less the new scenario than subjects in the control Condition 0. This effect also occurs when a repeated correction (Condition 2) was included, and also when an alternative explanation (Condition 3) was provided. In the general discussion section, we return to these results.

The effect of old information is, thus, statistically significant, but at the same it is also true that the absolute scores of old information are low, and the absolute scores of new information are quite high, also in Condition 1. This indicates that, in general, readers register the new information, but also that old information still exerts a significant, though small influence. The important point here are the differences between (control and experimental) conditions in producing old and new information, respectively. To have a more precise impression of the degree of holding on to old, both effects (that of using more old information, and less new information, than the control condition) at the same time have to be acknowledged. An index indicating this is the relative amount of old responses compared to new responses (the ratio of old divided by new). The degree of holding on to old for the experimental Condition 1 is then .12 (.84/6.94), and for the control Condition 0 only .02 (.20/7.57).

Compared to Wilkes and Leatherbarrow and Johnson and Seifert we found considerably fewer references to old information than they did, especially in Condition 1. Examining several possibilities, such as the effects for each story separately, we tentatively concluded that the explicitness of the correction and readers' processing strategies may have played an important part. The current experiments used a correction that explicitly stated that the earlier information was incorrect (see Appendix A), whereas Johnson and Seifert used a correction that was only a literal negation of earlier material.

Concerning the processing strategies, the previous experiment used a within-subjects design instead of a between-subjects design. This change in design may have resulted in more extensive and thorough processing of information. Consequently, probably fewer inferences were based on old information as compared to new. In other words, better updating was obtained. The next experiment was designed to give more insight on whether the processing strategies played an important role.

EXPERIMENT 2

If readers have to read a text knowing in advance that they have to answer inference questions afterwards, they will probably pay more attention to, and spend more time on the text than readers not having this expectation. This principle possibly explains the difference between Experiment 1 and previous research (Johnson & Seifert, 1993, 1994; Wilkes & Leatherbarrow, 1988). As stated earlier, because of the within-subjects design, subjects knew that they would receive inference questions, which might have caused deeper processing, producing less answers based on old information.

In the next experiment, we tried to restrict processing time in a natural way, by presenting the same texts orally—on tape. A number of studies support the idea that comprehension of spoken language, at least when it involves news reports, is harder than that of written language. For instance, research that compared the effectiveness of print media to radio or televison media consistently reports that reading the news produces better performance than either listening to or watching it, even when exposure times are the same for all modalities (Furnham & Gunter, 1985; Jacoby & Hoyer, 1982; Stauffer, Frost & Rybolt, 1980; Wilson, 1974).

For practical reasons, we only used the first three conditions from Experiment 1 (omitting the alternative causal condition). The main hypothesis of this follow-up study is that rather restricted—and experimenter-paced— processing time will hamper updating situation models. Particularly, changing a model is difficult and time consuming. Consequently, a correction is less likely to be processed effectively and there will be less suppression of old information, compared to a written, self-paced presentation. Therefore we could expect that oral presentation results in less successful processing of corrections than a written presentation, and, thus, in the production of more old information in Experiment 2 than in Experiment 1.

Method

Subjects. In this experiment, 46 students participated, randomly assigned to three conditions.

Material. The same texts and questions were used as in Experiment 1.

Procedure. The procedure and instruction were similar to those of Experiment 1. This means that every subject was presented with three stories, each in a different condition. Scoring of the answers to the questions was done similarly to Experiment 1.

Results

First, just as in Experiment 1, it is important to identify whether the subjects' textbases are similar in all conditions. Only if this is the case can we ascribe possible differences in response to inference questions to differences in situation models. Just as in Experiment 1, there is no significant difference between conditions. Therefore, we may assume that the different conditions have not resulted in textbases of different strength.

Second, Table 13.3 compares the results on the factual questions in both experiments. The data in Table 13.3 show that there are not significant differences between conditions on the factual questions, replicating the results of Experiment 1. Analysis of variance showed that for all texts, oral presentation results in poorer scores ($p < .05$) on factual questions than the written presentation does, suggesting that subjects had less opportunity to construct an equal textbase. Thus, Experiment 2 led to lower levels of correct responses than Experiment 1 but this decline was consistent across conditions. Therefore, we may assume that any

TABLE 13.3
Mean Score on the Factual Questions (max. 6) Per Experiment

Story	Experiment	
	1	2
1	4.77	3.91
2	4.57	4.02
3	5.14	4.52

TABLE 13.4
Mean Score on the Inference Questions (Experiment 2)

Scenario	Condition		
	0	1	2
old	0.20	1.09	0.72
new	7.52	6.65	6.96
non-responses	0.28	0.26	0.33

condition differences in inference questions that tap situation models are not attributable to differences in the textbase for the various conditions.

Table 13.4 shows the main results on the inference questions in Experiment 2. We would like to make three comments on these results. First, the amount of old information used in answering the inference questions in this experiment is not significantly higher than in the first experiment. More specifically, the old information in Condition 1 and 2 is in this experiment not significantly higher than in the previous experiment. This suggests that oral presentation does result in weaker processing of factual information but does not hamper the construction and updating of situation models. Second, Condition 1 and 2 result, again, in significantly more old and less new information than the control condition 0 does. Similar to Experiment 1, the effect of misinformation cannot be completely eradicated. Using the same index as in Experiment 1, the degree of holding on to old information compared to using new information is .17 and .10 in Condition 1 and 2 respectively, and only .02 in the Control condition 0. Third, in this experiment too, there is no significant effect of the repeated correction. Conditions 1 and 2 do not differ significantly with regard to either old or new information.

GENERAL DISCUSSION AND CONCLUSIONS

First, we want to say something about the relation between these two experiments. In Experiment 2, subjects performed more poorly on factual questions than in Experiment 1. We may conclude that oral presentation with restricted presentation time results in the construction of weaker propositional textbases. Apparently, subjects have less opportunity to construct an elaborated textbase. However, the oral presentation did not result in the production of a larger amount of old information. Thus, the restricted presentation rate did not resolve the discrepancy with the results of Wilkes and Leatherbarrow (1988) and Johnson and Seifert (1993, 1994).

We now know that differences in presumed extensiveness of processing are not likely to be responsible for this, which leads us to the conclusion that the discrepancy is probably not caused by a change in design (within-subjects versus between-subjects). Apart from possible differences in scoring, the most probable cause of the discrepancy is the explicitness of correction. As mentioned, in our experiments, very clear-cut corrections were used; more explicit than in previous studies.

The major results of both experiments are similar. This is striking, because Experiment 2 forced shorter processing times. Nevertheless, the corrections were processed similarly to those in Experiment 1, given the similar performance on the inference questions; only the factual questions were responded to with less accuracy in Experiment 2. Consequently, the conclusion might be that oral presentation results in a weaker textbase, without impeding the construction and updating of a situation model. Obviously, the strength of a situation model does not solely depend on the strength of the textbase.

It is also worthwhile to note that the experimental manipulations resulted in differences on the inference questions, presumably indicating differences in situational representations, but not in differences concerning the factual questions, presumably reflecting no difference in textbase representation. These results confirm findings of Wilkes and Leatherbarrow (1988). They found no difference in free recall, but differences in performance on inference questions.

The main results concern the effect of incorrect, old information on the inference questions. Subjects given old information as well as new information hold on more strongly to old information and, at the same time, use less new information than control subjects who only receive new information. In spite of the low absolute scores of old information, the pattern found here is in accordance with the expectations, suggesting that incorrect information, once given, is incorporated in the reader's situation model in such a way that a correction cannot easily eradicate the influence of it. This is completely in accordance with what we expected on the basis of previous research (Johnson & Seifert, 1993, 1994, this volume; van Oostendorp & Bonebakker, 1996; Wilkes & Leatherbarrow, 1988). It should be noted that our results are not merely a replication of Wilkes and Leatherbarrow's or Johnson and Seifert's results. The more adequate control condition in our experiments gives more strength to their conclusions. The most interesting point of the experiments here is that there was still a significant influence effect of old information despite the fact that the corrections were about as explicit as they can be.

Concerning the effect of an alternative causal explanation, the results of Johnson and Seifert (1993, 1994) were not replicated. In Condition 3, the amount of produced old information was not significantly smaller than the production in Conditions 1 and 2. None of the four stories separately—including the stories Johnson and Seifert used—showed a significant difference. The exact cause of this failure to replicate this effect is unclear. Differences in scoring, but also the exact inference questions used, could be sources of discrepancy.

Concerning the effect of a repeated correction, we saw in both experiments that Conditions 1 and 2 resulted in similar patterns of old and new information. This could mean that a rejection process is active: Information incompatible with a situation model previously constructed is consistently rejected and not integrated, also in the repeated correction condition. We hypothesized that it would not be plausible that with a repeated correction, the correction would be loosely encoded or skipped. This result may indicate that rejection rather than superficial processing here determines the fate of replacing information.

In general, we may conclude on the basis of these experiments—when comparing Conditions 0 and 1—that a correction cannot easily eradicate the influence of misinformation, whether presented in written form or orally. Furthermore, neither a repeated correction (Condition 2) nor an alternative explanation (Condition 3 in Experiment 1) can undo the damage.

On a more general level, these results indicate that backward inferences and integrations, based on new incoming information, are not always made. This suggests a kind of minimalistic processing causing an incomplete updating, rather than a full constructionistic processing (McKoon & Ratcliff, 1992, 1995). It is worthwhile to note that precise updating is hard to influence: Explicit instruction to read carefully or immediate presentation of subsequent information often do not constitute sufficient conditions for complete updating (cf. van Oostendorp, 1996a). Further research has to make clear what strategic or non-strategic factors control the completeness of processing (i.e., the updating of the old model) and we briefly expand on this.

It is worthwhile first to mention here the strategies Brewer and Chinn (1991) and Chinn and Brewer (1993) distinguished for responding to contradictory information. Briefly these strategies were: (a) ignore anomalous, new information or data, (b) reject new information, (c) peripheral theory change; that is, a partial peripheral change preserving the core of an old model, (d) reinterpret the new information while retaining the old model, (e) exclude the new information from the domain of the old model, (f) hold the new information in abeyance, that is, some kind of compartmentalization, and finally (g) accept the new information and restructure the old model. In our experiments, the focus was on holding on to the old information and on updating the already formed model under influence of new information. Holding on could be caused by ignoring (strategy a) or by rejecting (strategy b) or partially rejecting (strategy c), and we did find somewhat more evidence for rejecting (strategies b or c), with the kind of simple stories we used. Switching over to new information, that is, updating, seems to correspond to accept the new information and change the old model (strategy g). More detailed research has to make clear whether and when the other strategies are applied. For instance, occasionally we found evidence in the production protocols of the abeyance strategy (f). Subjects mentioned sometimes both sources at the same time, and found both equally plausible.

It is reasonable to assume that the regulation strategies as examined here (ignoring or rejecting new information vs. accepting new information and changing the old interpretation) depend on both individual characteristics of subjects and textual and contextual constrictions.

Concerning individual characteristics, we know that limitations in working-memory capacity, for instance, may influence a reader's representation of a text (Hoyes & Mannes, in preparation; Mannes, 1994). Limitations of working memory may force a reader to give priority to old or new information, respectively, for further processing. The suppressed information then has less chance to be used and to influence the final representation. Another individual characteristic relevant here is epistemological beliefs such as the belief that integration of ideas is important to understanding (see e.g., Kardash & Scholes, 1996; Rukavina & Daneman, 1996; Schommer, 1990). In these studies, it was demonstrated that readers who fail to revise their existing mental models lack the epistemic commitment to the notion that all of the information should be integrated into a coherent representation and also fail to engage in the kind of processing that produces integration (updating). The resulting knowledge is consequently incorrect. On the other hand, good readers are able to do so.

It was also shown in previous work (Garcia-Arista, Campanario, & Otero, in press) that the regulation strategies were dependent on the context (setting) in which the comprehension task was carried out. Garcia-Arista et al., for instance, presented subjects with the same text containing contradictions, either in a science or in a newspaper setting. Subjects detected more contradictions in the science setting, and also better regulated their comprehension than in the newspaper setting.

Textual conditions may also play a role, for instance, in the distance in the textbase between the old and new information. We held this distance constant in our experiments but it would be interesting to see whether a greater distance leads to less updating. More propositions interpretable from the old perspective could function in the same way as explicitly reinforcing old information, as in the experiments reported here. Thus, a lot of information fitting onto an old perspective may lead to less willingness to accommodate the new perspective. The exact character of the correction itself also seems to be relevant. For instance, does the correction involve a logical inconsistency, that is, two facts that could not both be true at the same time in the same world. These may be easy to detect but difficult to understand, in the sense of a change that is not easy to explain. In contrast, does the correction involve a change or evolution in the world? These may be difficult to detect, but easy to understand (i.e., one can find an explanation for the change). In cases of evolution, sometimes one might want to retain the old as well as the new information supplied with a time tag.

The extent of updating is without doubt also dependent on the credibility of the new data (Chinn & Brewer, 1993). Certainly with news reports this could be an important factor. A related aspect concerns the credibility of the source of the news.

Another textual factor might be the explicitness or ambiguity of the correction. Encountering a clear-cut correction probably enhances the ease of updating (see also our previous remark). Indeed, a recent study by Campanario and van Oostendorp (in press) showed that with a strong manipulation, consisting of a clear-cut contradiction in an expository text, subjects used the new perspective instead of the old information.

Furthermore, another textual factor might be the relevance or saliency of the original, incorrect event. Encountering many information units confirming an old perspective indirectly strengthens the old perspective. It makes the old perspective, so-to-say, more relevant, and in that case a new perspective must be very strong to counterbalance the old perspective. A follow-up experiment by van Oostendorp and Campanario (in prep.) indicated that strengthening of old information, by inserting sentences that indirectly reinforced the old information, lessens the degree of updating. More generally, the results of these studies to the role of textual constrictions point to a regulation mechanism that is based on weighting of evidence pro and contra the old and new source of information, and according to the outcomes, readers choose one or the other point of view, and use that for inferencing.

Finally, on a more global level, the believability of the information that is presented, in general, seems to be important for the degree of updating, and for the specific strategy used to update or to reject. Simple stories such as used in the present experiments probably have a low reality value for subjects, whereas the Somalia texts van Oostendorp (1996a) used have a high reality value. This difference could have consequences for the way updating takes place; in the first case, it seems probable that only a new episodic situation model (a new instantiation of it, e.g., of a fire in a building) is constructed without lasting changes in a reader's cognitive structure, whereas in the latter case, a much more difficult and diffuse change of permanent knowledge has to take place when one updates, consequently the updating process will be probably more slow and incomplete, and not all or nothing. An interesting line of further research is to examine precisely the effects of believability on updating and rejection strategies of readers.

APPENDIX: EXAMPLE STORY "FIRE IN A WAREHOUSE"*

Message 1: Jan. 25th 9:00 p.m. Alarm call received from premises of a wholesale warehouse. Premises consist of offices, display room, and storage hall.

Message 2: A serious fire was reported in the storage hall, already out of control and requiring instant response. Fire appliance dispatched at 9:00 p.m.

Message 3: The alarm was raised by the night watchman, who referred to the presence of thick, oily smoke and sheets of flame.

Message 4: Jan. 26th 4:00 a.m. Attending Fire Officer suggests that the fire was started by a short circuit in the wiring of a side room off the main storage hall. Police now investigating.

Condition 0 (Control):
Message 5: 4:30 a.m. Police and firemen are involved in the investigation.
Conditions 1, 2, and 3:
Message 5: 4:30 a.m. Police say that they have reports that lightly inflammable materials including paint and gas cylinders had been carelessly stored in the side room before the fire.

Message 6: Firemen attending the scene report the fire developed an intense heat that made it particularly difficult to bring under control.

Message 7: It has been learned that a number of explosions occurred during the blaze, which endangered firemen in the vicinity, but no casualties resulted from this cause.

Message 8: Two firemen are reported to have been taken to the hospital as a result of breathing toxic fumes that built up in the area in which they were working.

Message 9: The Works foreman has disclosed that the storage hall contained bales of paper and a large amount of photo-copying equipment.

Condition 0 (Control):
Message 10: 10:40 a.m. A message was received from the police about the progress of the investigation. It stated that the side room had been empty before the fire.

---

*(by H. van Oostendorp, originally in Dutch, adapted from Wilkes and Leatherbarrow, 1988).

Conditions 1 and 2:
Message 10: 10:40 a.m. A message received from the police about the progress of the investigation stated that the side room had been empty before the fire. The previous message had been incorrect.

Condition 3:
Message 10: 10:40 a.m. A message received from the police about the progress of the investigation stated that the side room had been empty before the fire. The previous message had been incorrect. Furthermore, evidence was found of gasoline-soaked rags, indicating that the fire had been started deliberately.

Message 11: 10:00 a.m. The owner of the affected premises estimates that total damage will amount to many thousands of dollars, although the premises were insured.

Message 12: A small fire had been discovered on the same premises, 6 months previously. It had been sucessfully tackled by the workmen themselves.

Conditions 0, 1, and 3:
Message 13: 11:30 a.m. Attending Fire Officer reports that the fire is now out and that the storage hall had been completely gutted.

Condition 2:
Message 13: 11:13 a.m. Attending Fire Officer reports that the fire is now out. He confirms the police report that there were no lightly inflammable materials in the side room. The storage hall had been completely gutted.

REFERENCES

Bell, A. (1991). *The language of news media.* Oxford, England: Basil Blackwell.

Brewer, W. F., & Chinn, C. A. (1991). Entrenched beliefs, inconsistent information, and knowledge change. In L. Birnbaum (Ed.), *Proceedings of the 1991 international conference on the learning sciences* (pp. 67–73). Charlottesville, VA: Association for the Advancement of Computing in Education.

Campanario, J. M., & van Oostendorp, H. (in press). Updating mental representations when reading scientific text. In J. F. Rouet, J. Levonen, & A. Biardeau (Eds.), *Proceedings of the using complex information systems '96 conference.* Poitiers, France: University of Poitiers Press.

Chinn, C. A., & Brewer, W. F. (1993). The role of anomalous data in knowledge acquisition: A theoretical framework and implications for science instruction. *Review of Educational Research, 63*(1), 1–49.

Findahl, O., & Höijer, B. (1981). Studies of news from the perspective of human comprehension. In G. C. Wilhoit & H. de Bock (Eds.), *Mass communication review yearbook* (Vol.2, pp. 393–403). Beverly Hills, CA: Sage.

Fletcher, C. R., & Chrysler, S. T. (1990). Surface forms, textbases, and situation models; recognition memory for three types of textual information. *Discourse Processes, 13,* 175–190.

Furnham, A., & Gunter, B. (1985). Sex, presentation mode, and memory for violent and non-violent news. *Journal of Educational Television, 11,* 99–105.

Garcia-Arista, E., Campanario, J. M., & Otero, J. (in press). Influence of subject matter setting on comprehension monitoring. *European Journal of Psychology of Education.*

Graber, D. A. (1988). *Processing the news.* London: Longman.

Gray-Wilson, S., Rinck, M., McNamara, T. P., Bower, G. H., & Morrow, D. G. (1993). Mental models and narrative comprehension: Some qualifications. *Journal of Memory and Language, 32,* 141–154.

Gunter, B. (1987). *Poor reception: Misunderstanding and forgetting broadcast news.* Hillsdale, NJ: Lawrence Erlbaum Associates.

Hoyes, S. M., & Mannes, S. (in preparation). *Representations of expository text.* University of Delaware.

Jacoby, J., & Hoyer, W. D. (1982). Viewer misconception of televised communication: Selected findings. *Journal of Marketing, 46,* 12–26.

Johnson, H. M., & Seifert, C. M. (1993). Correcting causal explanations in memory. *Proceedings of the 15th annual conference of the cognitive science society* (pp. 5011–5016). Hillsdale, NJ: Lawrence Erlbaum Associates.

Johnson, H. M., & Seifert, C. M. (1994a). Sources of the continued influence effect: When misinformation in memory affects later inferences. *Journal of Experimental Psychology: Learning, Memory, and Cognition, 20*(6), 1420–1436.

Kardash, C. M., & Scholes, R. J. (1996). Effects of preexisting beliefs, epistemological beliefs, and need for cognition on interpretation of controversial issues. *Journal of Educational Psychology, 88*(2), 260–271.

Kintsch, W., & Franzke, M. (1995). The role of background knowledge in the recall of a news story. In R. F. Lorch & E. J. O'Brien (Eds.), *Sources of coherence in reading* (pp. 321–333). Hillsdale, NJ: Lawrence Erlbaum Associates.

Kintsch, W., Welsch, D., Schmalhofer, F., & Zimny, S. (1990). Sentence memory: A theoretical analysis. *Journal of Memory and Language, 29,* 133–159.

Larsen, S. F. (1983). Text processing and knowledge updating in memory for radio news. *Discourse Processes, 6,* 21–38.

Mannes, S. (1994). Strategic processing of text. *Journal of Educational Psychology, 86*(4), 377–388.

McKoon, G., & Ratcliff, R. (1992). Inference during reading. *Psychological Review, 99,* 440–466.

McKoon, G., & Ratcliff, R. (1995). The minimalist hypothesis: Directions for research. In C. A. Weaver III, S. Mannes, & C. R. Fletcher (Eds.), *Discourse comprehension* (pp. 97–116). Hillsdale, NJ: Lawrence Erlbaum Associates.

Morrow, D. (1994). Situation models created from text. In H. van Oostendorp & R. A. Zwaan (Eds.), *Naturalistic text comprehension* (pp. 57–78). Norwood, NJ: Ablex.

Rukavina, I., & Daneman, M. (1996). Integration and its effect on acquiring knowledge about competing scientific theories from text. *Journal of Educational Psychology, 88,* 272–287.

Schmalhofer, F., & Glavanov, D. (1986). Three components of understanding a programmer's manual: Verbatim, propositional, and situational representations. *Journal of Memory and Language, 25,* 279–294.

Schommer, M. (1990). Effects of beliefs about the nature of knowledge on comprehension. *Journal of Educational Psychology, 82,* 498–504.

Stauffer, J., Frost, R., & Rybolt, W. (1980). Recall and comprehension of radio news in Kenya. *Journalism Quarterly, 57,* 612–617.

Trabasso, T., & Suh, S. (1993). Understanding text. Achieving explanatory coherence through online inferences and mental operations in working memory. *Discourse Processes, 16,* 3–34.

Van Dijk, T. A., & Kintsch, W. (1983). *Strategies of discourse comprehension.* New York: Academic Press.

van Oostendorp, H. (1996a). Updating situation models derived from newspaper articles. *Medienpsychologie, 8,* 21–33.
van Oostendorp, H. (1996b, April). *Holding on to misinformation during processing news reports.* Paper presented at the AERA 1996 annual meeting, New York.
van Oostendorp, H., & Bonebakker, C. (1996). Het vasthouden aan incorrecte informatie bij het verwerken van nieuwsberichten. [Holding on to misinformation during processing news reports]. *Tijdschrift voor Communicatiewetenschap, 24*(1), 57–74.
van Oostendorp, H., & Campanario, J. (in preparation). *Updating mental representation during reading expository texts that contain corrections.*
Wilkes, A. L., & Leatherbarrow, M. (1988). Editing episodic memory following the identification of error. *Quarterly Journal of Experimental Psychology, 40A*(2), 361–387.
Wilson, C. E. (1974). The effect of medium on loss of information. *Journalism Quarterly, 51,* 111–115.
Zwaan, R. A., & van Oostendorp, H. (1993). Do readers construct spatial representations in naturalistic story comprehension? *Discourse Processes, 16,* 125–143.

Chapter 14

Distinguishing Between Textbase and Situation Model in the Processing of Inconsistent Information: Elaboration Versus Tagging

Isabelle Tapiero
University of Lyon II, France

Jose Otero
University of Alcala, Spain

Current theories of text comprehension assume three levels of representation of the text and of its content (Fletcher & Chrysler, 1990; Kintsch, 1988; Kintsch & van Dijk, 1978; Tapiero, 1991; van Dijk & Kintsch, 1983). The surface level refers to the representation of the exact wording and syntax a reader captures from a text. The semantic level results from two types of processing: microprocessing and macroprocessing. The microprocessing implies the construction of a locally coherent propositional network called the textbase (see Kintsch, 1974; Kintsch & van Dijk, 1978). The macroprocessing involves propositions of the textbase (micropropositions) organized in a hierarchical and coherent sequence. These two processes, local and global, lead to two levels of discourse organization: the microstructure and the macrostructure. Thus, while reading a text, step by step the reader constructs the microstructure by applying local coherence relations (e.g., referential, and/or temporal and causal relations). The construction of global discourse coherence (macrostructure) is made by restructuring the microstructure into a meaningful global structure. At this level of comprehension, the reader's goal is to construct a representation that is faithful to the text (Kintsch & van Dijk, 1978; O'Brien & Lorch, 1995; van Dijk & Kintsch, 1983) and there is no need for the intervention of the reader's prior knowledge.

Contrasting with these two levels of discourse organization, the level of the situation model implies the integration of readers' prior knowledge with textual information. What is represented at the situation-model level is the result of the interaction between information provided by the text and the reader's knowledge. From this point of view, readers' knowledge is an important factor in constructing the meaning and interpretation of textual information (Kintsch & Franzke, 1995). Indeed, several experimental studies show that, whereas all readers are able to develop a propositional structure appropriate to the text, only some elaborate an adequate situation model that could allow them, for instance, to use the information in new situations (Kintsch & Kintsch, 1995). Thus, the specific knowledge readers have in the domain to be acquired, or readers' more general knowledge of the incoming textual information, may influence the construction of the situation model. However, several studies on text comprehension showed that depending on the domain-specific background knowledge comprehenders have, or on task specificity, the representation they construct would rely either on textbase relations or on situation-model relations (Fincher-Kiefer, Post, Greene, & Voss, 1988; Kintsch & Franzke, 1995; Mannes & Kintsch, 1987).

On the one hand, several studies showed that performance differences attributable to domain-specific knowledge reflect differences in the construction of the situation model and not in the formation of the textbase (Fincher-Kiefer et al., 1988; Tardieu, Ehrlich, & Gyselinck, 1992). For example, Fincher-Kiefer et al. (1988) found performance differences attributable to domain-specific knowledge (baseball) only when the task required the development of retrieval structures (recall of the final word of sentences plus recall of whole sentences) compared to a task that did not require this elaboration (recall of the final word of sentences). Interpreted within Kintsch and van Dijk's framework, their results show that, whereas high- and low-knowledge subjects have developed a propositional structure of the text content, only high-knowledge subjects have developed an appropriate and elaborated situation model evoked by the text (Fincher-Kiefer et al., 1988). Also, Tardieu et al.'s (1992) results are consistent with the interpretation proposed by Fincher-Kiefer et al. (1988). Whereas they did not observe any difference between experts and novices for the propositional level of representation (evaluated by questions involving paraphrases), they did observe reliable difference between these two groups in the situation model that was elaborated (evaluated by elaborative inferences). Their results showed that, whereas both experts and novices retrieved propositional information equally well, situational information was processed faster when subjects had to read with a knowledge-acquisition goal rather than with a summary goal.

On the other hand, different experimental variables have been used to distinguish between reader-constructed textbase-level and situation-model representations (see Kintsch, 1986; Mannes & Kintsch, 1987; Schmalhofer & Glavanov, 1986). Kintsch (1986) showed a dichotomy between remembering the text and what was learned from it. Whereas the former is dependent on how coherently the text is written, the latter is a function of the kind of encoding operation the reader performed. According to Kintsch, encoding just the propositional structure of a text at both the local and the global level only ensures that the text can be recalled or recognized. However, to answer inference questions (e.g., causal or spatial) about the text or to learn subject matter on the basis of the text, requires the reader to elaborate a mental model of the situation described in the text (see Perrig & Kintsch, 1985). Further evidence for the distinction between remembering a text and learning from it is also provided in Mannes and Kintsch's (1987) study. In their experimental work (Mannes & Kintsch, 1987, Experiment 1), subjects had to complete different tasks (summarization, sentence verification, cued recall, solving a specific problem, ranking) after reading a long scientific text on bacteria. The text was preceded by the study of an outline either consistent with the organization of the text to be read later, or inconsistent with the text to be read later. Half of the subjects performed the tasks just after reading the text, whereas the other half had a 2-day delay before receiving the same sequence of tests. The results of the memory tests (cued recall and summary) showed, first, that subjects in the consistent outline condition built a more stable and a more complete textbase than the subjects in the inconsistent condition (cued-recall task). Second, for the summarization task in the immediate test condition, both groups (consistent outline and inconsistent outline) formed an adequate macrostructure of the text they read. However, in the 2-day delay condition, subjects who studied the outline inconsistent with the textual organization introduced a very high number of deviations in their summaries. The results from the tasks requiring subjects to use their knowledge (verification, problem solving, and ranking) showed higher performances for subjects in the inconsistent conditions compared to subjects in the consistent conditions. Thus, consistency between previous knowledge and text content is an advantage in tasks involving memory retrieval; however, the opposite is true in tasks that require using what has been learned from the text: Inconsistency between previous knowledge and text content increases performance.

This chapter analyzes differences between the textbase and situation-model levels regarding the representation of inconsistent textual information. We argue that inconsistencies have different effects at the textbase or situation-model level, following a hypothesis suggested by Wilkes and Leatherbarrow (1988). Inconsistencies may merely result in the creation of a "tag" in the textbase or, alternatively, they may lead to elaborating the situation model. Both of these operations produce increased memory of the contradictory information. This is shown both experimentally and in terms of the C-I model of text comprehension (Kintsch, 1988).

MEMORY IMPROVEMENTS OF UNEXPECTED ITEMS: ELABORATION VERSUS TAGGING

Improved memory has been repeatedly found for inconsistent, atypical, unexpected, or contradictory information, beginning with the well-established von Restorff (1933) effect: Memory improves for unrelated items within a list of others that are categorically related. The effect is also found outside the list-learning experiments. Bower, Black, and Turner (1979) found better memory discrimination for atypical actions in a script. Lexical items are recognized more quickly when they are unexpected, that is, preceded by a nonpredictive context, compared to a predictive context (Cairns, Cowart, & Jablon, 1981; O'Brien & Myers, 1985).

Improvement of memory for inconsistent items has been explained in two ways. The most frequent explanation has been given in terms of distinctiveness in memory because of increased elaboration (i.e., inferences) needed to integrate the inconsistent information in the rest of the text (Cairns et al., 1981). O'Brien and Myers (1985) found that words that were unpredictable in a certain passage were recognized significantly more quickly than predictable words. Also, ideas that appeared in the text prior to the target word were better recalled when the target word was unpredictable. This was interpreted as showing that subjects reprocess previous portions of the unpredictable passages to maintain coherence. Increased recognition of the unpredictable word was explained by the fact that much of the difficulty encountered in a text is resolved through the use of bridging inferences and elaborations. It may result in a richer, more distinctive memory record, and it may also provide more possible retrieval routes (Anderson & Reder, 1979; Bradshaw & Anderson, 1982; O'Brien & Myers, 1985). Similar results were found by Albrecht and O'Brien (1993) in a study that examined whether or not readers attempt to maintain global coherence in a passage, and the effect on recall that a disruption of global coherence may have. In addition to finding increased recall of sentences disrupting global coherence, they also found a benefit for recall of information presented before the inconsistent sentence. The elaboration explanation is also consistent with the findings of van Oostendorp (1994). He presented script-based stories to subjects. In these stories, atypical events were included, like asking the waiter for a comic book instead of the menu. Reaction times to a secondary task showed that information that did not fit an instantiated schema received more extensive processing than conventional prototypical information.

However, the results mentioned on improved memory for atypical information appeared inconsistent with schema-based theories because opposite predictions result from the "filtering hypothesis": Only the information fitting schemata's slots is preserved; atypical information should be filtered out. Graesser (1981) developed a "schema pointer + tag" model, later modified into a "schema copy + tag" (Graesser & Nakamura, 1982), to account for these conflicting findings. According to the schema copy plus tag model, the memory representation of external information consists of a pointer to a subset of the information in the schema appropriate for the input, together with tags for the atypical information not fitting the schema. These tags designate deviations from the schema and should account for the special memorability of the atypical items. In one study, Graesser and Nakamura (1982) compared predictions of the elaboration and tagging explanations on recognition of information that is atypical with respect to the available schema. In one of the experiments, they manipulated the possibility of elaborating the atypical information by varying the rate at which the information was presented to subjects auditorily. The elaboration explanation would predict a smaller difference in the fast presentation condition compared to a slower presentation condition. At a fast presentation rate, subjects would not have time to elaborate the atypical information and thus the memory advantage should decrease. However, no difference in recognition rates of typical and atypical items was found between rates of presentation. This was interpreted as supporting an explanation based on the existence of memory tags whose construction seems to be achieved very quickly (Graesser & Nakamura, 1982). The tagging explanation has also been incorporated as an alternative to the elaboration explanation in one of the studies mentioned previously: If readers tag information involved in the inconsistency, at retrieval this tagged information should be more easily recalled (Albrecht & O'Brien, 1993). Thus, in this view, tagging may be considered as an automatic process not requiring readers' strategic actions.

The explanation of the memorability of inconsistent information in terms of the elaboration hypothesis is based on the assumption that subjects strategically generate elaborative inferences when they find an inconsistency. In this way, the inconsistency is related to the rest of the text and an increase in coherence is obtained. We assume that this mechanism requires using textual information in relation to a situational dimension (it may be compared to a problem-solving situation). Thus, not only a textbase representation but also a mental model of the situation described by the text should be formed in order to achieve this goal. We also assume that the elaboration activity requires important cognitive resources that are time consuming.

We tested elaboration versus tagging as explanatory hypotheses of memory for inconsistent information. Different mechanisms are hypothesized to operate in each case. Elaborations should lead to an integration of the inconsistency in the rest of the text and to an updated model of the situation described by the text. This will facilitate memory tasks that involve use of this model. By contrast, tagging will be conceptualized as a textbase phenomenon: It may allow readers to form a correct semantic representation but it will not produce an updating of the situation model. Consequently, readers will rely more on the information preceding the inconsistency than on the information dealing with it. Thus, the tagging explanation for the memorability of inconsistent information should be valid for recall tasks, but not for tasks that require inferencing, such as answering comprehension questions.

The elaboration explanatory hypothesis was tested by giving or not giving enough time to subjects for processing an inconsistent sentence, for example, one contradicting another. We expected that subjects would use the time to elaborate the contradiction, as in Graesser and Nakamura's (1982) study. This would result in a shorter response time to the contradiction in a recognition task, compared to a control situation where the same target sentence and probe are used but no contradiction exists. We would also expect better memory for this information in a cued recall task and better integration of the contradictory information in the situation model, as measured by answers to comprehension questions.

To test the effect of tagging, subjects were prevented from elaborating: They had only enough time to read the inconsistency but not enough to integrate the inconsistency in the rest of the text. We assumed that this lack of reading time would disrupt global coherence and situational-model building, but would not disrupt local coherence, so that readers would have an accurate semantic representation of the text (O'Brien, 1995). Moreover, the tag created by readers who noticed the inconsistency (i.e., a cue linked to the inconsistent information) would increase the memorability of this information. Thus, we expected that subjects would recognize more quickly and have a better memory for inconsistent propositions compared to a noncontradictory control version where subjects are also prevented from elaborating. The main difference between the elaboration and tagging conditions should concern the activation of an accurate situation model of the inconsistent text. We expected subjects in the elaboration condition would update their model of the situation described in the text, that is, they would integrate the inconsistency in their text representation. However, subjects in the tagging condition should be unable to do so. Tagging is only expected to have an influence at the textbase level because it is hypothesized to consist of the automatic addition of a "tagging node" to the textbase with the formation of a weak situation model.

THE C-I MODEL'S ACCOUNT OF INCONSISTENT INFORMATION PROCESSING: CONTRIBUTION OF READERS' KNOWLEDGE

An explanation for the recall performance of readers who process texts involving inconsistencies may also be obtained in terms of the construction-integration model of text comprehension developed by Kintsch (1988). Within the construction-integration theory, comprehension is seen as a cyclical process, involving two phases: a rule-based construction phase and a spreading activation, or integration phase. The construction phase is composed of rules for the construction of concepts and propositions corresponding to the text; rules for interconnecting the propositions in a network. Link strengths between propositions as well as self-strength of propositions may be varied according to theoretical considerations (see Kintsch, Welsch, Schmalhofer, & Zimny, 1990; Otero & Kintsch, 1992; Tapiero, 1992; Tapiero & Denhière, 1995). At this point, the textbase on propositional network is formed. Knowledge activation is assumed to be associative. Items from the textbase network in working memory activate some neighboring nodes in the knowledge network of the reader with probabilities proportional to the strengths with which they are linked to them. Finally, this construction phase includes rules for constructing inferences. The basic assumption of the model is that weak rules are applied, noncontextual, and sometimes incorrect so that the representation generated can be correct, but also redundant or even irrelevant. The integration phase, following the construction phase, occurs through spreading activation, in order to make the network coherent: The activation values of relevant propositions are strengthened and those of irrelevant propositions are deactivated. Each cycle of construction-integration roughly corresponds to the processing of a clause or sentence. Some elements, or propositions, of the sentences are retained in working memory, to be processed together with the new sentence. This produces overlap among the sentence elements and coherence is obtained via the reprocessing of propositions. The greater the overlap, the higher the activation level of the overlapping elements; hence, the greater the coherence with the rest of the elements. This integration process is assumed to occur without much effort and leads to a contextually integrated representation in long-term memory of the meaning of the text.

The model makes recall predictions depending on the activation of propositions during the encoding phase (Kintsch & Welsch, 1991). A higher activation of inconsistent propositions should be expected due to increased elaboration in an attempt to integrate this information in the rest of the text, as O'Brien and Myers (1985) found. However, if elaboration were prevented, the construction-integration model would not predict any memory improvement for inconsistent information. In fact, it would predict decreased recall of contradictory information due to the existence of negative links between contradictory propositions, as in Otero and Kintsch's (1992) work. In this study, 16- and 18-year-old secondary-school students read brief paragraphs containing contradictory statements. Many of the subjects failed to notice the contradiction, according to their self reports after having read the paragraphs. The C-I model provided a mechanism to explain this result: The first contradictory proposition inhibits the second

one in the integration phase because the former is disproportionally activated (higher activation level). This would be the case when subjects believe
very strongly in the initial text interpretations they create, leading to the
suppression of later contradictory incoming information. On a subsequent
recall test, the nondetectors frequently recalled only one proposition, more
often the first proposition than the second, in agreement with the "suppression hypothesis" supplied by the model. However, in the case of detectors, the predictions of the model did not conform to experimental
data (Otero & Kintsch, 1992). For those subjects who did detect the contradiction, enhanced recall of the contradictory propositions was found,
compared to the predictions of the C-I model. This discrepancy should
be expected because the existence of a contradiction was only accounted
for by the model as a negative link between the contradictory propositions.
No inferences resulting from the elaboration activity of detectors were
included in this simulation.

Thus, we intend to examine, first, how the C-I model may account for
the elaboration explanation when inferences are included in the simulation. Second, we intend to provide an account for the role of tagging in
terms of the C-I model. We first use the procedure used by Otero and
Kintsch (1992) to simulate processing of contradictions (i.e., introduction
of a negative link between the two contradictory propositions). Second,
we add a tagging node in the textbase network in order to account for
the improvement in memory due to tagging. This simulation should not
lead to suppression of the inconsistent information (see Otero & Kintsch,
1992) but to an opposite result: a higher activation and, consequently,
increased memory for this information. We then compare subjects' recall
and comprehension data with predictions of the C-I model including the
modifications that may account for our theoretical hypotheses.

EXPERIMENT

The representation built by subjects reading contradictory information was
tested in an experiment involving three types of tasks. First, subjects had
to recognize words related to the inconsistent information according to
an experimental procedure closely following that used by O'Brien and
Myers (1985). Second, comprehension questions involving the contradictory information were used to test the situation model elaborated by the
readers. Third, a cued recall task was also used in order to test for the
textbase representation of the text. The purpose of the recognition, inferential, and recall tasks was to ascertain the relative contribution of the
elaborative inferences versus the tagging node on the textbase versus situation-model levels of representation of the text. The experiment tried also

to replicate O'Brien and Myers' (1985) results regarding recognition time for predictable and unpredictable words. In O'Brien and Myers' experiment, subjects read paragraphs line by line, at their own pace. The paragraphs contained target words that were either predictable or unpredictable according to the context. Shorter response times in a recognition task were found for unpredictable target words compared to predictable target words. Also, subjects took longer to read sentences containing an unpredictable word compared to the same sentence containing a predictable word. Finally, better recall was found for information preceding the target word when this was unpredictable. These results were interpreted as showing that increases in comprehension difficulties lead to improvements in memory for the target word and for portions of the text involved in elaborating the inconsistent target information.

Our experiment differed from O'Brien and Myers' in several respects. First, we used passages containing explicit contradictions instead of unexpected information. Consequently, we tested for memory and comprehension (recognition, recall, and answers to inferential questions) of the contradictory propositions. Second, we presented the paragraphs, one word after another, at a fixed rate. Third, we manipulated the possibility of elaborating the contradictory information by limiting the available time to do it.

Fifty-four undergraduate students from the Faculty of Chemistry and the School of Electrical Engineering of the University of Alcala participated in the study. The students were given six paragraphs to read on a computer screen. Two of them, "Satellites" and "Cavitation," located in the third and fifth position in counterbalanced order, involved explicit contradictions between the third sentence and the last (fifth) sentence. A noncontradictory, control version of the two paragraphs was written by replacing the contradictory information in the second sentence by a neutral statement. The contradictory and control versions of the Satellites paragraph and the four probe words used in the recognition task are presented in Table 14.1.

TABLE 14.1
Satellites Paragraph

---

1. There are surveillance satellites in orbits at different heights.
2. They have telescopes and sensors in order to detect radiations.
Contradictory condition: 3. The telescope of a surveillance satellite is able to distinguish buildings.
Control condition: 3. The telescope of a surveillance satellite is able to distinguish cities.
4. The capacity to distinguish depends on the optical sensitivity of the instrument.
5. The telescope of a surveillance satellite is not able to distinguish buildings.
Probe words: TELESCOPE, PRECISION, ORBITS, CHALK

The propositional analyses of the Satellites and Cavitation paragraphs (contradictory and control passages) followed Kintsch's (1988) procedure, with concepts and propositions as network's units. The propositions and concepts corresponding to the two contradictory sentences for the Satellites text (sentences 3 and 5) are presented as an example:

P10 Telescope

P18 Building
P19 ABLEDISTINGUISH [P10,P18]

P29 UNABLEDISTINGUISH [P10,P18]

Subjects were randomly assigned to one of four testing conditions (CE, CNE, NCE, NCNE) depending on the existence of contradiction in both target texts (C: both texts in contradictory version; NC: both texts in non-contradictory version) and the possibility to elaborate the target information (E: available time to elaborate in both texts; NE: no available time to elaborate in any of the two texts). They were asked to read the passages on the video monitor and to answer questions related to the passages as quickly and accurately as possible. Words appeared from left to right, one word 350 ms after another, until a sentence was completed. After this it was erased and the next sentence was shown in the same way. A recognition task was presented after the last sentence of each paragraph, following O'Brien and Myers' (1985) testing procedure. Subjects had to indicate whether a probe word had been presented before or not. The first probe word for the contradictory and control paragraphs consisted of an argument of the contradictory propositions. Each trial ended with a comprehension question probing the acquisition of the target information (contradictory in the case of the contradictory conditions). The comprehension question for the Satellites paragraph is presented in Table 14.2.

Once this testing session was completed, two sheets of paper were provided with the following instructions: "Write everything that you remember about the capacity to distinguish of telescopes in surveillance satellites,

TABLE 14.2
Comprehension Question at the End of the Satellites Paragraph

---

Would it be possible for a surveillance satellite like those described in the text to distinguish the Faculty of Sciences or the Polytechnic School of the University of Alcala through its telescope?
  a. Yes
  b. No
  c. Satellites are not equipped with telescopes.
  d. According to the paragraph one can not say.

---

from the paragraph 'SATELLITES.' " A similar request was made for the other contradictory paragraph. After this, they were given two pages informing them of the contradictions in the paragraphs and asking if they had detected them while reading. In case they did realize it, they were asked to write what they had thought about it.

Elaboration was manipulated by introducing the following interrupting message after the two target paragraphs: PLEASE WAIT A MOMENT. THE PROGRAM IS SAVING YOUR RESPONSES TO THE RESULT FILE. WAIT SOME SECONDS AND THE PROGRAM WILL RESUME IMMEDIATELY. The time interval between the presentation of the last word in the last sentence of the target paragraphs and the presentation of the interrupting message before the testing procedure was different in the E and NE conditions. In the E conditions, the whole sentence stayed on the screen for 4,000 ms after the onset of the last word (*buildings* in the Satellite paragraph), creating the contradiction. In the NE condition, elaboration was prevented by presenting the warning message immediately after the offset of the last word in the sentence. The interrupting message stayed on the screen for 3,000 ms and then the testing procedure followed as usual. Assuming tagging to be a process taking place in a much shorter time than that needed for elaboration, tagging would be the only mechanism operating in the condition when the warning message is presented immediately after the contradictory sentence. Thus, tagging effects were compared to elaboration effects and to the control situation in which the same target sentence was presented but no contradiction existed.

RESULTS

Recognition Task

Only response times based on the first probe word (i.e., the target) of subjects detecting the contradiction were used in the C conditions. Also, response times higher than 2 SD from the mean were eliminated from the analysis. These were 2.3% of the data. Response times to the target probe words in the four conditions, averaged for the two target paragraphs, are presented in Fig. 14.1. Recognition rates for the target probe words were 100% for both paragraphs in the four conditions.

No significant differences were found for response times among the four conditions ($F < 1$), perhaps due to the test's lack of statistical power. However, the observed trend shows a decrease in response time in the contradictory conditions compared to the noncontradictory conditions. No difference is found between the CE and CNE conditions (in fact, average response time in the CNE condition is less than in the CE condition). This suggests that tagging has an effect on memory for the contra-

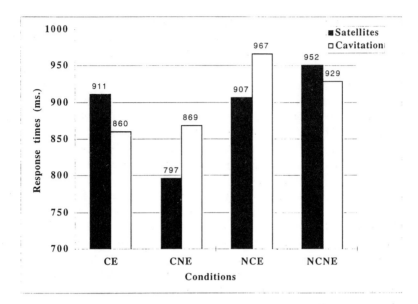

FIG. 14.1. Mean response times of the target probe words for both texts
as a function of the four experimental conditions (CE, CNE [Tagging],
NCE [Control], and NCNE [Control]).

dictory proposition, as measured by a recognition task, similar to the effect
of elaboration. The findings also show that subjects are faster recognizing
the target word when the text is contradictory than when it is neutral,
both in the E and NE conditions. Finally, good agreement exists between
the response times to the target word in the CE and NCE conditions and
those obtained by O'Brien and Myers for unpredictable words and predictable words: 838 ms for the unpredictable condition, and 941 ms for
the predictable condition. All subjects in O'Brien and Myers' experiment
had time to elaborate after having read the target information. This lends
concurrent validity to our measure.

The previous results show a similar improvement in response time to
contradictions in the two situations considered: when subjects may elaborate the contradictory information and when they do not have time to do
it but only to realize that there exists a contradiction. This suggests an
effect of tagging on recognition memory similar to the effect of elaboration.

Cued Recall Task: Evaluation of the Textbase

Recall protocols were analyzed in two ways. First, a statistical analysis was
done on the proportion of text propositions recalled. Then, a more specific
analysis was carried out on the recall protocols of subjects detecting the

contradiction in order to see whether memory for inconsistent information was actually enhanced.

An analysis of variance was conducted on the proportion of propositions recalled for detectors and nondetectors together. The condition (CE, CNE, NCE, NCNE) was a between-subjects variable because the same text was presented in a control and a contradictory version and paragraph topic (Satellites vs. Cavitation) was a within-subjects variable. The results showed a main effect of condition, $F(3, 50) = 2.82$, $p < .05$. The breakdown of this effect showed a significant superiority in the recall of the NC group over the C group, $F(1, 50 = 8.10$, $p < .01$, a significant inferiority in the recall of the CE group (.34) compared to the three other groups, $F(1, 50) = 4.9$, $p < .05$, and a significant inferiority in recall by the CNE group (.39) compared to the two NC groups, $F(1, 50) = 3.9$, $p = .05$. Proportions of recall for the NCE group (.50) and the NCNE group (.49) were not significantly different ($F < 1$).

The data presented here show that reading a contradictory text has a disrupting influence on the overall recall of the text. This negative influence is greater if subjects have time to elaborate. However, it is possible that this influence would not show up in the recall of contradictory information. Table 14.3 presents proportions of subjects (detectors in the case of the contradictory conditions) recalling the target propositions for the Satellites paragraph. The propositions P19 and P29 refer to the two contradictory statements (located in sentences 3 and 5). Proposition P30 refers to the contradictory statement transformed into a neutral statement in the NC conditions (a different identification resulted in the NC version, because an additional argument [BUILDINGS] had to be introduced).

The values presented in Table 14.3 indicate, first, that the second contradictory proposition (P29) is recalled less than the first one (P19). This should be expected in the NE condition (although in this case the difference does not reach significance: $X2(1) = 1.00$, p = .31): Subjects have less time to process P29. However, the effect is also found in the E condition

TABLE 14.3

Proportions of Detectors Recalling Either the First Contradictory Proposition (P19), the Second Contradictory Proposition (P29), Both Propositions, or None of the Propositions for the Satellites Paragraph. Proportions of Subjects Recalling the Target Propositions (P19, P30) for the NC Version Are Also Given.

	CE	CNE	NCE	NCNE
Only P19	0.45	0.50	0.25	0.38
Only P29/P30	0.18	0.33	0.25	0.08
P19 & P29/P30	0.36	0.17	0.33	0.31
None	0.00	0.00	0.17	0.23

($X2(1)$ = 5.3, p = .02). This result is consistent with the creation of a textbase representation by detectors of the contradiction in which the first contradictory proposition (old information) is more salient than the second one (new information). This finding is in agreement with the recall patterns obtained for detectors in previous experiments with the same type of texts. For example, a proportion of .35 of the detectors (12th-grade students) recalled only the first contradictory proposition in the text "Superconductivity" used by Otero and Kintsch (1992), whereas only a proportion of .02 recalled the second (Campanario, 1990). An alternative explanation for the improved recall of P19 could simply be the fact that it appears earlier in the text leading to a serial-order effect at recall. If this were the case, an effect should also appear in the NCE condition. However, no advantage in the recall of P19 is found in the NCE condition. Second, the existence of a contradiction has a positive effect on recall of the contradictory information in both the CE and CNE conditions (although the difference does not reach the conventional significance level: $X2(1) = 2.7$ p = 0.10 for the CE condition, and $X2(1) = 2.3$, p = 0.13 for the CNE condition). This is in contrast to the observed effect on the global recall of information: Subjects recall less information in the contradictory conditions.

Comprehension Questions:
Evaluation of the Situation Model

Answers to end-of-paragraph questions provide information about the relative weight of the two contradictory propositions in the situation model. Table 14.4 shows proportion of subjects (detectors in the C conditions) answering the comprehension questions for the Satellites paragraph in agreement with the first contradictory proposition, the second contradictory proposition, or those who declare that it is impossible to decide.

These proportions show that answers to end-of-paragraph questions are at variance with recall data. More subjects in the CE condition answer end-of-paragraph questions in agreement with new information than in agreement with old information, a difference that approaches significance ($X2(1) = 3.57$, p = .058). This is consistent with the idea that the recall task

TABLE 14.4
Proportion of Responses to End-of-Paragraph Questions
(Only Detectors in the C Conditions)

	CE	CNE	NCE	NCNE
Agreement with old information (P19)	.11	.50	.27	.30
Agreement with new information (P29)	.67	.00	.73	.50
Impossible to decide	.22	.50	.00	.20

only tests the semantic text content without accounting for the situation model. Old information may be more salient than new information in the textbase representation but not in the situation model. Subjects in the CE condition seem to update their situation model using this updated version when the task requires it—when subjects need to apply this knowledge to answer a question. This interpretation is also consistent with the fact that more agreement is found with old information than with new information in the CNE condition, as expected ($X2$ (1) = 4, p = .04). Updating the situation model is more difficult in this case because of a lack of time to do it. Also, the rates for "impossible to decide" are lower in the CE condition than in the CNE condition (although they do not reach significance ($X2(1)$ = 1.4, p = 0.23). A lower rate of such declarations in the CE condition was expected: Subjects may "fix up" the contradiction when given time to elaborate, as it has already been found in other studies (Baker, 1979; Otero & Campanario, 1990).

The relative facility with which subjects in this experiment update their situation model seems to be at variance with findings about the difficulty of discrediting old information by corrections presented later in a text (Johnson & Seifert, 1994; van Oostendorp & Bonebakker, 1996; Wilkes & Leatherbarrow, 1988). A possible explanation of the discrepancy may lie in differences in the type of texts used: narratives in the experiments which have just been cited, and expository-scientific in our work. In fact, Campanario and van Oostendorp (in press) found similar results regarding the importance of new information in updating situation models, when subjects read scientific texts including clear-cut contradictions like the ones in our paragraphs.

Conclusions From the Data

Three main conclusions follow from the foregoing results. First, elaboration and tagging have the same facilitation effect in memory of the contradictory information when it is measured by a recognition task: No significant difference has been found in recognition of the inconsistent information between the two conditions. This finding is consistent with Graesser and Nakamura's (1982) results mentioned earlier. Second, regarding recall of contradictory information, both elaboration and tagging have a facilitation effect. Although overall recall is disrupted by the contradiction, recall of the target propositions increases in both the CE and CNE conditions compared to the respective NC conditions. Third, elaboration has been found to have a different effect on memory depending on the task subjects have to perform. In recall, old contradictory information is more memorable than new contradictory information. However, new information is more frequently used than old information in the comprehension questions. This is interpreted as showing a different effect of elaboration on the two text representation levels, textbase and situation model. Old information is more salient than new information in the textbase representation, guiding recall. However, new information prevails in the situation model of the text used by subjects to answer the comprehension questions. Although the situation model is updated by subjects when given time to elaborate, this updating does not have an effect in the recall protocols.

In the non-elaboration condition, old information prevails in the recall task and also in answers to the comprehension questions. This is what should follow from the assumption of tagging as a textbase-level process that does not affect the situation-model level. Readers do not have time to update their situation model with the new information but only to add a tag to the textbase. Consequently, improved recall of the contradictory information should be expected compared to a control situation where no contradiction exists, as shown by the data. But no influence should be expected of the tag on tasks requiring use of the situation model.

A simulation in terms of the C-I model was done in order to account for these experimental findings: different results for recall and comprehension tasks in the elaboration condition, and more memorability of the target information in the contradictory non-elaboration condition compared to the control condition.

SIMULATIONS

Different simulations were performed motivated by our explanatory hypotheses of tagging and elaboration as processes respectively taking place at the textbase and situation model level. Only the simulations performed for the Satellites text are presented here, although simulations were run for both texts. The propositional network used in the simulations was the same as the one used in the recall data analyses. We applied the criterion of argument overlap (Kintsch, 1974; Kintsch & van Dijk, 1978) to relate the propositions in the network. For each simulation, the texts were processed sentence by sentence, keeping from each cycle (i.e., sentence) the most activated proposition, which was reintroduced in the next cycle. Once a sentence was processed, we integrated the representation of this portion of the text into the text representation in long-term memory. Whenever a proposition participated in more than one cycle, its representation in long-term memory was updated after ending its cycle. We now describe the simulations for each condition.

Elaboration Condition. We performed three simulations. A first one was run with no change in the network as a baseline for the comparisons. In the second simulation the textbase input was related to a situation model

(SM) network that corresponded to the verbal protocols given by the same subjects after the recall task. Examination of these protocols showed the following elaboration frequently generated by subjects who found the contradiction (Lightfoot & Bullock, 1990; Otero & Campanario, 1990): Either the first contradictory proposition or the second contradictory proposition may be true depending on the circumstances. Thus, the following statement referring to the assumed situation model was introduced in the second simulation: "Depending on the degree of optical quality of telescopes of surveillance satellites, they are either able or unable to distinguish buildings." We parsed this statement in concepts and propositions and added it to the input net during the processing of the last sentence (at the time subjects processed the *second* contradictory proposition). This was done in two stages.

In the first stage, we introduced a Macroproposition SM:CONTRAD[P29,P19] with a self strength of 2 that was linked to P29 and P19 (textbase propositions). It is supposed to correspond to the proposition immediately retrieved from memory when subjects notice the contradiction. This is the tagging proposition in the simulation of the non-elaboration condition. We also added a negative link between the two contradictory propositions. After ending this cycle, we initiated a new integration cycle (second stage) by introducing the propositions available from the situation model (the S propositions) and the propositions remaining activated from the preceding cycle (i.e., the first stage). The S propositions were not only related to some other propositions of the S network but also to some textbase propositions with a strength of 1. Figure 14.2 is the graphical

First stage

SM: CONTRAD [P29,P19]

Second stage

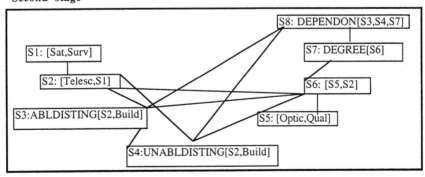

FIG. 14.2. Graphical representation of the propositions and concepts for the contradictory version of Satellites paragraph. Label S corresponds to the situation-model propositions.

representation of the situation-model network for the Satellites paragraph, introduced in two stages, corresponding to the elaborations readers were assumed to generate when they detected the contradiction.

The third simulation followed the same principles as the one just presented, but differed by the information contained in the situation model: It focused now on the information needed to answer the comprehension questions. The information needed to answer the comprehension questions corresponded to the idea that telescopes of surveillance satellites were unable to distinguish buildings, which was in agreement with the second contradictory proposition and with subjects' answers to comprehension questions. Thus, we introduced in the textbase net a statement referring to the content of the second contradictory proposition and the two stages of the simulation were initiated according to what we explained previously. These two different situation models were used to account for the discrepancy between the recall data and the answers to comprehension questions. Introducing different prior knowledge in the model is assumed to lead to different text interpretations. In addition, we wanted to show that the model (contrary to Otero & Kintsch's, 1992, findings), could account for a better memorability of inconsistent information when knowledge specifically related to the task was incorporated.

Nonelaboration Condition.   Three simulations were performed in this condition, two corresponding to the CNE condition and one corresponding to the NCNE condition. In the first simulation, we introduced first in the textbase network a negative link between the two contradictory propositions (P19 and P29) with a strength of −1, as in Otero and Kintsch (1992). We then introduced as a second stage a weak situation model, assuming that the subjects were not able to integrate the contradiction in their text representation (i.e., no updating) and only relied on the first contradictory proposition. This was done by weighting the first contradictory proposition. A second simulation was run in order to account for the tagging hypothesis: Even with no time to elaborate, subjects should be able to process the last information and to infer that it is contradictory with previous information in the text. This amounts to introducing the tagging proposition, CONTRADICTS [P29,P19] in the first stage of the simulation. The tagging proposition is related to the two contradictory propositions in the textbase network, that are connected themselves through a negative link. The tagging proposition, as in the simulation of the elaboration condition, has the status of a macroproposition with a self-strength of 2. We also assumed that the situation model created by readers in this condition could only be related to the first contradictory proposition, as subjects do not have time to update it when they find the contradictory information. Thus, a "weak" situation model related to the first contradictory proposition was introduced in the second stage of the simulation. In this way, this stage was comparable to the second stage in the previous simulation (CNE condition). In the third simulation, processing of the target paragraph in the NCNE condition was simulated by introducing a proposition corresponding to "Telescopes are able to distinguish cities" in the last cycle. This weighted the first target proposition, as in the second simulation, and corresponds again to the assumed situation model of readers when they find the second target proposition, P30.

RELATION BETWEEN PREDICTIONS AND DATA

We compared the activation values obtained in long-term memory for the two target propositions with experimental data regarding: (a) recall of the corresponding propositions, and (b) proportion of responses to end-of-paragraph questions. Table 14.5 presents the activation values of each of the three simulations for the two target propositions, proportions of recall (issued from Table 14.3) and answers to comprehension questions (issued from Table 14.4) of target information (i.e., P19 and P29) in the contradictory elaboration (CE) condition.

The results presented in Table 14.5 provide a good qualitative fit between the predictions of the C-I model (activation value for the two target propositions) and the data (mean proportion of recall and answers to end-of-paragraph questions of the target propositions) with the exception of the first simulation (without any modification) for which the activation value of the two target propositions remains very low. The introduction of a situation-model network in relation to the verbal protocols collected after the recall (Simulation 2) qualitatively fits the recall data, that is, higher activation corresponds to better recall (.45 for P19 and .18 for P29), whereas a similar agreement does not exist when the model predictions are compared with the responses to comprehension questions (a proportion of .11 in agreement with P19 and a proportion of .67 in agreement with P29). Thus, the introduction in the textbase net of a situation model

TABLE 14.5
C-I Predictions and Subjects' Data for the
Two Target Propositions in the CE Condition

Simulation		*Predictions*	*Recall Data*	*Comprehension*
S1: no modification in	P19	550	.45	.11
the text-base network	P29	1,000	.18	.67
S2: introduction of a	P19	2,984	.45	.11
SM related to recall data	P29	2,435	.18	.67
S3: introduction of a SM	P19	1,616	.45	.11
related to end-of-paragraph questions	P29	3,218	.18	.67

TABLE 14.6
C-I Predictions and Subjects' Data for the Two
Target Propositions in the NE Conditions

Conditions	Simulations	Predictions		Recall Data	Comprehension
CNE	S1: weak SM +	P19	3,155	.50	.50
	a negative link	P29	608	.33	0
CNE	S2: weak SM, a	P19	4,616	.50	.50
	negative link + a tag	P29	1,066	.33	0
NCNE	S3: S.Model	P19	2,260	.38	.30
		P30	814	.08	.50

related to what subjects are supposed to activate in order to answer the comprehension questions is relevant here. The activation values indicate in this case a good fit (Simulation 3) with the proportions of responses but not with the recall data, that is, higher activation corresponds to a higher degree of use of the new information. These results show that Kintsch's construction-integration model may account for the fact that different prior knowledge leads to different text interpretations, and more specifically, it provides some evidence for the fact that specific knowledge is used by readers as a function of the task they have to perform.

The relation between predictions (activation values) and data (recall and comprehension) in the CNE condition compared to that existing in the NCNE condition is shown in Table 14.6. The recall of target information, in particular P29, improves in the CNE condition (.33) compared to the NCNE condition (.08). However, the introduction of a negative link (Simulation 1) results in a poorer fit between the model predictions and recall data: The activation value of P29 (P30 in the NCNE condition) decreases from Simulation 3 to Simulation 1, whereas proportion of recall increases. A better agreement between simulation and data is obtained when a tagging node is introduced in Simulation 2. Moreover, and as predicted, an agreement exists between the model predictions and the responses to comprehension questions only in the CNE conditions (Simulations 1 and 2): A low activation value for P29 corresponds to no updating of the new information compared to the NCNE condition, in which a low activation (814) corresponds to the highest proportion of responses (.50).

GENERAL DISCUSSION

The objective of this study was twofold. First, we intended to compare the elaboration and tagging explanatory hypotheses of enhanced memory for inconsistent information in relation to the construction of the semantic and situation-model levels of representation. We assumed that whereas elaborations should lead to an integration of the inconsistency in the rest of the text and to an updated model of the situation described by the text, tagging should be conceptualized as a textbase phenomenon allowing readers to form a correct semantic representation but not producing an updating of the situation model. Second, we wanted to show that the construction-integration model could account for our data when adequate modifications were introduced.

A situation where subjects noticed an inconsistency has been studied by measuring response times in recognizing arguments of the inconsistent propositions and examining responses to comprehension questions. A similar experimental design to O'Brien and Myers' (1985) study has been used and their results have been replicated. Elaboration has been shown to have an effect on answers to comprehension questions—reflecting an influence on the situation model. Also, as in O'Brien and Myers' experiment, elaboration has been found to improve recognition memory for inconsistent information. However, similar effects on recognition and recall memory for the inconsistent proposition have been found even in the absence of elaboration opportunities. In this way, we provided support for the tagging mechanism that could explain increased memory of inconsistent, contradictory, or unexpected information. Thus, tagging is as good an explanation as elaboration when it concerns a textbase-oriented measure (recognition and recall), whereas elaboration of a situation model is needed to account for the comprehension data.

An additional important finding in relation to tagging emerges from the previous results. These data support an interpretation of tagging as a process operating at a different text representation level than elaboration. Enhanced recognition and recall memory has been found in a situation where elaboration is difficult, and only tagging is assumed to be operating. However, no influence of the contradictory information on the situation model initially built by the reader is observed in this situation. An adequate interpretation of the data can be made by assuming different effects of the contradiction at the textbase and situation-model levels in agreement with an explanatory hypothesis already proposed by Wilkes and Leatherbarrow (1988). In their study, subjects could accurately recall a correction about information provided earlier in a text without this having an effect on the updating of the associated situation model. The discrepancy was explained by assuming that the contradictory propositions and the correctional link were stored at the textbase level only. This should also apply to our case. When subjects are deprived of the possibility of elaborating, they seem to do all that can be done under the circumstances: storing the contradictory propositions together with a tag indicating their inconsistent character. Thus, tagging inconsistent information affects recall or recognition, as shown by increased memory of contradictory propositions, but does not affect tasks involving the situation model, like answering comprehension questions.

Our findings also show how different methods probe different representations of the contradictory information in subjects' memory. Subjects recalled better the first contradictory proposition than the second, influenced by the textbase representation. However, quite a different pattern was found when subjects were probed for application of knowledge acquired from the text. In this case, subjects who had been given time to elaborate after reading the contradictory information generally used the updated version, placing a greater weight on the second contradictory proposition to answer the comprehension questions.

The comparison between our behavioral data and the C-I model's predictions support the idea that inconsistencies have different effects at the textbase or situation-model level depending on the task requirement. By introducing some modifications in the C-I model of text comprehension we showed that it could account for the differential effect of prior knowledge on the memorability of inconsistent information. In the contradictory elaboration (CE) condition (Table 14.5), the activation values that better correspond to the behavioral data are a function of the type of information introduced in the situation-model network, that is, a best fit between the recall data and the situation model related to the verbal protocols, as well as between the comprehension data and the SM in relation to end-of-paragraph questions. In the contradictory non-elaboration (CNE) condition, introducing a tagging node in the C-I model simulations (Simulation 2, Table 14.6) was shown to improve agreement between simulation results and recall data. Just introducing a negative link between the contradictory propositions causes the predicted activation of one of the contradictory propositions to decrease (as in Otero & Kintsch's, 1992, simulation of the same situation), against the observed recall results. Moreover, the introduction of a tagging node in the C-I model is also in good agreement with the comprehension data: Higher activation is found for old information compared to new information.

Thus, an account of the positive effects of an explicit contradiction on memory in terms of the C-I model of text comprehension can be achieved in two ways: first, by incorporating propositions from the situation model in case the reader has the opportunity to elaborate the inconsistent information; second, in case this elaboration is impossible, an agreement between simulation predictions and data is better achieved by combining two factors: the negative effect of the inhibitory link between the inconsistent propositions and the positive effect of a tag on the inconsistent propositions, at the textbase level. In this way, introducing a tagging node in the C-I model's textbase network appears as a natural way to account for the positive effects that surprise or inconsistency may have on memory. Once again, the model predictions qualitatively fit the data and allowed us to test crucial hypotheses on the cognitive processes readers applied in a situation of text comprehension.

ACKNOWLEDGMENTS

The research reported in this chapter was supported by a French–Spanish Picasso Grant to both authors, and by Project PB93-0478 of DGICYT of the Ministry of Education, Spain, to the second author. We thank Luis Cardiel and A. Gallego of EITT, University of Alcala, for developing the program used in the experiments.

REFERENCES

Albrecht, J. E., & O'Brien, E. J. (1993). Updating a mental model: Maintaining both local and global coherence. *Journal of Experimental Psychology: Learning, Memory, and Cognition, 19*, 1061–1070.

Anderson, J. R., & Reder, L. M. (1979). An elaborative processing explanation of depth of processing. In L. S. Cermak & F. I. M. Craik (Eds.), *Levels of processing in human memory* (pp. 385–403). Hillsdale, NJ: Lawrence Erlbaum Associates.

Baker, L. (1979). Comprehension monitoring: Identifying and coping with text confusions. *Journal of Reading Behavior, 11*, 365–374.

Bower, G. H., Black, J. B., & Turner, T. J. (1979). Scripts in memory for text. *Cognitive Psychology, 11*, 177–220.

Bradshaw, G. L., & Anderson, J. R. (1982). Elaborative encoding as an explanation of levels of processing. *Journal of Verbal Learning and Verbal Behavior, 21*, 165–174.

Cairns, H. S., Cowart, W., & Jablon, A. D. (1981). Effects of prior context upon the integration of lexical information during sentence processing. *Journal of Verbal Learning and Verbal Behavior, 20*, 445–453.

Campanario, J. M. (1990). *Análisis de los protocolos de recuerdo de textos contradictorios.* Unpublished manuscript, Universidad de Alcalá, Grupo de Investigación sobre el Aprendizaje de las Ciencias.

Campanario, J. M., & van Oostendorp, H. (in press, September). Updating mental representation when reading scientific texts. In J. F. Rouet, J. Levonen, & A. Biardeau (Eds.), *Proceedings of the using complex information systems '96 conference,* Université de Poitiers, France.

Fincher-Kiefer, R., Post, T. R., Greene, T. R., & Voss, J. F. (1988). On the role of prior knowledge and task demands in the processing of text. *Journal of Memory and Language, 27*, 416–428.

Fletcher, C. R., & Chrysler, S. T. (1990). Surface forms, textbases, and situation models: Recognition memory for three types of textual information, *Discourse Processes, 13*, 175–190.

Graesser, A. C. (1981). *Prose comprehension beyond the word.* New York: Springer.

Graesser, A. C., & Nakamura, G. V. (1982). The impact of a schema on comprehension and memory. In G. H. Bower (Ed.), *The psychology of learning and motivation* (Vol. 16, pp. 59–109). New York: Academic Press.

Johnson, H. M., & Seifert, C. M. (1994). Sources of continued influence effect: When misinformation in memory affects later inferences. *Journal of Experimental Psychology: Learning, Memory, and Cognition, 20,* 1420–1436.

Kintsch, E., & Kintsch, W. (1995). Strategies to promote active learning from text: Individual differences in background knowledge. *Swiss Journal of Psychology, 54*(2), 141–151.

Kintsch, W. (1974). *The representation of meaning in memory,* Hillsdale, NJ: Lawrence Erlbaum Associates.

Kintsch, W. (1986). Learning from text. *Cognition and Instruction, 3*(2), 87–108.

Kintsch, W. (1988). The role of knowledge in discourse comprehension: A construction-integration model. *Psychological Review, 95,* 163–182.

Kintsch, W., & Franzke, M. (1995). The role of background knowledge in the recall of news story. In E. J. O'Brien & R. F. Lorch (Eds.), *Sources of coherence in reading* (pp. 321–333). Hillsdale, NJ: Lawrence Erlbaum Associates.

Kintsch, W., & van Dijk, T. A. (1978). Toward a model of text comprehension and production. *Psychological Review, 85,* 363–394.

Kintsch, W., & Welsch, D. (1991). The construction-integration model: A framework for studying memory for text. In W. E. Hockley & S. Lewandowsky (Eds.), *Relating theory and data: Essays in human memory in honor of B.B. Murdock* (pp. 367–385). Hillsdale, NJ: Lawrence Erlbaum Associates.

Kintsch, W., Welsch, D., Schmalhofer, F., & Zimny, S. (1990). Sentence memory: A theoretical analysis. *Journal of Memory and Language, 29,* 133–159.

Lightfoot, C., & Bullock, M. (1990). Interpreting contradictory communications: Age and context effects. *Developmental Psychology, 26,* 830–836.

Mannes, S. M., & Kintsch, W. (1987). Knowledge organization and text organization. *Cognition and Instruction, 4*(2), 91–115.

O'Brien, E. J. (1995). Automatic components of discourse comprehension. In E. J. O'Brien & R. F. Lorch (Eds.), *Sources of coherence in reading* (pp. 159–176). Hillsdale, NJ: Lawrence Erlbaum Associates.

O'Brien, E. J., & Lorch, R. F. (1995). *Sources of coherence in reading.* Hillsdale, NJ: Lawrence Erlbaum Associates.

O'Brien, E. J., & Myers, J. L. (1985). When comprehension difficulty improves memory for text. *Journal of Experimental Psychology: Learning, Memory, and Cognition, 11,* 12–21.

Otero, J., & Campanario, J. M. (1990). Comprehension evaluation and regulation in learning from science texts. *Journal of Research in Science Teaching, 27,* 447–460.

Otero, J., & Kintsch, W. (1992). Failures to detect contradictions in a text: What readers believe versus what they read. *Psychological Science, 3,* 229–235.

Perrig, W., & Kintsch, W. (1985). Propositional and situational representations of text. *Journal of Memory and Language, 24,* 503–518.

Schmalhofer, F., & Glavanov, D. N. (1986). Three components of understanding a programmer's manual: Verbatim, propositional, and situational representations, *Journal of Memory and Language, 25,* 279–294.

Tapiero, I. (1991). Acquisition et transfert de connaissances à l'aide de textes [Knowledge acquisition and transfer from texts]. *Psychologie Française,* Tome 36-2, 177–187.

Tapiero, I. (1992). *Traitement cognitif du texte narratif et expositif et connexionnisme: Experimentations et simulations* [Cognitive processing of story and expository text and connectionism: Experimentations and simulations]. Unpublished doctoral dissertation, University of Paris 8.

Tapiero, I., & Denhiere, G. (1995). Simulating recall and recognition by using Kintsch's construction-integration model. In C. A. Weaver, S. Mannes, & C. R. Fletcher (Eds.), *Discourse comprehension: Essays in honor of W. Kintsch* (pp. 211–233). Hillsdale, NJ: Lawrence Erlbaum Associates.

Tardieu, H., Ehrlich, M-F., & Gyselinck, V. (1992). Levels of representation and domain-specific knowledge in comprehension of scientific texts. *Language and Cognitive Processes, 7*(3/4) 335–351.

van Oostendorp, H. (1994). Text processing in terms of semantic cohesion monitoring. In H. van Oostendorp & R. A. Zwaan (Eds.), *Naturalistic text comprehension* (pp. 35–55). Norwood, NJ: Ablex.

van Oostendorp, H., & Bonebakker, C. (1996). Het vasthouden aan incorrecte informatie bij het verwerken van nieuwsberichten [Holding on to misinformation during processing news reports]. *Tijdschrift voor communicativetenschap, 24*(1), 57–74.

von Restorff, H. (1933). Uber die Wirkung von bereichsbildungen in Spurenfeld. *Psychologishe Forschung, 18,* 299–342.

Wilkes, A. L., & Leatherbarrow, M. (1988). Editing episodic memory following the identification of error. *Quarterly Journal of Experimental Psychology, 40 A*, 2, 361–387.

van Dijk, T., & Kintsch, W. (1983). *Strategies of discourse comprehension.* New York: Academic Press.

Chapter 15

Conclusions, Conundrums, and Challenges for the Future

Susan R. Goldman
Vanderbilt University

Herre van Oostendorp
Utrecht University

The contributions to this volume allow us to draw several conclusions about processes and strategies involved in constructing representations from textual input. However, they also pose a major conundrum around the issue of monitoring and detection of inconsistencies. Resolving this puzzle poses an interesting set of challenges to the field of discourse psychology. Finally, we consider several issues of learning from text that might be addressed by discourse psychology.

SOME CONCLUSIONS

In our introductory comments, we noted that earlier research on processing tended to rely heavily on measures of memory to make inferences about the kind(s) of representation that had been constructed. Several chapters in this volume (e.g., Caillies et al.; Coté & Goldman; Ferstl & Kintsch; Langston & Trabasso; Magliano, Zwaan, & Graesser; van den Broek et al.) looked at indices of online processing, either by modeling them or by collecting specific dependent measures of processing, including processing times and online, think-aloud protocols. The clear conclusion from these investigations is that readers' prior knowledge comes into play in varied and complex ways during the construction of representations. For example, sometimes prior knowledge supports rich, inferential elaboration of information in the text; other times it supports the detection of inconsistencies (Coté & Goldman). Yet other times it creates an illusion of knowing and may actually result in more superficial processing of the text (Ehrlich; van Oostendorp & Bonebakker).

Several of the chapters presented models that use online measures to predict final representations and memory. As such, the models reflect a "third generation" of cognitive research on reading (van den Broek et al., this volume). The predictions are most successful in the case of particular kinds of narratives, namely, goal-based stories. An important issue is the degree to which the assumptions and mechanisms of these models will need to be modified to account for online and memorial representations of different kinds of narratives and other text genres, especially texts designed to instruct readers (cf. Goldman, Varma, & Coté, 1996). In the next section, we explore this issue in more depth.

CONSTRUCTING AND REPRESENTING NARRATIVES

At least two types of narratives are represented in this volume. One type is goal-based stories. The other is news reports of world events. The data suggest that the online construction of representations for the two kinds of narratives may be governed by different variables.

With respect to goal-based stories, Langston and Trabasso and van den Broek et al. present models of processing of goal-based stories that are quite convincing in accounting for a range of online processing measures as well as memory measures. Both are connectionist, activation-based models and as such are members of a class of models that are derivatives of Kintsch's (1988) construction-integration model. However, both models make significant departures from Kintsch and also differ among themselves with respect to the mechanisms of connection and spread of activation.

The Langston and Trabasso model relies on knowledge of psychological and physical causality and places causal connectivity at the heart of representation construction. A network of event nodes is constructed based on causal connectivity among the events. Activation spreads among the nodes, with nodes having greater numbers of connections to other nodes accruing greater strength in the representation. Langston and Trabasso permit all nodes to participate in each processing cycle. The activation strengths on each cycle contribute to the construction of a long-term memory representation. With just these three assumptions, the model is impressive in the extent to which it can account for results obtained from a variety of online and memory measures.

One issue raised by Langston and Trabasso is the degree to which the causal connectivity mechanism is applicable to a wider range of texts. What other mechanisms of connectivity will be important? How does knowledge in the domain alter the kind of connections, causal or otherwise, that can be made during online processing? A second issue concerns the purpose for reading and potential implications of purpose for completeness of processing. In the case of the individuals generating the data modeled by Langston and Trabasso, we can assume a similarity in purpose among the readers for these types of texts in the laboratory experiment situation. With different types of texts, readers' purposes will vary. Varying purposes are likely to imply variability in readers' criteria for coherence. For example, for some purposes, readers may not be concerned to construct all of the causal connections among nodes. Rather, they may be content with a looser coupling of the information. Implications for construction of the network representation are not clear in the latter case. Indeed, coherence criteria differences may lie at the heart of the conundrum present among the results of the studies of updating, an issue that we discuss in more depth subsequently.

The landscape model of van den Broek et al. reflects the fluctuating pattern of concept activations that occur over the course of comprehending a text and uses this pattern to predict the final representation. In reading any given sentence, activation spreads from concepts directly activated by virtue of being in the sentence to their cohorts—other concepts to which they are connected. Connections result from an interaction of the text with readers' attentional capacities, background knowledge, and criteria for comprehension. As in the Langston and Trabasso model, an important aspect of background knowledge in the case of goal-based stories is causal coherence. The patterns of activation define a network of concept nodes varying in activation that are related to one another by links of varying strengths. The final representation is a direct result of the dynamic, fluctuating patterns of activation that occur during reading. The networks derived according to these assumptions were found to predict significantly frequency and order of recall of a goal-based story. The model also holds great promise for accounting for readers noticing inconsistencies, making forward inferences, and using background knowledge to guide processing.

Nevertheless, application of the landscape model to a broader range of texts faces similar issues to those discussed for the Langston and Trabasso model. This is likely even though the landscape model includes a parameter for differences in coherence criteria. One way around the issues associated with going beyond just causal connections among nodes is for van den Broek et al. to continue using the empirical method of having readers rate the connectivity among concepts at various points in the text. These ratings are, in effect, stand-ins for the four sources of activation assumed by this model to drive representation construction. An issue for future research is to unpack the operation of these four sources of activation during online processing. Consistent with Magliano et al., raters/readers may be basing their connectivity judgments on multiple dimensions of continuity or they might be based on singular dimensions. In either case, it would be extremely informative to be able to isolate which dimensions are used and the relative contributions of each. It is probably the case that those concepts that are most central, that is, have connections to the most other nodes, have high continuity in multiple dimensions. But does continuity in some dimensions count more than in other dimensions? What cues do readers use during processing to determine which dimensions count more?

The Magliano et al. work begins to address the dimensionality issues. In addition to demonstrating the importance of considering multiple dimensions of the situation being represented, some of their evidence suggests a priority relationship among the dimensions. Readers seemed to attend to some dimensions on a first read but to different ones on a second pass through the text. Such "adding" to the situation model suggests an active updating process. Active updating of this type may be restricted to goal-based stories. At least that is one implication of the discrepancy between evidence of active updating in the goal-based stories as compared to the apparent lack of updating when people read nonfiction narratives (e.g., newspaper articles), as discussed in the Johnson and Seifert, and van Oostendorp and Bonebakker chapters. This discrepancy is certainly a conundrum; its resolution is important. We discuss it in the next section.

A CONUNDRUM: DETECTION OR NOT? UPDATING OR NOT?

Several chapters suggest that the resolution of conundrums about detection and updating may lie in the type of processing readers are engaged in, which itself may be related to readers' purposes and goals in reading and their criteria for coherence. Garrod and Sanford, Johnson and Seifert, and van Oostendorp and Bonebakker each suggest that readers may not be noticing discrepancies (discontinuities) because they are not processing the text to a degree of meaning resolution that taps the level at which inconsistency detection might occur. Across the various chapters, they use terms like *sloppy*, *global*, or *shallow* processing to reflect the distinction. Ehrlich's work with instructional text also points to a "levels of processing" explanation for a lack of inconsistency detection. In her study, it was particularly interesting that the higher-knowledge students were less likely than the lower-knowledge students to detect discrepancies. One interpretation of this finding is that the higher-knowledge students processed the text superficially because early in the text they decided that they already knew the material. Hence, they merely skimmed through the text.

Tapiero and Otero suggest a somewhat different explanation for failures to detect inconsistencies. They suggest that the detection of an inconsistency depends on whether that inconsistency exists in the textbase or situation model level and whether the task the reader is doing requires the representation level at which the discontinuity exists. Of course, it is quite possible that different kinds of processing are needed to develop different levels of representation. However, the Tapiero and Otero explanation suggests a fruitful direction for subsequent work on updating.

Another type of explanation for the conundrum is suggested by the work of Perfetti, Britt, and Rouet on document models. They argue that the source of information is very important to the interpretation process and the construction of a representation. Although source information may be more relevant in some domains (e.g., history and science) than others (e.g., mathematics), the expectation that sources do not necessarily agree might make readers read more critically and increase their sensitivity to discrepancies among texts.

Implicit in the discussions of updating and construction of models of documents as well as models of the situation is the idea that the reader needs to be actively reasoning about the material. Reasoning is an important process in the online construction of representations. Readers need to reason with and about information contained in texts and how it relates to prior knowledge if they are to detect inconsistencies and correct misconceptions. Chinn and Brewer (1993) provide very nice examples of the strategies readers may follow in accommodating their existing models as compared to assimilating incoming data to established models. Some quite complicated reasoning patterns are often necessary. Additional research on how such reasoning influences the construction of representations is an important area of investigation.

Issues of purpose, coherence criteria, and expectations about different kinds of sources are all related to aspects of the larger communicative context of reading. Thus, to fully understand the online construction of representations, including when discrepancies are likely to be detected, discourse psychology needs to heed van Dijk's arguments about the importance of developing a theory of context that can specify the impact of, and interactions among, prior knowledge, discourse context, and social communicative context. The communicative context may be what informs readers' decisions regarding comprehension, monitoring, and updating criteria. Accordingly, van Dijk stresses the importance of continuous monitoring of the context by means of a mental context model.

CHALLENGES FOR THE FUTURE: LEARNING FROM TEXT

Issues of updating representations are really synonymous with issues of learning from text. Questions abound with respect to when, how, and for how long readers modify their knowledge. Structural Knowledge Assessment, proposed by Ferstl and Kintsch, is a promising method for allowing us to examine changes in knowledge more precisely. These issues require that models of online processing be integrated with models of long-term memory and how learning occurs. For example, Caillies, Denhiere, and Jhean-Larose report on the memorial consequences of presenting individuals with texts that differentially match the structure of their knowledge in a domain, where the structure of that knowledge is related to level of expertise in the field. To optimize learning by matching text structure to knowledge structure, there must be some way of determining the structure of prior knowledge.

As alluded to earlier in the discussion of goal-based stories, we still know little about potential differences and similarities in online processing activities when readers are in knowledge-rich versus knowledge-lean domains (Coté, Goldman, & Saul, 1998). Garrod and Sanford suggest that being able to construct a link to a situational topic can influence the whole processing episode. In the absence of a strong link, the representation needs to be constructed in a more bottom-up fashion. In this case, the representation is probably relatively episodic with some links to permanent knowledge.

The work reported in this volume does suggest some processing circumstances that facilitate greater integration of "new" information with a more permanent knowledge store. For example, Coté and Goldman showed that successful knowledge builders engaged in processing that transformed the text through self-explanations that relied on prior knowledge and active efforts to interconnect information from different parts of the text. Perfetti et al. indicated that reading multiple documents that presented different perspectives led to situation models that less closely resembled any particular document, especially if the task required the construction of an argument rather than a narrative of the events. In each of these cases, not only does knowledge affect processing, but earlier processing produces information that can be accessed and used in processing later portions of the text. Aspects of an evolving situation model impact encoding of subsequent text and perhaps construction of the textbase. For van Dijk, this interrelationship is an aspect of the communicative context of the event.

Learning involves incrementing, reorganizing, and replacing information. We face many challenges with respect to understanding the knowledge-acquisition processes that are involved in these aspects of learning. The work of Perfetti et al. on a documents model points out several important considerations relevant to learning over multiple sources of information. It will be interesting to extend our theoretical and empirical understanding of knowledge acquisition that occurs over multiple documents. Equally interesting is consideration of the impact on representation construction of nontextual forms of information such as pictures, graphics, and animated images. As the Gyselinck and Tardieu chapter indicates, we are still lacking a good understanding of how pictures and other forms of graphic representations contribute to the construction of a situation model. As the use of additional forms of media increases, we will need to ask about the processes associated with processing and integrating information from text with information present in video and animated images. These processing issues are fundamental to understanding learning and knowledge acquisition in a multimedia information age. However, we have many significant challenges in this area.

A final group of challenges concerns the need to better understand how multiple levels of representation are constructed, interact, and mutually influence one another. Although theories describe different levels of representation that are somehow related to one another in the meaning-making process, precisely how they are related is an open question. We need a better understanding of the coordination of different levels of representation and of the potential for interaction among levels. In other words, how do partially constructed situation models influence the construction of coherent textbases and vice versa? This emphasis is consistent with third-generation models of cognitive research on reading (van den Broek et al., this volume).

Another aspect of this final group of challenges concerns attempts to characterize representations dichotomously, as either textbase *or* situation-model level representations, rather than along some sort of continua. The most obvious continua are quality of the textbase and degree of appropriate integration of prior knowledge with the newly incoming textbase. Such a knowledge-construction model emphasizes the interaction of text and knowledge in constructing a mental model and in the result of the construction process. Coté et al. (1998) recently described such a model (cf. Goldman & Coté, 1997). It is similar to a conceptualization proposed by Kintsch (1997; McNamara & Kintsch, 1996).

Coté et al. (1998) proposed a space of mental representations defined by the simultaneous consideration of two dimensions: prior knowledge use and quality of the textbase, where quality is reflected by both coherence and completeness. As shown in Fig. 15.1, the vertical continuum reflects knowledge use, from high to low. The horizontal continuum reflects quality of the textbase, also high to low. The upper right quadrant of the figure captures highly coherent, well-formed mental representations. These result from high-quality textbases in combination with high levels of appropriate integration of prior knowledge. Textbase coherence results, in part, from appropriate cross-sentence connections. In this quadrant, coherence and integration increase as distance from the origin on both axes increases. The lower right quadrant differs from the upper right in the degree of

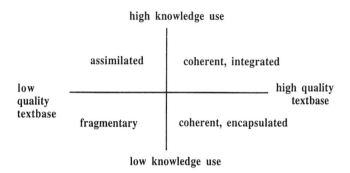

FIG. 15.1. A two-dimensional mental representation space. From Coté, Goldman, and Saul (1998).

prior knowledge use. A highly coherent representation may result from a high-quality representation of the text but relatively little integration with prior knowledge. This might occur if the input text is highly explicit and cohesive. Although the resulting representation would be of high quality, it would be relatively encapsulated in memory and have little impact on readers' knowledge structures for the domain. For example, the reader could hold two opposing views, one based in prior knowledge and one in the encapsulated text, and not recognize the discrepancy or contradiction. Representations in this quadrant may result in readers showing surface updating but not global updating (see chapters by Johnson & Seifert, and van Oostendorp & Bonebakker, this volume).

The quadrants to the left of the vertical axis reflect poor-quality representations of the textbase. The upper left quadrant depicts the result of high use of prior knowledge in conjunction with a poor-quality textbase. Representations in this quadrant differ from those in the upper right in that in this quadrant, text is *assimilated* into the reader's existing knowledge. If that knowledge is accurate, the resulting representation is of relatively high coherence but the reader has learned little new information. If the reader's prior knowledge was erroneous, the representation would reflect those errors and misconceptions even if there had been information in the text that contradicted that prior knowledge. So this quadrant reflects the idea that it is possible to have a situation model that is not faithful to the text but is highly coherent and resistant to change (cf. Scardamalia & Bereiter, 1991).

Finally, the lower left quadrant reflects poor-quality textbase construction and lower use of prior knowledge than the upper left quadrant. If the text is not highly cohesive or explicit and if the reader brings relatively little prior knowledge to the meaning-construction process, the resulting representation is of poor quality, largely isolated, and populated by fragmentary phrases and concepts. This type of representation would be likely for students with low knowledge in a content area who read texts that were poorly structured and left many gaps in logic and content that the reader was expected to fill but which they could not. Coté et al. (1998) use online and recall protocols to locate readers' interactions with particular instructional texts in each of these quadrants.

Conceptualizing mental representations along continua and examining the relative balance among levels of representation refocuses theoretical and empirical attention on the character of the knowledge network that exists during and after processing. Some of the important issues about knowledge networks include

- the coherence of the network;
- whether the network reflects new, emergent understandings of the situation, based on the integration of new information from a text with prior knowledge;
- whether levels of representations interact in ways that enable the detection of consistencies and inconsistencies in emerging knowledge networks.

These issues, and others like them, reflect persistent, central, and challenging issues for the future.

Taken as a whole, the chapters in this volume indicate that there are several fairly robust theoretical and computational models for conceptualizing representation-construction processes and their final outcomes. These models and the methods for assessing online processing reflected in the contributions to this volume have made it possible for discourse psychology to take major steps toward addressing important questions about the construction of mental representations and how these construction processes relate to the mental representations they produce. In this final chapter, we pointed out some conundrums and a number of challenges for the future. We look forward to the evolution of theory and methods as discourse psychology continues to grapple with these important issues.

REFERENCES

Chinn, C. A., & Brewer, W. F. (1993). The role of anomalous data in knowledge acquisition: A theoretical framework and implications for science instruction. *Review of Educational Research, 63*, 1–49.

Coté, N., Goldman, S. R., & Saul, E. U. (1998). Students making sense of informational text: Relations between processing and learning. *Discourse Processes, 25*, 1–53.

Goldman, S. R., & Coté, N. C. (1997, July). *Reading to learn: Evidence from think-aloud protocols.* Invited presentation at the Society for Text and Discourse meeting in Utrecht, Netherlands.

Goldman, S. R., Varma, S., & Coté, N. (1996). Extending capacity-constrained construction integration: Toward "smarter" and flexible models of text comprehension. In B. K. Britton & A. C. Graesser (Eds.), *Models of text comprehension* (pp. 73–113). Mahwah, NJ: Lawrence Erlbaum Associates.

Kintsch, W. (1988). The role of knowledge in discourse comprehension: A construction-integration model. *Psychological Review, 95,* 163–182.

Kintsch, W. (1997). *Comprehension: A paradigm for cognition.* New York: Cambridge University Press.

McNamara, D. S., & Kintsch, W. (1996). Learning from texts: Effects of prior knowledge and text coherence. *Discourse Processes, 22,* 247–288.

Scardamalia, M., & Bereiter, C. (1991). Literate expertise. In K. A. Ericsson & J. Smith (Eds.), *Toward a general theory of expertise* (pp. 172–194). New York: Cambridge University Press.

Author Index

A

Abelson, R. P., 31, *68*, 72, 89, *96*, 127, 128, *147*, 251, *276*, 306, *317*
Acton, W. H., 260, *275*
Adelson, B., 248, *274*
Afflerbach, P., 169, 189, *193*
Albrecht, J. E., 74, 87, *94*, *96*, 344, 345, *363*
Altmann, G. T. M., 103, 104, *120*, 247, *274*
Altschull, J. H., 136, *143*
Anderson, A., 219, 223, *242*
Anderson, C. A., 303, 310, 314, 315, 316, *317*
Anderson, J. R., 38, *67*, 99, *120*, 271, *274*, 344, *363*
Anderson, P. A., 249, *275*
Anderson, R. B., 201, 207, 211, *217*
Anderson, R. C., 114, *122*
Anderson, S. J., 128, *143*
Andrusiak, P., 91, *97*, 225, *244*
Anglin, G. J., 198, *217*
Argyle, M., 124, 130, *143*, *144*
Arthur, E., 82, *94*
Auer, P., 124, *143*
Austin, E. W., 136, *143*

B

Baars, B. J., 75, *94*
Baddeley, A. D., 209, *216*
Baggett W. B., 220, *243*
Baillet, S. D. 114, *121*
Baker, L., 189, *192*, 284, 285, 286, 297, 298, 299, 305, *317*, 355, *363*
Ballstaedt, S. P., 248, *274*
Balon, R. E., 136, *143*

Balota, D., 88, *94*
Baran, S. J., 138, *147*
Barclay, C. R., 127-128, *143*
Bartlett, F. C., 177, *192*
Barton, S. B., 20, 21, *25*, 298, *300*
Bartrip, J., 297, *300*
Barwise, J., 124, *143*
Baudet, S., 152, 153, 154, *167*, *168*
Baughn, C., 31, *69*
Beck, I. L., 187, *192*
Bell, L., 140, *146*
Bell, A., 320, *337*
Bereiter, C., 177, 178, *192*, *193*, 374, *376*
Bertus, E. L., 238, *243*
Betz, A. L., 127, 133, *147*
Bever, T., 3, 11, *25*
Beverly, S., 140, *146*
Biolsi, K. J., 248, 268, *276*
Bisanz, G. L., 249, *274*
Black, N. L., 91, *97*
Black, J. B., 344, *363*
Bloom, C. P., 62, *67*, 72, 73, 78, 88, *94*, 225, 227, *243*
Bodenhausen, G. V., 129, *148*
Bonebakker, C., 306, 309, 316, *318*, 332, 339, 355, *365*
Boshuizen, H. P. A., 152, 153, 162, 165, *168*
Bourg, T., 189, *193*
Bower, G. H., 31, *68*, 100, *121*, 126, 128, *144*, *146*, 213, *216*, 219, *244*, 319, 338, 344, *363*
Boyle, E., 15, 16, *26*
Bradley, M. M., 305, *317*
Bradshaw, G. L., 344, *363*
Bransford, J. D., 94, *97*, 198, *216*, 247, *274*
Brewer, W. F., 129, *143*, 219, 221, 225, *242*, *244*, 306, *317*, 322, 323, 333, 335, *337*, 371, *375*

377

Bridges, J. A., 134, *143*
Britt, M. A., 101, 102, 103, 109, 114, 117, *121*
Britton, B. K., 123, 126, *143*, 187, 189, *192*, *193*, 249, *275*
Brown, A. L., 53, 54, 55, *67*, 189, *192*, 284, *299*
Brown, C. A., 188, 189, *193*
Brown, C. M., 89, *98*, 233, *245*
Brown, P., 124, *143*
Bruder, G. A., 223, *243*
Bruner, J., 129, *143*
Budd, D., 89, *98*
Budesheim, T. L., 316, *318*
Bullock, M., 357, *364*
Burgoon, J. K., 136, *143*
Burgoon, M., 136, *143*
Burnstein, E., 305, 316, *317*
Bybee, C. R., 137, *144*

C

Cairns, H. S., 344, *363*
Campanario, J. M., 102, 113, *121*, 334, 335, *337*, *338*, *339*, 354, 355, 357, *363*, *364*
Carlson, G. N., 74, *95*
Carney, R. N., 198, *217*
Carpenter, P. A., 4, 7, *26*, 38, 63, *67*, 73, 76, 91, *95*
Casteel, M. A., 84, *94*
Chafe, W. L., 225, *242*
Chandler, P., 207, *217*
Charolles, M., 282, *299*
Chi, M. T. H., 90, *94*, 169, 171, 187, 189, *192*, 248, *275*
Chiesi, H. L., 90, *94*, 117, *122*, 152, *167*, 247, *276*, 306, *317*
Chinn, C. A., 322, 323, 333, 335, *337*, 371, *375*
Chiu, M., 169, 171, 187, 189, *192*
Chrysler, S. T., 248, *275*, 319, *338*, 341, *363*
Clark, H. H., 124, 130, 132, 137, *143*
Clark, L. F., 35, *67*, 72, 78, 89, *95*, 211, *216*, 219, 220, 228, 233, 239, *243*, 248, *275*
Clark, M. B., 91, *98*
Clayman, S. E., 137, *143*
Clifton, C., Jr., 103, 104, *121*
Cloitre, M., 11, *25*
Cohen, R., 124, *143*
Colby, B. N., 72, *94*
Collingwood, R. G., 221, *242*
Collins, A. M., 38, *67*
Conway, M. A., 128, *143*
Cooper, M., 207, 212, *217*

Cortazar, J., 86, *94*
Coste, T. G., 137, *144*
Coté, N., 38, 41, 58, 61, 64, *67*, 73, 93, 95, 169, 170, 173, 175, 176, 179, 187, 188, 189, *192*, *193*, 298, *300*, 368, 372, 373, *375*, *376*
Coupland, N., 124, *144*
Cowart, W., 344, *363*
Cox, B. E., 283, *299*
Crigler, A. N., 136, 137, *146*
Cuckle, P., 297, *300*

D

Dahlgren, K. 221, *242*
Daneman, M., 334, *338*
Darley, J. M., 137, *148*
Davenport, D. M., 265, *275*
Davis, H., 139, *143*
de Vega, M., 212, *216*
Dee Lucas, D., 117, *121*
deLeeuw, N., 169, 171, 187, 189, *192*
Dell, G. S., 11, *25*, 127, *146*
Denhière, G., 151, 152, 153, 154, 158, 160, *167*, *168*, 197, 212, *216*
Deschênes, A. J., 158, *167*
Di Luzio, A., 124, *143*
Dijkstra, K., 94, *95*
Dillon, A., 117, *121*
Dines, G., 136, *144*
Dong, Q. Q., 136, *143*
Dopkins, S., 220, 225, *243*
Duchan, J. F., 223, *243*
Duffy, S. A., 32, 43, 44, 45, 46, 54, 55, 56, 59, *68*, 74, *96*, 220, *244*
Dumais, S. T., 80, *95*
Duranti, A., 124, *144*
Duszak, A., 140, *144*

E

Edwards, D., 129, *144*
Ehrlich, K., 12, *25*
Ehrlich, M-F., 197, *217*, 286, 292, 297, *299*, *300*, 342, *364*
Einstein, G. O., 89, *96*
Epstein, W., 286, 297, *298*, *299*, 305, *317*
Ericson, T. A., 20, *25*
Ericsson, K. A., 64, *67*, 77, 90, 165, 167, *168*, 170, 171, *192*

F

Fairclough, N. L., 133, 139, *144*
Favart, M., 117, *122*
Feltovich, P. J., 90, *94*, 248, *275*

Ferreira, F., 88, *97*, 103, 104, *121*
Ferstl, E. C., 255, 269, *275*
Fillenbaum, S., 248, *275*
Fillmore, C. J., 239, *243*
Fincher-Kiefer, R. H., 247, *277*, 342, *363*
Findahl, O., 134, *144*, 319, *337*
Fivush, R., 129, *146*
Flavell, J. H., 282, 284, 298, *299*
Fletcher, C. R., 38, 58, 62, 63, 65, *67*, *69*,
    72, 73, 74, 78, 82, 83, 88, 90, *94*,
    97, *98*, 123, *147*, 170, 189, *192*,
    193, 225, 227, *243*, 248, *275*, 319,
    338, 341, *363*
Foltz, P. W., 102, *122*
Fong, G. T., 316, *318*
Forgas, J. P., 124, *144*
Fowler, R., 133, 139, 140, *144*
Franklin, N., 197, *216*
Franzke, M., 137, *145*, 151, 158, *168*,
    269, *275*, 322, *338*, 342, *364*
Fraser, C., 124, *143*
Fraurud, K., 17, *26*
Frazier, L., 5, 6, *26*, 103, 104, *121*
Fredin, E. S., 140, *144*
Freudenthal, D., 15, 16, *26*
Frost, R., 329, *338*
Furnham, A., 124, 130, 135, *143*, *144*,
    329, *338*

G

Gallini, J. K., 200, 207, *217*
Galtung, J., 135, *144*
Gammack, J. G., 248, 251, *275*
Gans, H., 133, 137, *144*
Garcia-Arista, E., 334, *338*
Garner, R., 284, 296, *299*
Garnham, A., 125, *144*, *146*, 282, 283,
    299, *300*
Garrod, S. C., 9, 12, 15, 16, 17, 23, 24,
    26, *27*, 77, *95*, 219, 242, 282, 298,
    299
Georgi, M. C., 102, 109, *121*
Gernsbacher, M. A., 11, *26*, 73, 83, 84,
    94, *95*, 100, *121*, 221, 225, 231,
    236, 242, *243*, *244*, 253, *275*, 282,
    299
Gibson, R., 140, *144*
Giles, H., 124, *144*
Gilliom, L. A., 12, *26*
Givon, T., 221, 223, *243*
Glaser, R., 90, *94*, 248, *275*
Glasgow University Media Group, 135,
    139, *144*
Glavanov, D., 114, 119, *122*, 248, *276*,
    319, *338*, 342, *364*

Glenberg, A. M., 31, *67*, 100, *121*, 199,
    200, 207, 209, 212, 213, *216*, 219,
    242, *243*, 286, 297, 298, *299*, 305,
    317
Glenn, C. G., 72, 78, 89, *97*, 233, *244*
Gliner, G., 249, *275*
Goetz, E. T., 211, *217*
Golden, R. M., 80, *95*
Golding, J. M., 52, *67*, 220, *243*
Goldman, S. R., 37, 38, 41, 58, 61, 63,
    64, *67*, 72, 73, 74, 78, 80, 84, 91,
    93, 94, *95*, *96*, *97*, 169, 170, 171,
    173, 175, 176, 179, 187, 188, 189,
    190, *192*, *193*, 226, 227, *243*, 249,
    275, 298, *300*, 368, 372, 373, *375*,
    376
Goldsmith, T. E., 248, *260*, 265, *275*
Goodwin, C., 124, *144*
Gordon, P. C., 12, *26*
Graber, D. A., 134, 136, 137, 138, *144*,
    320, *338*
Graesser, A. C., 30, 31, 32, 35, 62, *67*, 68,
    69, 72, 73, 74, 78, 83, 89, *95*, *97*,
    123, 126, 128, *143*, *144*, 169, *192*,
    219, 220, 221, 225, 226, 227, 228,
    229, 230, 232, 233, 234, 235, 236,
    238, 239, 241, *243*, *245*, 248, 249,
    253, *275*, *277*, 307, *317*, 344, 345,
    346, 355, *363*
Graham, J. A., 124, 130, *143*
Grant, J., 297, *300*
Gray-Wilson, S., 213, *216*, 319, *338*
Greene, E., 84, *97*, 253, *276*
Greene, S. B., 11, *26*, 283, *300*
Greene, T. R., 247, *277*, 342, *363*
Greenspan, S. L., 31, *68*, 100, *121*, 126,
    146, 219, *244*, 285, *300*
Groen, G. J., 152, 153, 162, 165, *168*
Grosz, B. J., 12, *26*
Guindon, R., 154, *168*
Gulgoz, S., 249, *275*
Gumperz, J. J., 124, *144*
Gunter, B., 134, 135, 137, *144*, 320, 329,
    338
Gyselinck, V., 197, 203, 204, 206, 207,
    213, *216*, *217*, 297, *300*, 342, *364*

H

Hacker, K. L., 137, *144*
Haenggi, D., 100, *121*
Hakala, C., 74, *96*
Halldorson, M., 220, *244*
Halliday, M. A. K., 124, *145*, 281, 283,
    300
Hanson, C., 128, *145*
Harris, R. J., 134, *145*

Hasan, R., 281, 283, *300*
Hebb, D. O., 38, *67*
Hegarty, M., 202, 204, 207, 208, 209, 215, *216*
Henderson, R., 18, *27*
Henley, N. M., 249, *275*
Herman, E. S., 139, *145*
Hewitt, L. E., 223, *243*
Hickmann, M., 297, *300*
Hirst, W., 128, *145*
Hodge, B., 139, 140, *144*
Höijer, B., 134, *144*, 319, *337*
Houghton, H. A., 199, *218*
Hoyer, W. D., 329, *338*
Hoyes, S. M., 111, *121*, 334, *338*
Hsu, M. L., 137, *145*
Huang, Y., 88, *97*
Hubbard, M., 303, 316, *318*
Hubert, L. J., 249, 268, *275*
Humez, J. M. M., 136, *144*
Hummel, J. E., 74, *94*
Husebye-Hartman, E., 74, 76, 83, 84, 91, *98*, 298, *300*
Hustinx, L., 12, *27*
Hymes, D., 124, *145*

I

Iyengar, S., 136, *145*

J

Jablon, A. D., 344, *363*
Jacoby, J., 329, *338*
Jain, R., 33, 43, 59, 60, 61, *69*, 171, 174, 187, 189, *193*
James, W. A., 38, *67*, 74, *95*
Jennings, T. M., 52, *67*
Jhean-Larose, S., 154, *168*
Johnson, B. K., 220, *243*
Johnson, E., 136, *145*
Johnson, H., 297, *300*
Johnson, H. M., 88, *95*, 113, *121*, 303, 304, 305, 306, 308, 309, 310, 311, 314, 316, *317*, 323, 324, 325, 328, 329, 331, 332, *338*, 355, *364*
Johnson-Laird, P. N., 3, *26*, 100, *121*, 125, *145*, 196, 197, *216*, 239, *243*, 247, *275*
Johnson, P. J., 248, 260, *275*
Johnson, M. K., 198, *216*, 247, *274*
Johnson, N. S., 72, 78, *96*
Jones, M. C., 297, *300*
Josselson, R., 129, *145*

Jucker, A. H., 140, *145*
Judd, C. M., 262, *275*
Just, M. A., 4, 7, *26*, 38, 63, *67*, 73, 76, 91, *95*, 202, 204, 207, 215, *216*
Just, M. R., 136, 137, *146*

K

Kamm, D. F., 137, *144*
Kaplan, S., 124, *147*
Kardash, C. M., 334, *338*
Karmiloff, Y. N., 297, *300*
Karmiloff-Smith, A., 297, *300*
Katz, E., 136, *145*
Keefe, D. E., 88, *95*
Keenan, J. M., 51, *67*, 114, *121*
Kerby, A. P., 129, *145*,
Kihlstrom, J. F., 128, *145*
Kinder, D. R., 136, *145*
Kintsch, E., 151, *168*, 188, 189, *193*, 249, 250, 269, *276*, 342, *364*
Kintsch, W., 9, 24, 25, *26*, 36, 38, 41, 63, 64, *67*, *68*, *69*, 72, 74, 77, 78, 80, 83, 84, 88, 90, *94*, *95*, *96*, *97*, *98*, 99, 100, 101, 114, 118, 119, *121*, *122*, 125, 128, 137, *145*, *147*, 151, 154, 158, 160, 165, 166, 167, *168*, 169, 170, 188, 189, *192*, *193*, 196, 197, *216*, *218*, 219, 238, 240, *243*, *244*, 247, 248, 249, 250, 251, 263, 269, *275*, *276*, 277, 305, 312, *318*, 319, 322, *338*, *339*, 341, 342, 343, 346, 347, 348, 350, 354, 356, 358, 362, *364*, *365*, 368, 373, *376*
Kinzer, C. K., 94, *97*
Kirsner, K., 248, *276*
Kirson, D., 270, 271, *276*
Klatzky, R. L., 73, 92, *95*
Klin, C. M., 88, *95*, 220, *243*
Klosson, E. C., 137, *148*
Klusewitz, M. A., 91, *95*
Koeske, R. D., 248, *275*
Körkel, J., 247, *276*
Koster, C., 15, *26*
Kress, G., 139, 140, *144*
Kreuz, R. J., 138, *145*
Kruley, P., 209, 212, *216*, 242, *243*
Kulhavy, R. W., 199, *217*
Kusbitt, G. W., 22, *27*

L

Labov, W., 129, *145*
Landauer, T. K., 80, *95*

Langston, M. C., 32, 33, 43, 56, 57, 63, 65, *68*, *69*, 73, 80, *98*, 219, 220, 221, 227, 228, 239, *245*, 249, *277*
Langston, W. E., 242, *243*, 199, 200, 207, 212, 213, *216*
LaPorte, R. E., 249, *274*, *276*
Larkin, J. H., 117, *121*, 210, 212, *216*
Larsen, S. E., 134, *145*
Larsen, S. F., 102, *121*, 127, 133, *145*, *147*, 319, *338*
Lau, R. R., 137, *145*
LaVancher, C., 169, 171, 187, 189, *192*
Le Ny, J. F., 160, *168*
Lear, J. C., 220, *244*
Leatherbarrow, M., 88, *95*, *98*, 303, 304, 308, 309, 311, 316, *318*, 323, 324, 325, 329, 331, 332, *339*, 343, 355, 361, *365*
Lee, M. A., 136, *145*
Legros, D., 152, 153, *167*
Lemmonier-Schallert, D., 195, *217*
Lentz, R., 198, *217*
Lepper, M. R., 303, *318*
Levelt, W. J. M., 139, *145*
Levie, W. H., 198, *217*
Levin, J. R., 198, 199, *217*
Levine, L., 31, 33, *68*
Lichtenstein, E. H., 221, *242*
Liebes, T., 136, *145*
Lieblich, A., 129, *145*
Lightfoot, C., 357, *364*
Lindem, K., 100, *121*, 219, *243*
Linden, K., 31, *67*
Liwag, M. D., 33, *68*
Loftus, E. F., 129, *145*, *146*
Long, D. L, 189, *193*, 220, *243*
Lorch, E. P., 91, *95*, *98*
Lorch, R. F. Jr., 78, 84, 88, 91, *94*, *95*, *96*, 126, *145*, 167, *168*, 169, 189, *193*, 220, *243*, *244*, 281, *300*, 341, *364*
Lovett, S. B., 199, *217*
Lucas, M. M., 74, *95*
Lucas, A., 18, *27*
Lutz, M. F., 32, 43, 48, 49, 50, 51, 52, 62, 63, *68*, 220, *243*

M

Mackie, J. L., 30, 35, *68*, 221, 224, 232, *243*
MacNealy, M. S., 138, *145*
Magliano, J. P., 32, 33, 34, 43, 56, 57, 62, 63, 65, *68*, *69*, 94, *95*, 169, 189, *193*, 219, 220, 225, 228, 231, 232, 233, 234, 235, 236, 238, 239, *243*, *244*, *245*, 253, *277*

Maki, R. H., 297, *300*
Mandl, H., 152, *168*, 199, *217*, *244*, 248, *274*
Mandler, J. M., 72, 78, 89, *96*, *243*
Mannes, S. M., 111, 114, *121*, 123, *147*, 189, *193*, 334, *338*, 342, 343, *364*
Marcus, N., 199, *217*
Markman, E. M., 285, *300*, 305, *318*
Markus, H., 128, 132, *145*
Marron, M. A., 102, *122*
Marschark, M., 212, *217*
Marslen-Wilson, W. D., 14, 15, *26*, *27*
Marsolek, C. J., 74, *94*
Martin, J. R., 124, *146*
Martin, L. L., 129, *146*
Mason, R. A., 102, *122*
Massad, C. M., 316, *318*
Mattson, M. E., 20, *25*
Mayer, R. E., 200, 201, 202, 207, 208, 211, *217*
Mazingo, S., 136, *146*,
McClelland, G. H., 262, *275*
McDaniel, M. A., 88, 89, *95*, *96*, 199, 208, *218*
McKeown, M. G., 187, *192*
McKoon, G., 11, 23, *25*, *26*, 38, 52, *68*, 72, 74, 77, 83, 88, 91, *96*, 127, 128, *146*, *147*, 167, *168*, 283, *300*, 333, *338*
McNamara, D. S., 90, *96*, 151, *168*, 188, *193*, 249, 250, 269, *276*, 373, *376*
McNamara, T. P., 213, *216*, 319, *338*
McNelly, J. T., 138, *146*
Means, B., 129, *146*
Means, M. L., 152, *168*
Meyer, B. J. F., 72, *96*, 187, *193*
Meyer, D. E., 38, *68*
Meyer, M., 3, *67*, 100, *121*, 219, *243*
Middleton, D., 129, *146*
Miller, J. R., 78, 84, *96*
Miller, G. A., 239, *243*
Miller, G. E., 201, *217*
Millis, K., 30, 31, *67*
Moar, K., 12, *27*
Moore, D., 285, 296, *301*
Morris, R. K., 12, *26*
Morris, C., 297, *298*, 299
Morrow, D. G., 31, *68*, 100, *121*, 126, 135, *146*, 213, *216*, 219, 223, *244*, 319, *338*
Moxey, L. M., 23, 24, *27*, 298, *300*
Mross, E. F., 88, *97*
Munger, G. P., 31, *69*
Murphy, G. L., 248, *276*
Myers, J. L., 12, *26*, 32, 43, 44, 45, 46, 54, 55, 56, 59, *68*, 74, 78, 84, 88, 92, *95*, *96*, 220, 228, *243*, *244*, 344, 347, 348, 349, 350, 361, *364*

N

Nakamura, G. V., 127, *144*, 345, 346, 355, *363*
Narvaez, D., 74, 84, *98*
Nathan, M. J., 189, *193*
Neisser, U., 128, 129, *146*
Nelson, K., 127, 129, *146*
Neuman, W. R., 136, 137, *146*
New, B. L., 310, *318*
Newtson, D., 127, *146*, 316, *318*
Nickels, M., 31, *69*
Noordman, L. G., 88, *98*
Norman, D. A., 248, *276*

O

O'Brien, E. J., 12, *26*, 33, 43, 52, 53, *68*, 74, 78, 83, 84, 87, 92, *94*, *96*, 126, *145*, 281, *300*, 341, 344, 345, 346, 347, 348, 349, 350, 361, *363*, *364*
Oakhill, J., 125, *146*, 283, 284, 285, 287, 296, *300*, *301*
Ohtsuka, K., 219, 225, *244*
Olson, J. R., 248, 268, *276*
Omanson, R. C., 59, *68*
Ore, O., 257, *276*
Otero, J., 305, *318*, 334, *338*, 347, 348, 354, 355, 357, 358, 362, *364*

P

Painton, S., 249, *276*
Paivio, A., 195, 211, *216*, *217*
Patel, V. L., 152, 153, 162, 165, *168*
Paterson, K., 298, *300*
Payton, P., 33, 43, 59, 60, 61, *69*, 171, 174, 187, 189, *193*
Peeck, J., 201, *217*
Perfetti, C. A., 20, *26*, 78, *96*, 101, 102, 109, 117, 118, *121*, *122*, 140, *146*, 247, *276*
Perrig, W., 100, *122*, 197, *217*, 248, *276*, 343, *364*
Perry, D. K., 137, 138, *146*
Pichert, D. E., 114, *122*
Plunkett, K., 127, *145*
Polanyi, L., 129, *146*
Post, T. A., 247, *277*, 342, *363*
Potts, G. R., 52, *67*, 270, 271, *276*
Pressley, M., 169, 189, *193*, 201, *217*
Price, V., 137, *145*
Price, J. M., 249, *276*
Propp, V., 72, *96*

Q

Quillian, M. R., 38, *67*

R

Raaijmakers, J. G. W., 82, *96*, 271, *276*
Radvansky, G. A., 32, 43, 48, 49, 50, 51, 52, 62, 63, *68*, 220, *243*
Rapoport, A., 248, *275*
Ratcliff, R., 11, 23, *25*, *26*, 38, 52, *68*, 72, 74, 77, 83, 88, 91, *96*, 127, 128, *146*, *147*, 167, *168*, 283, *300*, 333, *338*
Ratner, H. H., 285, *301*
Rayner, K., 5, 6, *26*, 74, *96*
Reder, L. M., 22, *27*, 270, *276*, 344, *363*
Reich, R. S., 22, *27*
Reisdorf, P., 91, *97*
Reitz, L., 88, *94*
Rémond, M., 286, *299*
Rinck, M., 213, *216*, 319, *338*
Rips, L. J., 248, *276*
Risden, K., 58, 63, 65, *69*, 73, 74, 76, 82, 83, 84, 86, 90, 91, *96*, *97*, *98*, 298, *300*
Risko, V. J., 94, *97*
Ritchie, B. G., 91, *98*
Ritchot, K. F. M., 83, *97*
Rizzella, M. L., 33, 43, 52, 53, *68*, 74, *96*
Robertson, S. P., 249, *275*
Robinson, J. A., 126, 127, *146*
Rodgers, K., 140, *146*
Rodkin, P. C., 31, *69*
Roeh, I., 140, *146*
Rogers, E. D., 306, *318*
Rohleder, L., 74, 84, *98*
Rosenhan, D. L., 316, *318*
Ross, L., 303, 316, *318*
Rossi, J. P., 151, *168*
Rouet, J.-F., 102, 107, 114, 116, 117, 118, *121*, *122*
Rubin, D. C., 127, *146*
Ruge, M. H., 135, *144*
Rukavina, I., 334, *338*
Rumelhart, D. E., 248, *276*
Rybolt, W., 329, *338*

S

Sachs, J., 92, *96*
Sadoski, M., 211, *217*
Sanford, A. J., 9, 12, 18, 19, 20, 21, 23, 24, *25*, *26*, *27*, 77, *95*, 219, *242*, 282, 298, *299*, *300*

Sanocki, T., 297, *298*, *299*
Saul, E. U., 74, 91, *95*, 169, 170, 171, 173, 175, 176, 179, 187, 188, 189, *192*, *193*, 372, 373, *375*
Scardamalia, M., 177, 178, *192*, *193*, 374, *376*
Schank, R. C., 31, *68*, 72, 89, *96*, 127, *146*, 251, *276*
Scher, M. S., 199, *217*
Schmalhofer, F., 36, *68*, 114, 118, 119, *121*, *122*, 197, *216*, 248, *276*, 319, *338*, 342, 347, *364*
Schmidt, H. G., 152, 153, 162, 165, *168*
Schneider, W., 247, *276*
Schneider, P., 297, *300*
Schnotz, W., 199, *217*
Schoenbach, K., 138, *147*
Scholes, R. J., 334, *338*
Schommer, M., 334, *338*
Schul, Y., 305, 316, *318*
Schulz, J., 268, *275*
Schvaneveldt, R. W., 38, *68*, 258, *276*
Sciama, S. C., 209, 212, *216*
Sears, D. O., 137, *145*
Secco, T., 53, 62, *69*, 72, 92, *97*, 220, *244*
Seel, N. M., 212, *217*
Segal, E. M., 31, *68*, 220, *244*
Seifert, C. M., 88, *95*, 113, *121*, 128, *147*, 303, 304, 305, 306, 308, 309, 310, 311, 314, 316, *318*, 323, 324, 325, 328, 329, 331, 332, *338*, 355, *364*
Serra, M., 297, *300*
Shanahan, T., 283, *299*
Shank, D. M., 12, *26*, 74, *96*
Shapiro, B. P., 88, *94*
Sharkey, A. J. C., 74, *96*
Sharkey, N. E., 74, *96*
Sharp, D. L. M., 94, *97*
Shatzer, M. J., 136, *143*
Shiffrin, R. M., 82, *96*, 271, *276*
Shillcock, R., 11, *27*
Shinjo, M., 32, 44, 45, 46, 54, 55, 56, 59, *68*, 220, *244*
Shoben, E. J., 248, *276*
Siegel, A. W., 124, *143*
Simon, H. A., 171, *192*, 210, 212, *216*
Simons, W., 12, *27*
Sims, V. K., 202, 207, 208, 209, 211, *216*, *217*
Singer, J. L., 129, *144*, *147*
Singer, M., 31, 43, *67*, 73, 74, 83, 88, 91, *95*, *97*, 126, *144*, 169, *192*, 225, 230, *243*, *244*, 307, *318*
Skowronski, J. J., 127, 133, *147*
Small, M. Y., 199, *217*
Smiley, S. S., 53, 54, 55, *67*
Smith, E. E., 248, *276*

Solomon, N., 136, *145*
Songer, N. B., 151, *168*, 188, *193*, 249, 250, 269, *276*
Speelman, C. P., 248, *276*
Speer, J. R., 310, *318*
Sperber, D., 130, *147*
Sperry, L. L., 32, 43, 53, 55, 62, 65, *69*, 152, *168*, 220, 225, 228, *244*, 253, *276*
Spilich, G. J., 90, *94*, 117, *122*, 152, *167*, *168*, 247, *276*
Srull, T. K., 128, *147*
St. John, M. F., 270, 271, *276*
Stanners, R. F., 249, *276*
Stauffer, J., 329, *338*
Steedman, M., 103, 104, *120*, 247, *274*
Stein, N. L., 31, 33, *68*, *69*, 72, 78, 89, *97*, 233, *244*
Steiner, I. D., 306, *318*
Strittmatter, P., 212, *217*
Subramaniam, G., 127, 128, *143*
Suh, S., 31, 33, 36, 37, 43, 44, 45, 46, 47, 48, 50, 51, 56, 59, 60, 61, 62, 63, 66, *68*, *69*, 74, 78, 84, *97*, 171, 174, 187, 189, *193*, 220, 225, 226, 229, *244*, 323, *339*
Sulzby, E., 283, *299*
Sunder-Meier, B., 242, *245*
Swanson, K. L., 126, 127, *146*
Sweller, J., 207, 212, *217*

T

Tabaczynski, T., 140, *144*
Tan, E. S., 31, *69*
Tanenhaus, M. K., 74, *95*
Tapiero, I., 152, 158, *167*, *168*, 341, 347, *364*
Tardieu, H., 197, 203, *216*, *217*, 286, 297, *299*, *300*, 342, *364*
Taylor, H. A., 197, *217*
Tenney, Y. J., 134, *147*
Tesser, A., 129, *146*
Thompson, C. P., 127, 133, *147*
Thompson, W. C., 316, *318*
Thurlow, R., 58, 63, 65, *69*, 73, 74, *94*, *98*
Tierney, P., 207, *217*
Till, R. E., 88, *97*
Trabasso, T., 31, 32, 33, 34, 36, 37, 43, 44, 45, 46, 47, 48, 50, 51, 53, 55, 56, 57, 59, 60, 61, 62, 63, 65, 66, 67, *68*, *69*, 72, 74, 78, 80, 83, 84, 92, *95*, *97*, *98*, 109, *122*, 126, *144*, 152, 167, *168*, 169, 171, 174, 187, 189, *192*, *193*, 220, 223, 225, 226, 229, 230, 234, 235, 236, 242, *243*, *244*, 253, *276*, 307, *318*, 323, *339*

Trafimow, D., 127, 128, *147*
Trew, T., 139, 140, *144*
Truitt, T. L., 242, *245*
Tuchman, G., 133, 137, 141, *147*
Tulving, E., 127, *147*
Turner, A. A., 84, *97*, *253*, *276*
Turner, T. J., 344, *363*
Tversky, B., 197, *216*, *217*
Tyler, L. K., 14, 15, *26*, *27*, 283, *300*

U

Unverzagt, W. H., 303, 305, *316*

V

Van den Broek, P., 31, 35, 36, 37, 38, 44,
    53, 58, 59, 62, 63, 65, *69*, 72, 74,
    76, 78, 82, 83, 84, 88, 89, 90, 91,
    92, 93, 94, *97*, *98*, 109, *122*, 167,
    168, 169, 174, 188, *193*, 220, 228,
    231, 232, 236, 242, *244*, *245*, 298,
    300, 308, *318*
Van Dijk, T. A., 38, *69*, 72, 74, 78, 83,
    90, *95*, *98*, 99, 100, 102, 114, *121*,
    122, 125, 128, 129, 133, 135, 136,
    137, 138, 139, 140, *147*, *168*, 169,
    170, 188, *193*, 196, *218*, 219, 240,
    243, *244*, 247, 251, 263, *276*, *277*,
    319, *339*, 341, 356, *364*, *365*
Van Oostendorp, H., 23, *27*, 88, 91, *98*,
    102, 113, *121*, *122*, 123, 126, 138,
    147, 219, 231, *245*, 306, 309, 316,
    318, 319, 320, 321, 322, 323, 332,
    333, 335, *337*, *339*, 344, 355, *363*,
    365
Van Zoonen, L., 136, *147*
Varma, S., 38, 41, 58, 61, 63, 64, *67*, 73,
    80, 93, *95*, 169, 170, 189, *192*,
    298, *300*, 368, *376*
Varnhagen, C. K., 37, *67*, 72, 84, *95*, 226,
    227, *243*
Vesonder, G. T., 117, *122*, 152, *168*, 247,
    249, *274*, *276*
Von Restorff, H., 344, *365*
Vonk, W., 12, *27*, 88, *98*, 283, *300*
Voss, J. F., 90, *94*, 115, 117, *122*, 152,
    167, *168*, 247, 249, *274*, *276*, *277*,
    342, *363*
Vye, N. J., 94, *97*

W

Waddill, P. J., 199, 208, *218*
Wagner, J., 305, *318*
Waletzky, J., 129, *145*
Walker, W. H., 154, 166, *168*
Walton, P., 139, *143*
Wason, P., 22, *27*
Weaver, C. A., 123, *147*
Weidenmann, B., 207, *218*
Weinert, F. E., 247, *276*
Welsch, D., 36, *68*, 118, *121*, 197, *216*,
    248, *276*, 319, *338*, 347, *364*
Whitney, P., 89, 91, *98*
Wiley, J., 115, *122*
Wilkes, A. L., 88, *98*, 303, 304, 308, 309,
    311, *316*, 323, 324, 325, 329, 331,
    332, *339*, 343, 355, 361, *365*
Wilkinson, A. C., 305, *318*
Willows, D. H., 199, *218*
Wilson, C. C., 136, *147*
Wilson, C. E., 329, *339*
Wilson, D., 130, *147*
Wineburg, S. S., 105, 114, 116, *122*
Wish, M., 124, *147*
Wodak, R., 136, *147*
Wright, J. C., 248, *276*
Wyer, R. S., 127, 128, 129, *147*, *148*,
    303, 305, 316, *318*

Y

Young, M., 76, 82, *98*
Yuill, N., 283, 284, 285, 287, 296, *300*,
    301

Z

Zabrucky, K., 285, 296, *301*
Zanna, M. P., 137, *148*
Zillmann, D., 140, *144*
Zimny, S., 36, *68*, 118, *121*, 197, *216*,
    248, *276*, 319, *338*, 347, *364*
Zwaan, R. A., 30, 31, 32, *67*, *69*, 89, 94,
    95, *98*, 123, 126, 134, 135, 138,
    147, *148*, 188, 189, *193*, 219, 220,
    221, 225, 227, 228, 231, 232, 233,
    239, 241, 242, *244*, *245*, 249, 253,
    277, 319, *339*

Subject Index

A

Activation, 73, 76–77, 368–369
  activation threshold, 75
  activation vector, 78, 82, 84, 88, 90–92
  fluctuating, 73
  levels of, 76
  online, 72, 78
  pool of, 76
  (re)activation, 74, 87
  sources of, 73, 77, 83
  spreading, 38
  value, 37, 39–40
Aims, 137
Anaphora,
  and comprehension skill, 286–296
  processing, 282–286
    monitoring of, 286–296
Appropriateness, 138
Association, 260, 269, 271
  cued, 250–254, 261–262
  free, 252
  matrix, 252, 253, 255
  strength, 252, 269
Asymptotic learning, 79–80, 82, 85
Attention, 74
  attentional resources, 72–73
Attitude, 129, 137
Autobiographical memory, 125, 133
Availability
  antecedent sentences on-line, 45–53

B

Background knowledge, 74, 76, 80, 83, 90
Bottom-up effects, 72

C

Carryover, 77, 83
Causal connection,ivity, 368–369
Causal connections
  causal network, 36–37
  reasoning, 29–30
  recall, 59–60
  relatedness, 54–56
  semantic representation, 34
  sentence "fit", 56–57
Causal Inference Maker, 72
Causal path, 152–154, 157, 166
Causal structure, *see also* Causal coherence
Causal-network model, 223–224, 229
  causal episodes, 223–224
Centrality, 257, 261, 266
Circumstances, 135
Clause structure, 140
Cognitive efficiency, 158, 162–164
Coherence, 72, 157, 250, 258, 269, 373
  causal, 83–84, 159, 253
  causal connections, 31
  causal-referential, 85–86
  propositional, 253
  recall, 60–61
  referential, 83–84
  semantic, 152–158, 163, 167
  teleological, 159
  temporal, 253
  text, 151, 152, 154, 158, 167
Cohort, 77
  cohort activation, 76–77, 81–82, 85, 88–91
    cohort-activation parameter, 77
  cohort competition, 79, 81–82
    competition learning curve, 76
Common ground, 124

Communicative event, 124, 134–135
Compartmentalization, 270
Comprehension, 29–30, 247–272
  discourse, 32
  integration, 33, 38
  on-line, 45–48
  problems, 169, 171, 184, 186, 188
  processes, 73
  questions, 354–356, 359–362
  skill, 286–296
Computational model, 76
Concept, 268–269
  elicitation, 251–252
  node, 252
Connection asymmetry, 80
Connection strength, 78–79, 81–82
Connectionist model
  activation value, 37
  assumptions, 40–42
  comparison of models, 63–65
  connection strength, 37–38, 40
  overview of, 33–40
  validation, 43–44
Connectionist model, 76
Constraints, 72, 88
Construction-Integration model, 72,
  269–270, 346–348, 356–363
Constructionist theory, 72, 74, 86
Context, 123–148, 271, 371
Context model, 123–148
  structure of, 130–131
Context modeling: theory vs. practice,
  140–141
Context vs. text, 132–133
Continuity, 370
Contradictions, *see* Inconsistencies
Contradictory information, 333
Credibility, 136, 138
Cued recall, 352–354, 359–362
Current State Strategy, 72

D

Decay, 77
Deictic expression, 139
Discourse
  analysis, 35–36
  coherence, 341–346, 361–362
  meaning, 134
  processing, 3–25
    anaphoric processing, 9–18
    immediacy of, 4, 9–18
    partial interpretation, 20–22
    theories of, 23–25
Discrediting information, 323
Documents

documents model, 102–111
  intertext model, 103–110
  learning from, 111–118
    expertise, 117–118
    integration, 111–113
    learner factors, 114–117
    updating, 113–114
Domain-specific knowledge, 292–296,
  342–343, 357–362

E

Elaboration, 269, 344–362
  effect of, 345–348, 351–356, 360–362
  production of, 344–345
  simulations, 356–358
  strategic process, 345
Emotion, 126, 129, 137
Episode, 127
Episodic memory, 88, 127
Epistemological beliefs, 334
Event interpretation, 125
Event model, 125–126
Event-indexing model, 220–242
  inference generation principles, 225,
    234–239, 242
  long-term memory principle, 228,
    239–240, 242
  processing time principle, 225–226,
    229–233, 242
Expectancy, 79
Experience model, 124, 126–129
Expertise, 152, 154, 157, 158, 162–166
Expository-scientific text, 349

F

Formulation, 138–139
Frequency, 252

G

Genre schema, 140
Genre, 134–135
Goals, 129, 137

H

Harmony, 269
Hebbian learning 79–80, 85
Hierarchical Clustering, 258

I

Ideologies, 137
Illustrations, 195–216
  and dual coding theory, 196, 210–212, 215
  facilitative effect of, 195–201
  functions of, 198–199
  and individual differences, 198, 208–210
  and mental model theory, 196, 212–215
Importance, 158, 160, 162, 164, 165
Inconsistencies, 343–363, 370–371
  detection of, 87
  explicit, 348–363
  memory improvement, 343–348, 352–356, 361–363
Individual characteristics, 334
Inferences, *see also* Elaboration
  backward inferences, 88–89
  coherence-building, *see* Backward inferences
  forward inferences, 88–89
  generation, 225–225, 233–239
  individual differences in comprehension, 90–93
Instantiation, 128
Instructional text, 370
Interaction, 137
Interest, 138
Intermediate effect, 152, 153, 165

K

Keyword, 250, 252
Knowledge, 151–154, 158, 159, 165, 166
  assessment, 247–272
  background, 247-272
  domain, 247, 250, 372
  mutual, 130
  networks, 374
  of journalists, 137
  organization, 167
  personal, 127
  prior, 151–154, 156, 158, 161, 162, 164–167, 372–374
  representation of, 248, 251
  structure of, 152, 165, 250, 254
Knowledge-building, 178–181, 183, 184, 187–189, 372

L

Landscape model, 71–73, 76–78, 84, 86, 88–89, 91, 369

Learners
  advanced, 152–154, 156–159, 161–165
  beginners, 152–159, 161–165
  intermediates, 152–159, 161–165
Learning from text, 247–272, 371–373
Levels effect, 159
Lexicalization, 139
Links
  associative, 252, 258–260, 263
  text, 253, 256, 266
Location, 135
Long-term memory, 170, 172, 175, 176

M

Macrorepresentation, 128
Macrostructure, 152, 154, 157, 165, 269–270
Meaning,
  discourse, 134
Media, 135
Memory, 153, 154, 157
  long-term, 152–154, 157, 165
  for text, 227–228, 239–240
  text representation, 59
Microstructure, 269
Minimalist theory, 72, 74, 86
Minimalistic processing, 333
Misinformation, 303, 323, 333
  correction of, 303–310
    alternate representations, 310
    global updating, 304, 307–310
    surface updating, 303, 315, 316
Model,
  context, 123–148
  event, 125–126
  experience, 124, 126–129
  updating of, 130
  schema, 127, 131–132
(Modified) Delta learning rule, 79
Monitoring, 169–170, 173–175, 177–178, 180, 188, 189, 281–298
  comprehension monitoring, 284–296
  metacognitive monitoring, 281–286
  components of, 282–286
MOPS, 127
Multidimensional Scaling, 249, 258
Multiple texts, 101–118, *see also* Documents
Mutual knowledge, 130

N

Narrative, 251, 253
Network, 258

associative, 251–253, 268, 270
of concepts, 78, *see also* Memory representation
  self-connection, 77–78
  node strength, 77–78, 80–81
  propositional, 253
  size, 256, 262
News discourse, 125, 133–143
Node, 252
  degree of, 257, 267
Nominalization, 139

O

Offline representation, *see also* Memory representation
Opinion, 129, 137
Oral text presentation, 329
Order effects in recall, 86
Overlap
  argument, 251, 253, 257
  of networks, 264–265

P

Paraphrase, 174–175, 179, 180, 186
Pathfinder, 258, 261, 268
Personal knowledge, 127, 133
Personal script, 127
Plans, 129
Power, 136
Prediction, 174–175
Prior knowledge, 170–189
Processing resources, 76, *see also* Attentional resources
Proposition, 251, 269–270
Propositional analysis, 349–350, 352–354, 356–359
Propositional structure, *see* Textbase
Proximities, 249, 252, 254, 258, 269
  asymmetry of, 249, 254

Q

Quadratic assignment, 268

R

Reading, 153, 154, 158, 162, 164, 166
  cycles, 75–77, 83
  purpose, 369
  rereading, 56–58
  strategies, 91
  trace, 170, 175, 187

Reasoning, 371
Recall, 152, 153, 157, 164–166
  cued, 154, 158, 161, 166
  free, 154, 156, 166
Recognition task, 351–352, 361–362
Referential structure, *see also* referential coherence
Reinstatement, *see also* (Re)activation, 74, 83, 170, 172, 175–177, 179–180, 183, 186, 188
Rejection, 306, 314, 322, 324, 333
Relevance, 130
Representation, 77
  coherent, coherence, 170–174, 177–179, 187–189
  construction, 169–172, 177–181, 183–184, 186–189, 367, 371–374
  episodic memory, 80
  levels of
    propositional, 170
    situational, 170, 181, 186, 188
    textbase, 188
  memory, 73, 78–79, 86, 92
    correcting, 86
    reconfiguring representation, 81
    restructuring representation, 81
    updating memory representation, 80
  mental, 72, 91, *see also* Memory representation
  mental structure 78, *see also* Memory representation
  network, 369
Rereading, 170, 172, 175–176, 181, 189
Resolving contradictions, 86
Resonance model, 87
Retrieval, 82, 92, 154, 157, 158
  structure, 165
Revision, 250
Rhetorical devices, 140
Roles, 135
Ruminations, 129

S

Scenario, 327, 331
Schema, 89, 344–345
  deviations, *see* Tag
  genre, 140
Schematic structure, 130
Script, 251–252, 264
  personal, 127
Self, 128
Self-explanation, 173–175, 177–180, 186–187

Semantic memory, 80
Semantic representation, 133–138
Sentence Processing
  ambiguity resolution, 7
  syntactic parsing, 4–5
Setting, 334
Similarity, 264
  judgment, 249–250
Situation model, *see also* Event model,
    31–32, 90, 99–102, 126, 151,
    219–220, 241–242, 247–248, 263,
    267, 271, 319–322, 341–346,
    354–363, 370–374
  construction, 319, 341–346, 356–359
  evaluation, 354–356, 359–360
  and multiple texts, 101–102
  situations model, 107–111
  strength, 321
  relevance, 322
  and text models, 99–100
  updating, 319–324, 332–334,
        355–356, 361–362
    (in)complete, 324, 333
    strict, 322
Situation schema, 124
Situational continuities, 221–224,
    241–242
  causal, 223–224,
  characters and objects, 222
  spatial, 233
  temporal, 222–223
  relationship with inference generation,
        224–228
  relationship with memory, 227–228
  relationship with processing time,
        224–225
Sloppy encoding, 322, 324, 33
Social Domain, 134
Social relations, 136
Social situation, 124, 130
Sorting task, 249–250, 269
SPEAKING model of context, 124
Spreading activation, 270
Standards of coherence, 83, 91
Story
  episodic structure, 57–58
  goal-based, 368
Storytelling, 129
Strategies, 128, 334
Structure
  goal–subgoal, 152, 153, 157, 159, 166
  hierarchical, 152–154, 157, 159, 166
  surface, 165
  teleological, 152–154, 157, 158, 165,
        166
  temporocausal, 152–155, 157–159,
        165, 166

text, 154, 157, 158, 162, 163, 165
Structure Building Framework, 73
Structure elicitation, 251, 253–254
Structure of narratives, 72
  story grammar, 72
  hierarchical theories, 72
Structure-building model, 225, 231–232,
    242
Superstructure, 140
Surface structure, 138–140, 319
Surprisingness effect, 79, *see* Expectancy
System
  causal, 159
  functional, 152, 153, 156, 158, 165
  teleological, 152, 159

T

Tag, 344–363
  automatic process, 345
  construction, 344–346
  effect of, 345–348, 351–356, 360–363
  simulations, 358–360
Task, 129
  specificity, 342–346, 355–356,
        361–362
Text
  causal, 153–157, 161–163, 165, 166
  cohesion, 281–298
  comprehension, 152, 157, 195–216
    and inference making, 199–215
  connection, *see* Links
  expository, 169, 174, 179, 187, 188
  informational, 169, 170, 172–173,
        186, 187, 188
  instructional, 169, 186, 187
  memory, 249–250, 264, 269–270
  representation, 251
    availability of sentences, 45–50
    integration of sentences time, 44–45
    levels of, 247
  structure, 251
    propositional, 253
  teleological, 153–157, 161–166
Text vs. context, 132–133
Textbase, 90, 151, 247, 261, 263, 267,
    270, 319, 341–348, 352–356,
    358–363, 371–374
  construction, 341–348, 361–363
  decay of, 263
  distance in, 334
  evaluation, 352–354, 358–360
Text-focused processing, 178–181, 184,
    188
Think-aloud protocols, 169–190
Thinking aloud, 234–236

Time, 135
Top-down processing, 72, 89
Transformation, 320, 321

U

Updating, 248, 370–371, 374
    of models, 130
    process, 81

V

Verb-clustering task, 239

W

Word order, 140
Working memory, 74, 76, 170, 174, 175,
    see also Attentional resources